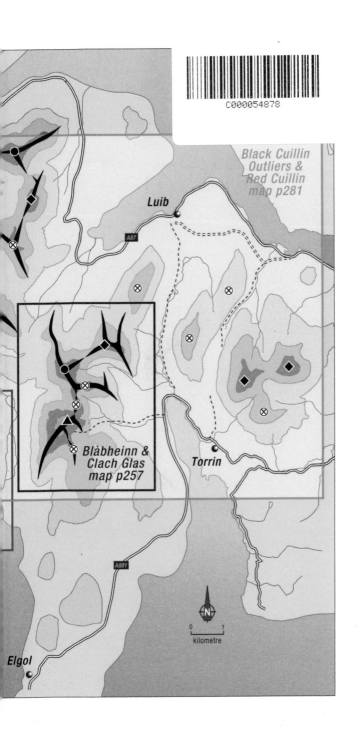

C000054878

Black Cuillin
Outliers &
Red Cuillin
map p281

Luib

A87

Blàbheinn &
Clach Glas
map p257

Torrin

A881

N

0   1
kilometre

Elgol

SKYE
THE CUILLIN

Mike Lates

Series Editor: Brian Davison

SCOTTISH MOUNTAINEERING CLUB
CLIMBERS' GUIDE

Published in Great Britain by The Scottish Mountaineering Trust, 2011

© The Scottish Mountaineering Club

ISBN 978-0-907233-13-5

A catalogue record for this book is available from the British Library

*Front Cover: Es Tressider & Blair Fyffe on the first ascent of
Captain Planet, E4, Bastier Tooth
(photo Ian Woods)*

Route descriptions of climbs in this guide, together with their grades and any references to in situ or natural protection are made in good faith, based on past or first ascent descriptions, checked and substantiated where possible by the authors.
However, climbs lose holds and are altered by rockfall, rock becomes dirty and loose and in situ protection deteriorates. Even minor alterations can have a dramatic effect on a climb's grade or seriousness. Therefore, it is essential that climbers judge the condition of any route for themselves, before they start climbing.
The authors, editors, friends and assistants involved in the publication of this guide, the Scottish Mountaineering Club, the Scottish Mountaineering Trust and Scottish Mountaineering Trust (Publications) Ltd, can therefore accept no liability whatever for damage to property, nor for personal injury or death, arising directly or indirectly from the use of this publication.

This guidebook is compiled from the most recent information and experience provided by members of the Scottish Mountaineering Club and other contributors. The book is published by the Scottish Mountaineering Trust, which is a charitable trust.
Revenue from the sale of books published by the Trust is used for the continuation of its publishing programme and for charitable purposes associated with Scottish mountains and mountaineering.

Design concept: Curious Oranj, Glasgow
Production: Scottish Mountaineering Trust (Publications) Ltd
Layouts & typesetting: Susan Jensen, Ken Crocket, Tom Prentice
Diagram and map graphics: Susan Jensen, Tom Prentice, Noel Williams
Printed & bound by Elkar, Bilbao, Spain

Distributed by Cordee, 11 Jacknell Road, Dodwells Industrial Estate, Hinkley, LE10 3BS
(t) 01455 61185   (e) sales@cordee.co.uk

For details of other SMC guidebooks see p324

Contents

Diagrams & Maps

Introduction & Acknowledgements

The Black Cuillin of Skye is a complete mountain range compacted into a remarkably small area on one of the most beautiful islands in the world. The miniature scale disguises the enormous extent of climbing available and visitors never fail to be amazed by the challenges these mountains throw down.

The roughness of the gabbro rock is legendary and confidence inspiring. More than 20 peaks are connected by a narrow crest that gives one of the finest Alpine-style ridge climbs in Europe. There are face routes on an alpine scale too, where glaciations have stripped the mountainsides of vegetation right down to sea-level in places. Labelling them as alpine mountains is no whimsical exaggeration; generations of experienced climbers have favourably compared Cuillin climbing with that of greater ranges. Beautifully crafted footpaths now take climbers and walkers into the dramatic corries in little over an hour where the scale suddenly becomes apparent.

Choices have to be made over which ambition is achievable; large packs of gear are no fun to haul along the narrow ridges but ascending a peak lightweight can leave the cragsman frustrated at passing so many superb looking cliffs. The climbs themselves rarely disappoint. Gabbro is very compact and routes will often cross blank looking sections where the line, holds and protection are revealed only on close inspection. Big faces can give a choice of classic climb on different tiers. The ridges provide continuous challenges where the only limitations are the climbers own ability and fitness. Ultimately mountaineers have to trust their own skills and judgement in all these situations.

A mantle of snow gives the Cuillin a truly Alpine appearance and the simplest ridges can become great climbs. Conditions vary from one peak or face to another and selecting the right climb is usually best done once in the corrie of choice. Water-ice is rare but the mixed climbing is on a par with anywhere else in Scotland with over 70 new winter routes added in recent years. The nature of the Cuillin means that big climbing adventures can be found no matter how thin the conditions. Just as in the Alps, climbs pioneered more than a century ago remain high on most visitors' agendas but, back in vogue, the Cuillin has seen a new generation of climbers realise the potential. There are now summer and winter routes at the highest levels. Weather, route type and equipment are all crucial considerations before leaving the ground. Be versatile during the planning and definitely on the mountain. Treat the Cuillin with respect and climb with a sense of adventure and they will repay you handsomely. There are routes to rival the quality of any in the British Isles but accomplishing a climb in the Cuillin leaves a unique aftertaste that draws the connoisseur back for more.

Mike Lates, August 2011

Most significantly thanks go to Cuillin historian Stuart Pedlar who has been a permanent inspiration. His complete climbing history of the Cuillin, in digital format, has been invaluable. Thanks to Mark Hudson with whom I set out to write the combined guide to Skye. Splitting into two volumes was not what anyone wanted, but was the only way to cover the huge number of new climbs on the island. Skye Sea-cliffs will be an essential part of any climbers trip to Skye. Thanks to the authors of previous editions of this guidebook; I am amazed at how they produced such accurate volumes without computers or digital cameras. Many thanks to the SMC publication team; particularly Tom Prentice and Brian Davison for patience with a new author and Andy Nisbet and Noel Williams for repeatedly feeding me information. Thanks to UKC for hosting the action shots competition. Thanks go to Eddie Lynch for some of the best photos for diagrams and particularly Beads, Icky, Rob Lawson and John Seal for repeatedly helping with "research". Thanks, too, to Bill Birkett, Steve Broadbent, Ginger Cain, James Edwards, Rowland Edwards, Mick Fowler, Tony Hanly, John Harwood, Mike & Catharine Hayne, Pete Hunter, Susan Jensen, Steve Kennedy, Neil King, John MacKenzie, Pete Macpherson, Colin Moody, Martin Moran, Jonathan Preston, Dave Ritchie, Guy Robertson, Clive Rowlands, Mark Shaw, Nick Smith, James Sutton, DJ Temple, Mike Thornton, Colin Threlfall, Helen & Neil Urquhart, Ben Wear and Martin Welch. The biggest thanks go to Catriona for her patience and support. Finally, thanks to the SMC for the increased appreciation of these superb mountains that I now have.

Geology of The Cuillin & Red Hills

Much of Skye is built from igneous rocks which were formed around 60 million years ago during a dramatic, but relatively short-lived, outburst of volcanic activity along the west coast of Scotland. Numerous volcanoes erupted throughout the Inner Hebrides at that time from Skye down to Ardnamurchan and Mull. Similar igneous activity also occurred on the Isle of Arran and in Antrim, Northern Ireland. This fiery episode is thought to have been associated with an early attempt to create a rift between Greenland and Europe. Eventually the rift took place well to the west of Scotland and over time this has created the North Atlantic Ocean. This rifting process still continues today with Iceland marking the position of separation.

The igneous activity in the Hebrides occurred in three phases. The first phase involved great outpourings of **basalt lava** which erupted from long fissures in the ground and built up flow upon flow. Each flow was around 10–15m thick. Sometimes there were long intervals between eruptions, giving time for the surface of the flows to weather and allow plants to become established. When the pile of flows had become especially thick it became more difficult for new lava to break through to the surface and so some later pulses of lava forced their way sideways in between the underlying strata of Jurassic sedimentary rocks. This created intrusions called **sills** of which the famous Kilt Rock is a fine example.

In the second phase of igneous activity basalt magma erupted from more localised centres to create spectacular volcanoes. The Cuillin massif represents the eroded remains of the magma chamber that once fed one of these volcanoes. The magma cooled more slowly within the Earth's crust than it did when it erupted to the surface. This allowed time for much larger crystals to form, and so produce a rock called **gabbro**. Although this rock has a similar chemical composition to basalt because of its larger crystal size it weathers to produce a rough surface with superb friction.

The mass of gabbro was subsequently invaded by three different types of minor intrusion. Basalt magma escaped through narrow vertical cracks in the gabbro and cooled to create features called **dykes**. It also followed inward dipping circular breaks and cooled to create features called **cone sheets**. The third structures to penetrate the Cuillin gabbro were **volcanic vents** – pipe-like features filled with a great jumble of rock fragments. There are a number of these vents among the northern Cuillin peaks in particular, as well as extensive outcrops in Srath na Crèitheach below Druim Hain.

These minor intrusions have a significant influence on the character of the Cuillin main ridge. Some of the dykes have proved softer than the gabbro and so have weathered out to create deep notches. Others have proved more resistant and now form steep walls such as the sides of the Inaccessible Pinnacle. Where cone sheets dip into the side of the ridge they often form convenient ledges, but where they dip away from the crest they form exposed slabs. The basalt tends to be much less sound than the gabbro because it is often permeated by microscopic cracks called joints and can break without warning. Some of the basalt also has a more rubble-like character and is riddled with gas holes many of which were subsequently filled by white minerals. The gabbro still provides reasonable friction when wet, whereas the basalt is notoriously slippery in such conditions. There is an extensive sheet of basalt on the crest of the main ridge between Sgùrr Alasdair and Sgùrr Thormaid.

The third phase of igneous activity involved the formation of a completely different type of 'acid' magma. This lava was more viscous in character and much of it remained in the crust where it eventually cooled to form large bodies of granite. The various Red Hills on Skye are all formed from this rock. These are more rounded hills than the Cuillin, partly because they are cut by far fewer minor intrusions.

Igneous activity in the Hebrides ceased around 56 million years ago and since that time a huge amount of material has been removed by erosion. Repeated glaciations over the last two million years brought about the final sculpting. In the most recent glacial episode the corries were scraped smooth by ice but the highest peaks remained uncovered and were subjected to freeze-thaw action.

History

Many local people still view the Cuillin similarly to their ancestors as a savage and inhospitable arena that only the foolhardy would enter. Despite this, it is not difficult to believe that these strong people had reached some of the peaks long before such exploits were recorded.

The history of climbing exploration in the Cuillin is well documented. Geology and glaciology became justifiable reasons for educated men to take to the mountains, often on an annual basis. In 1836 Duncan MacIntyre, a local forester known to have made previous attempts to scale Sgùrr nan Gillean, was summoned to Sligachan. His client was James Forbes, a professor of glaciology at just 24, and an experienced alpinist. The Forbes Arete on the Aiguille de Chardonnay, Chamonix, is named in his honour. The combination of Forbes' skills and confidence mixed with MacIntyre's local knowledge led to success.

Tourists were then guided regularly on Gillean but it was not until 1865 and explorations by Sheriff Alexander Nicolson that the Cuillin were brought to the attention of a wider range of climbers. A Gaelic scholar, he is considered the forefather of Cuillin exploration purely as an indulgent pastime. He wrote lavishly about his experiences and the beauty of the Cuillin in popular magazines. Most famously he climbed Sgùrr Alasdair, which was subsequently named in his honour.

John Mackenzie started his climbing career in 1866 at the age of 10 with an ascent of Gillean. His incredible career as a guide (all as an employee of the Sligachan Hotel) lasted over 50 years. It spanned the era of conquering virgin peaks, enchainment of the peaks by narrow ridges, creating directissma and finally exploring the great open rock faces. Although Mackenzie learnt skills from the great climbers he guided his climbing talent was recognised and regarded just as highly as his intimate knowledge of the area.

Charles and Lawrence Pilkington were amongst the top British alpinists when they first conquered the Inaccessible Pinnacle in 1880. Mackenzie was with them that day and on many outings through the next decade as they climbed most of the remaining virgin peaks. Charles returned with members of the Alpine Club in June 1887 making first ascents of Pinnacle Ridge, Clach Glas and of two unclimbed peaks above Coire Lagan. Thearlaich is the Gaelic name for Charles and he was honoured by having it named after him. He jokingly suggested "Pic Mackenzie" for the other and so it was that a lowly ghillie was equally honoured with the adoption of Sgùrr MhicCoinnich as the name. A month later Henry Hart, with Mackenzie as guide, traversed much of the Ridge in two days, most significantly linking MhicCoinnich to Thearlaich by a narrow ledge. Hart pompously recorded the feats in the hotel records, boasting that the rope had not been used even on the In Pinn. He then added disparaging comments to Pilkington's entry 'ropes used all the time' to which Pilkington replied 'This remark is hartless and need not have been added'. An anonymous guest added 'a rope and long drop would have suited this idiot'. Hart never returned.

The same year Norman Collie joined forces with William Wickham King gaining the top of the Basteir Tooth by descending from Am Basteir. Collie had started his climbing career just a year earlier, but his new pastime rapidly became an obsession that would take him to unclimbed peaks across the world. Collie was infamous for never leaving records of his routes but clues indicate that he spent the summers between 1887 and 1891 intensely exploring the ridges and gullies, especially those close to Sligachan. "Within four years of meeting Mackenzie, Collie had become the acknowledged expert on the Cuillin. He had the gift of solving the problems of uncharted country and his abilities in finding the right line up some seemingly impossible rock face were to stand him in good stead when it came to climbing further afield. He was an outstanding mountaineer, and his eye for detail was unsurpassed". Stuart Pedlar, Cuillin Historian.

In 1888 Collie and Mackenzie spent five hours searching before they breached the castellated walls of the Basteir Tooth to make the first proper ascent. They extended Hart's traverse from the previous season to reach Dubh na Dà Bheinn but were forced to bypass the Theàrlaich-Dubh Gap. In 1889 Collie joined forces with King to finally overcome the Gap. This made a continuous Traverse along the Main Ridge, without detouring over an outlying peak, a possibility.

Between 1890 and 1892 winter ascents of 12 of the major peaks were made by Porter, Benson and Tatham, a group of Eton school masters. In 1895 an ascent of Waterpipe Gully by Kelsall and Hallitt and their description in the Sligachan Climber's Book started a fascinating saga. It gives one of the best insights into the sport of climbing at the time. The gully has the look of a classic route, symmetrically splitting a sharp peak that bisects Coire na Creiche. In modern terms it is a worryingly loose adventure taking nine hours or more to ascend. Attempting the second ascent Falcon and Gray failed but accused Kelsall and Hallitt of poorly recording their route. The controversy grew as others made ascents, direct pitches or failed and recorded their opinions in the Climber's Book. Those who succeeded were masters of gully climbing, rated the route amongst the very best, and found the description ideal. Falcon and Gray both made two successful ascents and eventually conceded, but classic status was already assured. Extreme gully climbing was where it was at for top climbers at the time.

In 1896 Collie returned after his futuristic attempt on Nanga Parbat in 1895 had ended in tragedy with the death of Mummery and two porters. A highly productive week with other SMC members culminated in an ascent of climbed the awesomely steep north wall of Sgùrr Coire an Lochain to gain the last unclimbed mountain summit in Britain.

Naismith took climbing out onto vertical faces when he added his route to the Basteir Tooth in1898. W.W.King added one of his hallmark chimneys as a high quality directissma to the summit of MhicCoinnich, now a classic climb on a Ridge Traverse. Harold Raeburn was also present and traversed the Tooth by ascending Naismith's Route then descending King's Cave Chimney that had been excavated and first climbed only two days before.

The SMC held their first ever official Skye meet at Easter 1903 and another at Easter 1905. The Cuillin were clad in snow on both occasions. Raeburn was at the forefront with the first exploration of the remote north face of MhicCoinnich "insurmountable without the plating of ice and snow which forms so thickly" as Ling described one outing. The first breach of the great eastern ramparts of An Caisteal was impressive enough but it also transpires that Raeburn's parties climbed the TD Gap under snow on both occasions. Accommodation became available in Glen Brittle around this time and gave rise to an enormous wave of development in the hitherto remote southern corries.

The productive summer 1906 started a wave of activity that shaped climbing in the Cuillin forever. The best known ascent of the season was the Cioch on Sròn na Ciche by Collie and Mackenzie. The face was to become the most famous climbing arena on Skye. The Cioch remains a focal point for advances in Cuillin standards to this day. Guy Barlow and Harry Buckle made the first of scores of new routes with a full ascent of Cioch Gully and what they thought to be the first ascent of the Cioch. Leslie Shadbolt and Alastair MacLaren paid their first visit with Shadbolt's Chimney adding a frighteningly steep route to the Basteir Tooth. Henry Harland, along with the Abraham brothers, added South Crack on the Inaccessible Pinnacle typifying the type of climbing that these pioneers would introduce to the Cuillin. Collie was prolific once

---

Henry Harland and Alfred Binns posing for the camera of Ashley Abraham on the 80 foot pitch of Waterpipe Gully, VS, in June 1906. Abraham recalled: "My position was somewhat exposed, so I took the precaution of attaching myself with a rope to the top of the pinnacle. It was exceedingly fortunate that I did so. I had just made an exposure and was putting the slide back into the rucksack, when a sudden gust of wind blew the camera over towards the gully. It was just slipping over the edge when I made a grab and caught it, but in so doing lost my balance.

"A wild clutch, intended for the top of the pinnacle, but which only succeeded in securing my focusing cloth, was followed by a hazy and hurried wonder what was to happen next, when all need for prayerfulness was removed as the rope tightened around my waist and held me suspended over the gully. It was a most uncomfortable position; ..."

more in 1907 but it was routes by Harland and Ashley Abraham that really raised the standards with Cioch Direct and Black Chimney in particular. Their second direct ascent of Waterpipe Gully confirmed it as a remarkable achievement. Central Gully on Sròn na Ciche was climbed by a party led by the aptly named Everard Steeple whose name was to become synonymous with the Cuillin.

The first ever SMC guidebook to Skye was compiled in 1907 by William Douglas but was both sold out and outdated within the year. Ashley Abraham's *Rock-Climbing in Skye* was published in 1908. The most significant addition in 1909 was an impressive direct line from the bottom to top of the huge Western Buttress on Sron na Ciche by Steeple and Bowron called Median.

June 1911 saw a complete traverse of the Main Ridge for the first time. Leslie Shadbolt and Alastair MacLaren spent a little over 12 hours crossing from Gars-bheinn to Gillean with the approach and descent accomplished in 2hrs 30mins each, all times which are very respectable today. They returned in the September in the austere company of J.M.Archer Thomson and H.O.Jones. Thomson had dominated Welsh climbing developments for over a decade and the resulting "tour de force" could possibly be the greatest ever week of achievements in the Cuillin. They climbed no less than eight major new routes and a further five of lesser importance. The team climbed together on four big routes from a base at Sligachan then added major new routes in Coire Lagan as separate parties. Shadbolt was impressed by Thomson in particular "who would always choose a line, however difficult, and stick to it regardless of much easier alternatives on either hand". They had rain every day and ended with a repeat of Shadbolt's Chimney on the Tooth and descended by Naismith's Route.

The Irish team of O'Brien and Julian made two major ascents on the Coireachan Ruadha faces of Sgùrr Dearg and MhicCoinnich when they sailed into Loch Scavaig in 1912. North-East Gully was by far the hardest route climbed in the Cuillin, possibly achieved because O'Brien always chose to climb barefoot. The route was not repeated until 1951 and then only on Mike Dixon's second attempt. Steeple and Barlow were also very active, adding the significant Traverse of Sròn na Ciche with over 600m of difficult climbing.

The Great War inevitably reduced Cuillin activity and saw the loss of many fine young climbers. Steeple and Barlow squeezed in a trip in 1915 but significant advances didn't begin again until 1918. George Leigh Mallory and his wife Ruth, along with Pye and Shadbolt added a parallel line to Archer Thomson's on Mhadaidh and then the team switched their attention to the sweeping face of Sròn na Ciche. They climbed the Cioch and ascended Wallwork's route in order to inspect from above the unclimbed Crack of Doom that had repelled attempts since 1908. Mallory's Slab and Groove was climbed the next day making the first break through the lowest slabs of Western Buttress. Three days later Shadbolt and Pye finally climbed the Crack of Doom with Mallory having departed.

In 1919 Dorothy Pilley was on the first ascent of the very fine Cioch West. The discovery of the South Crag of Sròn na Ciche in Coire a' Ghrunnda in 1920 by Barlow and Steeple produced 11 long new routes over the next few seasons but their attentions were spread far and wide. Barlow had pioneered over 40 new routes by the end of his Cuillin climbing days. Gully experts Harland and George Abraham made the biggest addition with the 600m B Gully on Clach Glas. In 1921 the gritstone specialist Fred Piggot, in his rubber plimsoles, made a fine direct finish to the Crack of Doom and climbed two steep lines on the south face of the Inaccessible Pinnacle.

In 1923 the comprehensive SMC guidebook to *The Island of Skye* was published. The climbs were edited by Steeple, Barlow and J.H.B.Bell. A lull in developments over the next 15 years could be attributed to the economic depression but, overall, climbers visiting the island were happy to tackle the vast array of climbs in the guide. It was reprinted with very few changes through to 1952.

Climbing was no longer just a pastime for rich gentlemen. Engineers' Slant, climbed in 1931 by Sale, Reid and Brown, is the first sign of working class pioneers reaching the Cuillin, some years after they had started influencing developments closer to the cities. In 1937 William MacKenzie and Archie MacAlpine's Left Edge Route, Stone Shoot Variation on Alasdair and a hard final pitch of South Gully were

SMC Image Archive

Derek Haworth and Ian Hughes making the first ascent of Integrity, VS, Sròn na Cìche, on July 11, 1949

an indication of hard routes to come in the future.

Intense activity restarted in the post war years. Mass production of pegs and kara-biners during war now made them widely available and nylon ropes greatly improved both strength and handling. Sròn na Cìche was an obvious target with so many unclimbed lines and yielded ten major new routes before the end of the 1940s. Crack of Double Doom (VS), Doom Flake (VS) and Integrity (VS) were all climbed by Derek Haworth and partners and remain as classics to this day.

By far the most significant era in development of Cuillin rock climbs was the 1950s and 1960s. Not only were standards raised beyond all recognition but all the major faces in the Cuillin were discovered. The combination of increased security, a culture of aid being acceptable and incredibly good climbers meant almost every obvious line in the range was cleaned up. Since then the majority of new routes have filled in the gaps or straightened out existing lines. Grades were capped at Very Severe and all of the harder climbs are now climbed free in the Extreme grades. The cleaner rock on these steeper lines has helped ensure their popularity. The most significant face to be rediscovered was the Coireachan Ruadha face of Sgùrr MhicCoinnich when Aberdeen climber Bill Brooker and young Leeds climber Mike Dixon teamed up in 1950. Fluted Buttress (HVS) was climbed free, boldly tackling the steep buttress beside North-East Gully. Both recognised the quality and returned many times over the following years, significantly adding Crack of Dawn (HVS) together in 1951. The adjacent Bealach Buttress received their attentions in the same period with a number of partners that included Tom Patey climbing Thunderbolt Shelf with Brooker in 1953.

In 1951 Iain McNaught-Davies and Godfrey Francis climbed Cioch Grooves (now HVS) on Sròn na Cìche. A visit by the Creag Dhu top brass in 1956 produced a rise in

The first winter ascent of Frankland's Gully, V, Sgùrr Sgumain, on March 1, 1981

Brian Ledingham

standards with John Cunningham climbing Bastinado (now E1) on the same day Patsy Walsh freed Trophy Crack (E1); swapping routes immediately for the second ascents. The trophy was a peg left by Hamish MacInnes who had lowered off the route not long before. MacInnes was controversial in his blatant use of aid to force routes but he developed some of the best lines in the Cuillin. His good friend Ian Clough accompanied MacInnes on many projects throughout Scotland.

In 1957 the pair was prolific on Skye creating eight new routes with Creag Dhu Grooves (now E3) the pick of the bunch. The other notable visit was by the mercurial Robin Smith climbing Left Edge (E1) and a solo first ascent of Ladders (VS) on the rarely visited Chasm Crag. MacInnes and Clough added 14 new lines during 1958 including Grand Diedre (VS) and Vulcan Wall (HVS).

Tom Patey and a young Chris Bonington made their famous tour of the north of Scotland in 1960 and King Cobra (E1) was the most significant addition in the Cuillin. In the same year Robin Smith returned to climb Thunder Rib (E1); a frightening name for a frightening route. Patey, with Fred Harper, was the first to discover the huge walls at the top of the North-east wall of Blàbheinn with Chock-a-Block Chimney in 1961.

Big Elly Moriaty ran courses for the Mountaineering Association based in Glen Brittle in the early 1960s. John Harwood was a pupil on a course in 1963 but made his first Cuillin contributions with a direct start to Parallel Cracks. He returned as an instructor in '64 and '65 with an eye for unclimbed lines. In particular he developed the few solid areas of rock in Coire a' Ghreadaidh with Gail (E1) probably the best rock climb in the corrie.

It was earlier in 1965 that one of the last great Cuillin challenges had been finally achieved with the first winter traverse of the Main Ridge. Patey and Robertson, MacInnes and Crabb finally found the Ridge in ideal condition to achieve this mammoth challenge. It had been tried on a number of occasions before and, in 1962, Bill Wood wrote a very detailed account of every section but he had never managed to link them. It remains as the most highly prized route in British mountaineering.

Later in the year Clough was working as an instructor and added Shangri-La (VS) to Sròn na Ciche. These achievements were overshadowed by John Maclean's ascents of The Asp (E2) and Con's Cleft (E1) the two most prominent crack-lines on the sunny south face of Alasdair with the former being the Cuillin's hardest free ascent at the time. Also of note was the addition of The Snake (HVS) on Eastern Buttress led by Edinburgh Squirrels member Bill Sproul.

In 1967 Ginger Cain and Clive Boulton attacked the very steep face beside Slanting Gully to produce the serious line of Thor, the second E2 in the Cuillin. Harwood returned in 1968 with Roger High. Highlights were the fine Leviathan (VS) on the Chasm Crag but also modern routes on the granophyre crags of Marsco. Clough returned in September to develop the mass of unclimbed rock on Blàbheinn. Amongst 13 new routes the magnificent line of the Great Prow (VS) was the highlight. A St Andrews UMC party led by Phillip Gribbon had, however, beaten Clough's team to it a few weeks beforehand.

MacInnes and Clough returned to Blàbheinn in 1969 with sights set on even bigger prizes. They were joined by the strong team of Dave Alcock and Martin Boysen. All four made the first ascent of Jib (E1), the superb corner left of the Great Prow. Big routes were made on the adjacent Main Wall with Bargain Offer (E1) taking an uncompromising line close to Cathy and Hamish MacInnes's route called Clough's Cleft (VS). Clough discovered the very large and clean Glen Sligachan Buttress and Bealach Buttress had the steep upper wall breached by Tinn Lamh Crack (now E1) by J.Barraclough and J.B.Cooper. They then powered up Cocoa Cracks (now E2) left of Fluted Buttress.

The 1970s saw an improvement in protection and the use of twin axes for ice climbing so leading to increased standards in both summer and winter. As ever the new wave of developments took a few years to filter as far north as Skye. Paul Nunn climbed Ecstasis (E1) in 1972, but it was his completion of the Thor trilogy, with Megaton (E1) and Quark (now E3) during visits in '72, '74 and '76 with Boulton, Boyson and others, that was his major contribution. Jeff Lamb and Pete Botterill added Mongoose (E1) to the list of long classics on MhicCoinnich in 1974 with the direct pitch added by Mick Fowler and Phil Thomas on their highly productive first visit in 1977. Stairway to Heaven (E5) on the Great Prow was, by far, their greatest achievement. They also added Dilemma (E3) to Vulcan Wall just left of Creag Dhu Grooves (E3) which, itself, was freed by Richard McHardy and Gabriel Reagan in the same season. Geoff Cohen and Murray Hamilton finally freed Overhanging Crack (E2) on the Cioch in 1978 and Hamilton returned the following season with Dougie Mullin to climb Enigma (E3). The naked rocks in the Cuillin make water ice a real rarity but 1979 saw the first proper application of twin axes to steep ice by Jim Duff and Doug Scott. The Smear (V,5) is a long steep icefall between the Upper Rake and Foxes Rake.

Early season in 1980 had glorious weather and teams had a field day. Pete Hunter started by climbing four good routes in Glen Sligachan then climbed even better lines on Sròn na Ciche with Cameron Lees. The Krugerrand (E3) tackles the huge overhang directly behind the Cioch, Spock (E3) takes the blunt arete left of Vulcan Wall, Strappado Direct (E2) is almost independent of the original line and Acapulco Wall (E3) was added in the August. Clive Rowland had discovered the easily accessible south face of Sgùrr an Fheadain back in 1974 but returned in 1980 with friends to really develop the crag. The same bunch opened up Creag Druim Eadar da Choire in both 1980 and '81, with the clean central wall and steep east faces giving a fine selection of mid-grade routes. Rowland was a regular winter visitor with an eye for long new routes around this time and Frankland's Gully (V) was regarded as a step up in standards.

The most active climbers on Skye over the next few years ignored the Cuillin as mile upon mile of rock was discovered around the coastline. With such easy access this led to summer developments in the Cuillin noticeably slowing down.

In 1982 Dave 'Cubby' Cuthbertson produced some of the major Cuillin additions for the decade. With Duncan McCallum he climbed Zephyr, the second Cuillin E5, on the flying arete just right of Creag Dhu Grooves. A week later he was joined by Gary Latter and they climbed Magic (E4), Confession (E4) and the Chambre Finish (E2). Next day was spent making an incredible girdle traverse of the Eastern Buttress called Team Machine (E4). Although other routes were added to Sròn na Cìche through the '80s, with Dinwoodie giving the first Cuillin 6b grade to Erotica in 1983, it was only in 1989 that Grant Farquhar and Latter climbed the first E6 in the Cuillin. The Highlander fittingly climbs directly up the nose of the Cioch.

Only three major difficult routes were climbed elsewhere in the Cuillin in the whole decade. Lightfoot (E3) on Bealach Buttress was climbed by Murray Hamilton and Pete Whillance in 1983; G.Jones and A.Waters climbed Storm Watch (E3) on the steep side of Stack Buttress in Coire a' Ghrunnda and Steve Hill and Tom Dickson attacked the wall left of Naismith's Route to produce Rainbow Warrior (E3) on the Basteir Tooth in 1989.

The winter of 1986 was phenomenally heavy and saw the rare addition of major ice routes. Fowler and Vic Saunders' top priority was the first winter ascent of Waterpipe Gully (IV) which they achieved with time to spare so they moved across the corrie for a quick solo of a heavily iced South Gully (III) before some "inspiring possibilities open up above". A rope and two screws had survived the gear rationalisation which was enough to justify an ascent of Icicle Factory (VI,6). White Wedding (IV) the following day completed a typically successful weekend raid. Unknown to Fowler, Waterpipe had seen two ascents the week before. Greg Strange and Brian Findlay had ploughed to the foot on 23 February but backed off, then realised the scale of their error overnight in the car park and made the first ascent next day. The unfrozen bottom pitch had been bypassed but the complete ascent was made by Doug Scott and Colin Downer just four days later.

Coastal routes continued to be added at a frantic pace through the '90s, again having an inevitable effect on Cuillin and no advance in grades through a whole decade. In 1990 Tom Prentice and Kevin Howett added Uhuru (E3) to the unclimbed central section of Vulcan Wall. In the same year John MacKenzie added Rites of Passage (E1) and Black Magic (E2) on Creag Druim Eadar da Choire while Tom Walkington and Andy Cunningham cleaned and developed the low lying Sgùrr Hain Crag. A visit to Latter, Farquhar and Paul Thorburn in 1997 added the only new E5, with Finger in the Dyke taking an even more improbable line right of Stairway to Heaven.

Most other significant additions were made by comparative locals. Mull is not far as the crow flies from Skye but involves a ferry crossing and a three hour journey by road that hasn't tempered the enthusiasm of Colin Moody (Cog) right to this day. In 1994 he climbed virtually to the top of MhicCoinnich to climb seven new routes in one day and open up Top Buttress. Strathcarron guide Martin Moran started the decade by snatching the Ridge record but it was two big routes on the north face of Am Basteir that really left his mark on the summer scene. Hung, Drawn and Quartered (E3) in 1996 and The Squeeze Box (E2) in 1997 both tackled frighteningly steep and loose basalt chimneys rising vertically to the summit. Mike Lates had added a few routes since moving to Skye, with The Naked Saltire (E2) in 1999 the best.

Winter saw the real advances in the '90s. The Cuillin are rocky mountains that just don't form thick columns of ice regularly. A growing number of climbers realised the potential for climbing big routes in virtually any conditions. Deep Gash Gully (HVS) the most formidable of Cuillin gullies saw winter ascents by Fowler and John Lincoln and a week later Moran and Martin Welch in 1991. A few weeks beforehand Dave Ritchie and Steve Kennedy had scaled B Gully on Clach Glas that rises from just 200m above sea-level. Ritchie has since become the most prolific winter climber in the Cuillin, making raid after raid with a hardcore bunch of mates from Lochaber and Argyll and producing over 25 new routes. Through the '90s they favoured Am Basteir and Blàbheinn with winter ascents of Birthday Groove and Virgo, both IV,5, showing how amenable the low grade rock climbs could be.

Skye resident Colin Threlfall climbed a series of mixed routes through the early '90s with Paddy McGuire and a number of clients, particularly opening up the Glaic Moire Face. Moran also found the Cuillin frequently offered good guiding options and climbed 12 new routes on Blàbheinn and Pinnacle Ridge. A back roped solo of Forked Chimney (IV,5) in 1999 was a fine achievement exemplifying his drive and determination. Christmas 1993 saw a huge dump of snow which stayed to provide good ice conditions. Lates headed for a prominent icefall on the low-lying Winter Buttress on Blàbheinn finding it just too thin. Escape from Colditz (III) was a good consolation but Skye based lads, Donald Bissett and Mark Francis (Beads) beat him to the main prize a few days later to produce Sailaway (IV).

Fowler returned in 1995 with Andy Cave for a quick and misty mystery tour to climb Exiguous Gully (VI,6) on the back of MhicCoinnich and Serious Picnic (III) on Blàbheinn. In 1999 with Paul Ramsden he climbed a verglassed Whispering Wall (VI) and Chock-a-Block Chimney (V) on Blàbheinn the next day. Another fine addition was a winter ascent of O'Brien and Julian's Climb (VI,5) in 1996 by Brian Davison and Andy Nisbet to give possibly the most serious winter route in the Coruisk Basin.

The new millennium saw Coire a' Bhasteir busy again with Ritchie climbing Deep Chimney (IV,5), Moran on MacLaren's Chimney (IV,5) and Lates on Gingini Chimney (VI,6). Clough's Cleft (VI,6) on Blàbheinn gave Ritchie his finest Cuillin addition. Between 2001 and 2004 Ritchie attacked the high gullies and buttresses on Theàrlaich, only reluctantly admitting that "Ritchie V's" were probably grade VI years later. In January 2008 a fierce storm left the high cliffs plastered in rime. Pete Macpherson, Graham Briffett and Lates climbed Grand Diedre (V,6) but Guy Robertson and Mark Garthwaite stole the show the next day with an ascent of Dawn Grooves (VIII,8) bringing Cuillin standards in line with the rest of Scotland. Moran and Nick Carter confirmed the future potential at the end of 2008 with an outrageous ascent of Hung, Drawn and Quartered (VIII,8) on Am Basteir.

On rock the new decade saw Oxford Mountaineering Club open up the compact gabbro buttresses on Low Crag, close below the Tourist Route. Journey into Space (E5) and Electric Mainline (E5) both tackle the impressive Panoramix Wall. With Steve Broadbent at the helm they produced no less than 35 routes in the next few years. Steve Kennedy discovered Lota Buttress below the Tourist Route in 2002 and returned with the gang from Argyll and Lochaber a week later to clean up. In 2001 Kev Howett returned to Vulcan Wall with Scott Muir producing Clinging On (E4) one of the most desirable Cuillin lines which was also claimed by Julian Lines with an outrageous solo. Es Tressider and Blair Fyffe climbed a line of equal quality with Captain Planet (E4) on the Tooth in 2006. In 2007 Guy Robertson and Pete Benson climbed Paradise Found (E2), a superb long route on Coir' Uisg Buttress and the three star Rainman (E5) on Bealach Buttress next day. In 2008 Lates spied virgin rock high on Gillean, climbing five routes including Drag Queen (E4) and Big Worries Mate (E3) with quality clients. With Paul Cunningham he added four routes on the good rock in the TD Gap. Iain Taylor and Tess Fryer added yet more quality with Temerity (E4) on the Upper Cioch Buttress.

Back in 2004 Cuillin rock climbing had been brought back into line with the rest of the country by Dave Macleod. The Gathering (E8, 6b), again fittingly, breaches the overhanging east side of the Cioch by an outrageous sequence of small holds. Dave Birkett had climbed a very fine crack-line on Sgùrr an Fheadain to give What Have I Becombe? (E6, 6b, 6b) a month beforehand, but his finest Cuillin contribution came in 2007. Skye Wall (E8, 6b, 6c, 6a) on Coir' Uisg Buttress is a superb example of the top grade climbing still to be developed in years to come.

Big winters in 2009/10 and 2010/2011 have seen developments continue at all technical levels as the word seems to be finally getting out there is plenty to do in the Cuillin.

With fully professional climbers, exceptional indoor training facilities, and more technical tools than a heart surgeon, climbing is on the crest of a wave at this time. Hopefully this guidebook will inspire a new generation to appreciate all the Cuillin can offer.

Environment

Access

Part 1 of the Land Reform (Scotland) Act 2003 gives you the right to be on most land and inland water for recreation, education and for going from place to place, providing you act responsibly. This includes climbing, hillwalking, cycling and wild camping. These access rights and responsibilities are explained in the Scottish Outdoor Access Code. The key elements are:

- Take personal responsibility for your own actions and act safely.
- Respect people's privacy and peace of mind.
- Help land managers and others to work safely and effectively.
- Care for the environment and take your litter home.
- Keep your dog under proper control.
- Take extra care if you're organising an event or running a business.

Stalking, Shooting & Lambing

It is important to avoid disturbance to sheep, particularly during the lambing season between March and May. The stag stalking season is from 1st July to 20th October, although few estates start at the beginning of the season. Hinds continue to be culled until 15th February. Despite there being little commercial stalking on Skye climbers may encounter shooting parties, more likely carrying out a cull rather than for sport. Little notice is given because of the infrequency. Due respect should be given and confrontation avoided.

Flora & Fauna

Some rare alpine plants are exclusive to the range. In no circumstances should any plant-life be deliberately disturbed or damaged. Voles and other small mammals rely on the small amounts of vegetation that do exist in this delicate environment.

When climbing do not cause direct disturbance to birds, especially those nesting on crags such as Golden Eagle, Peregrine Falcon, Buzzard, Kestrel, and Raven. The most sensitive time is between early February and the end of July. Intentional disturbance of nesting birds is a criminal offence and if convicted, you face a fine of up to £5000 and confiscation of climbing equipment. It is the individual's responsibility to find out from the MCofS (see below) about voluntary restrictions at any particular location and to obtain advice as to whether their presence might disturb any nesting birds.

Erosion

Part of the revenue from the sale of this and other Scottish Mountaineering Club books is granted by the Scottish Mountaineering Trust as financial assistance towards the repair and maintenance of hill paths in Scotland. Enjoyment of future climbers shall not be spoiled by our damage of the landscape. Paths in the Black Cuillin are particularly well constructed. Climbers should take any opportunity to clear cross-drains to prevent these paths being washed away. If a path exists then try to stay on it. The danger of scratching by crampons should be carefully considered on winter ascents of rock routes, particularly on low lying cliffs where winter climbing is not established.

Cairns

The proliferation of navigation cairns detracts from the feeling of wildness, and may be confusing rather than helpful as regards route-finding. The indiscriminate building of cairns on the hills should be discouraged.

Car Use

Parking is generally not a problem but particular consideration must be used near the farm buildings in Glen Brittle. Avoid blocking access to private roads or land. Cars should drive with care on the narrow roads which often have livestock roaming on them. Passing places should be used to allow following traffic to overtake.

General Privacy

Respect for personal privacy near people's homes is nothing less than good manners.

Camping, Litter & Pollution

Responsible wild camping is permitted under the new access legislation, although 'No Camping' signs can still be found in the hills. If camping, do not cause pollution and bury human waste carefully out of sight and far away from any habitation or water supply. Avoid burying rubbish as this may also pollute the environment.

Stashes of water for attempts on the Cuillin Ridge are a major litter problem. These should be labelled and dated clearly and removed if not used.

Bothies

The Mountain Bothies Association <www.mountainbothies.org.uk> bothy at Camasunary is the only one within the Cuillin. Sadly its future is uncertain beyond 2012. By way of consolation it is not at all well placed for much Cuillin climbing.

Mountaineering Council of Scotland

The MCofS is the representative body for climbers and walkers in Scotland. One of its primary concerns is the continued free access to the hills and crags. Information about bird restrictions, stalking and general access issues can be obtained from their website <www.mcofs.org.uk>. Any climber or walker encountering problems regarding access should contact the MCofS at The Old Granary, West Mill Street, Perth PH1 5QP, tel (01738 638 227), fax (01738 442 095), email <info@mcofs.org.uk>.

Safety

Participation

"Climbing and mountaineering are activities with a danger of personal injury or death. Participants in these activities should be aware of and accept these risks and be responsible for their own actions and involvement."
UIAA participation statement.

Liabilities

You are responsible for your own actions and should not hold landowners liable for an accident, even if it happens while climbing over a fence or dyke. The same is true of routes with any protection in place. It is up to the individual climber to assess the reliability of bolts, pegs, slings or old nuts, which over time, may have become corroded and therefore fail.

Mountain Rescue

Contact the police, either by phone (999) or in person. Give concise information about the location and injuries of the victim and any assistance available at the accident site. It is often better to stay with the victim, but in a party of two, one may have to leave to summon help. Leave the casualty warm and comfortable in a sheltered, well marked place.

Mobile telephone reception is, with few exceptions, only found on top of ridges and peaks but magnetic rock can still create blank spots. Texts can often be sent when a conversation is proving impossible. A whistle or torch is still very useful to alert other people using the international distress signal (6 sharply repeated blasts or flashes repeated once every minute).

Accidents

A high percentage of accidents in the Black Cuillin result in serious injuries. Most common are those caused by climbers dislodging loose blocks. Extreme weathering, rock type and lack of regular traffic means that blocks of all sizes can move with alarming ease. Even commonly used abseil anchors should be treated very gently. See Skye MRT website <www.skyemrt.org>.

Weather Forecasts

Weather is important in the Cuillin. Modern forecasts are vastly improved but accuracy depends upon the speed that weather changes. Settled weather and atrocious conditions tend to be easy to predict but all need careful interpretation when changes are afoot. Vastly different opinions can be given from respected sources, even the evening before. Remaining optimistic frequently pays off in summer in particular with so much light available to climb long into the evenings.

Radio: BBC Radio Scotland has the Highland News at 7-55am which ends with a very accurate forecast for the Highland region Monday to Friday mornings. They also provide an excellent forecast for climbers, hillwalkers and sailors, broadcast 19.04 Monday-Friday 07.04 and 22.04 on Saturday and 07.04 and 20.04 on Sunday.

TV: A video forecast on BBC Text (p400) is shown on a loop for an accurate visual prediction of how weather systems are progressing. Reporting Scotland forecast at 6.50 to 6.55pm Monday to Friday with good satellite predictions.

Mountain specific internet forecasts: The areas covered are huge and need careful interpretation for the Cuillin.

<www.mwis.org.uk>

<www.metoffice.gov.uk/loutdoor/mountainsafety/westhighland>

Short term internet forecasts:

<www.metcheck.com> updates every 3 hrs. Reasonable long range forecasts.

<www.xcweather.co.uk> used by fishermen particularly for wind up to five days ahead.

<www.bbc.co.uk/weather> for good animations of cloud cover, precipitation etc.

Long term internet forecasts:

<www.weather.unisys.com/gfsx/index.php?r=eu>

<www.wetterzentrale.de>

Avalanches

Avalanches are thankfully rare in the Black Cuillin but the risk should be taken as seriously in this area as any. Climbers venturing on to the hills in winter should be familiar with the principles of snow structure and avalanche prediction. Deposition of windblown snow causes the largest risk. Slopes between 30 and 60 degrees with fresh snow, whether freshly fallen or simply blown, should be considered suspect. The greater the amount of fresh snow, the higher the risk. Avoiding these slopes may be simple, such as choosing a ridge rather than a gully, or finding a section of cliff blown clear, but remember that some buttress routes involve steep snow at their base or more seriously, just below the cliff top.

On meeting snow of dubious stability, climbers should dig a snow pit and examine the snow profile, looking especially for different layers of snow with different degrees of bonding. Slab avalanches are caused when a surface layer of snow is insufficiently attached to layers below and often when a climber triggers the slide. If a witness to an avalanche it is vital to start a search immediately, given it is safe to do so. Victims will often be alive at first, but their chances of survival lessen rapidly if buried. Unless severely injured, some 80% may live if found immediately, but only 10% after a three hour delay. Mark the burial site if known, listen for any sound, look for any visual clue, and search until help arrives if possible. A working knowledge of first aid may save a life, as many victims have stopped breathing. *A Chance in a Million?* by Bob Barton and Blyth Wright, published by the SMC, is the classic work on Scottish avalanches (see Books, below).

Midges and Ticks

Midges can be an annoyance between June and October but only usually peak badly in late July and August. Campers need to be especially well prepared, with head nets superior to any repellent. They are not often bad in the Cuillin but carrying a net is recommended for belays. When choosing a route try to climb in the wind and direct sunlight. The lack of vegetation and animals in the Cuillin generally keeps tick numbers low but they should be removed as completely as possible. Climbers should familiarise themselves with the effects of Lyme disease and consult a doctor if affected <www.lymediseaseaction.org.uk>.

Books

The sister-book to this edition, *Skye Sea-cliffs & Outcrops*, is an invaluable guidebook covering all other parts of Skye and neighbouring Raasay. Skye has arguably the best variety of sea-cliffs in Scotland including the soaring vertical columns of Kilt Rock, jug-covered overhangs at Elgol and hundreds of lines at Neist. Also covered are small sections on bouldering (including the Cuillin), stacks and pinnacles and one of the best ice arenas in the UK on the Trotternish Ridge.

Skye Scrambles contains many walks and scrambles not included in this book. Some descriptions and diagrams for overlapping routes are given in greater detail. *Hostile Habitats – Scotland's Mountain Environment* gives a particularly good insight into Scotland's mountain environments with the Cuillin well covered. *The Munros, The Corbetts, Scottish Hill Names, Scottish Hill Tracks*, and *A Chance in a Million? – Scottish Avalanches* are useful for hill walking routes and general mountain interest in this area. For more information and to order SMC and SMT publications, visit the SMC website <www.smc.org.uk>. See also the publications list at the end of this guide.

Technical

Grades and timings are for ideal conditions; dry rock or good snow and clear visibility.

Timings

Times have been introduced specifically for ridge scrambles. Individual ridges are described with timings and distances relating only to the scrambling section and not the approach walk. The Main Ridge is broken down into five sections that are described and given times in the Traverse chapter. Rounds of individual corries crossing sections of the Main Ridge are described briefly at the start of each chapter with times given for the complete round including approach. Times pertain to ideal conditions.

Scrambing Grades

Scrambling grades have been introduced to this edition with a deliberate crossover into the lower grade rock climbs. Long mountain ridges formally graded as easy rock climbs are now have a scrambling prefix to indicate this style of climb as opposed to a pitched rock climb. The Black Cuillin terrain is more serious than in other mountains in the UK. Grades are given for the easiest line and any deviation is likely to lead to more difficult and loose terrain.

Grade 1: Only minor use of hands is required and the right route fairly easy to find. A limited degree of exposure will be encountered. Descent and retreat should be comparatively simple.

Grade 2: More sustained use of hands will be required including short steep steps and narrow edges. Route finding and retreat can be quite difficult.

Grade 3: The most advanced standard of scrambling, usually on steep rock. For some sections climbers might prefer the protection of a rope in anything but perfect conditions. A route exists that does not involve making a graded climbing manoeuvre but finding the right line may not be easy particularly in sections of descent. Very exposed down-climbing is often needed and abseiling of these sections is not uncommon.

Grade 3/Moderate/Difficult/ Very Difficult or **Severe**: A scrambling style of route made harder by individual moves, sections or complete pitches (where the leader is required to place protection for security) of graded rock climbing.

Rock Climbing Grades

Compression of the grades in Britain happened in the 1950s and '60s with Very Severe being the highest even when points of aid were used. Climbs suspected as being under-graded are indicated in descriptions but be prepared for some surprises. Adjectival (overall) grades used are Easy, Moderate, Difficult, Very Difficult, Severe, Hard Severe, Very Severe (VS), Hard Very Severe (HVS) and Extremely Severe. The Extremely Severe grade is subdivided into E1, E2 and so on up to E8 in this book. UK technical grades are given for the hardest single move on a pitch or route.

Adjectival and technical grades are combined for routes of VS or above (and for Severe and Hard Severe where known). The normal range for technical grades expected on routes of the given overall grade are as follows; Severe – 4a, 4b; Hard Severe – 4a, 4b, 4c; VS – 4b, 4c, 5a; HVS – 4c, 5a, 5b; E1 – 5a, 5b, 5c; E2 – 5b, 5c, 6a; E3 – 5c, 6a; E4 – 5c, 6a, 6b; E5 – 6a, 6b. Routes with a technical grade at the lower end of the range will be sustained or poorly protected, while those with grades at the upper end are likely to have a shorter and generally well protected crux.

Winter Grades

The huge variation in how snow and ice forms will only ever make grades in winter an indication of seriousness. Multiple ascents give a common consensus but many Cuillin winter routes have seen no repeats. Grades are likely to be unique to what the first ascensionists found the route. Be prepared for great variation.

As with summer climbing a two-tier system is used with adjectival grade, in Roman numerals, giving an indication of the overall difficulty of the climb. Technical grades are shown by the Arabic numbers and apply to the hardest move or sequence of a route.

Grade I – Uncomplicated, average-angled snow climbs normally having no pitches. They may, however, have cornice difficulties or long run-outs.

Grade II – Gullies which contain either individual or minor pitches, or high-angled snow with difficult cornice exits. The easiest buttresses under winter conditions.

Grade III – Gullies which contain ice in quantity. There will normally be at least one substantial pitch and possibly several lesser ones. Sustained buttress climbs, but only technical in short sections.

Grade IV – Steeper and more technical with vertical sections found on ice climbs. Mixed routes will require a good repertoire of techniques.

Grade V – Climbs which are difficult, sustained and serious. If on ice, long sustained ice pitches are to be expected; mixed routes will require a degree of rock climbing ability and the use of axe torquing and hooking and similar winter tec niques.

Grade VI – Thin and tenuous ice routes or those with long vertical sections. Mixed routes will include all that has gone before but more of it.

Grade VII – Usually mixed routes which are very sustained or technically extreme. Also sustained routes on thin or vertical ice.

Grade VIII and beyond – Very hard and sustained mixed routes.

Pegs and Bolts

Bolts are considered unacceptable on mountain cliffs, so there are none in the Cuillin and none should be placed in future. Scotland has a tradition of climbs with leader placed protection with pegs also considered as unacceptable in summer rock first ascents. This is due to improved equipment and the option of move rehearsal as an alternative to hammered protection. Particularly compact gabbro buttresses in Glen Sligachan have seen this position compromised. The boldness of resulting climbs is still obvious and preferable to drilling bolted protection, so they have been included. The use of pegs in winter is still considered acceptable if removed by the second.

Using this Guidebook

Guidebook Layout

Crags and climbs on the Main Ridge are arranged by the corrie in which they lie rather than by the peak they are on. They are described in an anti-clockwise direction, starting with the inner sanctum of Harta Corrie, around the outside of the Main Ridge before reaching the huge inner corrie of Coruisk. Each area has a prominent starting point with approaches to crags and bealachs (passes) described at the start of the chapter, also marked on corrie photodiagrams where possible. Specific details of approach and descent are given with individual crags.

Diagrams

Corrie diagrams: All chapters apart from Cuillin Outliers have photodiagrams to show crags, approaches, descents and some climbs. They should be used in conjunction with maps and written descriptions. Each crag is numbered for the index and then retained in the text and maps.

Crag diagrams: If a route has been numbered in the text this indicates that there is a diagram depicting the cliff but not necessarily every climb. The diagram will be page-referenced and usually close to the relevant text. Many diagrams depict cliffs hundreds of metres high. The route marked will often only give an indication of the correct line concentrating on the start, key features and finish.

Maps

Guidebook maps (symbols are used indicate different categories of summit. Munro – black triangle; Corbett – black circle; Graham – black diamond; Other – crossed circle) give the overall layout of the peaks, corries and glens but a detailed map will always be needed for fine navigation. Map references have been taken from the Harvey's *Skye The Cuillin* Superwalker map. The whole area is covered on one side at 1:25,000 and the Main Ridge is enlarged to 1:12,500 on the other. The 1:50,000 and 1:25,000 OS maps for the Black Cuillin are both difficult to interpret with little differentiation between rocky ground and sheer cliffs.

Route Description

There are many big faces, particularly those set at low angles, where an almost infinite number of variations are possible. Detailed descriptions on this type of terrain can create more confusion than assistance. An attempt has been made to establish key features that can be used to keep on the recorded routes. Original descriptions have been retained where they are likely to be of use but climbers will need to use their experience in order to make important route finding decisions. Pitch lengths are often rounded to the nearest 5m. The descriptions assume the use of 50m ropes.

Left and Right

The terms generally refer to a climber facing the cliff. The Cuillin have a lot of ridge routes with both ascents and descents in which case the direction is specified or clarified by using compass directions. Routes are described from the direction in which the cliff is normally approached as indicated in the text.

Recommended Routes

A star quality system has been used. No star routes may be good although nothing special, eliminate in line, or lack information. Only a few are worthless or unpleasant.

   * Good climbing, but the route may lack line, situation or balance.

   ** A good route but lacking one or more of the features that make it a climb of the highest quality.

   *** A route of the highest quality, combining superb climbing with line, character and situation.

   **** The best climbs of their class in Scotland.

   In winter, quality will vary with conditions so stars, like grades, are applied for the conditions when the route is commonly climbed. In the best conditions the routes may justify more stars.

First Ascensionists

The year of the first ascent is given in the text. The full date and first ascensionists are listed by area in chronological order at the back of the guide. If climbed originally using aid or rest points, this is listed, usually with the first free ascent. Details of variations are usually given under the parent route. An ascent in winter conditions is indicated by a W at the start of an entry and a summer route by S. Winter ascents are listed separately from their corresponding summer route.

Specific Cuillin Advice

Skye Weather and Where to Climb

Skye has an unfair reputation for wet weather, being statistically drier than both Glen Coe and Fort William. It is fair to say that Skye has dramatic weather, often hugely varied across the island and through the day. Choice of location and type of route are the key to a successful trip. Weather patterns do exist and are affected by wind direction in particular. Modern forecasts tend to be very reliable for the proceeding 24 hours but long term forecasts are often wrong.

The driest weather comes from north and easterly airflows with moisture having been deposited on the Scottish mainland. It is quite unusual for this rule of thumb to fail. South and westerly airflows come in off the Atlantic. Fronts can move through very fast and an up to date forecast, predicting a rapid change to dry weather, should be noted and trusted. Forecasts for precipitation should be examined closely as there is a big difference between persistent rain and intermittent showers. Cloud base is important as it will affect navigation and can make rocks wet but there are many low-lying crags to choose from. The sharp structure of the Black Cuillin can break up strong winds with ridges and walls often sheltered compared to the open slopes of more rounded hills. Microclimates in the Cuillin are very specific with one end of the range often sheltering the other. In winds from the south and west the north (Sligachan) end of the Ridge is more likely to be clear. In winds from the north and east the south (Glen Brittle) end is more likely to be clear. The cut-off point is often distinct around Sgùrr a' Mhadaidh. In north-westerly winds Blàbheinn and Clach Glas are most likely to be clear.

Evening weather is frequently better through the summer months. With long hours of daylight a full day can still be had even when starting after lunch. In midsummer, with clear skies, it is never completely dark but torches may be needed between 11pm and 4am. In mid-winter, with cloud cover, it may be necessary to use torches until 8-30am and again by 4pm. As a rule of thumb, British Summer Time gives at least 12 hours of daylight in which to climb. Approach paths in the Black Cuillin are all very well constructed and allow an easy hour of walking in the dark. Winters have generally been colder and drier over the past few years. Really heavy snowfalls that block roads are rare and reliably cleared in less than 24 hours. Winter conditions can be expected from October onwards. Snow patches requiring crampons to cross safely often last until late April or May.

If mountain conditions are unfavourable or limbs are weary the island offers a huge variety of alternatives, summer and winter, often with very different weather as described in the sister-book to this edition, *Skye Sea-cliffs & Outcrops*.

Black Cuillin Terrain

These rocky peaks have little vegetation above 300m. Above this height any approach or descent will involve following discontinuous trails through boulders, screes and slabs with hands needed regularly. Narrow rocky ridges linking the peaks provide popular scrambling routes but also give the easiest descents from many climbs. Although technically easier than rock climbs, these routes see the vast majority of accidents in the Cuillin. Good hill skills are important and those in doubt should approach with modest ambitions. On good days in summer, when the daylight lasts for nearly 20hrs, the mountains induce a relaxed and carefree attitude. As with all big mountains the serious nature becomes apparent very rapidly as soon as cloud and rain draw in.

Gabbro is the Cuillin bedrock. It is exceptionally rough and gives good adhesion for feet but is very hard on clothing, equipment and skin. Basalt is compact, finer grained and more fractured so generally less reliable. It exists both as horizontal slabs and vertical dykes that often consist of blocky bands or ladders offering little protection. Lichens on any rocks are exceedingly slick when wet.

Route Type

The Cuillin offers three main types of outing for the summer climber.

1. "Cragging" with short climbs and easy descents. Leaders will know from experience how large a rack to take and whether one or two ropes are appropriate.

2. Mountaineering days aiming to cover a lot of easy climbing and probably more than one peak. A minimal rack and the minimum amount of rope needed for abseils should be used to keep pack size down; moving quickly over easy climbing terrain is the aim on these days.

3. Multi-pitch mountain rock climbs generally finishing close to, or on the top of, a peak. Climb a route with at least one grade in hand in case of trouble route finding. Familiarise yourself with the descents and possible escape routes. Climbing on two ropes is normal to allow for long abseils to be made in emergencies but they are not always used on the whole climb.

Bouldering

Thousands of gabbro boulders lie among glaciated slabs giving some of the finest mountain bouldering in the country. The rock is generally solid and clean and there are rarely any features on the roofs and steeper walls. Problems tend to be on lip traverses, arêtes, thin faces and sometimes cracks. Gabbro is well known for its incredible roughness; many a bouldering trip has been abandoned early due to raw fingertips so gloves/finger tape is advised. A bouldering mat is useful as the landings are often in a bog, stream or fierce rocks. The favourite venue is Coire Lagan and a dedicated guidebook, *Gabbrofest*, is available on-line at <www.betaguides.com>.

Equipment & Planning

An Alpine mentality of travelling light and fast works well in good conditions but contingency for rapid changes in weather should be made. Rescue is usually a long procedure and adequate warm clothing and shelter helps to slow the onset of hypothermia. Helmets are recommended for all routes. Gloves are recommended for all but the warmest of weather and can give useful protection to the fingers against the gabbro.

Gabbro is incredibly sharp and abrasive and great consideration should be given to the effect on ropes. Rope-drag, abseils and falls will all potentially shear a rope running over the razor edged crystals. Crystals can also give problems when seating nuts into cracks and camming devices have made protection far easier to place on many routes. Long slings are very useful for reducing rope drag and threading chockstones. In winter the majority of routes are mixed and require rock protection for security. Extra blade pegs are useful. Water ice is rare and only a few ice screws are generally required.

Navigation is complex especially if caught in cloud. Maps cannot show every detail and the presence of magnetic rock means a compass must be cleverly used as an aid rather than relied upon. The same applies to GPS too. Mobile phone coverage below the top of the ridges is almost non-existent.

Studying photodiagrams and written descriptions in advance will help with navigation at least as much as maps in the Black Cuillin.

Amenities

Reaching Skye

The Skye Bridge route is most popular being both free and quicker from most places taking 2hrs from Inverness or Fort William, 5hrs from Glasgow and 7hrs from the border. Taking the A9 to Dalwhinnie then crossing to Spean Bridge is the quickest route from the south but does miss the splendour of Loch Lomond and Glen Coe. Many sat-nav systems send drivers to Mallaig for the classic ferry journey. See <www.calmac.co.uk> for timetables and prices.

Travelling to Inverness by train or plane then hiring a car is an increasingly popular and viable option. Rail journeys to Kyle and Mallaig are beautiful routes <www.scotrail.co.uk>. Car hire on the island must be pre-booked. A Citylink

<www.citylink.co.uk> coach to Sligachan involves the least number of changes but be aware that there are no shops. Local buses are very limited with many run on school-days only and no service to Glen Brittle. A day-rover ticket for local buses is the best value <www.stagecoachbus.com>.

Choosing A Base

The Cuillin are situated centrally on this large island and a base in a band between Broadford and Portree will keep travelling times to a minimum. Glen Brittle is a logical base for climbing but somewhat isolated. Without transport Sligachan allows easy trips to Portree for provisions. Those with transport will find the main roads are very fast but single-track roads slow.

Accommodation

Tourist information offices are a good central source. The Portree office operates all year (01478 612 137) with seasonal branches in Broadford (01471 822 361) and Dunvegan <www.visithighlands.com> or (01845 22 55 121).The internet will be used by most visitors. Many good options appear several pages into searches and some very good deals can be found through the winter months.

Campsites at Sligachan and Glen Brittle are at the foot of the Cuillin. Other sites are listed on <www.scottishcamping.com> or <www.ukcampsite.co.uk>. Wild camping should be done considerately in line with the Scottish Outdoor Access Code and is not allowed beside the road in Glen Brittle.

Two mountaineering huts offering cheap accommodation are available to members of the BMC <www.bmc.co.uk>, MCofS <www.mountaineering-scotland.org.uk> and affiliated clubs. The BMC Memorial Hut at Glen Brittle has road access. The JMCS Coruisk Memorial Hut is usually reached using the Elgol boat services. The SYHA operates three hostels on Skye with Glen Brittle and Broadford hostels most useful <www.syha.org.uk>, (0870 155 3255). Independent hostels are now as popular as camping and most are listed on <www.hostel-scotland.co.uk> with the one at Sligachan a significant exception. The MBA bothy at Camasunary is due to close in 2012.

Food Shops

There are large branhes of the Co-operative supermarket in Portree, Broadford and Kyle and small branches of Mace in Broadford, Dunvegan and Staffin.

Eating & Drinking

There are an increasing number of top quality restaurants across the island and most pubs and hotels have improved quality hugely in recent years. Best climbing craic is to be found in the Old Inn in Carbost or Seamus bar at Sligachan. There is often live music in the Old Inn, Dunvegan Hotel, Edinbane Hotel and Isle Oronsay Hotel in Sleat. Quite a number of pubs and hotels close through winter making Portree or Broadford the best bases.

Climbing Equipment

Cioch Direct in Struan carry a supply of rock-climbing essentials but specialise in made-to-measure waterproofs. Inside Outside (Portree) and 914-Outdoor (Dornie) have a wider selection including camping gear. Camping gas, cheap waterproofs and boots can be found at Jans Mica, Bow and Stern or North-Eastern Farmers, all on Dunvegan Road in Portree, or the Magpie shop (beside the vets) in Broadford.

Climbing Walls & Leisure Centres

Portree High School has a leisure centre open to the public evenings, weekends and school holidays and has a tiny climbing wall (01478 614 810). Kyle of Lochalsh leisure centre has more times available for public access (01599 534 848)

Health

The Mackinnon Memorial Hospital in Broadford is the largest A&E facility and only x-ray department (01471 822491). There are medical centres in Portree (01478 612013), Broadford (01471 822 460) and Dunvegan (01471 521 203).

Fuel & Garages

Broadford Co-op has the only 24-hour fuel service with most in Portree and Dunvegan closing at 8pm in summer. Smaller outlets are still running in Carbost, Staffin and Struan. Recovery services use local contractors that know the island far better than call centre operatives.

Internet Access & Mobile Phone Reception

Wireless access or terminals to hire are widely available in cafes, pubs and shops throughout the island. One notable exception is Glen Brittle. Phone reception is most reliable on top of the Cuillin; texting is the best way to communicate when reception is intermittent.

Gaelic Pronunciations

The Gaelic (pronounced Galic not Gaylic as in Eire) language is an important part of the heritage of Skye. Knowing the meaning of mountain and place names and attempting to correctly pronounce them forms a connection for the climber with both the landscape and history. Emphasise the first syllable (English emphasises the second).

Gaelic	Phonetic	Meaning
allt	(allt)	river
banachdaich	(banachdich)	milkmaid / smallpox
basteir, bhasteir	(basteer, vasteer)	executioner (possibly)
beag	(bayk)	small
bealach	(bayallach)	pass, col
bidean	(bitjin)	sharp peak
bheinn	(vayn)	mountain
Blàbheinn	(bla-vayn)	Blue mountain
Bruach na Frithe	(brew-ach na free)	Brae of the forest
coire/choire	(coor or cooree)	corrie, valley
dearg	(jerrack)	red
druim	(drim)	ridge
dubh	(doo)	black
Sgùrr Dubh na Dà Bheinn	(doo-na da-vayn)	Black peak of the two ridges
eas	(eyas)	waterfall
eileann	(ellen)	island
fheadain	(aityan)	pipes
garbh	(garav)	rough
Gars-bheinn	(garsvayn)	Echoing mountain
ghreadaidh	(hreetah)	storms
ghrunnda	(hrroonda)	bare, naked
laogh	(llew)	calf
loch	(loch *not* lock)	lake
mhadaidh	(vaati)	fox
MhicCoinnich	(vick-hoe-inich)	Mackenzie
ràmh	(raav)	oars
Sligachan	(slig-acun)	Place of shells
sgùrr	(skoor)	peak
sròn	(shrone)	nose
Thearlaich	(hearlak)	Charles
Thormaid	(horrer-madge)	Norman
Thuilm	(hoolim)	Tulm (a Gaelic hero)

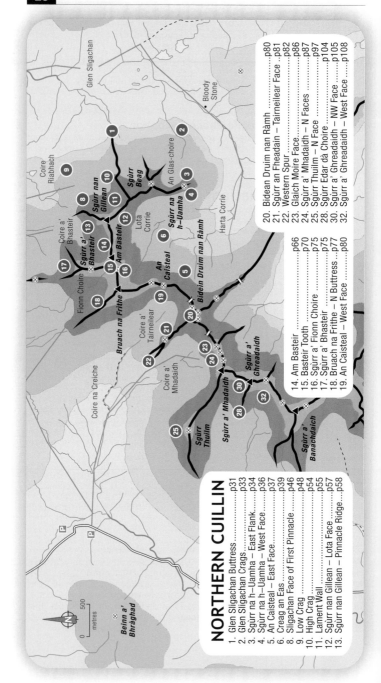

28

NORTHERN CUILLIN

GLEN SLIGACHAN & HARTA CORRIE
Diagram p32

This area offers two distinct styles of climbing. Long mountain routes leading to the summits of An Caisteal and Sgùrr na h-Uamha are alpine in both nature and scale. Dwarfed by comparison only are a selection of large buttresses that offer more cragging style climbs at very low altitude.

Glen Sligachan cuts a swathe through the heart of the Cuillin bowl giving a route that is considered by many to be the finest low-level walk in the British Isles. A well constructed footpath runs the full 12km from one coast to the other but the Sligachan river separates this from the crags and alternative approaches described are often preferable.

The glen footpath is also used to approach the rough granophyre buttresses on Marsco, described in the Cuillin Outliers chapter. Coruisk climbs can also be approached from Sligachan by crossing the Druim nan Ràmh from Harta Corrie as described in the Coruisk chapter.

In Harta Corrie there is arguably the most awesome scenery in the whole Cuillin with truly enormous walls of continuous rock. Routes are technically easy but have a big mountain feel to them. Speed and efficiency are needed to reach the summits comfortably.

The buttresses of compact, rough gabbro in Glen Sligachan are far bigger than they appear from a distance. Being at low altitude they offer superb routes at a variety of grades when the high mountain crags are shrouded in mist. The rock dries quickly and there are different aspects to suit various weather conditions.

Much of this area catches sunshine easily so is not a common choice for winter activity. However, closer inspection of aspect has given a number of possibilities. In heavy winter conditions the faces give some of the longest Alpine possibilities in the whole Cuillin and are worthwhile seeking out.

Approaches: Water levels in the River Sligachan must be considered when choosing an approach for glen climbs. Crossing the Ridge and descending to the climbs is drier and faster for many of the mountain routes but does require good visibility. Reaching the crags from below is navigationally simplest so approaches starting by the glen path are described here. Alternative approaches are described before the routes.

The footpath starts from the gated path on the north side of the old bridge at Sligachan, (NG 487 298). Follow the glen footpath for 6km until directly below Marsco at the sunken watercourse of the Allt Fiaclan Dearg (NG 496 253).
Head directly across the floor of the glen and cross the river to reach Glen Sligachan Buttress [1], (1hr 30mins). The buttress forms the start of an obvious rocky spur that could be construed as the true East Ridge of Gillean.

Continue for 400 metres beyond the Allt Fiaclan Dearg. A small path heads right down a stretch of short grass before taking a wet direct line to the bank of the River Sligachan at the mouth of Harta Corrie. Glen Sligachan Crags [2] are approached by crossing the River Sligachan at its confluence with the Allt a' Ghlais-choire and a short rise, 1hr 30mins. The East Flank of Sgùrr na h-Uamha [3] approach ascends An Glas-choire from the same crossing point over easy rough terrain, (2hrs 30mins).

The remaining cliffs lie above Harta Coire. Continue on the south bank of the River Sligachan past the magnificent Bloody Stone (good bouldering). The routes on the West Face of Sgùrr na h-Uamha [4] are approached by a small side corrie called Coire nan Clach, (2hrs 45mins). The Harta Face of An Caisteal [5] lies 2 kilometres beyond the Bloody Stone where the corrie turns north, narrows and forms an incredible amphitheatre, (2hrs 30mins). Rock faces rear up for over 700 metres to the serrated ridge above. Creag an Eas [6] is the broad cliff with a beautiful waterfall at the right-hand side that blocks easy access to Lota Corrie from the head of Harta Corrie, (2hrs 45mins).

1. GLEN SLIGACHAN BUTTRESS

1. Sidetrack   Very Difficult
2. Cheek of the Devil   HVS *
3. Blasphemy Chimneys   Severe
4. Opal Creamer   E1 *
5. Rat Trap   VS

GLEN SLIGACHAN

1. GLEN SLIGACHAN BUTTRESS

(NG 485 252)   Alt 150m   East facing   Map p28   Diagrams p30, 32
This very large buttress lies on the north side of the prominent stream. A very deeply recessed twin chimney system separates the Left and Right Buttresses. Routes are described from left to right.

Alternative Approach: Follow the Tourist Route footpath to Low Crag [9]. Traverse below this crag and continue south-east, descending slightly, across rough ground for 1km, (1hr 20mins).

Descent: Traverse left (south) to gain the stream-bed in the open gully. Alternatively, the continuation ridge gives a good scramble to the bealach between Sgùrr Beag and Sgùrr nan Gillean (Grade 2) passing close by High Crag [10].

Left Buttress

1 Sidetrack   135m   Very Difficult   *(1969)*
Start at the left side of the buttress.
1. 25m Climb a left-slanting crack followed by slabs to a recess.
2. 35m Climb directly above by a shallow corner and slabs, then veer right to belay below a steepening.
3. 20m Go up right to climb a short steep groove, then move left to a ledge.
4. 30m Climb up left to the final bulging barrier and make a long horizontal traverse right to a cracked block belay in a corner.
5. 25m Ascend the groove directly above the belay, then trend diagonally left to the top.

2 Cheek of the Devil   155m   HVS *   *(1980)*
A very steep wall with blank grooves and lots of exposure at the huge overhang. Start at a cairn on slabs below the left end of the huge roof.
1. 25m Climb the slabs to a niche just left of the nose.
2. 25m 5a Pull over the niche and go up steeply leftwards into a blank groove with a bulging headwall. From the very narrow ledge beneath the headwall, go right up a faint groove to a wide ledge and peg belays.
3. 35m Traverse right, then climb a small V-groove high on the right-hand side of the big wall. Climb the groove to a peg belay.
4. 35m 5a Bold moves up the steep wall on good holds lead rightwards to the arete. Climb around the arete and go up to a superb eyrie (peg runner). Go delicately around the arete to a thin crack, climb this and walls above to the girdling ledge.
4. 35m Finish up short walls and corners.

Right Buttress

This is the steep clean wall with a prominent vertical white streak in the centre. It is bound on the left by two parallel corners that cross in a grassy bay low down.

3 Blasphemy Chimneys   105m   Severe   *(1969)*
Takes the left-hand corners above and below the grassy bay.
Climb the prominent corner-chimney strenuously to a large grassy bay. Walk into the corner and climb the left-hand of two chimneys into a niche. Move up left and climb a crack to a grass ledge, then move back right to belay in a corner of the original line at a ledge. Finish up the corner.

4 Opal Creamer   80m   E1 *   *(1980)*
This route takes a fairly sustained line left of a white streak. Start from the large grassy bay.
1. 45m 5a Climb direct up a faint line for 12m, crux. Go slightly left and follow a

GLEN SLIGACHAN & HARTA CORRIE

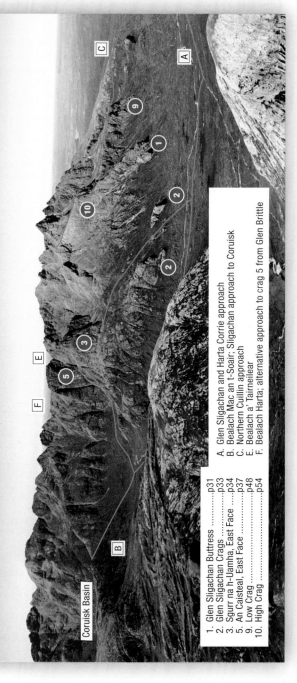

Coruisk Basin

1. Glen Sligachan Buttress p31
2. Glen Sligachan Crags p33
3. Sgurr na h-Uamha, East Face p34
5. An Caisteal, East Face p48
9. Low Crag p48
10. High Crag p54

A. Glen Sligachan and Harta Corrie approach
B. Bealach Mac an t-Soair; Sligachan approach to Coruisk
C. Northern Cuillin approach
E. Bealach a' Tairneilear
F. Bealach Harta; alternative approach to crag 5 from Glen Brittle

narrow zigzag line to a crack at 30m. Go right, then left and up to a good chock belay under the first overlap.

2. 35m Move over the overlap on the right and continue up to the overhang. Pull over this on good holds and finish up slabs on Rat Trap.

5 Rat Trap   95m   VS   *(1980)*
Start at the lowest rocks just right of the white streak.
1. 35m Climb up and right to a peg belay in a niche at the foot of a slanting groove system.
2. 25m Follow the slanting grooves to a short chimney, then climb this to a good peg belay beneath a prominent left-slanting crack.
3. 35m 5a Climb the very awkward crack, then follow easier ground to the top.

2. GLEN SLIGACHAN CRAGS

Map p28   Diagram p32
These fine crags lie either side of the Allt a' Ghlais-choire 1km south of Sligachan Buttress. The rock is rough gabbro offering excellent friction. Blade pegs are useful as the rock can be very compact, but protection is generally good when found.

Alternative Approach: As for Glen Sligachan Buttress and continue south on useful deer trails for a further 1km. (1hr 35mins).

Main Crag

(NG 488 245)   Alt 120m   East facing
This crag is over 100m high and roughly triangular in shape on its north-east face. The south-east face is composed of vast rolling slabs. Descend most easily by traversing northwards.

North-East Face

Lukes' Climb   50m   Hard Severe 4b *   *(2000)*
At the left side of the north-east face an obvious heathery ramp leads rightwards on to the face. Start at the far right of the ramp (peg belay).
1. 25m Climb the slab into a shallow corner and go up the right wall. Make an airy traverse right to the central slabs. Go up these for 5m to a crack.
2. 25m 4b Climb just right of the corner to an obvious break. Climb this awkwardly to a spacious ledge.
Scramble off left to easy slabs leading to the top of the crag.

South-East Face

The Runaway Slabs   100m   Very Difficult   *(2000)*
Climb the slabs centrally on good rock with excellent friction. Much variation possible.

Laceration Crag

(NG 487 242)   Alt 160m   East facing

This lies about 200m south of the Main Crag and slightly higher up the hill.

Descent: To the right passing below slabby walls.
The most prominent feature is a long off-width chimney that gives the next route.

Slash and Burn   40m   VS 4b   *(2000)*
Graded for the use of pegs.
1. 25m 4b Climb the slabby right wall of the chimney till forced to move left. Bridge up to a small tree which is passed on the right with difficulty to move just outside a chimney-cave (peg belay).

2. 15m 4b Climb the slabby corner above with good moves leading to a trap chimney.

Hartatak   90m   VS 4c   *(2002)*
Takes a diagonal line from right to left. The slabby buttress has a recessed area in the middle with two small bulges low down. To the right of the bulges are some pale streaks. A narrow grassy ledge runs diagonally left across the slab. From the right side of the slab, roughly below the right-hand bulge, follow a line leading diagonally left, above and parallel to the grassy ledge. A flake-line leads to near the left edge just below a small grassy recess (45m). Traverse back right along a narrow ledge to the middle of the slab then directly up via some short corners (45m).

Mortuary Slab

(NG 485 240)   Alt 225m   East facing

This large slab overlooks the Bloody Stone. From the top of Laceration Crag, the slab is seen in profile 100m to the west. A slight descent leads to its foot.

Descent: Move right and scramble over slabs to the top of Laceration Crag.

Post Mortem   30m   Very Difficult *   *(2000)*
Start 20m from the right edge at an obvious break (small cairn). Climb the crack for 5m to where it forks. Follow cracks and grooves leftwards to the easier slabs above (good protection).

SGÙRR NA H-UAMHA

The wonderful uniform shape of this peak when viewed from Elgol is due to the two large opposing faces that meet on a narrow summit ridge. There is huge scope for variation from the routes recorded on them; indeed few people ever feel that they have followed the line they were attempting. These are all long routes largely on good quality rock at the lower end of the grades and without too much danger of running into a climbing cul-de-sac.

Alternative Approach: Ascend the Tourist Route until it reaches the South-East Ridge, Traverse Sgùrr Beag and descend to Bealach a' Ghlais-choire. Gain the foot of the climbs by diagonal descents below the East or West flanks, (3hrs).

Descents: All routes finish on the summit. Descend north along the narrow steep ridge with some difficult route choices to reach Bealach a' Ghlas-choire, Grade 3/Moderate (20mins). The return to Sligachan is likely to be the same as the approach. Descent of An Glas-choire to the Glen is quickest but potentially very wet. Drier is to continue north to Sgùrr Beag then west towards Sgùrr nan Gillean. Large cairns mark where the Tourist Route descends at an altitude of about 800m.

3. EAST FLANK

(NG 478 241)   Alt 525m   East facing   Map p28, Diagrams p32, 35

North-East Face

The right-hand end of the East Flank becomes steeper and more continuous giving a concentrated area of climbs which can be difficult to tell apart.

1 Un-named Climb   130m   Very Difficult   *(1964)*
The most northern buttress of the face is separated from the main face by a prominent gully. Climb the gully for 80m then follow the left branch, going first by a chimney, then several jammed blocks, followed by rather loose rock, to finish just north of the summit.

3. SGÙRR NA H-UAMHA
East Flank

d

1

3 2

5 4

6

1. Unnamed Climb	Very Difficult
2. Aslan's Tongue	Severe *
3. North–East Face	
Original Route	Grade 3/Mod
3a. Cuill Climb	II/III *
4. The Crescent	Very Difficult
5. Left Hand Route	III
6. South Ridge	Grade 3/Mod

d. descent (North Ridge, Grade 3/Mod)

Laceration Crag

2 Aslan's Tongue 300m Severe *(1968)*
This route takes the line of a huge hanging tongue shaped ridge running out from the back of the recessed bay that lies below the north-east face. Start at the first break right of a cairn at the base. Trend right before breaking back on clean slabs to the crest, after which the climb is nowhere really difficult. After about 100m the route dwindles to a ledge with an undercut wall to the left; now follow two 50m steps leading to a further 90m of open slabs which end right at the summit.

3 North-East Face Original Route 250m Grade 3/Moderate *(1887)*
The route follows an obvious right-slanting break on a face that looks more north than north-east. Ascend a conspicuous slabby ramp then continue up a left-slanting groove. Climbs slabs on the right where the gully broadens. The angle steepens above here giving many different options. The original party moved left over easier ground before taking slabs direct to the summit
Winter: **Cuill Climb 250m II/III** * *(1999)*
Follows the summer line then makes a direct finish. Start 20m right of the gully on the North-East Face. Climb a short icefall and continue up a left-slanting groove to join a broader part of the gully after 30m. Climb this until it swings to the right and as it turns upwards again follow it past an exit left towards the eastern flank.

Continue until the gully makes a small diversion rightwards. At this point climb up the slabs ahead, moving slightly left to link up the two right-facing overlaps above, before finishing more directly to the summit.

The next routes lie to the south and are approached by traversing beneath the face from the upper reaches of An Glas-choire.

South-East Face

4 The Crescent   150m   Very Difficult *   *(2002)*
High on the left side of the east face is a prominent hanging groove topped by an overhanging wall. The face to the left of the groove drops down into a corner and forms an extensive area of slabs.
1. 45m Start directly below the groove in a small grassy bay and follow a basalt fault over a small bulge to gain the right side of a small hanging slab. Climb the slab into the main groove which almost forms a gully in the lower section.
2. 60m Move left from the base of the groove on to a slabby wall. Follow a crack-line until below the overhanging wall.
3. 45m Traverse up leftwards to the buttress edge in a fine position. Move up the edge then pull back right to reach the easier upper section of the face (45m). Some 200m of scrambling leads to the summit.

5 Left Hand Route   295m   III   *(2000)*
This is the left-hand of the two parallel gullies in the middle of the south-east face. Traverse leftwards until the left-hand gully is reached. Climb the gully which is mainly easy angled up and over steps for 150m, until a short steep section is reached. Climb this and continue until the gully ends. Climb slabby rocks above bearing right for two pitches and move over easier ground to reach the summit ridge.

The line of the next route is not clear from the floor of the glen but is obvious once the broad grass rake below the East Face is reached.

6 South Ridge   300m   Grade 3/Moderate *   *(1890)*
Start 150m right of the nose of the south ridge. Ascend the rib left of a shallow gully which deepens as it reaches the South Ridge. Take steep rocks directly once the ridge is gained and continue to the top as close to the crest as possible.

The next route takes a line approximating to the true South Ridge of Sgùrr na h-Uamha. Its precise start, line and end are unclear but the original description is included as an aid to navigation.

7 Smith's Climb   300m   Severe *   *(1949)*
This line, chosen to obtain the most continuous climbing, is roughly in the direction of the summit from the lowest point of the Druim nan Ràmh ridge. The crag is in three tiers, the lowest being broken, the middle being the main face and uppermost comprising the summit rocks. Climb a groove onto steep slabs for about 60m to a line of vertical rocks. From below this, follow a diagonal traverse left to the first steep, smooth groove. Gain the main face ahead and climb up until a left traverse is possible along a line of basalt. Climb up into a deep square-cut groove, visible on the skyline from the base of this section. Follow this for 60m to the summit ridge which eases to scrambling near the top.

4. WEST FACE

(NG 475 240)   Alt 600m   West facing   Map p28
This tiered face is technically high above Harta Corrie. It is bounded on the left by West Gully and on the right by the true South Ridge. The first route takes a central line up the South-West face directly to the summit.

1 Murray's Climb   240m   Difficult   *(1937)*
The face springs up steeply from the upper part of Harta Corrie. This route starts at the base of the rocks where one can see into Lota Corrie on the left and lower Harta Corrie on the right. The climbing is steep and exposed, with much variation possible. In general the climbing is more difficult further right.

2 Braehead Climb   120m   Very Difficult   *(1965)*
This route ascends the face just right of West Gully as directly as possible. Climb slabs and grooves to some overhangs, which are passed on the right by parallel cracks. Move left and climb a pinnacle to a ledge with a perched block. Climb a small chimney to a large ledge under some overhangs. Continue up right past the overhangs, and then back left along an easy ledge. Go right to a groove which leads to easier scrambling to the North Ridge.

3 West Gully   150m   Moderate   *(1948)*
Climb the gully for 75m, then follow the left branch, going first by a chimney then by several jammed blocks, followed by rather loose rocks to finish just north of the summit. A possible route for wet days.
Winter: **III** *   *(1999)*
Good climbing following the summer line.

HARTA CORRIE

5. AN CAISTEAL - EAST FACE

(NG 465 241)   Alt 375m   South-East facing   Map p28   Diagrams p32, 38

The Harta face of An Caisteal is a great slabby mass of rock, cleft into three buttresses by two long gullies (South and North). A steep tier at the base of the cliffs causes much confusion about how to access the slabs above. A number of long lower grade climbs have been done but countless variations are possible.

Alternative Approach: A shorter approach from Glen Brittle crosses the Ridge at Bealach Harta, (see Coire na Creiche chapter intro), followed by a long easy descent to the foot of the face, (2hrs 30mins).

Descents: All routes finish on the crest of An Caisteal. Head south along the Ridge to Bealach Harta followed by a straightforward descent west into Coire a' Tairneilear and Glen Brittle or Harta Corrie to the east.
    It is both more enjoyable and direct to return to Sligachan by following the Ridge north to Bruach na Frithe (Grade 3/Difficult) as described in the Cuillin Ridge Traverses chapter. The only major obstacle is the immediate descent from An Caisteal into the head of the Tairneilear Stone Shoot.

1 South Buttress   400m   Difficult   *(1911)*
The steep rock band at the start gives the crux. Ascend the gully between the South and Central Buttresses to a point just below a huge overhanging pitch. Then climb a vertical corner on the left to gain a downwards sloping ledge. Follow this leftwards across the wall to a square platform from where it is possible to break onto the main slabs of the buttress. Climb the slabs for some distance with occasional traverses to circumvent overlaps. An easier section of 60m follows, before the buttress arrows down to an arete with a steep drop on the left and a gully on the right. About 50m below the summit, cross the head of the gully on the right to reach an 8m chimney which gives the last of the difficulties.
Variation: **Direct Start   Very Difficult**   *(1946)*
The square platform can be gained more directly from the bottom of the gully by climbing a short vertical wall on the left where a large rock splinter of dubious security projects from the face. This is harder but avoids an uninteresting detour.
Variation: **Superdirect Start   VS**   *(1998)*
An even more direct start can be made by ascending the apron of slabs at the base

5. AN CAISTEAL - East Face

1. South Buttress — Difficult
1a. Direct Start — Very Difficult
1b. Superdirect Start — VS
2. Raeburn's Route — Difficult
3. White Wizard — III/IV **
4. Archer Thomson's Route — Difficult
5. North Buttress — Difficult **

E. Bealach a' Tairneilear, approach from Glen Brittle to Creag an Eas (6)
F. Bealach Harta, best approach from Glen Brittle

of the buttress and then breaking through the rock band a little to the left of the other two starts.

2 Raeburn's Route   360m   Difficult *(1905)*
This lies to the right of South Gully. Easy climbing leads to a steeper section where the rocks are slabby. Turn an overhang on the left to a point overlooking the gully. A fine chimney leads out above the overhang by easier rocks. The final wall, two-thirds of the way up, is cleft by several chimneys.

**3 White Wizard   350m   III/IV ** ** *(1983)*
This fine winter route finishes by a line between Raeburn's Route and Archer Thomson's Route. Follow an obvious right-trending 90m gully formed by a basalt dyke. Break out left up snowfields for 90m, then follow a narrow gully line to the top. The top section of this route is particularly good.

4 Archer Thomson's Route   360m   Difficult *(1911)*
This rather indefinite line is best described as being straightforward, very interesting but with no particular features. It lies to the left of North Gully and the climber is left to pick the most appealing line.

**5 North Buttress   300m   Difficult ** ** *(1953)*
Start right of North Gully, go up the left-hand edge of a steep wall, then return to the centre of the buttress. Continue up a long stretch of slabs, gradually getting steeper, to a terrace. Climb the front of the tower ahead, moving from left to right and then back left again. The continuation to the final tower is easier. This can be climbed either by a central chimney or a gully to the left, to its top. The summit of An Caisteal is easily reached a little further to the north.

6. CREAG AN EAS

(NG 469 244)   Alt 345m   South facing   Map p28   Diagram p32

A huge wall of rock rises between Harta and Lota Corries bounded by a beautiful waterfall on the right hand side. Slabs left of the waterfall are interrupted by two loose gullies before the cliff becomes very steep and dramatically undercut. Left again the walls form a buttress reaching down to grass ledges and steep slabs before becoming overhung once more above the bounding gully.

Alternative Approach: Gain Bealach a Tairneilear from Coire na Creiche (1hr 30mins). Descend scree for 150m until an easy traverse north into Lota Corrie is possible. Traverse the corrie and descend easily on the left (east) side of the water-fall and cross to the foot of the cliff (2hrs 30mins).

**Holiday Bonus   100m   HVS ** ** *(2010)*
An adventurous route on good rock after the initial 10m. Approach from the water-fall to gain the highest grass ledge about 15m before it drops into the bounding gully. Start 3m left of a series of corners, the lowest of which is smooth and uninviting.
1 20m 4b Turn a band of very loose blocky rock on the left before stepping back right into the second corner A welcome large crack leads to a comfortable stance.
2 25m 4c Follow the basalt fault left across the face. An improbable thread protects the hard moves through the squeeze after 5m. Belay on micros and a low spike on the ledge where a break through the wall above looks feasible.
3 30m 5a Rise steeply rightward to gain a broad ledge (7m). Gain a higher ledge by traversing left then back right. The final wall gives a well protected crux puzzle to reach a detached flake belay on the ledge above.
4 25m 4c Step off the flake and climb the 5m wall above to reach easier ground. A recessed fault leads to the top of the buttress.

Mike Lates

Malcolm Airey on the first ascent of Holiday Bonus, HVS, Creag an Eas

NORTHERN CUILLIN

Map p28   Diagram p42

Sligachan was the centre of almost all Cuillin exploration for over 50 years and routes on the mountains closest to the hotel were at the cutting edge of climbing exploits during this era. Many climbs pioneered here in Victorian times will impress, baffle and shock climbers of today with their audacity.

A highlight is the classic round of the Coire a' Bhasteir peaks. Pinnacle Ridge on Sgùrr nan Gillean is every bit as good in descent as ascent so can be used to either start or end the day. The Basteir Tooth has climbs on good rock at all grades with exposure completely out of proportion to the small physical scale. Low Crag offers a large accessible area of climbs at low altitude, again with routes of all grades.

Coire a' Bhasteir is the Cuillin's best winter corrie, holding snow and ice more reliably than any other. A good indicator is the state of a steep wall that lies just above the lochan that can be studied from a lay-by just north of the Sligachan road bridge.

Recommended Approach: Approaches to peaks and crags at the north end of the Cuillin Ridge (except Bruach na Frìthe [18]) share a common start by a well constructed footpath across the moor south of Sligachan for 2km. This then splits to the east and west sides of Sgùrr nan Gillean. The branch that heads to the east is known as the 'Tourist Route' that finishes by the narrow South-East Ridge of Sgùrr nan Gillean which is not suitable for non-climbing tourists.

Start opposite the mountain rescue building at Sligachan (NG 485 298). Cross the Allt Dearg Mòr by a newly constructed bridge then take the well made path across the Sligachan bogs to a second footbridge (30mins). Cross the bridge and head east for the Tourist Route Crags [7-12] and Sgùrr nan Gillean or continue up the path on the west bank to approach Coire a' Bhasteir crags [13-17].

The Tourist Route rises to a prominent boulder at the high point of a grassy spur, NG 476 270. This spur rises to the south forming a rocky shoulder that gives one approach to the start of Pinnacle Ridge [13]. Nead na h-Iolaire [7] is reached by turning north-east along the top of the spur for 1km. The Tourist Route continues initially with a small descent and then horizontally into Coire Riabhach. The Sligachan Face of the First Pinnacle [8] overlooks this corrie (1hr). A rise in the path leads to a short level section (alt. 300m) before the long scree slopes begin. Low Crag [9] is found below the path by making a leftward traverse from here around the base of the crags (1hr). Continue up the Tourist Route to the mouth of Coire nan Allt Geala where a large watercourse is reached (NG 477 254). The huge buttress of High Crag [10] lies on the skyline level with this point (1hr 30mins).

The path ascends Coire nan Allt Geala until a headwall is reached. Lament Wall [11] stretches west from here to the notch between Knights Peak and Sgùrr nan Gillean itself. The Tourist Route breaks sharply left through the headwall to reach a final section of boulders and scree leading to the South-East Ridge after about 2hrs to give magnificent views of the whole Ridge. The summit of Sgùrr nan Gillean is gained in about 30mins from where the South-East Ridge is joined (Grade 2). The Lota Face of Sgurr nan Gillean [12] is best approached by crossing the ridge here then making an easy diagonal descent.

For all the Coire a' Bhasteir crags [13-17], remain on the west bank beyond the second footbridge to reach the mouth of the Basteir Gorge. Routes on Sgùrr a' Bhasteir [17] lie right of the gorge. Routes on the lower pinnacles of Pinnacle Ridge [13] are reached by crossing below the gorge and ascending grass to reach the rocky shoulder above. Follow the shoulder to the toe of the First Pinnacle (1hr). A small trail rises across the screes and boulders beneath all the pinnacles eventually reaching Bealach a' Bhasteir (2hrs).

The more common approach to the same bealach and the rest of the corrie stays west of the gorge, initially climbing slabs to the lip of Coire a' Bhasteir. Traverse more slabs to reach a tiny lochan in the heart of the corrie (1hr 30mins). The headwall above the lochan is turned on the left by a large trail that leads up scree to the lowest rocks of Am Basteir [14]. The foot of the 4th and 5th pinnacles can be

NORTHERN CUILLIN

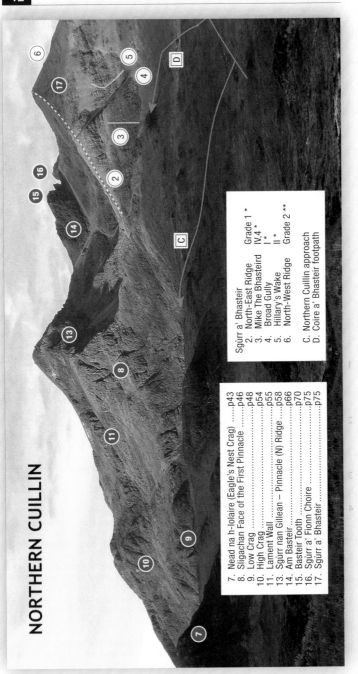

Sgùrr a' Bhasteir
2. North-East Ridge   Grade 1 *
3. Mike The Bhasteird   IV,4 *
4. Broad Gully   I *
5. Hillary's Wake   II *
6. North-West Ridge   Grade 2 **

C. Northern Cuillin approach
D. Coire a' Bhasteir footpath

reached by a rough traverse from here and Bealach a' Bhasteir lies 10min to the east up more scree. The Basteir Tooth [15] is reached by a well trodden trail that rises west beneath the imposing Am Basteir cliffs, passing the huge recess of King's Cave Chimney just 100m before Bealach na Lice (2hrs). This pass gives easy access to some routes high above Lota Corrie on the Basteir Tooth and Sgùrr a' Fionn Choire [16]. The summit of Bruach na Frithe [18] is a simple short walk from here but climbs described are best approached via Bealach a Mhàim from either Sligachan or the Fairy Pools car park.

The Round of Coire a' Bhasteir 8hrs Grade 3/Severe **
Done in either direction this is a classic round with hard scrambling, abseils and intricate route finding. Classically, climb Sgurr nan Gillean by Pinnacle Ridge, descend the West Ridge and traverse Am Basteir before a choice of abseil descents from the Basteir Tooth. A harder version goes anti-clockwise with the advantage of giving good practice for a Main Ridge Traverse.

Start by either northern ridge of Sgùrr a' Bhasteir, climb the Tooth by Naismith's, Collie's or other routes, find the difficult route onto Am Basteir before climbing the West Ridge of Sgùrr nan Gillean. Descend by Pinnacle Ridge to comprehend why it is considered as the classy finish to a full Ridge Traverse. Pinnacle Ridge is described below and further relevant descriptions are given in the Cuillin Ridge Traverses chapter.

TOURIST ROUTE CRAGS

7. NEAD NA H-IOLAIRE (EAGLE'S NEST CRAG)

(NG 484 275) Alt 230m West facing Map p28 Diagrams p42, 44

The crag is more vegetated than most but has reasonable climbs for practice or a short day. The descent route is to the right of the crag, down the wide scree gully.

1 Nihilist's Escape 40m Severe   *(1952)*
At the eastern end of the crag runs an indistinct gully visible from the Sligachan Hotel. This route climbs the left edge. Climb up the steep face until it relents to a slab then a tree belay at 40m.

2 Left Rib 60m Very Difficult   *(1918)*
This climb takes the rib bounding the left side of the central chimney. Climb slabs and heather to a large ledge. Continue via a steep 20m slab to a heather shelf, whence a higher ledge leads to the top.

3 Central Chimney 60m Difficult   *(pre1897)*
The prominent chimney is often wet.

4 Eagle's Eyrie 85m Very Difficult   *(1993)*
Start at a grassy ledge directly below the summit and left of a steep wall bounding the wide descent gully.
1. 35m Climb the slab to a grassy ledge at 20m, move left and climb the slab to a wide ledge and block belay.
2. 25m Climb the slab on its right-hand edge, continue boldly on good basalt and where the face steepens, traverse 6m right above a rowan to continue up a crack to a ledge and block belay.
3. 25m Climb the gabbro face and move right to a small ledge on a steep slab. Climb the slab on good holds to easier ground and pleasant scrambling to finish.
Variation: **Raptor finish 30m Severe**   *(1994)*
Start at the centre of a gabbro slab, 3m left of the second pitch of Eagle's Eyrie. Climb the crack in the centre of the slab to a heather terrace, no protection. Climb the broken left edge of a gabbro wall to a sloping heather terrace, then go up the short wall above. Belay up to the right.

7. NEAD NA H-IOLAIRE (EAGLE'S NEST CRAG)

2. Left Rib	Very Difficult	5. Elizabeth	Difficult *
3. Central Chimney	Difficult	6. August Rib	Severe
4. Eagle's Eyrie	Very Difficult	7. One Flew Over the	
4a. Raptor Finish	Severe	Cuillin Ridge	E3

5 Elizabeth   50m   Very Difficult *   (1994)

Probably the best of the routes here, with a bold first pitch. From the right-hand corner of the buttress adjoining the scree gully, go 15m along a path rising up left. Start at the middle of an undercut concave slab.

1. 25m Climb the slab to a heather ledge and continue up a gabbro and basalt staircase to a block at the foot of a steep corner; belay on the right.

2. 25m From the block, climb the corner to a sloping heather terrace and cross over left to a short steep gabbro wall. Climb this diagonally right on mouth watering holds to easy ground.

6 August Rib   90m   Severe   (1967)

The route lies up the right side of the face and starts a little way up a scree gully at a short slanting crack in the west wall (arrow). Go up the crack for 5m, then step awkwardly left round onto a rib which is followed to a stance and belay. Follow the rib on the right in two short sections to another good stance and belay. Climb the clean and exposed rib on the right to a ledge from which easy rocks lead to the top.

To the right of August Rib is the scree gully. The left-bounding wall offers one route.

7 One Flew Over The Cuillin Ridge   50m   E3   (1994)

Start near the entrance of the scree gully.

1. 30m 4c Follow a right-curving line up the wall, a good pitch. This promising start does not continue.

2. 20m 5b The continuation of the line unfortunately goes through a basalt sill for 15m, no gear, falling to bits, to a final 4m of good gabbro.

SGÙRR NAN GILLEAN

(NG 472 253)   965m

This is regarded by many as the finest of all Cuillin peaks, a symmetrical pyramid supported by three sharp ridges. The easiest ascent is by the misleadingly named Tourist Route that culminates with a complex and exposed section of the South-East Ridge. This final section warrants a route description in its own right.

South-East Ridge (The Tourist Route)   200m   Grade 2 **   *(1836)*
A short but difficult culmination to this classic route, 30mins. The ridge narrows and steepens significantly 200m after it is gained, (NG 473 251, Alt 825m). The first obstacle is a short gully ending in a chimney. Above here the easiest route takes a broad rake on the south side of the ridge and a basalt groove continuation. Traverse slabs right for 50m to a corner below the ridge. Climb a series of 3 short corner steps until forced onto the final 100m horizontal ridge that leads to the summit cairn. Following the narrow crest of the South-East Ridge instead is highly recommended, climbing on solid rock in a superb position, Grade 3.
Winter: **200m   II ****
Conditions vary a lot with the choice of the exposed crest or broad ledges dependent mainly on depth of snow.

Descents: The South-East Ridge (Tourist Route) is complex in its upper reaches. Follow the narrow crest for 60m until it is possible to descend to a broad rake that lies 50m down to the right (south). At 800m the ridge levels out and the boulder field to the north is descended. The West Ridge is more serious (Grade 3/Moderate) but easier to navigate. An abseil is commonly used to descend the chimneys at the lowest part of the route. Descending Pinnacle Ridge (Grade 3/Difficult) gives a quality climb but is only recommended in perfect conditions. Allow 2-3hrs to return to Sligachan by all routes.

Finale of Sgùrr nan Gillean's Tourist Route.
Climbers Michael Stirling-Aird and Paul Laughlan

8. SLIGACHAN FACE OF FIRST PINNACLE

(NG 474 259)   Alt 600m   North facing   Map p28   Diagrams p42, 47

Pinnacle Ridge and routes on the west faces are described further on in this chapter but this face gives a number of direct starts. The Tourist Route drops slightly into Coire Riabhach which is overlooked by this steep north face, 300m above. It is divided into two tiers by a broad shelf that narrows to the right before reaching the lip of Coire a' Bhasteir. The face is of huge historical significance with the climbs giving a real insight into just how accomplished the Victorian pioneers were. Some of these routes were used regularly as the start to an ascent of Pinnacle Ridge, often in the rain. Modern climbers may find a route on each tier to be more than enough entertainment for a day out.

Approach: The lowest rocks make a fine scrambling approach when dry but it is quicker to take heather covered boulders and scree on the right side. The climbs are described from left to right.

Descent: Between the tiers follow the broad shelf east to rejoin the Tourist Route or join Pinnacle Ridge by following the same shelf to its western extremity. Above the Upper Tier most parties continue climbing by Pinnacle Ridge (Grade 3/Difficult) but awkward scrambling descents are possible. Either descend the First Pinnacle to the west or climb for a further 100m to the top of the First Pinnacle. Descend west into Coire a' Bhasteir via the gully that lies between the First and Second Pinnacles or south-east to the Tourist Route by the broken rocky flanks.

Lower Tier

1 The Sickle   330m   III *   (2000)

Take the lowest rocks of the corrie by a combination of slabby icefalls and snow-fields to reach the foot of Maclay's Gully. The meat of the route follows the rib of Naismith's Route on the left, zigzagging to eventually reach the prominent horizontal basalt fault. From here the first ascensionists crawled left to reach a narrow groove which led to easier terrain and the broad ledge that separates the two tiers.

2 Naismith's Route   180m   Difficult   (1896)

This route starts by following the rib immediately left of Maclay's Gully then takes the left-hand gully and chimney in the upper tier.

1. 70m   Scramble then climb up clean rocks on the rib to belay on a prominent basalt shelf that crosses the entire lower tier at three-quarters height.

2. 20m   Break through the bulge above the shelf (surprisingly steep but well protected). Easier climbing leads to the open scree slopes above.

Walk up and left across the broad terrace to the open shallow gully in the upper tier some 40m away.

3. 60m   The gully is easy for 45m. It leads left to a hidden chimney.

4. 15m   Climb the chimney.

5. 15m   Ascend a nearly vertical wall above to the end of the difficulties.

3 Maclay's Gully   90m   Very Difficult *   (1898)

This is the prominent long gully in the lower tier. It has previously been confused with Black Chimney which is the far shorter dark gash up right on the same tier. Good easy scrambling in the lower reaches is interrupted by one awkward move to surmount a wedged boulder. The gully finally steepens and forks at 60m. No description is recorded for the right fork. The left fork fits the original description of a "steep and rather stiff gully" very well. Despite being dirty the climbing is excellent with positive holds appearing just at the right time. Pass a bulge and a wedged chockstone by the left wall before the final steep crack. It has been ascended in winter conditions.

4 Black Chimney   45m   Severe *   (1907)

This conspicuous chimney lies at the top right-hand end of the lower tier. It is best

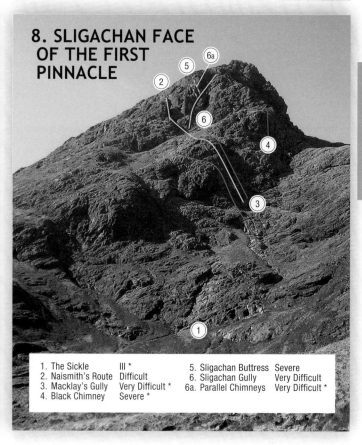

8. SLIGACHAN FACE OF THE FIRST PINNACLE

1. The Sickle	III *	5. Sligachan Buttress	Severe
2. Naismith's Route	Difficult	6. Sligachan Gully	Very Difficult
3. Macklay's Gully	Very Difficult *	6a. Parallel Chimneys	Very Difficult *
4. Black Chimney	Severe *		

reached by a short traverse from where the climbing begins on Pinnacle Ridge. The route was rated by Ashley Abraham as the most severe climb he made in the Cuillin apart from Cioch Direct but also one of the best. It succumbed to extreme combined tactics and may not have received a free ascent.

1. 15m Ascend the chimney-crack in the steep slab below the overhanging chimney. Traverse left to a large ledge when the way is barred by a large loose splinter of rock.

2. 20m Regain the chimney and ascend easily to a small cave with a steeply sloping floor.

3. 10m Gain a foothold on the right wall with difficulty to reach a small recess above. The chimney is now reduced to a crack that leads out to the lip of the overhang. Let battle commence!

Variation: **Thor Finish 40m Severe**   *(1963)*

2a. 25m From the large ledge at the top of pitch one climb a thin crack at its left end to a stance and belay.

Upper Tier

5 Sligachan Buttress 90m Severe   *(1911)*

Follows steep rocks in a fairly direct line to the top of the buttress left of Sligachan

Gully. Start from a shelf below the buttress just left of Sligachan Gully (possibly the one 20m above the level of the scree.) The original description is repeated here as the most reliable and accurate information available.

"We attacked from the shelf at the foot the buttress on the left side of Sligachan Gully. From the start the leader drew out nearly 80 feet (25m) of rope before coming to anchor in a recess. About 40 feet (12m) above, an airy stride had to be made right around a corner. The take-off, a little rock ledge, is very small for two but Jones managed to get a firm pose during the operation. Later we struck at a right angle into a cave which was identified as the last pitch of a Parallel Chimney. From this we emerged easily on a terrace.

"By a very unusual move in the nature of a considered spring across the top of the chimney we attained an abnormally steep wall which bought us finally to the summit of the buttress, whereon we set a cairn. The line throughout was nearly straight; the slight deviations were to the right. We began the climb at 1.30 and were at Sligachan at five o'clock, so the climb must have taken about two hours." This with four climbers!

6 Sligachan Gully   100m   Very Difficult   (1907)
This lies centrally on the top tier, rising slightly left to right. The original route may not appeal unless dressed in tweeds but the Parallel Chimney variations are clean and very worthwhile. The rift ceases abruptly in its lower reaches being blocked by an overhanging wedge shaped boulder.
1. 30m Combined tactics may just keep the true start within the confines of Very Difficult. Mere mortals will avoid this pitch by taking an easier line out right to just below an obvious cave feature. Break sharp left below the cave to gain the base of the gully proper.
2. 20m Ascend the easy angled chimney or walls to the right to reach a wide opening in the crags.
3. 30m Ascend the filthy narrow chimney above (crux). It leads to a scree patch below a large impending boulder. Turn this on its right edge to reach a vegetated ledge ("such a place that an Alpine botanist dreams of" Ashley Abraham). The capstone is turned on the right more easily.
4. 20m Easier terrain leads to a broad area of scree and boulders that is passed through on the normal route up the First Pinnacle.
Two parallel chimneys branch left from the gully from the start of pitch 2. Both are similar in nature and grade and on better rock than the parent route.
Variation: **Lower Chimney   80m   Very Difficult ***
Surmount a large square chockstone low down in rift. The chimney narrows above to give excellent back and footing. Climb through a narrow hole near the top of the chimney to belay (25m). Another fine chimney pitch above is even steeper and tighter (20m). The steep clean wall above is very hard to start and can be avoided to the east.
Variation: **Upper Chimney   80m   Very Difficult ***
Two easy pitches lead to a deepening of the chimney. Again ideal for back and footing technique an added twist is the need to reverse the position to face the opposite direction halfway up. Once accomplished go outside the wedged blocks above to belay. Another pitch of the same leads to the skyline. Take the steep clean wall above to the top of the buttress.
Variation: **Geologist's Variation   30m   Very Difficult**   (2007)
An obvious fault rises across the right wall from the base of the narrow chimney on pitch 3. Traverse horizontally right for 4m to reach a broken shallow chimney. Enter the chimney (crux) to reach easier rocks that lead to the top.

9. LOW CRAG

(NG 478 261)   Alt 300m   North-East facing   Map p28   Diagrams p42, 51

This crag was developed by members of Oxford University Mountaineering Club. Route descriptions have been reproduced from the club's own comprehensive guide. It is a vast crag consisting of numerous buttresses providing a range of climbing. They dry quickly after rain and remain in condition when many of Skye's higher crags are out of bounds. The buttresses offer superb walls of immaculate gabbro adorned with plentiful small but positive holds. The compact rock offers little natural protection so assume that routes are both bold and poorly protected unless otherwise stated in the description. Panoramix Wall shows well in profile from the footpath before reaching the floor of Coire Riabhach. Buttresses are described from right to left (north to south) as approached from the Tourist Route (1hr).

Riabhach Wall

This first area reached is a short well featured gabbro wall, reminiscent of a grit-stone edge with reasonably protected climbs. At the extreme right-hand end is a small in cut rectangular slab.

1 Escapist's Daydream   10m   Hard Severe *   (2002)
The centre of the thin slab is climbed on small edges. Belay some distance back.

2 Coolin Off   20m   E1 5a **   (2002)
To the left is a bulging rounded arete. It bounds the right-hand side of Riabhach Wall. Start at a fault immediately right of this and trend up and left to reach a hor-izontal break. From here, insecure moves lead to a huge bucket and easier rib above.

3 Oxford Blue   20m   E1 5b **   (2002)
Head straight up the wall right of The Purple Turtle to reach a small triangular niche. Move out of this more easily to belay above.

4 The Purple Turtle   25m   HVS 5a *   (2002)
A well protected route with a challenging crux at mid-height. Climb the left-slanting ramp in the centre of the wall and continue directly up the thin flake-crack above. Finish rightwards along a basalt ledge.

5 The Groove   25m   VS 4b *   (2002)
The short groove in the centre of the face provides an obvious but awkward line. Gain the ledge above and step right to finish up more broken ground.

Just to the left of The Groove lies a small but impending wall at the top of the crag. This is the objective of two bold routes.

6 Taliban Groove   20m   E1 5a *   (2002)
The shallow corner in the steep headwall right of Kandahar. Start as for The Groove but follow the left-hand crack to a small ledge and suspect rock. From here make precarious moves left before finishing up the exposed groove.

7 Kandahar   15m   E4 5c *   (2002)
The steep headwall 5m left of The Groove. Climb up easy slabs to excellent holds in the basalt dyke, and poor tiny wire runners. Make difficult moves on tiny holds, trending right up the undercut flake-crack to the top.

8 Small Slab   15m   HVS 5b   (2002)
Climbs the short undercut slab immediately right of two basalt seams in the left part of the wall. Starting from the right, pull through the overlap on undercut holds, climb the slab directly and finish up the wall above.

9 The Seamstress   10m   Very Difficult   (2002)
Climb up between the two basalt seams.

10 East Ramp   20m   Moderate   (2002)
The easy walls and ledges close to the left-hand arete provide a pleasant scramble.

Variation: **20m   Difficult**   *(2002)*
Ascend the first crack right of the start of East Ramp with a choice of finishes.

The small clean buttress halfway between Riabhach Wall and North Buttress offers three short Difficult corners.

North Buttress

A short distance around the corner from Riabhach Wall lies the larger North Buttress which is in two main sections. The first to be reached is the short North Wall with short easy climbs on sound rock bounded on the left by the blunt arete of Mercury Rib. The East Face lies above a long broad ledge that runs up left beyond.

North Wall

Routes are described from right to left, starting in the corner at the top of the grassy ramp.

11 Alison's Rib   25m   Difficult   *(2002)*
The vague rib to the right of a prominent square corner eases with height.

12 Electra   25m   Very Difficult   *(2002)*
The square-cut corner at the right side of the wall is often damp but provides a well protected climb.

13 Venus   25m   Hard Very Difficult *   *(2002)*
Start below ledges a few metres left of Electra and follow the easiest line straight up the blunt rib above.

14 Warmin' Up   25m   Severe   *(2002)*
From the large ledge on Venus make an airy but well protected step left into the large depression in the centre of the upper wall. Climb straight up this and exit via a small slab above.

15 Faithless   25m   E1 4c *   *(2002)*
Follow the vague basalt dyke up the centre of the face. Start just left of a rocky step on the grassy approach ramp.

16 Mercury Rib   25m   VS 4b   *(2002)*
Gains the blunt arete at the left side of the North Face. Start just right of the arete. Traverse up and left to a prominent niche on the arete. Continue up the arete to a large belay ledge.

East Face

A broad terrace rises leftward below the steep face. A steep damp corner bounds the right-hand side of an impressive blank slab

17 Varsity Crack   55m   VS   *(2002)*
A sense of humour and exploratory attitude may overcome the quality of the rock. Start 20m to the left of the damp corner. Follow the obvious right-slanting crack at the left side of the blank slab.
1. 25m   Follow the crack making several steps right onto the face. Belay in an unpleasant basalt dyke.
2. 30m 4c   The crack above the basalt is overhanging and dirty but with excellent holds. After a few difficult moves the angle eases to give pleasant scrambling to the top.

18 Frost Route   50m   E1 *   *(2005)*
Start 20m further left where the terrace narrows and becomes rocky. Well protected.

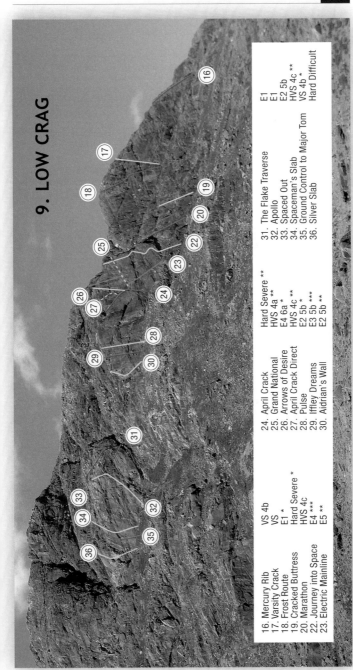

9. LOW CRAG

NORTHERN CUILLIN

16. Mercury Rib   VS 4b
17. Varsity Crack   VS
18. Frost Route   E1 *
19. Cracked Buttress   Hard Severe *
20. Marathon   HVS 4c
22. Journey into Space   E4 ***
23. Electric Mainline   E5 **

24. April Crack   Hard Severe **
25. Grand National   HVS 4a **
26. Arrows of Desire   E4 6a *
27. April Crack Direct   HVS 4c **
28. Pulse   E2 5b *
29. Iffley Dreams   E3 5b ***
30. Aldrian's Wall   E2 5b **

31. The Flake Traverse   E1
32. Apollo   E1
33. Spaced Out   E2 5b
34. Spaceman's Slab   HVS 4c **
35. Ground Control to Major Tom VS 4b *
36. Silver Slab   Hard Difficult

1. 25m 4c Gain the right-hand chimney-crack. Follow this to the top where the steep upper wall is reached. Step left and then up to a reasonable sloping ledge with a large cam belay.
2. 25m 5b Hard moves start up the corner at the left side of the ledge. Above the corner the angle eases on a short clean wall.

Panoramix Right

Traverse south below the lowest rocks for 60m to reach an obvious watercourse where the rocks are worn smooth and there is often a waterfall above. The rock here is more lichenous than most of Low Crag. Descend the ramp to the right.

19 Cracked Buttress   17m   Hard Severe 4a *   *(2004)*
The cracked buttress just to the right of the waterfall gives varied climbing. Climb on to the large chockstone via a series of ledges. From here, step up and follow the right-hand side of the pillar to its rounded top.

20 Marathon   35m   HVS 4c   *(2004)*
Start at the foot of the flakey crescent groove. Climb the groove and continue to a small ledge. Step right (crux) to gain access to the continuation groove above, which is followed (with ground fall potential) to the loose ramp of Rather Be Wet Than Sorry.

Panoramix Wall

The showpiece of the crag. This 60m wall of clean gabbro dries more quickly than most of the other buttresses. Protection is almost invariably worse than it looks from below. Several in-situ pitons provide a token attempt to protect some of the blankest sections but a selection of tiny camming devices will prove helpful. Most routes pass by the 'Haven', a rocky recess lying left of the steepest wall and reached most easily by April Crack. Routes are described from right to left.

21 Rather be Wet Than Sorry   45m   Very Difficult   *(2000)*
A rather damp climb that skirts around the side of the steep wall. At the bottom right side of the wall is a right-slanting ramp below an overhang. Start up this just left of the vegetation.

22 Journey into Space   60m   E4 ***   *(2003)*
This weaves its way up some of the blankest parts of the wall. The first pitch has three good runners and the second has none.
1. 35m 5b Start up the sloping ramp as for the previous route. After 4m head straight up to break through the overhang above (peg in wall just above). Traverse right on the basalt until a line of holds leads back left to another basalt dyke and a good runner. A wild rising traverse right along the basalt leads to a belay on a cluster of cams close to the right side of the wall.
2. 25m 5c Move back left and pull through the overhang on small holds. A very poor peg runner provides the only protection on the pitch. Trend up left on improving holds across the blank wall until the ledge of Grand National is reached. Step right and climb the shallow groove as for that route, before continuing straight up on excellent holds to the top.

23 Electric Mainline   65m   E5 **   *(2000)*
This bold route takes a logical line up the steep central wall, stepping left to belay in The Haven at half-height. Start 3m left of Journey into Space.
1. 35m 5c Start up a line of holds leading up to the left of the small overhang. Climb straight up to a diagonal break from where difficult moves lead past two vertical cracks and through a basalt dyke to a rest ledge and peg runner. Follow an obvious easy ramp left to a patch of grass below the central overhang (Friend 3). Surmount this with surprising ease on small but good holds. Easy climbing leads

left to belay on the Haven.
2. 30m 6a Step down right and pull through the steep ground on excellent holds (as for Grand National). Move right along the basalt dyke to a corner with white quartz in it. Climb this to a small ledge and tied off peg runner. The wall above forms the crux and is protected by a peg on the right. Climb the wall directly to finish at the highest point of the crag.

24 April Crack   45m   Hard Severe ** (2000)
1. 25m 4b A crack-line provides a steep struggle directly to an obvious central recess known as the Haven.
2. 20m Climb the attractive leftwards-slanting slab then finish up a short steep crack.

The following three routes are alternatives to pitch 2, starting from the Haven and described from right to left.

25 Grand National   30m   HVS 4a ** (2000)
A very bold pitch following the basalt dyke from the Haven right across the centre of Panoramix Wall. The hardest moves are at the start, but as height is gained the exposure becomes sensational and protection non-existent.
Step down and right to reach positive holds for a pull through steep ground onto a basalt ledge. Walk rightwards, with good hand holds, past a quartz vein to a short shallow groove near the right side of the wall. A tricky move up this groove gains a gabbro ledge which is followed scarily right to a belay.

26 Arrows of Desire   25m   E4 6a * (2005)
The steep prow above the Haven gives a sustained technical climb protected by small wires.
From the Haven climb straight up on small holds to a blank section, where a committing rock over gives access to better holds above. Clip a poor peg and finish more easily up the prow.

27 April Crack Direct   30m   HVS 4c ** (2000)
A good route taking a line direct to the summit of the buttress.
A steep crack rises behind the Haven. Climb the wall left of this until a step right can be made to its security. Poor holds and jams allow for strenuous progress to reach easier ground.

Panoramix Left

About 30m to the left (south) of April Crack is a short wall with an overlap at half-height. To the left the rock is clean and dry with several short hard routes.

28 Pulse   25m   E2 5b * (2003)
Interesting climbing skirting the vegetation on the right side of the wall. Start with a series of mantelshelves below the right-hand end of the overlap. Reach the overlap which is turned using the crack on the right. Move left up a ramp (tiny cams) to gain hand holds in the basalt. Climb direct to the top using well spaced holds.

29 Iffley Dreams   25m   E3 5b *** (2000)
A fine technical climb with a bold top section. Climb directly to the obvious hanging flake. Move left to pull through an overlap on big holds to reach a small ledge. Finish directly up the wall above on good small holds. An alternative finish trends right above the overlap and is slightly easier.

30 Adrian's Wall   20m   E2 5b ** (2000)
The zigzag arete at the left end of the wall is another bold undertaking with thin moves to reach the first protection at 11m. Start just left of two hair-line cracks.

Spaceman's Slabs

A short way to the left (south) of the descent ramp is a prominent slab with a number of overlaps. This slab gives several pleasant friction climbs. The rock is generally clean and dries fast. Routes are described from right to left.

Descent: Walk to the left (south) of the slabs.

31 The Flake Traverse   45m   E1   (2006)
To the right of the main part of the slabs is a huge broken niche. Start from a small cave below and right of this. Low in the grade but with some dubious rock.
1. 30m 5a Pull out of the cave and make an awkward move right to reach the hanging flake. Exposed moves lead to the slab above, where an easy but bold traverse right gains a vague crack. Climb this to a poor belay on a sloping ledge.
2. 20m 4b Move left to the end of the ledge and climb the steep basalt wall above on good holds turning a prominent block on the left and finishing up a short groove.

32 Apollo 13   35m   E1   (2000)
This route weaves around the overlaps on the right-hand side of the slabs.
1. 25m 4c Climb thinly to a jug then the slab above (crux). Follow the slab up and right past more overlaps. Trend left below the final, largest one to belay in a large niche.
2. 10m 4c Climb up right from the niche to a short roof crack. Climb this on the left by layaway moves.

33 Spaced Out   45m   E2 5b   (2006)
Start where a thin basalt dyke reaches the ground just right of Spaceman's Slab. Climb directly up the steep slab to the overlap where good runners protect the steep moves above.

34 Spaceman's Slab   45m   HVS 4c **   (2000)
The original route up the slabs provides interesting climbing. From a weakness in the initial bulge climb the centre of the slab to a basalt dyke below another bulge at about 25m. Climb through the bulge and belay on easy ground above.

35 Ground Control to Major Tom   45m   VS 4b *   (2000)
A good climb up the left-hand part of the huge slabs, encountering a wide variety of rock types. Climb straight up left of Spaceman's Slab over three distinct bulges. Block belay.

36 Silver Slab   25m   Difficult   (2006)
Takes the slabby buttress left of Ground Control. Hard for the grade.

COIRE NAN ALLT GEALA

10. HIGH CRAG
(NG 479 252)   Alt 525m   North-East facing   Map p28   Diagram p42

This is a massive black wall, 100m high and 70m wide, silhouetted on the eastern skyline from the mouth of Coire nan Allt Geala. There are only two routes on the main face but a selection of shorter routes have been climbed on a tier immediately below, which is hidden from the approach.

Bottom Tier

There are a number of single pitch routes, worthwhile when dry, described from right to left.

Bedrock   25m   Severe *(2002)*
An interesting route wandering up the right side of the crag. Start 1m left of a shallow broken groove. Climb a series of short steep walls above.

Jacob's Ladder   30m   Hard Severe 4a * *(2002)*
An exciting route following an obvious diagonal line across the centre of the crag. Start up the right-slanting basalt ramp then climb up into the steep corner above. Pull awkwardly up the left side of the block before finishing to the right.

Haribo   20m   VS 5a ** *(2002)*
The prominent right-facing shallow corner provides a well protected struggle. Reach the corner via a basalt ramp then climb it on good side pulls. Climb to the top on good small holds.

High and Dry   15m   Hard Severe *(2002)*
Near the extreme left of the wall is a corner with two slanting cracks to its right. Climb between these and pull over onto an easier right-trending steep ramp. Follow this to a tricky and exposed exit.

Pink Umbrella   25m   Hard Difficult * *(2002)*
Around the corner at the left end of the wall is a small slab with an obvious diagonal crack. Follow the crack left and continue over the bulge above.

Black Wall

The main wall of this cliff remains virgin but the bounding corners have been tackled.

Descent: There is a gully to the right; a trap fault in its true right side leads down a ramp to the foot of the wall.

Black Magic   100m   HVS 5b *** *(2000)*
Climbs the impressive crack on the right side of the wall. Scramble easily to its foot. Excellent sustained climbing leads to a big ledge at 40m. Easier climbing leads to broken ground (60m).

Left Gully   100m   Very Difficult *(1911)*
The steep and wet lower section was bypassed by slabs to the left. After regaining the gully good easy climbing led to a 25m pitch turned by back and foot work. This can be bypassed on the right side.

11. LAMENT WALL

(NG 472 253)   Alt 675m   North facing   Map p28   Diagram p42

This enormous face stretches from the summit of Sgùrr nan Gillean right down to High Crag but climbs have only been recorded to the west (right) of the point at which the Tourist Route reaches it. Ascend Coire nan Allt Geala to where the path abuts the headwall. The Tourist Route breaks left from this point. A fairly prominent trail in the scree, formed by many mistaken 'Tourists', heads right beneath this long face to eventually reach the col between the 4th and 5th pinnacles of Pinnacle Ridge. Routes are described from left to right.

Wee Buttress

This is a small area 70m up to the right from where the Tourist Route reaches the headwall.

No Regrets   25m   Severe 4b * *(2008)*
A very attractive corner-crack rises steeply in the first large solid buttress reached.

Turn an overhang low down to reach the steep crack, 7m of laybacking leads to a break in the angle of the left wall. Follow the crack more easily leftward to the top. Belay immediately on the last solid rock.

The less attractive crack just to the right contains very loose flakes and was escaped by a **Wee Bitty Regret** (25m Difficult, 2008) at an easy break right at half-height. The cracks continuation, taken by the second, gave an enjoyable section of 4b climbing to reach the slab above.

Big Buttress

Continue up and right for another 100m beneath the face until a continuous large (60m) buttress is reached.

Descent: Follow the top of the cliffs uphill for 50m to reach the top of a large (5m wide) blocked chimney (cairn) which has seen much traffic.

Big Worries Mate   55m   E1   (2009)
Tackles the prominent chimney bounding the steep central wall on the left.
1. 35m 4c A short steep start leads to easy broken ground on the right. Regain the chimney and climb carefully past large wedged flakes to belay 5m below the first overhanging block.
2. 20m 5b Bridge very high before delicately pulling left over the roof. The second block roof is more solid and slightly easier. Turn this on the left to gain a small bay and belay. Scramble easily out right to finish.

The next routes both start 20m right of the main face by an open corner. No Worries Mate takes the right-hand corner-line above.

**Drag Queen   60m   E4 ** **   (2008)
The crux pitch takes the crack splitting a prominent yellow headwall at the top of the face, left of No Worries.
1. 20m Climb easily to a good belay where No Worries moves out right.
2. 20m 5a Climb a steep groove directly behind the belay towards a prominent clean looking crack above (10m). Avoid the main crack (loose) by stepping left to follow a parallel crack to a pedestal where the cracks reconverge at the foot of the yellow wall.
3. 20m 6a Gain the next large ledge easily (4m). The left corner is ignored for the steep crack in the yellow wall. Step back right into the hanging pod and ascend on positive but very steep holds. Protection is good but difficult to assemble. Belay immediately above on hollow flakes.

No Worries Mate   50m   HVS ** * *   (2008)
Makes a superb single pitch route.
1. 20m Climb easily to a good spike belay.
2. 20m 4c Follow the crack on the right up past a bulge. Above here the corner-line is damp and dirty. A gearless groove lies 2m to the right. It has spaced positive holds which lead to a step left onto a welcome ledge.
3. 10m 4c The steep, well protected, corner above gives good climbing.

Upper Face

Follow the Tourist Route to the upper snowfields then rise right above the previous routes to where the face steepens.

Lament   120m   III/IV   (1986)
Start on the left and take an icy ramp which slants right to reach an icefall. About 10m before the icefall, break out left through overhangs to gain and climb a hidden chimney to easy ground to the summit.

NORTHERN CUILLIN

LOTA CORRIE

Although Lota Corrie lies directly above Harta Corrie it is far quicker to approach by crossing the Main Ridge from the north (2hrs 30mins) than via Glen Sligachan.

12. SGÙRR NAN GILLEAN - LOTA FACE

(NG 471 250)   Alt 700m   South facing   Map p28

A shallow depression runs directly to the summit up the south face giving the line of the winter climb. Lota Buttress is a clean area of rock immediately east of this. Bealach a' Bhasteir gives a suitable approach in winter but less so in summer when approach via the Tourist Route is recommended.

Lota Buttress

The buttress presents a slabby left-hand section and becomes progressively steeper towards the right culminating in a deep chimney. Another steep buttress lies to the right again with a prominent flake-crack near the top (Cuddy). The routes are described from right to left.

Cuddy   50m   VS 4c *   *(2003)*
The buttress right of the deep chimney contains a huge flake in the upper section. Start directly below the flake at the left end of a ledge. Climb flakes to another ledge which is followed rightwards, past a perched block, to a small corner. Climb the corner then move left into another short corner. Continue up slabs on the left to the base of the flake (25m). Pull on to the flake, step right and finish straight up (25m).

**Arbroath   50m   VS 4c/5a ** **   *(2002)*
Takes the striking line of cracks just left of the deep chimney finishing up a steep upper wall.

Fairy Nuff   45m   Severe 4a *   *(2002)*
Start at a detached pinnacle well left of Arbroath and beyond some steep corners. Climb the right side of the pinnacle to a block. Move out left, then up and back right into an obvious fault running to the top. Follow the fault.

Adamant   45m   Severe 4a *   *(2002)*
Shares the same start as Fairy Nuff. From the top of the pinnacle move out left to the edge then finish directly up cracks and slabs.

Faded Message   45m   Severe 4a *   *(2002)*
A short distance left is a basalt fault which runs up diagonally leftwards. Climb the initial section of the fault into a short chimney/groove at 5m. Step right onto a wall right of a tiny groove. Climb straight up following a short groove at mid-height and a blocky bulge to finish.

Ladies Day   48m   Very Difficult   *(2002)*
Climb the basalt fault all the way out left for 25m to the left edge. Climb a groove to slabs then finish up right.

One long winter route on the south face is recorded, starting immediately left of Lota Buttress. A snowfield lies 100m directly below the summit. Ice sometimes flows from this snowfield down a shallow depression in the face below then over rock steps to the foot of the face.

White Dreams   285m   IV,5 *   *(2000)*
1. 30m Climb steep thinly iced slabs to a snowy ledge.

2. 30m Continue up thin iced slabs, then steep snow to a ledge on the right.
3. 30m Climb the short steep ice pillar above (crux), then easy snow.
4. 55m Follow easier ice up the depression above to gain a snow basin and climb to its top.
5. 50m Exit rightwards up steeper ice and gain the main snowfield.
6. 40m Follow easy snow to the top of the snowfield.
7. 50m Climb mixed ground trending right to finish at a fine thread belay under the summit cairn.

COIRE A' BHASTEIR

This dramatic hanging corrie is guarded by slabs and a deep gorge at the entrance and surrounded by jagged pinnacles. The gorge was famously ascended by an Alpine Club party with a swimming pitch followed by the first recorded display of naturist climbing above. Swimming can be avoided by Raeburn's 4c traverse or **Coopers' Gully** (Moderate) which lies 10m before the pool in the east wall. The corrie floor above contains a small lochan and is backed by a steep wet 50m wall. In winter this can be seen from the road just before Sligachan and gives a good indication of ice conditions in the corrie. The wall has been climbed directly and by the watercourse on the left all at grade III in many varied conditions.

13. SGÙRR NAN GILLEAN - PINNACLE (NORTH) RIDGE

(NG 472 258) Alt 600m North-West facing Map p28 Diagrams p42, 62

The Sligachan Face of the First Pinnacle [8] has already been described. The western walls overlooking Coire a' Bhasteir offer many traditional climbs, all over 100m in length. The altitude and aspect of the pinnacles give the most reliable snow and ice conditions in the Cuillin. Descents from all routes are usually by continuing up Pinnacle Ridge but easier escapes can be made down the eastern flanks to join the Tourist Route.

1 **Pinnacle Ridge** 600m **Grade 3/Difficult** ******** (1887)

One of the real Cuillin classics with good quality rock, continuous challenge and plenty of exposure, 2hrs 30mins from the lip of the corrie. In strong south-westerly winds the route is well sheltered by the bulk of Sgùrr nan Gillean. Many more direct lines are possible to those described, mostly on solid rock and commonly up to Very Difficult standard. In poor weather the Third and Fourth Pinnacles can both be avoided completely by the eastern flank which also gives the safest means of escape. Epics are frequent. Start from the lip of Coire a' Bhasteir where the First Pinnacle rises steeply from the rocky shoulder.

Climb the First Pinnacle via its north-west face trending left initially until above Black Chimney. A steep band above a horizontal ledge at 80m is turned by a central basalt chimney. The ridge narrows and leads to a broad bay above Sligachan Gully. The summits of the First and Second Pinnacles can then be reached by easy boulder strewn terrain on the eastern flanks but are better taken directly by rocks overlooking Coire a' Bhasteir.

Third Pinnacle: The summit is reached by a chimney that splits the crest. An awkward 20m abseil from threaded slings down the central groove to reach the top of a chimney is now normal. Two climbing descents can be made into the central groove, both Very Difficult and scary in the rain. The safer option starts by an obvious ledge on the Coire a' Bhasteir side about 10m below the summit. The other descends a steep crack that starts 10m below the summit towards the Fourth Pinnacle. Continuing down the chimney to the next col is easy.

Fourth Pinnacle: Follow the prominent ledge, which does continue right around but is not recommended, out right for 30m on the Coire a' Bhasteir side. Traverse easily back to the crest then continue by an obvious basalt groove to the western shoulder of the peak and follow this directly to the summit. Descend south below the summit to reach a promontory. Avoid the abseil beyond by zigzagging on the

Pinnacle Ridge, Grade 3/Difficult.. Climber Ruaraidh Campbell

Coire a' Bhasteir side. Turn a tower that sits in the col (easily traversed) on the Coire a' Bhasteir side to the col below Sgùrr nan Gillean itself.

Fifth Pinnacle: The move to gain the first slabs is the hardest obligatory move on the whole route. Stepping left to gain a crevassed block is the easiest option. Zigzag right then left above here for 40m to gain a slabby recess with a loose chimney to the left. Taking the rocks above directly to a wide terrace is recommended. The next buttress is also best taken direct with caution on loose rock just before reaching a final terrace. A good direct finish breaks left up a basalt break 15m before reaching the West Ridge and leads directly to the summit cairn.

Winter: **IV,4** ********
More sustained than Tower Ridge on Ben Nevis, a winter ascent equates to a serious alpine outing. Solid névé is the classic way to enjoy the route but it also makes a fine mixed climb in thinner conditions. Deep powder snow can render the climb impossible.

First Pinnacle - West Face

The face is too broad to make routes worthy of detailed documentation but many attractive features have been climbed by parties taking a more direct line to start Pinnacle Ridge.

2 First-Second Gully   100m   Easy
This is the largest and most southerly of four gullies that all start right of the First Pinnacle. The other routes were explored and ascended in the late nineteenth century with no particular difficulties recorded. In winter the main gully is grade I.

Second Pinnacle

Details of routes on this pinnacle have not been checked and the lack of stars does not reflect the descriptions of the good climbing available. There is a choice of easy lines in the lower half of the face to gain the highest of the horizontal terraces. Routes are described above here from left to right.

3 Rudge and Wood's Route   100m   Severe   *(1944)*
Believed to be the narrow dyke 20m left of the central gully taken by the Original Route. "On reaching a point about half-way to the summit we discovered a long, steep chimney which appeared to lead right up to the summit ridge. This gave us a very good climb, rather strenuous in places, on very good clean rock. It ended among broken rocks slightly north-east of the summit."

4 Original Route   100m   Difficult   *(1896)*
Starts by a steep narrow gully to gain more of an open corner, which runs up the face fairly centrally.

5 Thomson and Jones Route   100m   Severe   *(1911)*
Climb the steep narrow gully on Original Route for 10m, then traverse right across a slab for a few metres. Traverse back left above it before making a long upward step (crux) to reach easier angled slabs. Traverse diagonally right to a groove defined by one high retaining wall. Climb this to its termination then make a traverse across slabs for 20m below an overhang. Climb easy rocks beyond for 30m. Ignore the easy continuation and finish on the left above an angular recess, an overhanging block, a sharp edge, and a short groove to finish virtually on the summit.

6 Second-Third Gully   100m   Difficult   *(1896)*
This is easy, apart from a large cave which requires much wriggling of the back and foot variety.
Winter: **Grade II** unless banked out around the cave.

Third Pinnacle

7 Fria   90m   Very Difficult *   *(1963)*
This climb lies on the Second-Third Gully face of the Third Pinnacle. Traverse out of Second-Third Gully to the foot of steep rocks some 60m from the base of the Third Pinnacle. Climb the conspicuous fault on small holds, then take steep rock overlooking Second-Third Gully for 60m to reach a large square cup, which has sloping floors falling into the gully. Gain the top right-hand corner of the cup by a long crack and leave by a short chimney to climb a further 15m to the top.

8 Slingsby's Route   120m   Severe   (1890)
There is no difficulty from the foot of the pinnacle to a ledge level with the top of the first pitch in Second-Third Gully. The next 30m concentrates the difficulties, starting some 12m left of a chimney. Steep rocks lead to a sharply inclined slab, which is awkward to start. Difficulties ease once a deep crack on the right is gained, whence it is easy to a broad ledge below a cave. The crux is the exit from the cave (as always) and is easier on the left. Easy rocks then lead to the top.

9 Luscher's No.1   115m   Very Difficult   (1920)
This is the chimney to the right of Slingsby's Route. The chimney crosses a ledge running beneath a steep slab. Climb the chimney direct to the ledge. Above, short pitches lead to another ledge. Continue up the rocks on the right to the ridge which falls steeply into Third-Fourth Gully.
Winter: **115m   IV,6 ★★**   (2001)
Climbs the obvious chimney on the front face just right of centre above the lower slopes of Third-Fourth Gully.
1. 10m Climb ramps to the foot of the chimney.
2. 45m Climb the chimney direct with committing exit moves.
3. 60m Follow a groove on the right to easy snows and the crest of the ridge 40m below the top of the Third Pinnacle.

10 Luscher's No.2   90m   Difficult   (1920)
This starts from the Third-Fourth Gully at a deep black crack. Climb the crack for 5m, cross the slab on the left, then climb straight up the ridge left of Luscher's No.1
Winter: **90m   III**   (1999)
Needs a good build-up of snow. Climbs the ramp-line running left across the face of the Third Pinnacle, starting 100m up Third-Fourth Gully. Finish up a short buttress to the crest of the ridge.

11 Third-Fourth Gully   100m   Very Difficult   (1905)
The climbing is confined to about 30m. The initial 20m consists of two slimy chimneys followed by a large cave. The crux above is a loose wall which has seen another large rockfall in recent years. If you are still with us, the climb finishes up a short chimney.

Fourth Pinnacle - Knight's Peak

This pinnacle gives long routes on largely solid rock with much variation possible.

12 North Face   150m   Difficult   (1898/1920)
Two variations have been climbed on this face. The earlier route starts below the difficult pitch in Third-Fourth Gully and follows a narrow ledge right before going straight up. The later route climbs a chimney in the right side of Third-Fourth Gully to a cave. The line continues up a chimney for a short distance before breaking out left on a series of fine slabs to the summit.

13 West Ridge of Knight's Peak   150m   III,4 ★★   (1997)
A good mountaineering route, gaining the ridge by the obvious ramp trending up right from the foot of Third-Fourth Gully, then weaving up grooves just left of the crest and finishing by two steep mixed pitches, the first on the crest and the second a chimney 1m right of it, which lead to the summit arete.

14 West Face Direct   200m   Hard Severe ★   (1927)
An interesting and popular route. At the toe of the pinnacle is a shallow cave, well known as a shelter. Start 2m right at an obvious slab.
1. 40m 4b Climb the slab just right of a slanting groove, then traverse up right to a nose on the skyline to a small platform below a grassy crack with a rusty peg (possible belay). Follow the line of the crack on the left then right to a large platform and belays. It is possible to traverse off right at this point.

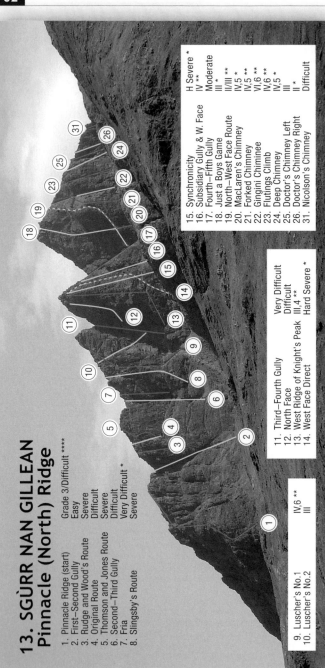

13. SGÙRR NAN GILLEAN
Pinnacle (North) Ridge

1. Pinnacle Ridge (start)   Grade 3/Difficult ****
2. First–Second Gully   Easy
3. Rudge and Wood's Route   Severe
4. Original Route   Difficult
5. Thomson and Jones Route   Severe
6. Second–Third Gully   Difficult
7. Fria   Very Difficult *
8. Slingsby's Route   Severe

9. Luscher's No.1   IV,6 **
10. Luscher's No.2   III

11. Third–Fourth Gully   Very Difficult
12. North Face   Difficult
13. West Ridge of Knight's Peak   III,4 **
14. West Face Direct   Hard Severe *

15. Synchronicity   H Severe *
16. Subsidiary Gully & W. Face IV **
17. Fourth–Fifth Gully   Moderate
18. Just a Boys Game   III *
19. North–West Face Route   II/III **
20. MacLaren's Chimney   IV,5 *
21. Forked Chimney   IV,5 **
22. Gingini Chiminee   VI,6 **
23. Flutings Climb   IV,6 **
24. Deep Chimney   IV,5 *
25. Doctor's Chimney Left   III
26. Doctor's Chimney Right   II *
31. Nicolson's Chimney   Difficult

2. 20m 4b A steep slab of gabbro lies a few metres above and to the right of the last pitch. Climb this rightwards with two awkward moves (small wire runner) to reach easier ground.

3. 150m Continue by a series of grooves and a final chimney (Difficult) to reach Knight's Peak.

Red Slab Variation: **40m   VS**   *(1950)*
Start just left of the original start. Exiting a cave at 20m by a crack forms the crux and is followed by stepping back right immediately before regaining the parent route.

15 Synchronicity   210m   Hard Severe 4b *   *(2002)*
A prominent corner-groove runs almost the full length of the buttress just right of centre (right of West Face Direct). Start at the foot of a slabby corner system just left of Subsidiary Gully. Climb the initial easy angled corner to a wide ledge beneath the main corner (cutting across West Face which comes in from the right) (40m). Climb the corner directly, surmounting a bulge near the top, to a ledge (40m). Continue directly up a groove and corners to the top of the pinnacle in three pitches (130m).

16 Subsidiary Gully and West Face   150m   Moderate   *(1897)*
This face is open to a large degree of variation. Most parties start by Subsidiary Gully which is a prominent line left of Fourth-Fifth Gully. Climb the face above by a variety of routes.
Winter: **150m   IV** **   *(1962)*
A good sustained climb, which takes the line of least resistance.

17 Fourth-Fifth Gully   100m   Moderate   *(1907)*
The only difficult section of this gully is the final steepening, best avoided by a deviation to the right. More serious climbing will be encountered on Pinnacle Ridge unless a decent down the eastern side of Fourth-Fifth Gully is chosen. In winter it gives an easy approach to the more serious climbing on Pinnacle Ridge (IV).

Fifth Pinnacle - Basteir Face of Sgùrr nan Gillean

This high face gleams like a white jewel in good winter conditions. The aspect and altitude turn it into an outstanding objective with routes of all grades available.

18 Just a Boy's Game   170m   III *   *(1993)*
Although escapes are possible to the left, this is a good route. Start at the ramp of North-West Face Route and gain an icefall. This gives the first of four ice pitches with snow terraces in between, the third being an ice bay. The route takes a fairly direct route to the summit rocks finishing at a pinnacle on the West Ridge less than 50m from the summit.

19 North-West Face Route   150m   II/III **   *(pre-1960)*
Start at the bottom of Fourth-Fifth Gully.
1. 50m Ascend rightwards up a ramp running above MacLaren's Chimney until it steepens into a chimney.
2. 50m Climb the chimney and move leftwards through a rock band to the buttress crest.
3. 50m Follow the crest to the summit rocks.

20 MacLaren's Chimney   50m   Very Difficult   *(1911)*
The obvious straight chimney immediately right of Fourth-Fifth Gully is rather loose in summer conditions.
Winter: **50m   IV, 5** *   *(2000)*
A good winter pitch; finish up North-West Face Route or Just a Boy's Game (200m to the summit).

Mark Pratt

Mike Lates on the first winter ascent of Gingini Chiminee VI, 6

21 Forked Chimney   75m   Very Difficult   *(1898)*
Start 15m right of Fourth-Fifth Gully. The chimney is very steep and deeply cut, and divides into two about 30m above the scree. Climb the left branch, back and footing past an overhang. The right branch of the chimney has also been climbed.
Winter: **75m   IV,5** **✶✶**   *(1999)*
An atmospheric winter climb. Follows the main chimney in three pitches. Finish up a snow amphitheatre to the West Ridge.

22 Gingini Chiminee   35m   VI, 6 **✶✶**   *(2000)*
The line between Forked Chimney and Flutings Climb is sometimes completed by an icicle dripping past the cave.
1. 15m Climb to the cave.
2. 20m Place good Friend protection in the cave roof, then spirit up the delicate icicle starting inside and working out. The difficulties end after 15m. The easy finishing pitches had to be missed due to icicle failure for the seconds.

23 Flutings Climb   90m   Difficult   *(1919)*
To the right of Forked Chimney are three shallow gullies; this climb takes the right one and is reached by a 30m pitch.
Winter: **90m   IV,6** **✶✶**   *(1997)*
The longest of the three chimneys is shallow to begin and has a leftward kink at half-height. An excellent winter climb at the top end of its grade.
1. 40m Climb steepening and poorly protected mixed ground into the shallow chimney. At its top move L across the kink and go up the deeper upper chimney for 5m to a chockstone belay.
2. 50m Climb the iced chimney to a steep exit, then the continuing snow gully to block belays just below the West Ridge.

24 Deep Chimney   70m   Difficult   *(1898)*
The chimney starts at the upper left-hand corner of a scree shelf on the right of the buttress. There is a large jammed block near the top.
Winter: **70m   IV,5** **✶**   *(2000)*
Follow the summer route. Above the large jammed block a finish was taken on the right wall.

There are two parallel gullies starting a few metres right of Deep Chimney.

25 Doctor's Gully Left   60m   Moderate   *(1888)*
The left-hand gully.
Winter: **70m   III**   *(2001)*
Follows the summer route, starting at the foot of Deep Chimney at a right-trending fault. Two good icy pitches early season. After heavy snowfall the route banks out and will become far easier.

26 Doctor's Gully Right   60m   Moderate   *(1888)*
Climb the right-hand gully.
Winter: **70m   II** **✶**   *(1994)*
Start at the large snow bay 50m left of Tooth Chimney and climb the gully going straight up to the ridge over three or four enjoyable bulges.

27 West Ridge of Sgùrr nan Gillean   200m   Grade 3/Moderate **✶✶**
Tackle the lowest rocks by one of the next five routes. Welcome easy ground above leads, after 300m, to a final narrowing, squeezing through The Window and the tiny summit plinth, 30mins. In descent it is common to abseil the lowest part of the ridge from the large block immediately west of Tooth Chimney.

The following climbs are most commonly approached from Bealach a' Bhasteir and used to gain the West Ridge of Gillean. They are described from right to left as they would be reached from the bealach. A ledge runs below the lowest pinnacles of the West Ridge on the north (Sligachan) side giving access to the first four routes. The final route takes an equivalent ledge system on the opposite (Lota Corrie) side of the West Ridge.

28 Easy Chimney and Tooth Arete   Grade 3/Moderate **

This is the technically the easiest route to gain the upper reaches of the West Ridge. Start from the ledge 5m before the recessed bay holding Loose Chimney and Tooth Chimney. Climb the easy chimney to reach the narrow ridge above. Balance around between the pinnacles in a very exposed position. Spare a thought for those who used to have to negotiate the celebrated Gendarme that sat here until 1987. In winter it is grade III.

29 Loose Chimney   20m   Moderate

The right-hand corner of the recessed bay is loose and leaves the pinnacles still to be negotiated.

30 Tooth Chimney   30m   Difficult **   (1956)

Follow the left-hand chimney in the recessed bay. Back up around a chockstone to finish.
Winter: **30m   III *
Can prove very awkward unless banked out.

31 Nicolson's Chimney   50m   Difficult   (1865)

Continue traversing left past the recessed bay for 5m. Ascend 10m of scrambling up the easy rib to reach the base of a steep greasy chimney. Very unpleasant but a must for the Cuillin aficionado. It is not a good escape off the West Ridge.

32 Lota Ledge   100m   Grade 3/Moderate *

A narrow horizontal ledge skirts beneath the pinnacles on the south side of the West Ridge. A couple of moves have to be made facing into the rock but it is largely easy. There is a worryingly large drop below the ledge and a good spike belay at the mid-point of the scramble. Would benefit from more traffic. A slabby rake eventually breaks easily back up left to arrive at the same point as Nicholson's Chimney. Harold Raeburn ascended directly to the pinnacles from this ledge at a considerably higher grade.

14. AM BASTEIR

(NG 467 253)   Alt 795m   North facing   Map p28   Diagrams p42, 67

This mighty blade has some harrowing climbs, appropriate for a peak whose English meaning was once thought to be 'The Executioner'. The basaltic dykes on the north face form logical but loose lines. Winter covers many of these evils and transforms it into a popular venue that frequently comes into condition.

Descent: Descend the **East Ridge** (Grade 2) to Bealach a' Bhasteir. The Bad Step halfway along this ridge is only 4m but at least Moderate. It is easy to climb when descending from the peak but does stop many non-climbers in ascent.

North Face

1 The Deadline   195m   III,4 *   (1999)

Takes the highest of the three left to right-slanting ledge systems on the north face.
1. 30m Start just left of the lowest rocks of the north face. Climb a short ice pitch, then snow.
2. 50m Move right and up easy ground to a large ledge system rising from the left.
3. 45m Move right climb a short corner then traverse 10m right to a tight right-slanting chimney (crux) to gain the upper ledge system, not obvious from below, and an alcove.
4. 50m Climb the ramp stepping off a pinnacle to cross Am Basteir Chimney.
5. 20m Continue up the ramp to finish at the notch on the east ridge of Am Basteir.

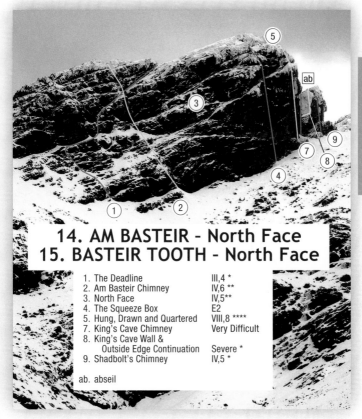

14. AM BASTEIR - North Face
15. BASTEIR TOOTH - North Face

1. The Deadline	III,4 *
2. Am Basteir Chimney	IV,6 **
3. North Face	IV,5**
4. The Squeeze Box	E2
5. Hung, Drawn and Quartered	VIII,8 ****
7. King's Cave Chimney	Very Difficult
8. King's Cave Wall &	
Outside Edge Continuation	Severe *
9. Shadbolt's Chimney	IV,5 *

ab. abseil

2 Am Basteir Chimney   145m   Very Difficult   *(1909)*

Largely hidden from below this route starts about 30m to the right of the lowest rocks, rising leftward to finish 50m east of the bad step on the summit crest.

This chimney is in three sections, the first is straightforward, the next 20m is the crux with classical chimney climbing, whilst the upper 25m is fine climbing on excellent holds. It is possible to bypass the crux chimney by rocks on the left.

Winter   **145m   IV,6 ****   *(1999)*

Follow the summer route.

1. 40m Climb the chimney and shallow gully above.
2. 40m Climb easier ground and snow slope to below a steep chimney.
3. 40m Continue up the fine technical chimney (crux) to belay on The Deadline.
4. 25m Climb the continuation fault above to the top.

3 North Face   260m   Difficult   *(1911)*

An extremely atmospheric climb with impressive rock scenery. Climb the initial chimney section of Am Basteir Chimney then continue to the base of the steep chimney. Traverse out right on a series of ledges across the very steep face below the summit. A choice of steep exit chimneys lead to the crest of Am Basteir close to the summit.

Winter: **260m   IV,5 ****   *(1999)*

The first two pitches are the same as Am Basteir Chimney.

1. 40m Climb the chimney and shallow gully above.

2. 40m Climb easier ground and a snow slope to below a steep chimney.

3. 50m Traverse hard right following the obvious ledge system for 40m. Climb a corner to gain a higher ledge system.

4. 50m Follow this fault rightwards over broken ground and ledges to belay in an alcove below a chimney.

5. 40m Continue easily rightwards along the narrowing ledge in a superb position to belay in the chimney of the Squeeze Box.

6. 40m The first ascent chose to finish by this chimney topping out just short of the summit.

4 The Squeeze Box   110m   E2   (1997)

Climbs the soaring chimney in the centre of the steep north face. Start at a break left of the chimney where there is a short wide crack at head height.

1. 30m 5b Climb the crack and groove above. Move on to the slabby wall on the right and up rightwards to the base of the chimney. A serious pitch.

2. 30m 5b Climb the back of the chimney in two sections. Vertical caving, probably always wet.

3. 30m 5a Pass a huge chockstone by moving out of the chimney on to a slab on the right, climbed to a ledge system. Continue up the deep narrow chimney with a through route.

4. 20m Finish easily up the continuation fault.

North Face, IV 5. North Face, Am Basteir. Climber Mark Shaw

Dave Ritchie

Hung, Drawn and Quartered, VIII, 8, North Face, Am Basteir.
Climber Ian Parnell

5 Hung, Drawn and Quartered 75m E3 ***   *(1996)*
A classic struggle up the striking chimney-line starting 10m left of King's Cave Chimney. The first three pitches are overhanging. Excellent belays; some brittle rock – beware parties on the screes below.
1. 15m 6a Climb the slanting slot just to the right of the main chimney. Belay 6m higher at a cave.
2. 17m 5c Swing up left, climb a ladder dyke, then follow the chimney to a grassy break.
3. 18m 5c Climb the overhanging trap dyke, an impressive pitch.
4. 25m 4c Follow the dyke and surmount a big chockstone to finish just west of the summit.
Winter: **VIII,8 ******   *(2008)*
An exceptional winter line; first climbed in heavily verglassed conditions. Protection generally plentiful but complicated by iced cracks – large cams/chocks/hex's and several long slings required.
1. 15m The main chimney-line was climbed direct through the roofs; strenuous but accommodating.
2. 17m The cracked roof above the belay was climbed direct instead of the ladder dyke on the left
3. 18m A very strenuous exit up a crack on right side of the dyke.
4. 25m An awkward finish at the chockstone.

Am Basteir - West Face (above the Basteir Nick)

The routes that are so crucial to a continuous Ridge Traverse are described here. From the Basteir Nick, the gap between Am Basteir and the Basteir Tooth, climb a short chimney giving easy access up to a grassy patch, which is also reached from the east by the Lota Corrie Route. An enclosed gully lies across basalt slabs 30m above here. Gain the gully and follow it for 15m to reach a small recessed cave directly above. Three common options are taken to surmount the overhung bulge above:

1. 8m 4b The prow immediately left of the cave starts with very steep climbing on reasonable holds before turning the chockstone by the right wall. Bold.

2. 6m 5b or use a traditional shoulder. Follow the slabby ledge up and left to where the ledge ends abruptly as Sligachan comes into view. The short corner above is severely undercut (The Mouth) but can be subdued by Victorian tactics giving fun and comparative safety in which to tackle the overhang.

3. 25m 4a Before reaching the recessed cave a number of grooves can be taken in the right wall of the gully. These lead directly toward the summit of Am Basteir avoiding the overhang completely. The only disadvantage is the extra time needed to climb the pitch.

6 West Wall   45m Severe   *(1960)*

The only full length climb on this face is a scrappy outing via the ramps and corners overlooking the Basteir Nick. From the grass patch just above the Nick take the first diagonal ledge leftwards to where a 4m wall leads to a higher cramped ledge. Move 6m left where an awkward pull-up leads to the foot of a prominent 10m corner. Climb this easily to reach the ledge below The Mouth.

BEALACH NA LICE

15. BASTEIR TOOTH

(NG 465 254) Alt 855m   North and South facing   Map p28   Diagrams p42, 73

This startling and fearsome fang (915m) juts out west of Am Basteir. Fortunately the Tooth is composed of sounder gabbro than Am Basteir. The south face, in particular, offers a number of very high quality routes that are often sunny and sheltered. In the wet the surest way of reaching its summit is to climb Lota Corrie Route.

Descents: Most parties will continue by climbing a route on the west face of Am Basteir (above). The easiest descent is to abseil 20m down King's Cave Chimney. A chamber must first be reached on the Sligachan side by dropping through a hole at the north side of the Basteir Nick. Good thread anchors are often in place. A 30m abseil drops west directly from the summit of the Tooth to the narrow neck below the overhung nose which is fun but serious. Care is needed to get the right line, avoid abrasion on the gabbro and retrieve the ropes. Descending Lota Corrie Route is possible, but not recommended.

North Face

7 King's Cave Chimney   30m   Very Difficult   *(1898)*

Editions of the climbing guide to Skye seem to have alternated between declaring this through route passable to it being blocked and in need of excavation. In 2009, on inspection from above, there was no clear route visible. The original climb involved three days of excavation by three men who would probably think highly of anyone wishing to maintain their route in the state in which they left it! The cleft is unmissable, just 100m below Bealach na Lice. Climb 12m over chockstones to a large chamber, crux. At the back there is a blockage, pierced by a small hole, which may require excavation. Persevere to wriggle up the final 2m tunnel which will lead to daylight and the col above.

8 King's Cave Wall and Outside Edge Continuation   55m   Severe *   *(1960)*
Start up the right wall of King's Cave Chimney, below the first chockstone, by a flakey crack; possible belay at 10m. Awkward climbing leads to a large semi-detached block. From just above this block make an airy but easy horizontal traverse 20m right to the edge of the undercut spur between King's Cave and Shadbolt's Chimney; belay. Climb the spur directly, adhering tenaciously to the extreme right edge, a very fine pitch.

9 Shadbolt's Chimney   50m   Very Difficult   *(1906)*
This is the clean cut uniform cleft 10m right of King's Cave Chimney. It finishes with a 7m tunnel through jammed boulders to emerge on top of the Tooth.
Start at the foot of King's Cave Chimney up sloping ledges to a small cave at the base of the rift. Exiting this is the crux; "The climber faces outwards to look for a good handhold high on the outside wall and then swings round on that. The leader can be held safely here by the rope threaded through a hole." The bed of the chimney leads to a 14m chimney giving "easy back and knee work leading to a hole in the roof. This leads to a narrow tunnel going outwards before doubling back to a small opening through which the party emerges into the sunshine (or rain) just opposite the finish of Naismith's Route."
Winter: **50m   IV,5 ***   *(2002)*
Follow the original summer route. Short but entertaining, the initial steepness forming the crux.
Outside variation: **Very Difficult**   *(1932)*
Instead of going into the back of the cave, back up outside to the roof, then go horizontally outwards under it and round to the end. The walls get rather too far apart for comfort, but a large slab which blocks the chimney affords relief by a crack between itself and the east wall. Constricted climbing leads to the jumbled blocks at the top and easier climbing to finish.
Winter: **VI,7 ****   *(2010)*
The eight metre roof of the chimney gave a unique and brilliant pitch with sustained back and foot techniques leading to a heavily rimed exit squeeze.

South Face

Most routes start from below the huge overhanging nose of the Basteir Tooth. This is reached from Bealach na Lice by gaining and then descending a narrowing ridge of rock to the final large ledge. A funnelling effect for the wind often makes this ledge seem very unfriendly but the South Face tends to be sheltered by comparison.

1 Naismith's Route   45m   Severe **   *(1898)*
A good route in an outrageous position. It is serious when tackled at the end of a Ridge Traverse but a delight as an objective in its own right.
Start from the ledge beneath the overhanging nose of the Tooth. It is advisable to split the route to avoid rope drag and to help with communications.
1. 10m Scramble down and round to belay on the blocky ledge on the south face.
2. 30m Zigzag right then left to reach the end of a long ledge. Walk along this to the narrowing. Either climb the wall above via a positive pocket (bold) or step right and ascend a large flake and crack above. The continuation crack is steep but well protected usually finishing with an ungainly exit onto the slab above. A spike belay here is best for communication.
3. 5m Scramble easily up onto the roof of the Tooth.
Variation: **Direct Start   20m**
This is a better option in strong winds. Descend easily into Lota Coire from Bealach na Lice until directly beneath the original start. Gain the corner from the left then climb to the blocky ledge.

2 Captain Planet   40m   E4 6a ***   *(2006)*
The finest climb on the Tooth takes a crack direct to the obvious groove 6m right

NORTHERN CUILLIN

Naismith's Route, Severe, South Face of the Basteir Tooth.
Climber John Carlin

of the arete and then finishes by the seemingly blank wall above. Straight, steep and well protected the three sections are well balanced in technical difficulty. Start from the first large blocks reached on Naismith's Route.

A thin crack rises directly up to the base of an obvious groove right of the arete (14m). Ascend the steep groove (PR) with difficulty to reach the crack above and a welcome niche (12m). Break right out of the niche for 3m before ascending the impending wall above. Good protection and positive holds give a grand finale (14m).

Variation: **Direct Finish   15m   E5 6a ***   (2008)
Continue above the resting niche until a slab of freshly broken white rock is reached. Climb this with delicacy, using small thin flakes, into the right-facing corner underneath the capping roof, rest. Make a few tricky moves right to finish beside the original route.

3 Rainbow Warrior   40m   E3 **   (1989)
The original hard route on this face boldly turned the logical crack and groove of Captain Planet because of wet rock. Start from a belay between the two ledges on Naismith's route.

1. 25m 6a Step left onto the large break. Climb to gain a left-trending line leading to the crack immediately above the groove. Climb this until a ledge leads left to a poor belay on the arete.

2. 15m 5c Traverse left until it is possible to surmount the roof above. Step back right and climb to a smaller roof. Pass this by a choice of parallel cracks direct to the summit.

Variation: **Gordon's Wet Dream   E3** *   (1995)*
Continue left and climb the groove when dry (crux, 6a) to rejoin the original route. Pitch 2 traverses up left to a shield of rock that leads to the top of the Tooth, 3m below the cairn (4c).

The next two routes are approached by descending into Lota Corrie from Bealach na Lice.

4 Naismith's Route Direct   85m   Severe   *(1934)*
This is almost an independent route which adds a lot more to the challenge before joining the original route at the ledge below the crux moves. The route starts up the deep forbidding chimney that is reached 100m after leaving the bealach and is often mistaken for the Lota Corrie Route.
1. 15m Follow the chimney to reach a broad ledge on the left.
2. 20m Break left up across mixed ground.
3. 10m Climb the wall above to reach an inward sloping ledge.

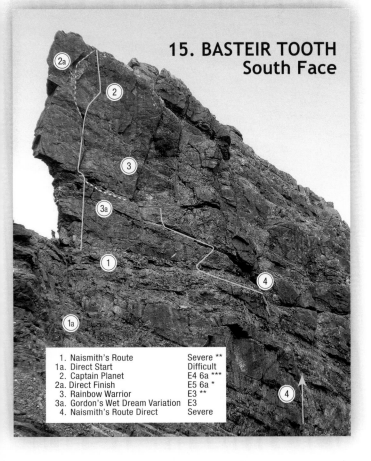

15. BASTEIR TOOTH
South Face

1. Naismith's Route	Severe **
1a. Direct Start	Difficult
2. Captain Planet	E4 6a ***
2a. Direct Finish	E5 6a *
3. Rainbow Warrior	E3 **
3a. Gordon's Wet Dream Variation	E3
4. Naismith's Route Direct	Severe

Rainbow Warrior, E3, South Face of the Basteir Tooth. Climber Mike Lates

4. 25m "The feature of the route is a 'stomach traverse' of 60ft (20m), where a long, narrow ledge slants up and leftwards across the south face. There is a big drop below and the rock immediately above the ledge projects like an eave, forcing one to lie on one's stomach and wriggle. The ledge thins out and, fortunately, so does the overhang, so that one first may kneel and then stand, being now on vertical rock with good holds." W.H.Murray, second ascent.

5. 15m Finish by the Original Route.

**5 Lota Corrie Route (Collie's Route)   200m   Grade 3/Moderate ** **   *(1888)*

This is an interesting and easy way of climbing the Tooth saving valuable time for parties running out of daylight near the end of a Ridge Traverse. It is as enclosed as Naismith's is exposed.

Descend for 300m from Bealach na Lice into Lota Corrie staying close beneath the vertical south-west wall of Am Basteir. A prominent overhang holds a comfortable walled bivvy site some 50m before the route finally starts to re-ascend.

A short clean wall gives the first possible breach to gain an easy angled open gully that leads back towards the Tooth. This is followed by either an upper or lower line with loose debris requiring delicacy at times. It leads to a grassy ledge just above the Basteir Nick, with the slabby back of the Tooth just beyond.

Winter: **II/III**
Difficulties vary with depth of snow but gaining Am Basteir beyond will always be harder.

Routes to Am Basteir are described under Am Basteir – West Face, immediately before the Basteir Tooth [15].

16. SGÙRR A' FIONN CHOIRE

(NG 464 252) Alt 825m   South facing   Map p28   Diagram p42

This is the prominent boss of rock between the Basteir Tooth and Bruach na Frithe, cleft by a gash at the top. Amazing cone sheets have formed a tiered castle that is frustratingly difficult for climbers to penetrate. Ascent from Fionn Choire is easy.

Approach: Descend 100m below Bealach na Lice into Lota Corrie. Traverse below the wall past the deep cleft.

Route Two   50m   Difficult   *(1907)*
This is the only route breaching the tiered wall facing Am Basteir. Climb the first corner system beyond the cleft. Climb a steep chimney through the first tier. Traverse rightwards across a 30 degree slab to a steep corner on right. The corner leads to the gash near the summit.

Route One   100m   Difficult   *(1896)*
Follow the base of the cliffs past Route Two to start at a fearsome nose formed by the rib running down from the summit. Climb the nose for a short distance then turn it on the left by a ledge immediately below the overhanging part. The precipitous west side of the Sgùrr is scaled by a steep corner to an easier finish.

SGÙRR A' BHASTEIR

17. SGÙRR A' BHASTEIR

(NG 467 263) Alt 525m   North Facing   Map p28   Diagram p42

This shapely symmetrical mountain is the right-hand most peak (NG 464 257, 898m) when viewed from Sligachan. It is connected by a superb horizontal ridge to the Main Ridge giving the best views of Pinnacle Ridge, Am Basteir and the Tooth. It makes an ideal start to a **Round of Fionn Choire** (Grade 1 ***). The first route lies above the lochan in Coire a' Bhasteir.

1 Gully Climb   70m   Severe   *(1902)*
There are three good pitches. The first is climbed on the left and the second up the centre, leading to a broad terrace. The third is about 15m high and overhangs considerably at the top. "John Mackenzie tried it directly up and, after nearly getting to the top slipped and fell, luckily not hurting himself at all as he was well hitched." This was then avoided by thin climbing on the left. "It is decidedly more interesting than the Doctor's Gully, the last pitch being, I feel sure, more difficult than anything in Waterpipe Gully."

2 North-East Ridge   600m   Grade 1 *
This is the left-hand ridge of Sgùrr a' Bhasteir as seen from Sligachan. It gives a good introduction to the Cuillin as all steep scrambling can be avoided if necessary, 1hr from the Basteir Gorge. Start by following the zigzag path up slabs on the west side of the Gorge. Where the path traverses into the corrie break right up a large selection of slabs in a south-westerly direction, returning to the crest of the broad ridge whenever possible.

Winter: **I** ****

The ridge frequently holds firm snow, consolidated by its exposed position, where other snow is still deep. A good route with superb views.

3 Mike The Bhàsteird   120m   IV,4 *   (2010)

A left facing corner lying 100m left of Broad Gully frequently holds ice.

1. 50m Follow the corner for 20m then the ice-sheet left of the corner to a large block belay.

2. 30m Continue in the same line which is thinner and harder.

3. 30m Easier ground leads to a terrace. Follow this right, below the impending wall until an abseil into Broad Gully is possible.

An independent line (III), 30m left of broad gully, follows a line of ice and turf to the terrace below the impending wall.

4 Broad Gully   200m   I *

A large gully splits the north face to reach the North-East Ridge at about 780m. It is not recommended in summer but holds snow well in winter and gives a pleasant easy route in most conditions. Extensive sections of easy angled ice also form readily on the face right of the gully about 80m higher and give excellent sport.

5 Hillary's Wake   120m   II *   (2008)

Start at a shallow gully just right (west) of Broad Gully. Follow the gully to a fork. Take the right-hand branch to an exit onto a large snow field (120 m). Continue easily up the snowfield in a direct line toward the summit. Above the snowfield a series of rock steps and ribs lead to the North-East Ridge about 100m below the top. Much variation is possible.

Am Basteir sunset. Climber Mark Shaw

6 North-West Ridge   400m   Grade 2 **
This is a slightly superior ridge to the North-East in dry conditions, offering more continuous climbing possibilities on steeper terrain. All difficulties can, again, be largely avoided. Approach by crossing the corrie to reach the bealach just south of Meall Odhar. Follow the Ridge as closely as possible, 45mins.
Winter: **I ***
The grade assumes that snow is followed as much as possible by the easiest lines.

FIONN CHOIRE

Fionn Choire is probably the safest route by which to reach the crest of the Cuillin Ridge. In winter it can hold huge quantities of snow and has been snow boarded down as far as the Allt Dearg. One area of cliffs lies high on the flanks of the North-West Ridge seen easily from Fionn Choire but can be difficult to locate in mist. Water ice also forms fairly easily on small buttresses lower down the North-West Ridge giving good entertainment.

18. BRUACH NA FRÌTHE - NORTH BUTTRESS
(NG 459 254)   Alt 780m   North facing   Map p28

Approach: Routes are best approached from Bealach a' Mhàim which is a well used pass between Sligachan and Glen Brittle. Start 200m beyond Sligachan at the Allt Dearg Cottage road end then follow the gorge to reach Bealach a' Mhàim (1hr). This point can also be reached from the Fairy Pools car park in Glen Brittle. Paths lead easily into Fionn Choire from the broad bealach. The North-West Ridge is gained easily from the corrie by bearing south at about 600m.

North Chimney   110m   Very Difficult   *(1908)*
This is the obvious chimney on the north face. The first ascensionists used tension and support from the rope to swing out and surmount the only major obstacle, a large chockstone above undercut walls.
Winter: **110m   III,5**
The route is graded for thin conditions which give a technical struggle; under deep snow it can be an easy grade I.

North-West Ridge of Bruach na Frìthe   Grade 1 *
The ridge is very broad and easy in its lower reaches above Bealach a' Mhàim. It finally narrows at an altitude of 700m with a well worn trail along the crest easy to follow. There is a steep section on the ridge crest above North Buttress. At this point the path takes to the southern flanks. It never properly regains the crest again, ascending a series of basalt dykes and scree covered rakes to the summit.
Winter: **I ****
A superb easy route by which to get views of the Cuillin in all their winter glory. Taking the crest direct has steps of grade II.

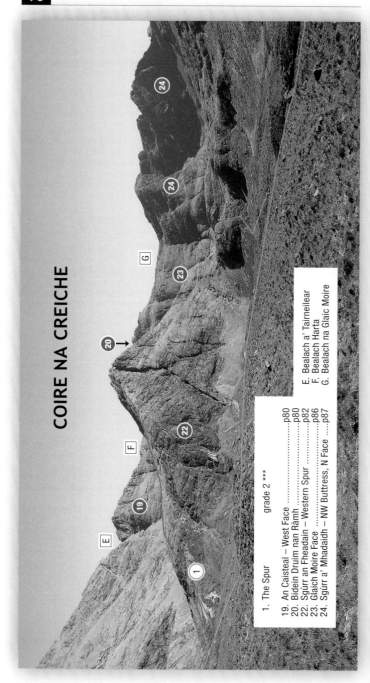

COIRE NA CREICHE

1. The Spur   grade 2 ***

COIRE NA CREICHE
Map p28

Sgùrr an Fheadian dominates this broad corrie with both the peak and Waterpipe Gully bisecting two upper corries. Coire a' Tairneilear is the more northerly and Coire a' Mhadaidh the larger and very significant climbing corrie to the south. The whole corrie is backed by Bruach na Frìthe to the north, Bidein Druim nan Ràmh centrally and Sgùrr a' Mhadaidh to the south.

The skyline is a classic route with difficult climbing and descents that form the most complex section on a Main Ridge Traverse. The huge north face of Mhadaidh is the mountaineer's choice for a big adventure in a period of fine weather. Route finding, rope work, climbing ability and nerve will all be tested. A southerly aspect makes the walls of Sgùrr an Fheadain an attractive place to climb, less than an hour from the road. Routes on the Glaic Moire Face are a mix of wonderful scrambles and classic gullies. A short day avoiding the worst weather can always be found hereabouts. The area has many crags with northern aspects and is a natural winter venue. There are many easily accessible winter climbs at all grades.

Recommended Approaches: All crags start by descending the footpath to the beautiful Fairy Pools. Crags in Coire a' Tairneilear are reached by following the path to the narrow entrance of this upper corrie (45mins). The classic Spur route also starts from here. All other crags lie to the south and are approached by leaving the footpath 500m beyond the Fairy Pools (NG 442 255) and following the Allt Coire a' Mhadaidh.

For crags [19-21] and Bealach Harta pass through the narrow entrance to Coire a' Tairneilear. The best path traverses scree slopes high above the river on the north bank leading to a grassy bowl enclosed by a serrated skyline (1hr). The Tairneilear Face of Sgùrr an Fheadain [21] lies up boulder fields to the south (1hr 30mins). Pass through a short section of gorge to reach another meadow. Bealach a' Tairneilear is the sharp V nick in the skyline to the left, reached by the Tairneilear Stone Shoot that holds no particular hazards. It gives quick access to the South Ridge of Bruach na Frìthe just below Sgùrr a' Bàirnich (1hr 30mins). The West Face of An Caisteal [19] lies immediately right (south) of the stone shoot. Bealach Harta is a good pass to Harta Corrie at the south end of An Caisteal and immediately north of Bidean Druim nan Ràmh. Ascend scree then slabs close to the main watercourse in the south-eastern corner of the upper bowl before a large boulder field leads to this, the lowest point on the Main Ridge (1hr 30mins). The North Face of Bidean [20] can also be reached this way but via the Spur is recommended.

Approach all crags south of the Spur [22-24] by rough ground beside the Allt Coire a' Mhadaidh for 1km. Routes on the Waterpipe Gully Area of Sgùrr an Fheadain [22] lie just above the level of the moorland (45mins).

Coire a' Mhadaidh and Bealach na Glaic Moire are approached by following the Allt Coire a' Mhadaidh scrambling through a small ravine to an open corrie surrounded by slabby buttresses and very steep faces. The most prominent tributary leads directly to the foot of South Gully on the Glaic Moire Face [23] in 1hr 15mins. The face is bound on the left side by a prominent scree gully that gives an easy path to Bealach na Glaic Moire (2hrs), a significant easy pass leading to Loch Coruisk.

Sgùrr a' Mhadaidh has four tops numbered from north to south with the fourth being the highest. The Northern Faces [24] are reached from the corrie floor by a rightward rising traverse beneath the increasingly intimidating walls (1hr 15mins – 2hrs). Such a huge face inevitably has a highly complex topography and some route descriptions remain ambiguous.

North-West Buttress leads to the first top and is bound to the south by the Amphitheatre. This gives access to the prominent diagonal faults of Foxes' Rake and Upper Rake that rise across the true North Face. Beyond the Amphitheatre a rising traverse beneath the steep walls passes the major fault-lines of Slanting Gully, Dyke Gully and, finally, Deep Gash Gully. High routes around the entrance to Deep Gash Gully may be better approached from the Coire An Doruis side described in the next chapter.

Round of Coire na Creiche 9hrs Grade3/Difficult **

A classic route, crucial for those researching a full Traverse with over 3km of sustained hard scrambling. Route finding is complex and detailed descriptions are given in the Cuillin Ridge Traverses chapter. Anti-clockwise starting up the West Ridge of Sgùrr a' Mhadaidh via Sgùrr Thuilm and finishing by descending the North-West Ridge of Bruach na Frìthe is recommended. Traversing Bidein Druim nan Ràmh forms the crux. The round can be split with a classy start by the Spur on Sgùrr an Fheadain with options to head north or south from Bidein (both 7hrs).

COIRE A' TAIRNEILEAR

Easy winter lines have been climbed on the southern flanks of Bruach na Frìthe in exceptional conditions and may look attractive on the approach walk.

19. AN CAISTEAL - WEST FACE

(NG 459 245) Alt 600m West facing Map p28 Diagram p78

Descents: All routes finish on the crest of An Caisteal. The easiest descent is to head south along the Ridge to Bealach Harta (Grade 3) followed by a straightforward descent into Coire a' Tairneilear. Heading northward is steep and exposed with a final difficult descent into the Tairneilear Stone Shoot often abseiled (Grade 3/Difficult).

North West Chimney 220m V,5 * (2009)

This route climbs the face left of West Buttress. Despite being escapable after pitch 2 the route is worthwhile particularly for its fine top pitch. Start from the Tairneilear Stone Shoot. At its narrowest point an easy snow gully leads off right onto the buttress.

1. 35m Follow the snow gully to a ledge and cave belay.
2. 60m Surmount some large blocks and follow the gully above to belay overlooking an easy gully rising from the left.
3. 50m Cross the gully and climb the mixed groove above.
4. 30m Continue up the fault above to belay below the prominent curving chimney.
5. 45m Climb the chimney to gain the ridge north of the summit.

West Buttress 200m Difficult

Easy scrambling on the right side of the first tier is on good rock. The second tier can be avoided on the right by scramblers but gives the climber an interesting challenge. Start by an open groove right of centre but break out left before it steepens. Cross loose ground left (15m) below overhangs to reach clean rock. Some 10m of good steep climbing leads directly back to scrambling terrain.
Winter: **200m II** (2006)

A good route when snow is consolidated. Avoid the steep second tier.

Arrow Slot 140m III (2006)

This gully lies immediately right of West Buttress, and finishes at the northern most deep gap on the ridge. Approach by snow slopes and a lower shallow gully. Above the first pitch (crux) belays were taken in snow. A direct finish to the gap was avoided by traversing left below a huge chockstone and loose looking blocks.

20. BIDEIN DRUIM NAN RÀMH

(NG 457240) Alt 750m North-West facing Map p28 Diagram p78

This is the most complicated section of the Ridge to traverse and is described in detail in the Cuillin Ridge Traverses chapter. A large boulder field lies below the north-west face giving a possible bypass. Three prominent rifts spilt the face of which two are known to have been climbed and descended. **North Gap Gully** and

Northern Peaks from Bidean Druim nan Ramn. Climber Matt Barratt

COIRE NA CREICHE

South Gap Gully lead easily to the gaps either side of the Central Top by Moderate climbing.

SGÙRR AN FHEADAIN

(NG 452 245)   688m

The symmetry of the Coire na Creiche centres on this dramatic peak and the deep cleft of Waterpipe Gully that splits the west face from top to bottom. The approach is attractively short. The Tairneilear Face [21] is a sombre place which is balanced well by the sunny aspect of most routes on the Western Spur [22].

21. TAIRNEILEAR FACE

(NG 455 244)   Alt 600m   North-East facing   Map p28

This hidden face has seen very little activity with the routes lying on separate buttresses either side of the dip in the connecting ridge between Sgùrr an Fheadain and Bidean Druim nan Ràmh.

Descent: A slabby descent north to the base of the crags is possible from the dip between the buttresses.

Sinistra Buttress

A large steep face overlooks Coire a' Tairneilear.

Sinistra Crack   150m   Severe   *(1980)*
There are two crack systems in the steep face. Climb the left-hand crack, which slants slightly left, in three long pitches to the crest of the ridge.

Hosepipe Ban   70m   III,4   *(2010)*
Two large gullies start from just below the dip in the ridge. They are hidden from
Coire a' Tairneilear but clearly visible from the summit of Sgurr an Fheadain. Climb
the left-hand of these in two pitches by back and footing.

150m further right a deep gully splits the summit of Sgurr an Fheadain.

Summit Buttress

Cameron's Gully   70m   I   *(2000)*
Climb the deep gully with two short steepenings and good rock scenery.

22. WESTERN SPUR

**(NG 449 249)   Alt 300m   South-West facing   Map p28   Diagrams p78,
83**

A huge variety of climbs are contained in this small area.

Descent: Shorter climbs finish low on the broad western spur. Traverse horizontally across the spur until a scrambling descent can be made down the first open
gully encountered. From the apex of the peak (not quite the highest point) descend
easily east for 100m to a dip. Easy screes lead south into Coire a' Mhadaidh.
Alternatively climb the continuation ridge (Grade 1) east for 1km to reach the Main
Ridge just south of Bidean (30mins).

1 The Spur   400m   Grade 2 *
A fine short route with plenty of continuous rock, 1hr. It stays more sheltered than
other ridges in windy weather.
Start up clean slabs forming the left-hand toe of the spur close to the entrance to
Coire a' Tairneilar (100m). A broad shallow bowl is reached above. Traverse south
(right) across screes from here, passing a prominent rowan tree, to reach the crest
of the spur. Easy climbing follows the crest directly in good positions to the
summit.
Winter: **I ***
Take easy snow gullies centrally to reach the broad shallow bowl. Snow conditions
dictate whether it is better to move right to the crest as in summer or follow
numerous snowy grooves running parallel to it on the northern flank.

2 Summit Gully   150m   Difficult   *(1907)*
Ascend the initial slabs on The Spur. A laid back gully rises out of the shallow bowl
leading directly to the summit of Sgùrr an Fheadain. Three climbing pitches are
encountered. Turn the largest chockstone with some difficulty at the bottom edge
of the left wall, 5m below the overhanging block.

Waterpipe Gully Area

The rock here varies in quality with some superb sections higher on the routes adjacent to the green cave. A small triangular grassy niche lies at the southern toe of
the Western Spur, just before the south wall is reached. Routes begin here and are
described from left to right.

3 Spur Gully   120m   Difficult   *(1907)*
Previously named as Drainpipe Gully. Climb the gully directly above the grassy
niche via some pleasant pitches. Follow the left branch at the bifurcation.

4 Edgeway   120m   Very Difficult **   *(1980)*
A cracking route. It is popular with locals at the start of the season to remind them
of what Cuillin routes are about. Protection is just adequate. Takes the right edge
of Spur Gully initially and continues straight up by an obvious line.

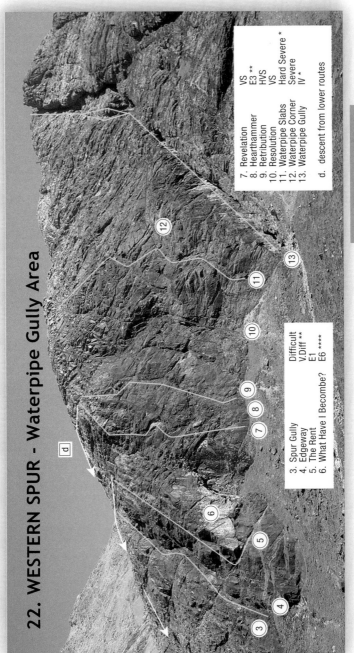

83

22. WESTERN SPUR - Waterpipe Gully Area

COIRE NA CREICHE

7. Revelation	VS **
8. Hearthammer	E3 **
9. Retribution	HVS
10. Resolution	VS
11. Waterpipe Slabs	Hard Severe *
12. Waterpipe Corner	Severe
13. Waterpipe Gully	IV *
d. descent from lower routes	

3. Spur Gully	Difficult
4. Edgeway	V.Diff **
5. The Rent	E1
6. What Have I Become?	E6 ****

1. 35m Take the easiest line up the steepening rib. Small wires protect moves that lead leftward towards a 5m bulge. Cleverly arrange protection before launching onto some steep moves. Belay well back.
2. 30m Regain the rib and continue more easily to the fork in Spur Gully.
3. 25m Regain the rib by descending slightly. Follow the crest in a great position until the angle eases. Belay on a small chockstone.
4. 30m An open vegetated groove leads to a large terrace.

The crag becomes far steeper around the next corner. The most notable feature of the face is a large recessed green cave.

5 The Rent   120m   E1 5b   *(1980)*
This climb starts left of the green cave on the main face.
Traverse up and left along a ledge, passing beneath a large roof to meet an open corner just right of Edgeway. Climb up the break in two pitches and take the third and crux pitch up a tricky chimney. More straightforward climbing leads to the top.

6 What Have I Becombe   80m   E6 ****   *(2004)*
The obvious overhanging off-width crack to the right of The Rent.
1. 40m 6b Climb the crack with a bold start leftwards past a peg runner and continue rightwards up the crack. Make hard moves over a bulge to a big flake ledge to the right.
2. 40m 6b Continue up the crack with a hard start leading to easier climbing over ledges to a big grassy ledge.

7 Revelation   150m   VS 4c   *(1980)*
To the right of the green cave is a wall. Climb this to gain a curving line parallel to the face. The second pitch takes a vegetated corner but a fine headwall gives a rewarding final pitch.

8 Hearthammer   105m   E3 **   *(1990)*
This route takes a slanting dyke high in the centre of the face which only shows on close inspection of the wall. Low in the grade. Start 3m left of the flake-crack of Retribution.
1. 35m 4c Climb a slabby wall directly to a grass ledge at 25m, gain the wall above by a large block on the right, then move back left and go up to belay in a short corner at the base of the dyke.
2. 40m 5c Follow the dyke diagonally rightwards to a ledge, move right and climb the right-hand side of an overhang to rejoin the dyke which is followed to its conclusion at a good ledge. A tremendous pitch.
3. 30m 4b Continue more easily to the top.

9 Retribution   145m   HVS 5a   *(1980)*
Start at a prominent flake-crack and follow this line up the central wall, left of the two chimney systems.

10 Resolution   150m   VS 4b   *(1974)*
Left of the start of Waterpipe Gully is a steep wall with two chimney systems. The route takes the right-hand chimney initially, then transfers to the left. Start at an easy slab; cairn.
1. 40m Climb the slab to a sapling, go up a corner for a few metres, then move up a wall on the right to a chimney. Follow this to a spike belay.
2. 20m Follow the grass rake to its top, then move across the wall on the left to a good stance and ash belay.
3. 40m Traverse left to join the other crack system and climb this diagonally right to a steep grassy recess. Climb a short corner on the left, or the slab on the right, to a good ledge and poor peg belay.
4. 10m Move a few metres right and go up to a good stance at the foot of a short corner.

5. 40m Climb the corner and an easy diagonal line left to the top.

11 Waterpipe Slabs   150m   Hard Severe 4b *   (1981)
This route starts centrally between Waterpipe Gully and Resolution. It follows a parallel course to Resolution, always taking the line of least resistance to the top.

12 Waterpipe Corner   400m   Severe   (1947)
This route was recorded with no less than 22 pitches, 10 short (<15m) pitches lead in 130m to an easing of the angle. A further 200m of scrambling with a couple of small climbing pitches then leads to another 120m of steep climbing, broken into seven further pitches. 100m of scrambling leads to the summit. Start at the lowest point of the arete left of Waterpipe Gully and keep as near to the gully edge as possible. In general the climb is very steep and exposed with wonderful views down the gully.

13 Waterpipe Gully   400m   VS 4b   (1895)
A huge and serious classic expedition that is too loose to recommend highly. The first ascent of the prominent central gully was a remarkable feat for the time and produced one of the major gully climbs in Scotland. It has been climbed directly but most parties will choose to avoid many of the main pitches. A time of 10hrs is normal for an ascent.

Start deep inside the cleft where a steep 8m wall blocks the way and sets the tone. A complete description would lead to confusion but notes made by J.H.Bell forewarn of the major difficulties and were of more use than any other description carried by the current author.

Near the foot (pitch 2) a very steep pitch occurs about 80ft (25m) high. To climb straight up here is very difficult. The pitch can be passed by following a sloping ledge on the right wall past a small rowan tree. About 300ft (100m) up there is a vertical pitch with a tiny waterfall. Climbers can scale this direct, regardless of a ducking, otherwise the right wall must be taken again.

About 850ft (270m) up a stack of rock divides the gully into two branches. This place can be passed by climbing up a small grassy ridge by a shallow chimney in the stack itself then traversing into the right-hand branch. Alternatively the latter can be followed throughout.

Near the top, at a place where the gully is narrow and both walls are unclimbable, there is a hopelessly steep pitch of 60ft (20m). The way here lies up a chimney in the left-hand corner of the pitch, then stepping right round a (loose) projecting rib of rock to regain the gully which is wet and mossy.
Winter: **400m   IV** *   (1986)
Requires a prolonged hard freeze. Most pitches are short and linked by easy snow. The hardest and longest pitch was the first.

14 Pig's Ear   250m   Very Difficult   (1972)
Takes in the steep rocks to the summit right of Waterpipe Gully. Pitch lengths were not recorded but numerous overlaps are turned by rakes or direct by trap dykes eventually leading to the final tower just right of Waterpipe Gully. Described as 'a fine route on good clean rock with sunny aspect.'

15 The Hose 360m   III   (1978)
About 50m right of Waterpipe Gully is another shallow gully. Two 45m ice pitches and several smaller ones were encountered en route. Escapes are possible to the right.

16 Moon Raker   60m   VS   (1963)
This line was reported as well seen from the Foxes' Rake on Sgùrr a' Mhadaidh. It has not been identified but the description is repeated here: Follow a prominent boomerang shaped corner well right of Waterpipe Gully. There are three pitches, one of 30m and two of 15m. The second pitch is the crux.

The following route lies 400m further into Coire a' Mhadaidh (NG 450 243). It takes rocks on the southern flank of Sgùrr an Fheadain directly above the footpath.

17 Stepped Buttress   200m   II   (1995)

The bottom of the route is a steep wall with a line of small left-slanting ledges. Start about 30m from the burn. Climb the initial steep wall by a line of left-slanting ledges with one awkward section. Continue to the top of the first step in another pitch then walk to the second step. Climb this in two pitches to a scree slope. It is possible to descend to the right back into the corrie below the Glaic Moire Face or to climb another route on the southern headwall of Sgùrr an Fheadain.

COIRE A' MHADAIDH

This important and impressive corrie lies up and right (south) of Sgùrr nan Fheadain.

23. GLAICH MOIRE FACE

(NG 451 241)   Alt 500m   North-West facing   Map p28   Diagrams p78, 88

This is the wide slabby headwall that stretches impressively as a defence to Bealach na Glaic Moire. The rock is formed into sweeps of slabs punctuated by prominent gullies. The face is bounded on the left by a broad scree gully that gives easy access to Coruisk and the normal descent route from the bealach.
Routes are described from left to right.

Descent: From Bealach na Glaic Moire descend west to a grassy terrace that drops slightly as it traverses north along the top of the face. Continue in the same direction across scree and boulders, passing the top of both North Gully and Stag Gully until an easy descent can be made down the broad scree slope. Difficult to locate in mist.

1 Stag Gully   120m   II/III   (1994)

Left of North Gully is a thin chimney slot. Climb this in three pitches to a terrace where a further pitch leads to the top. This gully is only a metre wide in places.

2 Stag Buttress   200m   III   (1994)

This is the buttress to the right of Stag Gully. Take a central line to the crux section halfway up at some slabby rocks. Below and above this section the climbing is much easier.

3 North Gully   120m   Moderate   (1914)

Scramble easily for 100m. The first obstacle is an overhanging slab extending across the gully, which is avoided by a crack on the left wall. The final cave pitch gives a through route.
Winter: **III** *   (1983)
The gully gives a fine ice pitch at mid-height and a through route up to the Bealach na Glaic Moire. Better ice forms on the right wall and slabs towards the top of the climb.

4 Central (Tuppenny) Buttress   220m   Grade 3 ***

Possibly the best way to approach Glaic Moire from Glen Brittle. Take the central buttress direct with vertical dykes often giving the easiest climbing.
Winter: **220m   III,5**   (1995)
This climb is on the broad area of rock between North Gully and Central Gully, taking a chimney-line to the right of the large area of slabs. Easy climbing for 100m leads to a steeper central section where the chimney gives three long pitches to the top. The middle pitch has a rock barrier which can prove tricky in thin conditions.

Variation: **Central Buttress Right-Hand Groove** **120m** **III,4** *(2001)*
Climb the first 100m of Central Buttress to where the original route goes up a deep chimney. Below and to the right is an obvious slanting groove. Gain this (crux) and climb the groove, a slabby section and an icy ramp to finish.

5 Central Gully **100m** **Difficult** *(1952)*
The initial bridging pitch is the best. Above, the angle eases and the walls become shallow and the gully ends on the slabs at mid-height.

6 South Gully **210m** **Severe** ****** *(1937)*
The Allt Coire a' Mhadaidh burn flows out from this route. which is sheltered in all weather. A gigantic boulder appears to block the way at the start but is easily turned on the right. The route is very worthy of attention with continuous clean solid rock, challenging climbing and route finding and sparse but solid protection. Climb a succession of excellent pitches all about Difficult to Very Difficult in standard. The 30m final crux pitch is turned by back and footing up past a gushing waterfall or avoided by most parties by an escape to slabs on the left.
Winter: **III/IV** ***** *(1979)*
Requires a hard prolonged freeze, especially if the final pitch is to be tackled.

Right of South Gully lies a four-tiered buttress with no recorded routes that is bound by a prominent but far shallower gully **Winter Gully** (180m I *), leading to the southern end of the bealach above.

24. SGÙRR A' MHADAIDH - NORTHERN FACES

(NG 450 240) **Alt 550m** **North-West facing** **Map p28** **Diagrams p78, 88, 90, 93**

When conditions have been dry for some days this is a venue highly recommended for the experienced mountaineer but most routes are not suited to beginners. There are four tops on Sgùrr a' Mhadaidh numbered from north to south as they lie on the Main Ridge. The faces below are all large and it is often difficult to distinguish where the routes go.

Descents: Numerous descents are used for the different routes. They include traversing the Main Ridge north to Glaic Moire or south to An Doras as described in the Ridge Traverse, in the last chapter. This involves a variety of Difficult climbing and abseils depending on which direction is chosen and should not be underestimated. Many routes finish on the large diagonal rakes which can be descended to the Amphitheatre but neither is easy in their entirety. Routes finishing close to the top of Deep Gash Gully involve a scramble back down the West Ridge of Sgùrr a' Mhadaidh (Grade 3) before traversing back beneath the face. Specific details are given with the different buttresses.

North-West Buttress

This is the broad buttress that runs directly to the summit of the first top. The first route acts as an approach and finish to the two following climbs.

Descent: Follow the Main Ridge north to Bealach na Glaic Moire (on the south flank, Grade 1) and descend as described for the Glaic Moire Face [23], above.

7 North-West Buttress **360m** **Very Difficult** ***** *(1896)*
The classic climb described here should not be confused with the scrambling route described in Skye Scrambles (Grade 2). The first two tiers are no more than a scramble (150m) but the third is very steep and intimidating. Start 20m right of Winter Gully. Take the most solid line of rock, bearing right until overlooking a shallow gully system that forks before the first broad terrace. The second tier has a narrow gully running leftward giving 90m of scrambling both in and out of the gully.
The third tier is a different prospect entirely, with an overhanging section some

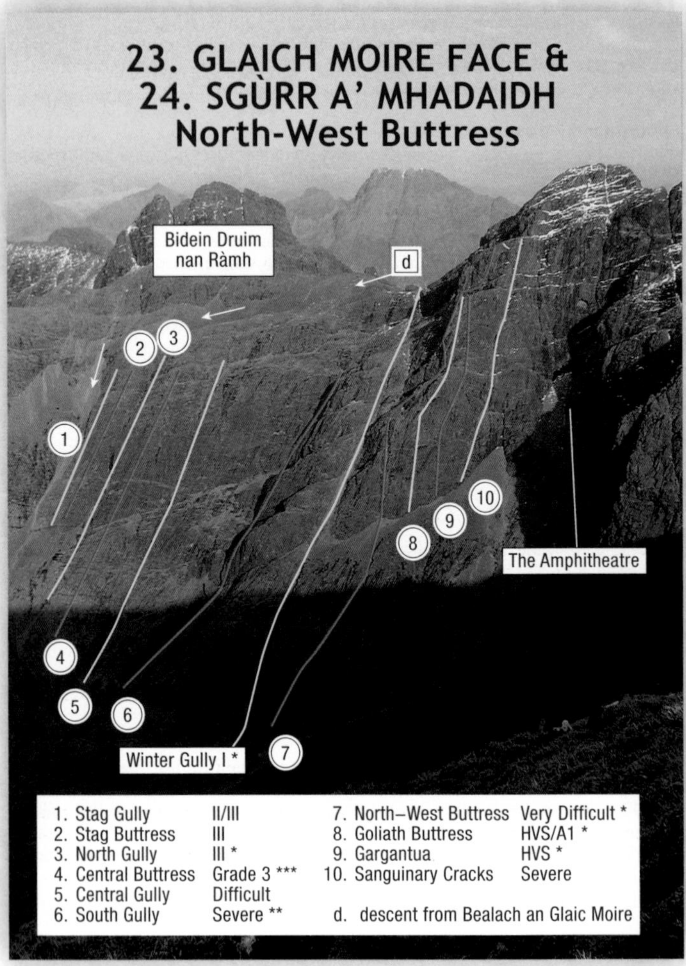

23. GLAICH MOIRE FACE &
24. SGÙRR A' MHADAIDH
North-West Buttress

Bidein Druim nan Ràmh

d

The Amphitheatre

Winter Gully I *

1. Stag Gully	II/III	7. North–West Buttress	Very Difficult *
2. Stag Buttress	III	8. Goliath Buttress	HVS/A1 *
3. North Gully	III *	9. Gargantua	HVS *
4. Central Buttress	Grade 3 ***	10. Sanguinary Cracks	Severe
5. Central Gully	Difficult		
6. South Gully	Severe **	d. descent from Bealach an Glaic Moire	

30m above the base. Head straight up on steepening rock until forced right. A shallow gully then climbs the right side for 20m. The traverse back left to the middle line of the buttress is by a narrow horizontal ledge, accomplished by keeping right leg and arm in the groove and left limbs in space, "the strain comes chiefly on a part of the anatomy little fitted to bear it"! A shallow groove reached in the crest of the buttress has been climbed but a steep corner further left gives better climbing for 10m. Above the rock is sheer but a curious groove gives a serious 20m pitch to a ledge. Follow this right until it is possible to reach the top of this memorable tier.

The top tier starts by a slab to reach a steep 8m wall. This is climbed by a short chimney at the right side before easier ground leads to the crest of the Ridge.

8 Goliath Buttress   345m   HVS/A1 *   (1964)
This climb takes the steeper right side of the second tier of North-West Buttress then tackles the third tier directly. Start on the second tier, beneath a crack at the

left end of the block overhangs and 25m left of Sanguinary Cracks.

1. 40m 4a Climb slabs to the foot of the crack and follow this to a stance in a niche under a large overhang; peg belay.

2. 25m 4a Step left onto a rib and continue straight up to a block belay.

3. 35m 4a Continue up the fault by a double crack to a large overhang, then traverse 5m to a stance on the right edge of the buttress; peg belay.

4. 25m Climb to a large terrace beneath the third tier then scramble to its base.

5. 20m 4a The line of overhangs above is broken by a dyke in the centre. Climb to a ledge beneath this; peg belay.

6. 20m 5a Surmount the overhanging dyke, exit using one peg for aid and continue to a good ledge.

7. 30m 4c Move up to a large block perched on a slab, cross the block to a very steep wall on the left and climb this strenuously, but on large holds, to a terrace.

8. etc. 150m Easier climbing now leads to a junction with North-West Buttress, 60m, which is followed to the summit, 90m.

9 Gargantua   360m   HVS 5a *   *(1969)*

This climb follows the right-hand edge of Goliath Buttress overlooking Sanguinary Cracks. Start at a shallow groove.

1. 30m Climb the groove, then follow the edge of the buttress to flake belays below a slightly overhanging wall.

2. 25m Traverse 6m left, then go up slabs and grooves to a large ledge below the right end of block overhangs girdling the front of the buttress; peg belay.

3. 20m 5a Follow the dyke right for 4m, go up then left below one overhang and out onto a lip of the overhang above the previous stance, crux. Climb the wall and slab above to a ledge; peg belay.

4. 35m Climb to a large terrace.

5. etc. 250m Now follow the crest of the buttress for several pitches to join North-West Buttress.

10 Sanguinary Cracks   210m   Severe   *(1958)*

This climb follows the prominent line of cracks on the right flank of Goliath Buttress. Start below the second tier, left of the Amphitheatre, at a chockstone belay at the base of the cracks.

1. 30m Climb a crack and the slabs on its right to a shelf.

2. 30m Continue up the shallow chimney above to a horizontal shelf.

Easier climbing leads for 75m to another shelf. Above, a short steep pitch leads to a ledge where the line of cracks finishes. Scrambling is possible either left or right, but it is better to continue directly to the summit. The last pitch is somewhat loose.

The Amphitheatre

A 25m band of rock splits the Amphitheatre at half-height. When descending from the Upper Rake a diagonal break is hidden on the right (north) side, Grade 2. Some good pitches of ice often form here and a disappointing climb, **Clap Trap** (240m Severe 1966), was recorded taking a direct line up the North-West Buttress.

11 Icicle Factory   205m   V *   *(1986)*

A superb route taking the prominent ice-choked corner in the back right-hand side of the Amphitheatre, up to the left of The Smear.

1. 30m Climb into an ice groove and continue to a ledge on the left.

2. 30m Climb an ice curtain on the left to gain a right-slanting ramp which is followed to a belay below the main difficulties.

3. 30m Ascend the narrowing ice ramp and surmount the capping icicle to belay on the right.

4. 25m Continue up an icicle and the steep ice above to belay beneath the very impressive final pitch.

5. 45m Climb the ice column to the overhang and transfer to an icicle on the right which leads to an easy gully. A superb pitch.

COIRE NA CREICHE

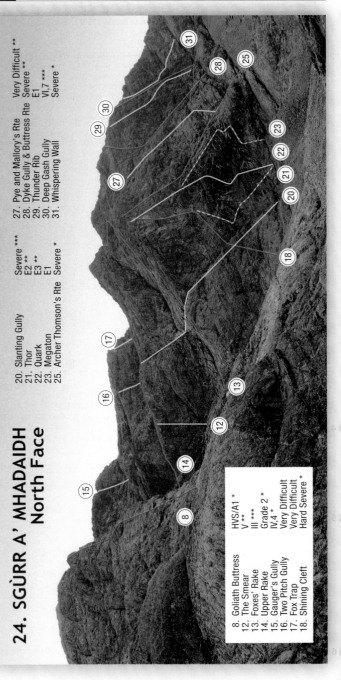

24. SGÙRR A' MHADAIDH
North Face

8. Goliath Buttress	HVS/A1 *	
12. The Smear	V **	
13. Foxes' Rake	III ***	
14. Upper Rake	Grade 2 *	
15. Gauger's Gully	IV,4 *	
16. Two Pitch Gully	Very Difficult	
17. Fox Trap	Very Difficult	
18. Shining Cleft	Hard Severe *	

20. Slanting Gully	Severe ***	
21. Thor	E2 **	
22. Quark	E3 **	
23. Megaton	E1	
25. Archer Thomson's Rte	Severe *	

27. Pye and Mallory's Rte	Very Difficult **	
28. Dyke Gully & Buttress Rte	Severe **	
29. Thunder Rib	E1	
30. Deep Gash Gully	VI,7 ***	
31. Whispering Wall	Severe *	

6. 45m Continue to join the Ridge on the first top. Descend to Bealach na Glaic Moire as for the previous routes.

2 The Smear 90m V ★★ *(1979)*
The prominent icefall that flows down between the Upper Rake and Foxes' Rake. Descend by the Upper Rake.

3 Foxes' Rake 300m Grade 3 ★
This is the lower of the two right-slanting rakes giving a good sheltered climb in strong westerly winds. Caution with loose rock is needed. Start 50m up into the Amphitheatre with a step across to gain the slabs. The slabs lead up and rightward fairly simply for 200m to a cairn where the outer edge of the rake becomes grassy and level. (Continuing too far leads to very loose ground above Deep Gash Gully.) Make a sharp left turn back towards the upper bounding wall. Large areas of compact blocky basalt need to be negotiated for 50m to reach an easing in the angle. Slabs lead to a large flat ledge on the West Ridge of Sgùrr a' Mhadaidh. Descent is easiest by An Doras.
Winter: **III ★★★**
One of the most reliable winter routes in the Cuillin. The rake has an outer lip that retains snow and ice regularly, a Cuillin rarity. The lip does make the conditions hard to judge from the road (the wall often appears black) but it is climbable in thin conditions and well worth a gamble. A more direct start from the Amphitheatre on good water ice is sometimes possible. On the rake stay closer to the wall than in summer. The best ice on the steepest section of slabs forms in the left corner. Rock protection is predictably sparse with blade pegs and bulldogs recommended.
Variation: **Day Tripper IV** *(2006)*
Stayed right on the easier line before discovering a hard section above Thunder Rib.

Routes Above The Upper Rake

Descents: These routes leave a choice of awkward escape. Traverse over tops north to Bealach na Glaic Moire or south to An Doras as described in the Cuillin Ridge Traverses chapter. Descending the Upper Rake or the Thuilm Ridge of Mhadaidh leads back to the foot of the north face.

4 Upper Rake 300m Grade 1 ★
An enjoyable easy scramble through stunning rock scenery. It finishes between the third top and the main summit of Sgùrr a' Mhadaidh from where far more serious scrambling is encountered along the Ridge.
Winter: **I ★**
Holds ice slightly less well than Foxes. A steep step before leaving the Amphitheatre is the hardest section before reaching the Ridge.

5 Gauger's Gully 100m Difficult *(1939)*
This deep-cut gully splits the middle of the second top of Sgùrr a' Mhadaidh but does not start from the Upper Rake. Halfway along the Upper Rake break up left by easy scrambling before dropping slightly to the foot of the gully. Alternatively, make a scrambling descent from the Ridge between the second and third tops. The gully has three principal pitches. Climb easily up the bed of the gully to a stance and belay below a chockstone. Climb the left wall and continue past the chockstone to a chimney above. Climb the back and foot chimney past a large chockstone to the top.
Winter: **75m IV,4 ★** *(2002)*
Follow the summer route. Good rock scenery throughout.

6 Two Pitch Gully 75m Very Difficult *(1911)*
This is the deep, vertical, chockstoned rift in the wall of the third top. It starts from

the Upper Rake and lies 90m right of the top section of Slanting Gully. The start of the climb is the crux, where a short entry gains the chimney above.

17 Fox Trap   60m   Very Difficult   *(1951)*
This is the obvious deep fault in the south-west face of the third top. Start 20m below the col between the third and fourth tops. Follow the chimney passing chockstones high up.

North Face

The face starts immediately right of the Amphitheatre.

Descents: All routes (apart from Slanting Gully) finish on Foxes' Rake with those north of Dyke Gully ending low enough to make descent easy. Routes right of Dyke Gully finish above the hard section of Foxes' Rake. From here the best descent to the bottom of the cliff is by the Thuilm Ridge of Sgùrr a' Mhadaidh (route 32).

18 Shining Cleft   270m   Hard Severe 4b *   *(1952)*
A long climb that has considerable atmosphere. It starts left of the long diagonal gully, Slanting Gully, crosses it, then continues up the great V-cleft above the overhangs of the Thor trilogy. Start at the lowest point of the slabby rocks left of Slanting Gully and cross them to a cairn. Climb up right to a ledge, then go up a 4m slab to a slanting chimney in a long low overhang. Trend right across slabs to a recess above the big cave in Slanting Gully and cross the gully at that point. Follow a narrow gangway, then a broad slabby ledge under big overhangs, to a slabby amphitheatre topped by a basalt sill.
   This amphitheatre runs up to form the great V shaped cleft of smooth basalt which is overhung at its top. Follow the cleft, easily at first, to the sill and belays. Now traverse delicately right on basalt to reach a right-slanting ledge (4b). Climb a short chimney to a platform on the crest of the rib, which forms the right wall of the V cleft. Follow the rib, at first by a chimney on the left, then by easier rocks on the crest, to finish on Foxes' Rake.

19 Foxes' Folly   105m   Severe *   *(1950)*
A very pleasant climb running parallel to Slanting Gully .Start at the base of the dyke 6m left of Slanting Gully.
1. 40m Climb the dyke to steeper rocks and a block belay near the gully.
2. 10m Traverse left until the steep rocks can be climbed back to the right to a small broken overhang with spike belays.
3. 10m 4a Climb the fault through the overhang above to reach a steep slab which leads to Slanting Gully above a wedged block.
4. 30m Easy climbing on the edge of the gully leads to the final pitch.
5. 15m Climb a crack on the left of the gully to Foxes' Rake.

20 Slanting Gully   210m   Severe **   *(1907)*
This prominent feature is regarded as one of the finer Cuillin gully climbs with largely clean solid rock. The Upper Rake gives the best descent. Start about 40m right of the Amphitheatre, low on the left side of the North Face.
   The gully is divided into two parts where Foxes' Rake intersects it rather more than halfway up. The initial pitch involves threading a tight gap. Easier terrain above leads into the back of a deep chasm (50m). Gain a large wedged chockstone. Either bridge boldly up the chasm or climb the left wall by an exposed slabby rib, 25m. Minor pitches follow with a good final pitch leading to Foxes' Rake.
   Across and above the continuation starts by the Cracks Pitch. Climb up cracks to a small cave with an overhanging roof. This pitch can be avoided by slabs on the right before stepping back left to enter the gully. Follow this more easily to another impassable section. Follow a narrow ledge along the face on the right to a corner with a tricky manoeuvre to gain the continuation. Continue more easily above and finish with a good 25m pitch to the Upper Rake.

24. SGÙRR A' MHADAIDH
North Face

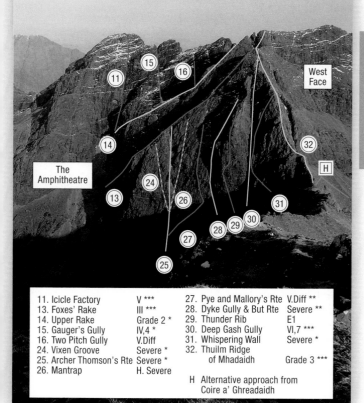

West Face

The Amphitheatre

H

11. Icicle Factory	V ***	27. Pye and Mallory's Rte	V.Diff **
13. Foxes' Rake	III ***	28. Dyke Gully & But Rte	Severe **
14. Upper Rake	Grade 2 *	29. Thunder Rib	E1
15. Gauger's Gully	IV,4 *	30. Deep Gash Gully	VI,7 ***
16. Two Pitch Gully	V.Diff	31. Whispering Wall	Severe *
24. Vixen Groove	Severe *	32. Thuilm Ridge	
25. Archer Thomson's Rte	Severe *	of Mhadaidh	Grade 3 ***
26. Mantrap	H. Severe		

H   Alternative approach from
Coire a' Ghreadaidh

Winter: **IV,5 ***   *(2004)*
The route was climbed with a thin covering of powder snow as far as Foxes' Rake.

The cliff dramatically steepens beyond Slanting Gully and presents a huge diamond shaped wedge of rock, 200m high, where three high quality lines find their way. There are considerable areas of loose or brittle rock on this section of the crag.

1 Thor 240m E2 *   *(1967)*
Start 12m right of Slanting Gully where a short gangway leads left into a corner above its undercut base. Follow the gangway into the corner and go directly up this on a narrow dyke to a stance on the left (25m 5a). Continue directly up the dyke to a stance on an easy traverse line about 10m below the lower overhangs.

Go up to the right to a stance on a wide sloping ledge (12m 4b). Move up left onto the wall, and then traverse a horizontal gangway with difficulty to an old peg. Make a tricky move across an overhanging dyke (5c, crux) to a sloping ledge on the left. Continue up the steep but easier corner directly above, stepping across left at the top to a stance and peg belay (4c). Finish by Shining Cleft.

22 Quark   210m   E3 ** (1976)

The second great route of the trilogy, which takes a direct and fierce line in an excellent position between Thor and Megaton. Start 25m right of Thor.

1. 45m 5b Climb a slab to below a steep wall, possible belay at 15m, and climb grooves on the left past large poised blocks to a vertical basalt dyke. Move left and follow a shallow fault to the upper slab, then go up left to a good ledge.

2. 45m 5c Go diagonally right to a steep groove (often wet), climb 7m to a standing place and then traverse right with difficulty, crux, to a small stance and possible belay. It is probably better to continue. Climb a hanging black groove to move right to a belay.

3. 45m 4c Continue up the groove, then move left to easier ledges. Follow the ramp back right to a belay. This pitch is unpleasantly loose with small stones on the ledges.

4. and 5. 75m Continue more easily to the top, taking the line of choice.

23 Megaton   250m   E1 (1972)

This has had no recorded ascent since the crux ramp collapsed leaving unstable and blank areas of rock. There have been two known attempts, one of which freed the lower section (6a), but both parties still retreated from the remains of the ramp. It is recorded for posterity and as a challenge. Start centrally, below the widest part of the overhangs, 75m above and right of Thor.

1. 35m Climb the lower slab to belay below overhangs.

2. 40m 5a Traverse right to a basalt breach in the overhanging wall, then climb to a large ledge; escape possible.

3. 25m 5a Gain the upper slab, then traverse horizontally to its lip, small stance and peg belay.

4. 25m 5b Using combined tactics, gain and climb the left-slanting ramp, peg runner, to a small stance and peg belay.

5. 35m 5a Climb up for 12m, then traverse left to easier slabs.

6. and 7. 90m 4b Continue more easily, finishing close to Shining Cleft on the rounded rib.

The cliff now becomes slabby once more and the rock improves. A major fault taken by Archer Thomson's Route lies 80m right of the overhangs passed by the Thor trilogy, mid-way between Slanting Gully and Deep Gash Gully. The next four routes all start easily by this line.

24 Vixen Groove   200m   Severe * (1968)

Take the obvious easy fault of Archer Thomson's Route for 45m to a broad shelf. Follow an obvious groove to the left in four pitches to Foxes' Rake with an awkward chimney-cave at about 100m.

25 Archer Thomson's Route   225m   Severe * (1911)

This route takes the prominent groove line more or less directly. The climbing is easy as far as a shelf 45m up. A steep 25m chimney is ascended by the left wall, which is continuously Severe to a good anchorage. 10m of easy rock lead to a platform. Pass a shelf, some difficult slabs and a 2m wall then an easy section of 13m to a shallow cave. Turn this on the left rib with good holds. An easy stretch (13m) leads to a wide gully climbed on the right for 10m before a traverse to the right under an overhang then more slabs and finally an easy scramble to the top by Foxes Rake.

26 Mantrap   200m   Hard Severe   *(1958)*
This climb lies up a fault-line about 15m right of Archer Thomson's Route after the initial easy pitch. Climb easy rocks right of the fault, which is at first wide and broken; belay on a broad ledge. Continue up right of the fault to a stance. Now the fault steepens and becomes harder. Climb up left over slabby undercut rocks to a bottleneck in the fault. Traverse awkwardly right, then climb steepening rock and pass a final bulge at the narrowest section of the fault, crux, usually wet. Easier climbing leads to a very wet, steep and loose overhanging exit; turn this on the left. Easier pitches lead to Foxes' Rake.

27 Pye and Mallory's Route   225m   Very Difficult ✱✱   *(1918)*
A fine and historic route with yet more intriguing route finding. The start is artificial but traditional, the alternative being to start up Dyke Gully. Start up Archer Thomson's Route for just 10m then make an easy 45m right traverse, parallel to the scree, until close to Dyke Gully. Keep left of the dyke for 60m, trending away from it. Move left to a shallow chimney and climb it, finishing by the left wall. After 45m the climbing becomes easier. An interesting finish is to traverse right and climb a shallow chimney which leads to Foxes' Rake.

A tier of rock now begins to separate the scree slope from the base of the main cliff. Continue beneath this until below another prominent fault. Climb a short groove in this lowest tier to reach the following routes.

28 Dyke Gully and Buttress Route   180m   Severe ✱✱   *(1956)*
The first half of this climb follows the slanting dyke gully 40m left of Deep Gash Gully, while the top half takes the buttress to its right where the situation is superb.
The first 30m is easily scrambled until the gully becomes more defined. The initial small overlap is guarded by two loose blocks. Above is easier scrambling for 50m. The final 15m pitch of the dyke is clean and steep with small positive holds. Above the gully is easy and broken leading to Foxes' Rake. The second half of the route gives 90m more good climbing. From the top of the last dyke pitch traverse up and right across the right wall of the gully to a massive flake belay beneath a vertical wall (15m). Turn the vertical rocks on the left by an awkward sloping shelf, then make straight up the buttress on interesting rocks to finish. Further scrambling, first left to avoid a prominent tower, then right above it, leads across the top of Deep Gash Gully to the final rocks of the Thuilm Ridge.

To the right of the dyke gully the crag rears up into a fine looking rib.

29 Thunder Rib   240m   E1 5a   *(1960)*
A fine name for a climb with a fierce reputation, which takes the rib left of Deep Gash Gully. Start at the centre of the rib and climb it to a stance. A few metres above gain a traverse line left and follow it, descending slightly, to the lip of some overhangs. Continue traversing hard left, crux, around the corner until it is possible to resume upwards progress. Go up, then right, passing right of three old pegs, and then continue diagonally up through bulges to the edge of Deep Gash Gully. Finish up the crest of the gully. There are several variations, all harder.

30 Deep Gash Gully   240m   HVS ✱✱   *(1949)*
This is the prominent, usually wet gully on the right of the north-west face. It is the Cuillin version of Glen Coe's Raven's Gully. The route descriptions of summer and winter ascents may be best used in combination although neither will remove the need for strength and determination. Sections of easier terrain lie between the pitches described.
1. 20m 4c Back up to the topmost of a series of chockstones which form the roof of a large cave. The exit is contorted and leads to a belay.

2. 20m 5a Continue up the narrow gully, across another interesting roof. Easier rocks lead to the top of the chimney.

Two easier pitches now follow, the second of which involves a left traverse and a 12m overhanging chimney which leads to a cave. Climb out of the cave by descending for 2m, then go up awkward loose rocks on the right wall until a strenuous chimney (arm pulls and knee jams) leads to a belay (4c). Three easier pitches now lead thankfully to the top.

Winter: **VI,7 *** *(1991)*

A formidable and atmospheric winter climb.

1. 30m Climb a short step, then easy snow to a large roofed cave.

2. 15m Back and foot to huge chockstones in the roof, then go out and under the lip of the overhangs to an awkward exit. Belay in the recess immediately above.

3. 40m Climb a short step and easy snow to a hollow on the right wall.

4. 40m Go up left into the extremely steep upper gully. Bridge up past an ice pillar, then climb iced grooves to a hidden cave recess below the final overhangs.

5. 30m Climb 3m on the right wall, then make very committing moves to bridge the gully and enter a narrow chimney. Surmount the final capstone direct and climb steep snow to belay at the next chockstone recess.

6. and 7. 90m Bridge past the chockstone, then climb the snow gully to a short exit pitch.

31 Whispering Wall   160m   Severe *   *(1960)*

This route stays close in above Deep Gash Gully after the initial pitch. Start 50m right of the start of Deep Gash Gully. A more direct start up the basalt wall immediately right of the gully is both loose and devoid of protection.

1. 30m An obvious horizontal ledge runs to a nose 45m above the start of Deep Gash Gully. Make a difficult rising traverse to this nose from the right.

2. 30m A fault just right of the nose leads to a leftward traverse protected by an in-situ Bulldog left on the first winter ascent. Continue up a vertical dyke to a spacious but poorly protected ledge.

3. 30m Follow the dyke around to the left for 10m then climb a good gabbro slab rightwards to belay on orange blocks below the final steep chimney.

4. 20m Fight up the blocked chimney which suffered a large rockfall in the summer of 2008. It may be safer to avoid this pitch by a rightward traverse as taken by the winter line.

5. 50m Easier ground leads to the crest of the Thuilm Ridge of Sgùrr a' Mhadaidh.

Winter: **155m   VI *** *(1999)*

Takes the lower two-thirds of the summer line before trending right to finish.

1. 30m Start in the dyke line and climb up trending left to below a large block.

2. 35m Pass the block on the left and move up to gain the left-hand end of a prominent snow shelf. Move along this for 7m, then climb the steep and poorly protected wall above trending left to the edge of the wall. Surmount a small overlap to the foot of a chimney.

3. 45m Climb the chimney to a snow ledge. Veer up leftwards to an exposed position overlooking Deep Gash Gully. Move left, then trend back right to the left-hand end of a snow ramp.

4. 45m Follow the ramp rightwards to gain the crest of the buttress.

The skyline between Coire a' Mhadaidh and Coire a' Ghreadaidh is a steep narrow ridge. It can be approached by traversing Sgùrr Thuilm or, more rapidly, by ascending to the Thuilm – Mhadaidh col from the corries on either side.

32 Thuilm (West) Ridge of Sgùrr a' Mhadaidh   200m   Grade 3 ***

This ridge rises impressively from the col. Weave a way up staying as close as possible to the crest, 30mins. Awkward and very exposed in places some bypasses are possible on the right. The ridge levels off all too soon and a broad area on the crest marks the top of Foxes' Rake. The rest of the ascent is easy and soon leads to a minor top (900m) on the Main Ridge. Turn right and follow the narrow crest,

reaching the main summit after 120m. The ridge provides a reasonable descent after climbing in the corrie.
Winter: **III** **
The rocky nature of the ridge doesn't make it a natural choice for winter but still gives enjoyable climbing.

Nero Buttress

(NG 444 239)

This steep little buttress lies 200m to the west and level with the base of Deep Gash Gully, just 5mins below the Thuilm-Mhadaidh bealach.

3 Nero   80m   Very Difficult   *(1968)*
1. 40m Climb the prominent groove in the centre of the crag to a ledge. Continue up right to blocks and belays.
2. 40m Go up right over detached blocks, up a slabby groove and out right. Continue rightwards and then directly to the top.

25. SGÙRR THUILM - NORTH FACE

(NG 438 247)   Alt 390m   North facing   Map p28

The whole northern flank of this mighty outlying peak is peppered with discontinuous slabs and small buttresses. There is mention of a 1920s route but no description recorded. This flank dominates the view on entering Glen Brittle with routes approached directly in less than 1hr. Two gullies split the north face when viewed from the road.

Descent: The south-west ridge of Sgùrr Thuilm is used most commonly to approach the very good Thuilm Ridge of Mhadaidh. It is a tedious climb up scree fields to its scenic summit but gives a rapid descent.

These accessible parallel gullies fill regularly and run directly to the summit, split by a broad terrace at one-third height. The lower tier contains two or three icy options with the steep gully below Thuilm Right so far unclimbed. The routes described start above the broad terrace.

Thuilm Left   250m   II/III *   *(2006)*
Well to the left side of the broad terrace lies a wide deep rift. Easy snow leads to a deep cave (110m). A 15m icefall on the right wall was incomplete on the first ascent and an awkward escape was made onto the easier flanks. On the second ascent, six days later, the gully was virtually banked out. Continue with little difficulty to the top. The summit lies 50m to the east once the ridge is reached.

Thuilm Right   250m   II **   *(2005)*
A narrower gully lies toward the right end of the broad terrace.
The gully was climbed in thin snow conditions with little difficulty, in the confines of surprisingly large walls.

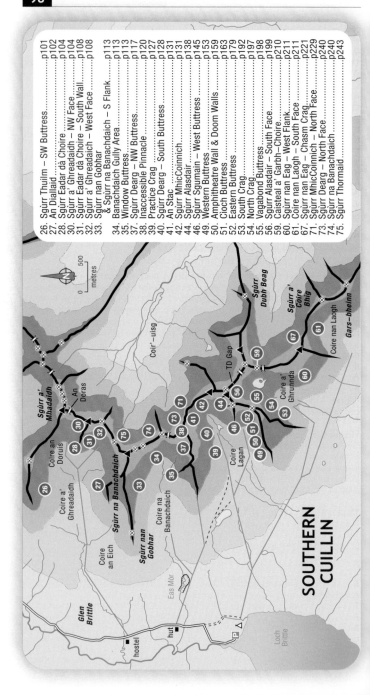

COIRE A' GHREADAIDH

Maps p28, 98   Diagram p100

Coire a' Ghreadaidh is a beautiful corrie enclosed by the bulky conical peak Sgùrr Thuilm to the north and the attractive ridge of Sgùrr nan Gobhar to the south. It is subdivided into two upper corries by the spur of Sgùrr Eadar da Choire. The corrie holds a surprising lack of continuous solid rock with only a handful of recommended rock climbs. Most other climbs are more suited to inclusion in mountaineering days.

The skyline traverse from Sgùrr a' Mhadaidh to Sgùrr na Banachdaich is one of the easier classic rounds with 1.5km of delightful scrambling over five different tops. The knife-edge crest on Sgùrr a' Ghreadaidh epitomises one major appeal of the Cuillin Ridge with continuous technically easy climbing in an exposed, precarious end, some might say, ludicrous position. Gail, Gauche, and Scimitar are the harder routes of quality in the corrie. In winter many of the faces can be studied from the road. In good conditions big face routes are possible on many lines with the slopes being neither too steep nor blocked by continuous bands of cliffs. White Wedding is the classic ice route but is a notorious tease that forms, but only thinly, quite often.

Recommended Approaches: A well made path follows the left bank of the Allt Coire a' Ghreadaidh from the Glen Brittle Youth Hostel (NG 430 234) before reaching the lower corrie floor. At one point the gorge drops for 20m through a 1m slot and gives a traditional climbing challenge in back and foot work above a deep pool. The path becomes broken once the slabby waterfalls are reached (45mins). Cross the river just below these falls and take a direct line north to reach the obvious South-West Buttress of Sgùrr Thuilm [26] in 1hr. Remain on the south bank of the river to reach all the other climbing crags. The path levels off in a delightful alpine meadow above the slabby waterfalls. Head south-east, straight up grass and heather, to reach the toe of the An Diallaid [27] in 1hr.

The upper corries are separated by the fine rocky western spur of Sgùrr Eadar dà Choire. Approaches from Coire An Doruis, which lies up to the north (left) are described first. Stay on the east side of the river to reach the level floor of Coire An Doruis. Easy scree leads up right to the toe of Sgùrr Eadar dà Choire [28] which has an obvious large cave just on the north side (1hr 30mins). A broad boulder field rises from the opposite side of the corrie to the west face of Sgùrr a' Mhadaidh [29] (1hr 45mins). The head of the river sinks in the top corner of Coire An Doruis. The path here, beneath the steep north wall of Sgùrr Eadar dà Choire, briefly becomes distinct once more before taking a direct line across boulders to the stone shoot below An Doras. The North-West Face of Sgùrr a' Ghreadaidh [30] lies immediately right of the stone shoot and comprises of two sections separated by the prominent sharp fault known as Eag Dubh. An Doras Buttress has a broad slabby base and a rightward traverse below it reaches the foot of Eag Dubh. The steep Summit Buttress lies 70m higher above a long broad ledge on the right (2hrs).

The South Branch of Coire a' Ghreadaidh lies to the right (south) of Sgùrr Eadar dà Choire. Take slabs on the north side of a deep chasm that guards the entrance to the upper corrie. The South Wall of Sgùrr Eadar dà Choire [31] lies above a tiny lochan, 100m up scree on the left. A shallow gully leads up left beyond the South Wall to where Sgùrr dà Eadar Choire abuts Sgùrr a' Ghreadaidh. Hidden Gully Buttress is about halfway up this with the west face of Sgùrr a' Ghreadaidh [32] stretching right across the corrie to the south (1hr 30mins).

Round of Coire a' Ghreadaidh   7hrs   Grade 3/Moderate ★★★★

A well trodden corrie round, similar in standard when tackled in either direction. The western peaks of Sgùrr na Gobhar and Sgùrr Thuilm are often bypassed using An Doras and Coire an Eich for approach and descent to give a shorter day. The Main Ridge from Sgùrr na Banachdaich to Sgùrr a' Mhadaidh (1.5km) is continuously challenging with the highlight traversing the narrow ridge along the top of Sgùrr' a' Ghreadaidh. Details in the Cuilin Ridge Traverse chapter, p292. The Thuilm Ridge of Sgùrr' a' Mhadaidh is the hardest section, particularly in descent.

COIRE A' GHREADAIDH

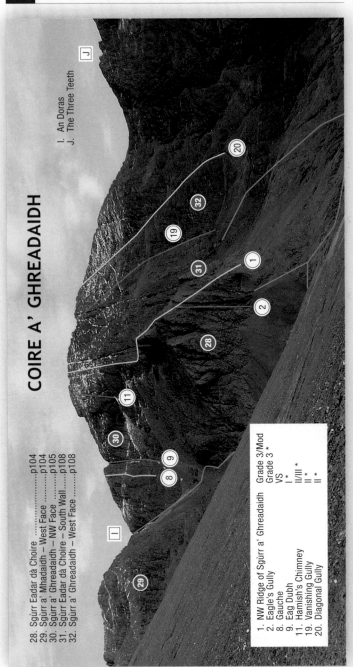

I. An Doras
J. The Three Teeth

1. NW Ridge of Sgùrr a' Ghreadaidh	Grade 3/Mod	
2. Eagle's Gully	Grade 3 *	
8. Gauche	VS	
9. Eag Dubh	I *	
11. Hamish's Chimney	II/III *	
19. Vanishing Gully	II *	
20. Diagonal Gully	II *	

26. SGÙRR THUILM - SOUTH-WEST BUTTRESS

(NG 430 238) Alt 390m   South facing   Map p98   Diagram p100

This is the first crag in the corrie and, being low, it often escapes the worst of the weather. It is fairly quick drying, has one very good route and others of interest. The rock is never above suspicion and much of the crag is for steady climbers only. The crag is split by a prominent central corner, taken by Gail, with a slab on the right.

Descent: Traverse west across broken ground until the slabby west end of the buttress has been skirted fully before descending. Continuing up to the summit of Sgùrr Thuilm is a very arduous slog.

1 Black Slab   60m   Grade 3 *   *(1992)*
The left end of the crag is composed of firm gabbro slabs. Near the left end is an undercut cave. Start just left of the cave and take a delightful line straight up the slabs.

2 Soft Options   60m   Hard Severe   *(1992)*
1. 30m 4c Climb the prow on the right of the cave (3m) then go straight up the easy slabs above.
2. 25m 4b Continue up the slabs rightwards to a bulge which is climbed direct to a stance and belay.
3. 5m 4b Climb the short headwall.

3 Fosdyke   60m   Hard Severe   *(1971)*
Start on the left side of the prominent vertical dyke in the centre of the cliff.
1. 25m Gain the crumbly dyke and climb it delicately to a small stance below roofs.
2. 5m 4b Traverse the slab on the left below the large roof, using undercuts, to a small stance.

COIRE A' GHREADAIDH

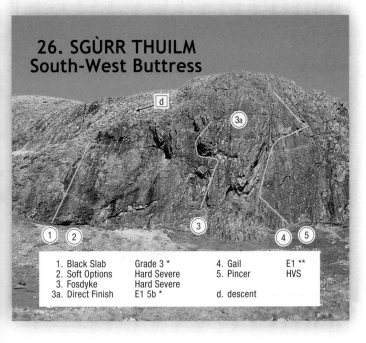

26. SGÙRR THUILM
South-West Buttress

1. Black Slab	Grade 3 *	4. Gail	E1 **
2. Soft Options	Hard Severe	5. Pincer	HVS
3. Fosdyke	Hard Severe		
3a. Direct Finish	E1 5b *	d. descent	

3. 30m Climb the slabby corner above until it becomes grassy, then move right and follow a steep groove to a scree terrace.
Variation: **Fosdyke Direct Finish   E1 *** *(2005)*
2. 30m 5b Tackle the roof directly to gain a groove. Ribs and slabs above are easier.

4 Gail   95m   E1 ** *(1965)*
This fine route takes the clean corner just right of centre. Most of the loose rock has been removed, and the climbing is well protected on the second and third pitches.
1. 25m 4a Climb the rib right of the mossy groove, then trend left to a big spike.
2. 20m 5b Climb the corner direct to a small ledge above the crux steepening.
3. 15m 5a Climb to the band of overhangs, then traverse right on underclings to a ledge.
4. 35m 4b Rather than climb the easy groove above, step boldly left onto a ramp and go around the edge onto a slab. Climb this to easy ground.

5 Pincer   65m   HVS *(1965)*
This is the vertical dyke just right of the Gail slab. It gives a sustained, interesting and worrying pitch which is much more solid than it looks, requiring a patient approach. Protection is adequate.
1. 25m 4c/5a Climb the right-curving dyke past a broken ledge and continue to a heathery nook.
2. 15m Climb easily up the dyke to the stance on Gail.
5. 25m Finish up the groove.

To the right of Pincer is a much easier line graded at Severe.

27. AN DIALLAID

(NG 433 230)   Alt 500m   North facing   Map p98

This impressive peak lies on the right of the approach path and remains much viewed but little climbed. The rock on the lower slabs is firm gabbro but the steeper buttress near North-East Gully has much basalt.

Descent: Many of the routes finish well below the loose upper reaches of An Diallaid. Head north down easy ground to return to the foot of the buttress. The easiest descent from the summit is down the screes of Coire an Eich immediately to the south.
Routes are described from left to right.

1 Footrot   120m   Difficult *(1970)*
The easy-angled slabs above the path are composed of immaculate gabbro, devoid of cracks or protection. Other lines can be taken straight up – but this route climbs the slab from left to right, taking the line of least resistance.

The next climbs lie further up, near North-East Gully, which splits the slabby buttress.

2 Diamond Buttress   240m   Very Difficult *(1965)*
This is the long rambling buttress left of North-East Gully. Start 30m left of the gully and follow the edge of a slab. After 30m, keep to a definite ridge and make for a large slab higher up. In the middle section there is a steep undercut wall. Turn this on the left and scramble up to the slab. Start the slab at an obvious corner, move into a groove on the left and follow a series of corners to the top. Apart from the top corners, the rock is excellent.

3 Nearer My God to Thee   155m   VS *(1980)*
Start immediately left of and below the start of North-East Gullys' first pitch, where a flake leans against a big slab which forms the gully's left wall. There is very little protection, but the first and last pitches are interesting.
1. 35m 4b Climb the flake and crack to the top, go up the wall above and step

27. AN DIALLAID

North-West Spur of Thormaid
Grade 3/Mod

1. Footrot — Difficult
2. Diamond Buttress — Very Difficult
3. Nearer My God To Thee — VS
4. North-East Gully — III*
5. Verucca — Very Difficult
5a. Direct Start — Severe
6. Branching Gully — Difficult

COIRE A' GHREADAIDH

right to a narrow ledge. Now climb the wall left of a mossy crack to a narrow ledge. Continue straight up the wall above on better holds to a spike belay.

2. and 3. 80m Follow the edge of the slabs to a ledge below a steep undercut wall.

4. 40m 4a To the right is a large poised flake with a crack on the right. Climb the crack to the top of the flake, then continue up an easier corner to the top.

4 North-East Gully   150m   Severe *(1929)*
This is the deep narrow gully, which appears as a deep chimney when viewed from below. There are about seven pitches, of which the first is the crux.
Winter: **III** * *(1978)*
A fine line which usually presents two good pitches in full conditions.

5 Verruca   120m   Very Difficult *(1970)*
This route starts right of North-East Gully. Climb the rib by the line of least resistance; belays are hard to find.
Variation: **Direct Start   60m   Severe** *(1970)*
Start almost at the entrance to North-East Gully at the edge of a steep wall.
1. 40m Climb the unprotected wall to a peg belay.
2. 20m Continue directly to the ridge.

6 Branching Gully   120m   Difficult *(1908)*
This is the prominent gully that lies up right of North-East Gully and faces north-west across Glen Brittle. It is easily seen from the path into the main corrie. There are several interesting pitches.

28. SGÙRR EADAR DÀ CHOIRE

(NG 440 234)   Alt 630m   West facing   Maps p28, p98   Diagram p100

This peak forms the true North-West Ridge of Sgùrr a' Ghreadaidh. The South Wall [31] of the peak is described later in this chapter

1 North-West Ridge of Sgùrr a' Ghreadaidh   400m   Grade 3/Moderate * *(1898)*
Taken directly there is some rotten rock at the start; Eagle's Gully is far superior. The most notable difficulty is an exposed slab traversing the final rocks before the top of Sgùrr Eadar dà Choire. A short dip beyond is followed by some good climbing until the ridge broadens in the upper reaches. The crest of the Main Ridge is usually reached 80m north of the summit, 1hr 30mins.
Winter: **II ** ** *(1976)*
Follow the left flank of Eagle's Gully to its termination. Traverse up and left to a small ridge below a short steep slab. Climb the slab to the crest of the ridge, then follow the ridge to its junction with the West Face of Sgùrr a' Ghreadaidh. Climb the face by a steep 60m gully on the left (north) side of the true ridge. Snow slopes above lead easily to the summit crest.

2 Eagle's Gully   150m   Grade 3 * *(1910)*
A series of parallel faults split the centre of the north face of Sgùrr Eadar dà Choire. This takes the left most gully. Other gullies are looser and the broad rib is good but broken. Start 40m down left of a prominent cave in the foot of the face. The gully has no great difficulties and is like climbing an enormous staircase. Continue by climbing the North-West Ridge which is somewhat harder.

29. SGÙRR A' MHADAIDH - WEST FACE

(NG 444 236)   Alt 800m   West facing   Diagram p100

A broad area of tiered rocks stretches from below the Thuilm-Mhadaidh Bealach across to An Doras. A buttress directly below the bealach gives a good scramble in dry conditions. Follow thin slabs fairly continuously left of the central gully in the lower half. Broken rocks right of the gully then lead to the bealach. This may be the location of **Aegis** (Difficult 1958).

Rise rightwards past this buttress to the foot of the west face. Diagonal faults cut back left giving the quickest access to the classic Thuilm-Mhadaidh Ridge and climbs in the Deep Gash Gully area of the North Face of Sgùrr a' Mhadaidh [24]. This face warrants mention largely because of winter lines that regularly form further right, giving over 200m of good quality climbing direct to the summit. Often thin looking from a distance, lines vary in degrees of continuity but give surprisingly rewarding climbing, (grade II/III).

30. SGÙRR A' GHREADAIDH - NORTH-WEST FACE

(NG 445 234)   Alt 750m   North-West facing   Maps p28, 98   Diagrams p100, 106

This is the large mass of rock immediately below the skyline between An Doras and the summit. It is a good cliff, split into two distinct sections by the notch of Eag Dubh. The buttress to the left of Eag Dubh, An Doras Buttress, is larger, firmer and friendlier than the long crag to the right, Summit Buttress.

An Doras Buttress

Descent: Head north along the crest of the Main Ridge to An Doras.
Climbs are described from left to right.

3 Ice Trap   120m   III ** * (2009)

A prominent icefall forms frequently in the steepest section of the Trapist dyke. Start at a recessed gully 15m up left of Trapist.
1. 50m Two steep steps lead to a snowfield. Belay on blocks right of the icefall.
2. 50m Climb ice for 20m to reach blocks then head right across snow to a recessed corner.
3. 20m The corner is well protected and leads to the crest above.

4 Trapist   85m   VS (1976)

This pleasant route follows the pronounced dyke on the left side of the buttress.
1. 45m 4a Climb the dyke on the left side of the buttress.
2. 40m 4c Climb easily to a steepening, then climb the wall left of the dyke to reach a diagonal ramp leading to the top.

5 Simplicity   170m   Severe * (1976)

Many parties have had problems following this route and finding the promised juggy wall in the top pitch. It is probable that pitch 4 heads right to reach steeper rocks. Start below the smooth looking slabs towards the left of the face.
1. 40m Follow a dyke up the slabs, then move right to belay under a large overhang; an excellent pitch.
2. 35m Climb the overhang on the right, then continue easily to a grass ledge.
3. 40m Climb the wall above.
4. 30m Scramble to the base of the final wall.
5. 25m Climb the rough juggy wall to the top; a good pitch.

6 Baptist   140m   Severe (2006)

Start at the centre of the slabs at a vertical trap dyke crossed by a diagonal trap dyke at 2m.
1. 20m Climb diagonally leftward along an obvious line, scant protection, to belay below an overhang.
2. 30m Move right round the overhang and easily up slabs and short walls heading for the ragged notch above. Belay on the grassy terrace above.
3. 45m 4a Initially follow the trap line over the bulge, then move left towards the skyline, then back right to climb a steep cracked wall to a hanging slab. Belay below a triangular overlap.
4. 45m 4a Move left round triangular overlap, then climb easily in the groove line, surmounting a steep little wall by a prominent crack on the way to the top.

106

30. SGÙRR A' GHREADAIDH - North-West Face

1. Sgùrr a' Ghreadaidh
   NW Ridge   Grade 3/Mod *
1a. Winter chimney variation   II **

I. An Doras

Sgùrr a' Mhadaidh
West Face

3. Ice Trap	III *
4. The Trapist	VS
5. Simplicity	Severe *
6. Baptist	Severe
7. An Doras Buttress	Very Difficult
8. Gauche	VS *
9. Eag Dubh	I **
10. Scimitar	VS **
11. Hamish's Chimney	II/III *
12. Virgin Arete	VS

7 An Doras Buttress   130m   Very Difficult   (1955)
Start at the lowest rocks right of Simplicity and follow a central route throughout, with much moderate scrambling on excellent rock. There is considerable scope for variation.
Winter: **130m   III**   (2000)
The simplest line was followed turning small bulges by some thin slab climbing to finish 50m from An Doras.

8 Gauche   150m   VS *   (1976)
A good line. Follow a prominent corner in the right side of the buttress.
1. 40m 4a   Climb the crack direct to a stance.
2. 35m 4b   Climb to the overhang and turn this on the left wall.
3. 40m   Scramble to below the final wall.
4. 35m 4b   The exposed arete between the chimney and grooves leads to the top.

Traverse right beneath the face to reach the open start to Eag Dubh.

9 Eag Dubh   100m   Grade 2
An unpleasant route by a series of small steps linked by loose scree. Open for the first 70m the gully enters a deep slot. Towards the top take an almost solid rib of basalt on the left side.
Winter: **100m   I ****
Highly recommended approach to the top of Ghreadaidh in preference to the awkward step out of An Doras.

Summit Buttress

To the right of Eag Dubh the imposing Summit Buttress of Sgùrr a' Ghreadaidh lies directly below The Wart, a prominent jutting nose of rock on the skyline. The unclimbed northern section shows clear signs of glaciation with steep bleached rock offering little encouragement.

Descent: The quickest return to the bottom of the climbs takes a broad broken rib from the southern (top) end of the Wart at a small level dip in the Ridge. The rake running below Summit Buttress is easily reached 100m below, immediately above a steep basalt chimney. Descending Eag Dubh is damp and loose but easier to locate.

The smooth northern wall is bounded on the right by a shallow right-angled corner giving the first route.

10 Scimitar   90m   VS **   (1968)
Start 60m south of Eag Dubh below first right-angle corner.
1. 30m 4c   Climb shallow grooves to the large overhang. Traverse 10m left, crux, then up and left on spaced holds to the start of the crack. Take care with rope drag. Good belay.
2. 30m 4c   Sustained climbing takes the crack directly with a steep finish to a broken ledge (poor spike belay).
3. 30m 4a   The left wall of the continuation groove gives the best line to the crest of the Ridge.

11 Hamish's Chimney   90m   Difficult   (1965)
This is the obvious deep chimney on the right-hand side of the crag. It provides interesting climbing but is very short of protection.
1. 30m   Climb the chimney with confidence to a spike and thread belay.
2. 30m   The chimney narrows after 10m and requires some squirming. An escape is then possible across loose ground to the left where a blunt rib is possibly preferable but definitely cheating! The chimney contains two more chockstones that are turned on the left. Follow the scree gully then escape to a solid bulge on the left.

COIRE A' GHREADAIDH

3. 30m Easy scrambling directly leads to the path as it bypasses the Wart, the summit is 140m to the south.

Winter: **II/III** *   *(1999)*

Follow the summer line enjoying a lot less loose rock.

12 Virgin Arete 75m VS   *(1965)*
This route lies up the buttress immediately right of Hamish's Chimney. The first pitch is good, but the climb is easier and looser above.
1. 20m 4c Climb a groove and a strenuous overhang on the edge overlooking the chimney.
2. 45m 4a Continue in the same line to the terrace.
3. 10m Scramble up easy rocks to the ridge.

COIRE A' GHREADAIDH - SOUTH BRANCH

A secluded corrie enclosed by large faces of discontinuous rock.

31. SGÙRR EADAR DÀ CHOIRE - SOUTH WALL

(NG 441 233)   Alt 650m   South facing   Map p98   Diagram p100

There are two recorded lines on this big wall. In the centre of the face lies a prominent corner at three-quarters height.

Descent: An open gully behind the buttress leads back down right to the gully running beneath Hidden Gully Buttress.

13 Ceo 110m Very Difficult   *(1965)*
This climb lies up the highest part of the buttress, following a left-slanting groove.
1. 25m Climb the groove to a ledge.
2. 30m Continue up the groove, which becomes indefinite, then go up a short wall to a ledge.
3. 45m Enter the undercut groove above from the right and continue to a ledge.
4. 10m Move right along the ledge and go up a final wall.

14 Gael Force 135m HVS *   *(1977)*
This climb takes the corner in the centre of the face, starting directly from below at a groove.
1. 45m Climb the groove and the steep wall above to the terrace.
2. 45m 4b Continue steeply to a detached flake, then trend right to the foot of the main corner and a peg belay.
3. 25m 5a Traverse under the corner, then climb directly up the crux crack to finish over a steep wall to a terrace.
4. 20m 4b Finish by a steep wall on good but loose holds.

32. SGÙRR A' GHREADAIDH - WEST FACE

(NG 443 232)   Alt 700m   West facing   Maps p28, p98   Diagrams p100, 109

About 100m above the lochan to the east lies the extensive west face. There is no simple route to or from the ridge but, despite the huge expanse of rock, the climbing has proved broken and limited. By contrast it is a good venue for long winter adventures.

Descent: Traverse the Main Ridge north for 300m to An Doras as described in the Cuillin Ridge Traverses chapter. Routes are described from left to right.

The first route takes an open shallow gully bounding the left end of the face that leads to the dip east of Sgùrr Eadar dà Choire.

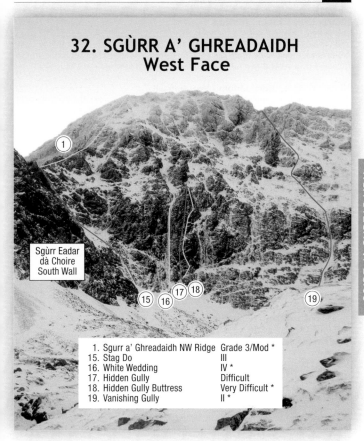

32. SGÙRR A' GHREADAIDH
West Face

Sgùrr Eadar
dà Choire
South Wall

1. Sgurr a' Ghreadaidh NW Ridge	Grade 3/Mod *
15. Stag Do	III
16. White Wedding	IV *
17. Hidden Gully	Difficult
18. Hidden Gully Buttress	Very Difficult *
19. Vanishing Gully	II *

15 Stag Do   100m   III   *(2004)*

Easy mixed ground leads to icy slabs. Climb these to reach an 8m ice pitch. Above this a snow runnel leads to the Sgùrr Eadar dà Choire ridge.

16 Overhanging Gully   135m   Very Difficult   *(1947)*

Climb the first two pitches of Hidden Gully as far as the chockstone below the black chimney. Traverse 5m left, and then climb a basalt dyke for a further 25m to a belay. Continue 30m up the dyke, using the left-hand gabbro wall. Climb the gully to an overhanging wall and cave turning this on the right to reach a scoop. Climb the scoop to a large ledge and finish up a gabbro ridge via a gendarme.

Winter: **White Wedding   IV ***   *(1986)*

This route is the prominent straight icefall at the left side of the corrie. The second pitch has a steep start and is often thin even when the top ice bulge appears well formed.

1. 25m Two ice steps lead up left to a ledge on the right at the start of the steep section.
2. 45m Excellent ice climbing leads to a ledge on the left.
3. 30m The ice ahead is steeper but shorter and leads to easier ground.

Take snow slopes to the crest of the Ridge between the two tops 150m above.

17 Hidden Gully   120m   Difficult   *(1908)*
This gully is, surprise, surprise, hidden on approach. It cuts obliquely into the crags and faces Sgùrr Eadar dà Choire. Start immediately right of the Overhanging Gully fault. A traditional style route the chief features are a large cave, a black chimney followed by a second cave and then scrambling to finish.

18 Hidden Gully Buttress   140m   Very Difficult *   *(1952)*
A good route but quite short for such a long approach. It takes the buttress right of Hidden Gully gaining in quality with height. Start in the gully. Steep but Moderate climbing leads to a small rock amphitheatre on the right-hand side of the buttress. Traverse horizontally left along a fault to a niche near the crest. Continue up the right retaining wall of the buttress above the niche, climbing a steep and exposed groove running diagonally right across a seemingly impregnable wall. Now climb a light coloured wall on excellent holds to the finish of Hidden Gully.

19 Vanishing Gully   120m   Difficult   *(1910)*
This gully starts 70m to the right and contains several interesting pitches. It fades into the face above at two-thirds height. Easy slopes above lead to the col between the two tops of Sgùrr a' Ghreadaidh.
Winter: **120m   II ***
Good ice pitches lead to easier snow slopes.

20 Diagonal Gully   275m   Moderate
This is the long slanting gully immediately below the col between Sgùrr a' Ghreadaidh and Sgùrr Thormaid. It leads diagonally up to the ridge and contains one pitch near the bottom which can be turned on the north side.
Winter: **275m   II ***   *(1967)*
Apart from a minor pitch near the bottom, snow leads to the top.

The face continues southward beneath the Three Teeth and Sgùrr Thormaid. It is bound by a broad spur that starts low in the corrie and rises to the summit of Thormaid (927m) giving one mountaineering route.

21 North-West Spur of Thormaid   250m   Grade 3/Moderate   *(1936)*
The lower black section gave 130m of good moderate gabbro on the line of a prominent crack which goes up the centre. The spur becomes better defined higher up finishing to the north-east of the Bealach Thormaid.
Winter: **250m   I/II**   *(1993)*
Follow the summer line throughout.

SGÙRR NA GOBHAR

(NG 427 224)

This peak forms the western spur of Sgùrr na Banachdaich. An obvious forked gully lies directly above the youth hostel giving a sheltered approach with some good Grade 2 scrambling but is loose in places. The ridge crest is very fine in dry weather but is unpleasantly greasy in the wet (500m Grade 2). In winter the gully banks out and can give a fine direct approach to Sgùrr na Banachdaich at grade I.

COIRE NA BANACHDAICH
& INACCESSIBLE PINNACLE

Maps p28, 98   Diagram p112

This is the smallest of the major corries and also the most accessible with well constructed paths. A direct descent from the Ridge is barred by a broad slabby headwall split by Banachdaich Gully. The West Ridge of Sgùrr Dearg gives the most direct approach to the Inaccessible Pinnacle but bypasses some very fine climbing on the corrie buttresses.

Window Buttress was once a popular venue because it is the best cliff for an introduction to rock climbing in the Cuillin. It is currently a quiet place to climb on some good quality gabbro. Combining routes in the corrie with a finale on the Inaccessible Pinnacle gives a classic day out with lots of climbing in a short distance. The Inaccessible Pinnacle is a contender for the most popular objective in the Cuillin. It is a remarkable blade that is far larger than most climbers envisage. The climbs on it are all high quality in the low or middle grades and, in fine weather, make the Pinnacle a worthwhile venue in its own right.

A round of this corrie avoiding the Inaccessible Pinnacle gives one of the easier Cuillin circuits with stunning views into both Coire Lagan and the Coruisk basin. Very few winter routes have been developed so far but the corrie aspect has good potential.

Recommended Approaches: Car parking is very limited for this popular footpath. Please park considerately. The nearest alternative is at a sharp right bend in the road just 200m beyond the farm buildings.

The path starts opposite the Memorial Hut through gorse bushes by the fine stone walled sheep fank. After 200m it crosses the Allt Coire na Banachdaich by a wooden bridge and 5mins of walking leads to a great viewpoint of Eas Mòr (big waterfall). It is a dramatic 40m waterfall hidden from the road in a deep ravine with one ascent recorded exiting via the right-hand branch of the right-hand gully. Above the waterfall the footpath splits. The right fork leads to Coire Lagan but is more commonly used as the most direct approach to the Inaccessible Pinnacle.

Take the left fork for all cliffs in the corrie which has a long level floor. Routes on South Flanks of Sgùrr nan Gobhar and Sgùrr na Banachdaich [33] are reached in less than an hour by direct approaches from the corrie floor.

The path remains obvious until it reaches the lowest slabs of the Window Buttress in about 1hr. A beautiful pool sits beside the path at the far side of these slabs. This is at the confluence of two equal sized tributaries. Leave the path and follow the left tributary directly for routes in the Banachdaich Gully [34] area (1hr 15mins). Window Buttress [35] is gained from the same pool by climbing up slabs then scree directly to a terrace below the first steep rocks (1hr 15mins).

Beyond the pool the southern branch of the stream enters a narrow gorge. The main footpath to Bealach Coire na Banachdaich lies above this, rising over broken slabs and scree in a south-easterly direction. Cross the stream immediately above the gorge to reach the slabby Inbetween Buttress [36] in 1hr 30mins. Ascend an open gully running parallel to the watercourse on the north side to reach a broad boulder field. North-West Buttress [37] lies 100m to the south (1hr 45mins). For Bealach Coire na Banachdaich traverse horizontally northward for 200m. The walls above run out at an easy boulder field which leads directly to the narrow (5m) bealach (2hrs). The Inaccessible Pinnacle [38] is easily reached from here in less than 30mins.

The more direct approach to the Inaccessible Pinnacle [38] climbs the West Ridge of Sgùrr Dearg (2hrs). Above Eas Mòr take the right fork for 300m. Here the path splits again. The left turn leads directly to the lowest reaches of the West Ridge which is described below.

COIRE NA BANACHDAICH

Round of Coire na Banachdaich   6hrs   Grade 2 ***

The easiest of the classic rounds is done anti-clockwise for the best scrambling and

COIRE NA BANACHDAICH & INACCESSIBLE PINNACLE

The Neck

Sgùrr Dearg Beag

Inaccessible Pinnacle

simplest descent. The round is far harder and will take an extra hour if the Inaccessible Pinnacle (Moderate) is climbed. The upper section of the West Ridge of Sgùrr Dearg is complex and awkward to follow in mist and can easily lead to harder terrain. The middle top of Sgùrr na Banachdaich has the narrowest section and can be bypassed easily some 50m down on the Glen Brittle side. Descent from Sgùrr na Banachdaich is easiest by Coire an Eich. Descend steep screes from Sgùrr nan Gobhar if the full round is completed.

33. SGÙRR NAN GOBHAR & SGÙRR NA BANACHDAICH - SOUTH FLANK

(NG 430 222)   Alt 400m   South facing   Map p98

A very broad area containing some readily forming winter lines.

Goat's Gully   210m   Difficult   *(1950)*
This rather esoteric climb follows the black gash splitting the south flank of Sgùrr nan Gobhar over all sorts of obstacles.
Winter: **180m   II/III**   *(1993)*
Climb the gully in four pitches. Turn the first small icefall on the right.

Ice forms easily in the shallow watercourses that rise diagonally towards the summit of Sgùrr na Banachdaich from the corrie floor. Short steep pitches can be found low down in hard winters but generally the lines are about grade I in standard.

34. BANACHDAICH GULLY AREA

(NG 440 219)   Alt 675m   West facing   Maps p98, 124   Diagram p112
The corrie headwall is composed of rough solid gabbro and is steep in its lower reaches. A number of lines are possible on either side of the deep cleft of Banachdaich Gully.

1 North Rib   120m   Difficult   *(1906)*
The north walls of Banachdaich Gully give much drier climbing than the gully on clean rock. Start just inside the mouth of the gully.

2 Banachdaich Gully   120m   Very Difficult   *(1898)*
This gully lies centrally within the band of slabs below the bealach. It contains four pitches, the last being the best. Some pitches are best turned on either wall if the gully is too wet.
Winter: **III** *   *(1979)*
The gully is far better under winter conditions, with several ice pitches.

3 South Slabs   120m   Grade 3/Moderate   *(1907)*
The slabs to the right of the gully give amusing scrambling that can be varied at will, providing a more interesting way to the bealach than the normal approach. Not advisable as a descent.

In a good winter **The White Line** (500m I 2010) is a superb line of easy ice and snow running parallel and 50m right of the Banachdaich Gully water course in three obvious sections to reach the Ridge.

35. WINDOW BUTTRESS

(NG 437 217)   Alt 570m   North Facing   Maps p98, 124   Diagrams p112, 115

This crag gives an ideal introduction to the skills of multi pitch climbing in the Cuillin and lies only an hour from the road. The face has been climbed extensively on Lower Window Buttress, all in the lower grades. Leaders will often be required to make their own choice of line, safe in the knowledge that the buttress is escapable in many places. Upper Window Buttress has longer pitches of good climbing but still has many easy options. Identical names for buttresses, routes and variations has been a source of confusion so some renaming has been used:

Window Buttress is now split into Lower and Upper Window Buttresses linked at the Neck. Window Buttress Original Route is common to all other variations on the lower tier. Upper Window Buttress Route actually starts from a wide rake 35m up and left of the Neck.

Descent: Lower Buttress routes finish at the Neck. Descending from here to the east or west sides give a quick easy return to the foot of the cliff. Upper Buttress routes finish high on the West Ridge of Sgùrr Dearg which is classically used to continue to the Inaccessible Pinnacle. Routes are described from right to left.

West Face

A long narrow gully lies 200m up and west of the lowest rocks, leads to the shoulder of Upper Window Buttress and is obvious on the approach walk. The gully has been climbed in winter under deep snow at grade II **Deep-Cut Gully** (1994). Not to be mistaken for the lower wide gully (descent) that leads to the Neck of Window Buttress.

4 Burglar's Entrance   160m   Severe   (1952)
This climb follows the right wall of Deep-Cut Gully.
1. 50m Scramble up the edge of the gully.
2. 30m The wall steepens and an ascending traverse brings one out into a minor gully, up to the right.
3. 30m Climb over the large boss of rock to a short face and up the central wall to belay.
4. 35m Scramble to a cairn, and up steep slabs to double perched blocks and large pinnacle belay.
5. 10m Walk up to a steep overhanging nose. The route goes from the right using a small hold on the face on to the overhanging slab, up and over the nose to belay.
6. 15m Climb over the slabs and the top section of Upper Window Buttress.

5 Deep-Cut Gully Buttress   160m   Difficult   (1907)
Climb the left buttress. "The buttress afforded a most enjoyable climb of considerable difficulty".

6 Evening Wall 80m Very Difficult   (1937)
Climb the rib on the left side of the western descent gully. Finish immediately above the Window.

Lower Window Buttress

7 Window Buttress Original Route   110m   Very Difficult *   (1906)
This route has large numbers of variations at the start all in the lower grades. The most popular are described below. They all converge below the Window which gives an entertaining test piece. A large cairn defines the start of the normal route which takes a steep crack just right of centre.
1. 20m Climb the crack immediately behind the cairn. A steep move at 5m gives a well protected crux before gaining a more enclosed groove. Good climbing leads to a block belay.
2. 20m A steep corner above leads to short walls that can be turned by choice of cracks.
3. 25m The Window is an arrow-slot gap in the nose of the buttress some 30m above. Take easy angled slabs and small corners to a bay below and left of the Window.

35. WINDOW BUTTRESS

The Window

The Neck

d

7. Window Buttress — Very Difficult ***
7a. Variation — Severe *
7b. Variation — Very Difficult ***
7c. Melpomene — Difficult
8. Bishops Climb — Difficult
8a. Variation — Difficult
9. Durham Slabs — Severe
10. Widow's Eye — Severe **

11. Upper Window Buttress Route — Severe *
12. Playgrope — III *

d. Eastern descent

4. 10m The corner below the Window is steep and difficult to start. Either squeeze through the Window or finish up the corner. This difficulty can be bypassed on the right (west) side of the Window.

5. 25m Scramble easily to base of final pinnacle.

6. 10m Make a steep initial move to gain the pinnacle.

Variation A: **Severe   40m**

An open corner lies 8m left of the cairn and bounds the nose on the left. The rock is good above the initial moves. A series of steep steps lead to a choice of belays in the corner as the angle eases (20m). Break right from the corner system to open slabs and walls close to the original route.

Variation B: **Very Difficult   40m**

The buttress 5m right of the cairn is climbed by cracks and ledges to a block belay and grass ledge (20m). The wall above can be turned by any of the three well-worn cracks and corners. Rejoin the original route in the slabby open ground below the window.

Variation C: **Melpomene   Difficult   40m**   *(1958)*

Starts by the steep corner 5m right again.

Winter: **IV,5**   *(2007)*

The full length of the buttress gave a long and sustained route.

Upper Window Buttress

Linking the top pinnacle to Upper Window Buttress is the Neck. An easy descent to the east or west sides give a quick easy return to the foot of the cliff. The easiest continuation is by a good Grade 3 scramble (150m, 30mins) going first right and then back left before reaching the West Ridge of Sgùrr Dearg. The next three climbs all start down left from the Neck.

8 Bishop's Climb   80m   Difficult   *(1914)*

Descend the gully behind Window Buttress east for 20m on easy rock to gain a slanting shelf via some steep but straightforward rocks, all highly polished. The first pitch is a 5m gully or cave with wedge shaped chockstone at top. Move right onto the buttress and climb 15m to a block (belay) and for a further 15m in same line to the wide rake. A ribbed rock ledge then slopes upwards to the right for 25m and a vertical chimney or corner of 20m finishes the climb.

Variation: A much cleaner start at the same grade climbs the fine open rocks a few metres left of the chimney.

9 Durham Slabs   35m   Severe   *(1962)*

Start from the same shelf as Bishop's Climb some 10m down to the left.

Climb diagonally up an orange block and slab on the right to belay on a platform (20m). Climb straight up to a triangular flake, move right round this and continue to finish on a wide rake.

10 Widow's Eye   50m   Severe ✱✱   *(1970)*

A very good climb that takes a prominent clean curving corner. Start 100m down east from the Neck. Climb the corner for 12m over three shelves on the left to a belay. Climb the corner direct avoiding a small overhang by delicate climbing on the right wall. Continue to a block belay at the top where care is needed to avoid sending loose rocks down the climb. A further 10m of scrambling leads to a wide rake.

One route starts from the wide rake tackling the steep walls above. Otherwise 70m of steep scrambling leads up and right to the top of the buttress.

11 Upper Window Buttress Route   130m   Severe ✱   *(1957)*

Follow the wide rake above the finish of the previous routes leftwards for 60m to the end of the ledge.

1. 30m Trend left up a steep wall, some loose rock, to a crack.

2. 10m Traverse easily right.
3. 30m Climb the prominent crack.
4. 30m Continue up the crack, turning a chimney delicately on the left, then climb a steep wall using an undercut crack on the left.
5. 30m Finish up a steep broken wall on the right.

2 Playgrope 230m III,4 * (2008)
This route follows the east side of the entire buttress beneath the steep walls. Take icy slabs and grooves for 90m. A narrow gully is followed for 30m. Take the rib on the left in small pitches to the ridge above. Continuing by the gully would be an option in better conditions. A good mountaineering outing.

36. INBETWEEN BUTTRESS

(NG 439 216) Alt 680m North-West Facing Map p124 Diagram p112

This buttress is easily reached across the screes after completing one of routes on Lower Window Buttress. It leads to the foot of the North-West Buttress and a route on each buttress is a highly recommended combination for approaching Sgùrr Dearg.

3 Val 90m Very Difficult (1980)
This good route follows the right-hand arete of the crag directly.

37. SGÙRR DEARG - NORTH-WEST BUTTRESS

(NG 441 215) Alt 825m North-West Facing Maps p98, 124 Diagrams p112, 118

A clean cliff of good rock where every route has been awarded at least one star for quality. All climbs lie on the right half of the buttress where the most obvious feature is a clean slabby corner climbed by Aesculapius.

Descent: Traverse above the face in an easterly direction, rising slightly for 100m to pick up a diagonal rake. Carefully descend this to the scree and boulders above the springs. Routes are described from left to right.

4 Toolie Grooves 90m VS ** (1953)
Start below an obvious deep chimney that has opened out to form a groove at the base.
1. 25m 4b Climb the groove, which has a hard start. Exit via an obvious gangway on the left to a niche.
2. 40m 4c The corner above the niche leads to a rightward slanting ramp and a small platform below the final overhang. Move right to where the crux mantelshelf leads to the base of a steep little slab. Climb the slab, then a notch in the ensuing overhang to a ledge.
3. 25m 4c Move to the right end of the ledge and climb a short crack to broken ground above.
Variation: **Direct Finish 20m VS 4c **** (2005)
Climb the crack immediately above the notch. Steep but on good holds and well protected.

Some 10m right of Toolie Grooves a loose gangway slopes up right. The next routes start from a ledge 20m up the gangway.

5 Black Chimney 90m Very Difficult * (1909)
This deep cleft is hidden from the spring approach but obvious from further west (right). Climb the basalt staircase to the chimney. Back and foot up this. Near the top, escape on the left wall to a large terrace. Alternatively follow a sloping ledge on the right to the same terrace. Finish by a short vertical chimney in the back wall or other escapes further left.

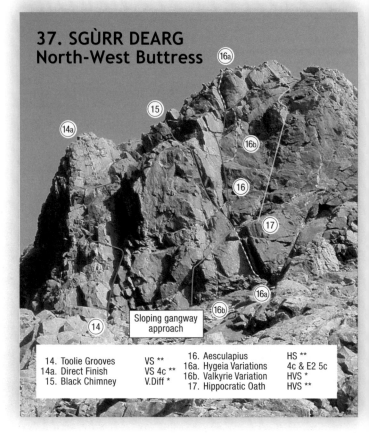

37. SGÙRR DEARG
North-West Buttress

14. Toolie Grooves	VS **	16. Aesculapius	HS **
14a. Direct Finish	VS 4c **	16a. Hygeia Variations	4c & E2 5c
15. Black Chimney	V.Diff *	16b. Valkyrie Variation	HVS *
		17. Hippocratic Oath	HVS **

Sloping gangway approach

**16 Aesculapius   70m   Hard Severe ** **   (1958)

A good climb on solid rock which reputedly can be climbed in the wet. Start on the same sloping gangway as Black Chimney at a scree ledge.

1. 35m Go right up the basalt staircase then climb the corner right of Black Chimney to a small triangular ledge.

3. 20m 4b Climb a crack in the steep wall on the left to a shelf under an overhang, then move back across the top of the wall to a ledge. This is artificial but gives the best climbing. Continuing directly up the main corner is easier and more logical. Climb a narrow chimney above either inside or outside the chockstone to a ledge.

4. 15m Traverse right up a rising ledge then continue right to easy ground.

Variation: **The Hygeia Variations   VS 4c and E2 ***   (1958)

The direct start climbs the steep corner with a prominent right wall of yellow basalt 10m right of the gangway. The direct finish takes the final overhang, originally climbed with aid.

Variation: **Valkyrie   HVS ***   (1959)

Some 5m left of Hygeia Variation start in a cracked corner, climb it strenuously to the loose gangway. Cross this and continue up the corner then right to the foot of Black Chimney. Follow Aesculapius to the small triangular ledge. Climb the overhanging crack to an outward sloping mantelshelf. Continue up steep cracks and a chimney to finish up the last pitch of Aesculapius.

7 Hippocratic Oath   70m   HVS   * (2005)
A fine direct line on the wall above the gangway, well to the right of the Aesculapius corner, gives steep climbing on perfect rock.
1. 40m 5a Climb up easily to steeper compact rock. Continue boldly up the steep open face to a hanging corner crack high up. Pull through to a ledge on the left.
2. 30m 5a Step right and climb a vertical 3m wall. Squirm behind a huge block to mantel on to a sloping shelf below a final corner-crack, climbed to the top.

This next route lies well above and left of the main buttress in the corner formed by a change in aspect of the cliffs from north-west to west facing.

8 Kibby's Route   140m   * (2006)
The climb is worthwhile for the 2nd pitch which is clearly seen as height is gained on the approach. The first low gully is not seen until below it.
1. 50m Go up easy snow gully to a belay at rocks on the left.
2. 50m Climb the fine corner for 25m and exit onto snow slope.
3. 40m Continue up close to rocks to a cul-de-sac. Pull over a chockstone or pass by a very tight through route. Steep moves on the right arete lead back into the snow gully, which soon finishes on the ridge.

Left again a broad way ice runs above the scree slopes for 200m before an easy approach is possible to Bealach Coire na Banachdaich. A fan of scree exits from a huge gully at the right end of this face. **Grey Rib** (60m Severe 2002) is a loose climb on the left edge overlooking this gully.

SGÙRR DEARG

(NG 444 216)   Map p124

Sgùrr Dearg is a broad bulk of a hill that catches more than its fair share of cloud especially in north westerly winds. When clear the rocks dry quickly and many a party can be seen rapidly ascending the West Ridge to make use of the conditions (2hrs). Approach from Coire Lagan is longer, harder and more difficult to navigate in mist.

Descents: The West Ridge is the easiest route to follow but in poor visibility care is needed to find the right line as far as Sgùrr Dearg Beag. Descending east below the Inaccessible Pinnacle is only possible on the Coire Lagan (south) side. Start by descending 30m of smooth slabs to reach a large open scree slope. Descend this for just 40m then move back left to take the continuation slabs close below An Stac. An Stac Direct is as serious as the Pinnacle itself and is not recommended in descent.
Heading north to Bealach Coire na Banachdaich is comparatively simple but route finding on descent in the corrie below is awkward especially in the mist. Descend Coire na Banachdaich for 100m and then bear horizontally south for 200m to the springs below the North-West Buttress. Descend an open gully north of the watercourse.

West Ridge of Sgùrr Dearg   Grade 2   **
Take the footpath easily to the lowest rocks of the ridge. Ascend steep loose scree slopes to reach the western-most top on the ridge. The path is well defined above here until the ridge steepens and the direct line is interrupted by broken buttresses. These are turned most easily on the right (south) before reaching the cairned top of Sgùrr Dearg Beag (90mins). A short descent from here leads to a prominent band of red peridotite in a minor col. Beyond here the ridge narrows significantly but can be bypassed by a continuous ledge system on the right (south). The ridge turns abruptly northward just 150m from the summit of Sgùrr Dearg (2 hours). This crucial turn is particularly difficult to identify on descent in poor visibility.

38. INACCESSIBLE PINNACLE

(NG 444 216)   **Alt 970m**   **Maps p98, 124**   **Diagrams p112, 121**

This remarkable blade of rock projects on the south-east side of the summit of Sgùrr Dearg, overtopping the latter by some 8m. It has been a popular outing for over 100 years and is unlikely to become any less so. It is the only place in Skye where tempers regularly become frayed as climbers and non-climbers mix unhappily, fuelled by justifiable adrenalin as they attempt to safely ascend and descend a fundamentally dangerous lump of rock.

Etiquette on the East Ridge is to give priority to parties on a Traverse attempt but is only happily given to those that either solo up or use very fast, minimal rope work. Climbing over or past other parties is a risky business, roped or not and a very polite and patient approach should be taken.

Climbing one of the many quality routes other than the East Ridge will rarely involve queuing. Otherwise climbers should consider going elsewhere during bank holidays and mid to late morning on most good days.

Descent: A fixed metal anchor is usually in place around the base of the Bolster Stone (the highest boulder). Queuing for this is the cause of most hold-ups and frustration on busy days. Alternative abseil anchors are possible from the summit. Arrange with waiting parties to throw any slings down once you have completed the descent. Another way to speed up the process is to allow others to use abseil ropes already in place. Down-climbing the East Ridge is not a good option even when the route is clear of other parties.

South Face

Approach: The slab below the Pinnacle is treacherous and covered in loose debris. Great care should be taken not to knock rocks onto parties approaching from the Coire Lagan direction. The easiest line currently lies 30m out from the face then traversing perched scree and rocks at the lowest edge of the slab.

1 East Ridge   65m   Moderate ****   *(1880)*
This is the classic route of the Pinnacle with wild exposure for such a technically easy route. The whaleback shape makes protecting inexperienced party members difficult and should not be underestimated. The route can be climbed safely in the wet by competent parties using short quick pitches but strong winds make for a hairy ascent. Start up a broken chimney on the south face to reach a ramp that runs parallel with the crest of the ridge. The crux lies shortly after the route gains the crest and is well protected by a slung spike. Climb to a ledge on the Coruisk side of the crest with spike belays (30 m). Continue more easily, passing a jammed boulder 5m before the ridge finally widens enough to relax. Good block belays overlook a ledge that leads easily round to the abseil point.
Winter: **III/IV ****
A different proposition under snow. Often the dry south face gives the only positive hand purchase whilst the ledges are disguised.

2 South Crack   30m   Hard Very Difficult ****   *(1906)*
This classic climb is recommended when there are queues on the East Ridge. It takes the prominent crack running up the centre of the face via a short detour onto the left edge at 10m. Belay just below the crest.

3 Hadrian's Wall   30m   VS   *(1962)*
A hybrid variation of Routes I and II.
Start 5m left of South Crack at a ledge 2m off the ground.
1. 20m 4c   Traverse left to a diagonal crack, then climb straight up the face on small holds to a platform.
2. 10m   Step off the right end of the platform, then climb the face, finishing over a slight overhang.

38. INACCESSIBLE PINNACLE

1. East Ridge — Moderate ****
2. South Crack — Hard Very Difficult ****
3. Hadrian's Wall — VS 4c
4. Route II — VS 4b *
5. Route I — VS 4b **
6. Varicose — VS 4c
7. Closer to the Edge — VS 4c *

ab. abseil

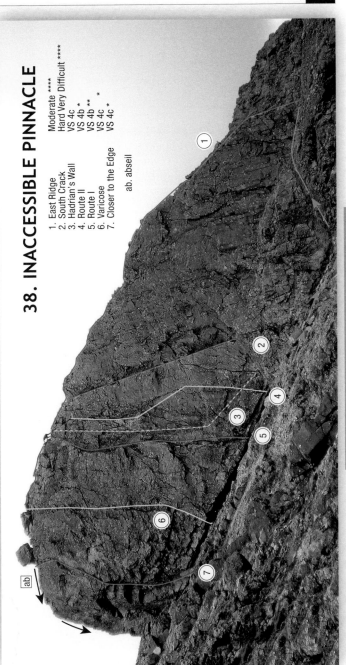

South Crack, Hard Very Difficult, Inaccessible Pinnacle. Climbers unknown

4 Route II   30m   VS 4b *   *(1921)*
The right-hand line of weakness. Climb straight up the wall to a small ledge, continue to a second ledge, then step right into a corner and finish up the face.

5 Route I   30m   VS 4b **   *(1921)*
This route takes the left-hand of two lines of weakness which run up the face left of the prominent South Crack. Climb the wall direct to join Route II at a ledge below the summit ridge.

6 Varicose   30m   VS 4c *   *(1964)*
This good and exposed climb lies up the left side of the face and has a hard start. Start below the right end of the band of overhangs at 6m. Haul onto the undercut face with difficulty then climb to the overhangs. Surmount this on good holds and continue to a ledge with a perched block. Climb the wall above directly to the summit.

7 Closer to the Edge   25m   VS 4c *   *(1980)*
Start at the extreme left end of the face. Climb a left-slanting groove capped by two roofs, pull right under the second, then climb a groove directly to the summit block.

8 West Ridge Route   20m   Severe **   *(1886)*
Quite a hard classic climb lacking in protection and positive holds. There are two alternative lines after the initial steep moves. Ledges lead easily left to a blank shelved corner with a bold move back up right to gain the large flake. Better protected is to stay close to the west face, pulling round to the horizontal crack at the base of the large flake. A very public place to get the jitters!

North Face

9 North-West Corner   20m   Difficult   *(1895)*
This route collapsed following a lightning strike in the winter of 2006/07.

10 The Naked Saltire   30m   E2 5c ***   *(1999)*
The straightest climb in the Cuillin takes a while to dry but is well worth waiting for. Start 25m down the scree slope on the dark side of the Pinnacle.
The perfect overhanging crack-line splitting the north wall is the same fault as South Crack. Athletic moves off the ground (crux) are protectable and lead to a pod. Bridge up the crack, sustained and well protected to the crest.

BANACHDAICH & INACCESSIBLE PINNACLE

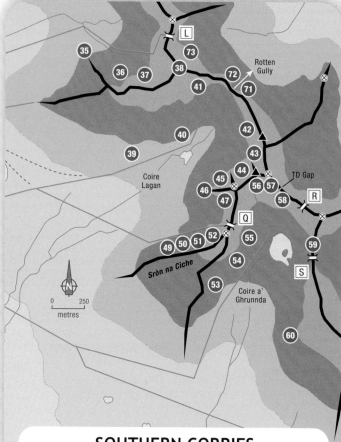

Rotten Gully

Coire Lagan

TD Gap

Sròn na Cìche

Coire a' Ghrunnda

0 250 metres

SOUTHERN CORRIES

COIRE LAGAN

Maps p98, p124   Diagrams p126, 135, 150

For rock climbers, Coire Lagan is the most significant corrie in the Cuillin by a wide margin. Huge expanses of high quality rock have been widely explored by top climbers for over a century. It can almost be considered as two separate areas with the Coire Lagan Face of Sròn na Ciche forming one enormous wall to the south and most other crags and faces overlooking the loch in the upper corrie. Sròn na Ciche accounts for at least half of the routes but there are many high quality climbs on the other buttresses that are often overlooked.

Sròn na Ciche is best in the evening light but the sheer scale makes an earlier start important for most. The face is home to some of the longest mountaineering routes in the country climbed either singly or by linking climbs on each tier to suit the day. Western Buttress will appeal to the alpinist with more than a dozen pitches on most routes. The iconic Cioch is a magnet for most visitors but is best avoided at busy times when queuing is commonplace. Eastern Buttress has a concentrated selection of comparatively short hard routes on impeccable rock and is well worth the extra few minutes of approach.

Upper Coire Lagan provides a wide choice with mostly sunnier aspects than Sron na Ciche. In particular the North and West Buttresses on Sgumain and South Buttress on Dearg have a selection of lower and middle grade routes on sound rock. The corrie round is very highly recommended with a succession of classic routes linked by continuously high quality ridges.

This end of the Cuillin receives less snow than the north but a good winter can turn the north faces of Alasdair and Sgumain into alpine style classics. Thinner conditions produce many good mixed climbs, particularly high on Sgùrr Theàrlaich.

Recommended Approaches: Park at the beach car park and start behind the campsite toilet block. Cross the Ruadh Dunan track after 100m then continue easily up the popular footpath. The first fork at 1km (NG 420 203) is where the Coire a' Ghrunnda path heads southward to skirt the broad flank of Sròn na Ciche. The next fork at 2km is less obvious (NG 433 207). It leads horizontally across lower Coire Lagan to the foot of the great walls of Sròn na Ciche.

The main path continues to Upper Coire Lagan. Pass by the prominent Matterhorn Boulder and then a large cairn marking the junction with the Memorial Hut footpath until the footpath starts to rise. Here the West Ridge of Sgùrr Dearg presents a slabby south face at the base of which lies Practice Crag (39) reached in less than an hour from the beach. Continue to the glaciated lip of the upper corrie which holds the beautiful Loch Coire Lagan, encircled by huge cliffs and a jagged skyline (1hr 15mins).

South Buttress [40] lies up to the left and is normally approached directly by screes from the loch (1hr 30mins). Two stone shoots lie opposite each other dropping impressively to the corrie floor. The Great Stone Shoot lies to the east and is unmistakable unless the mist is down. The foot of the An Stac Screes is reached by a good trail traversing the west side of the corrie. The ascent is made regularly because it gives the simplest access to Sgùrr MhicCoinnich and a popular approach to the Inaccessible Pinnacle. The least arduous route up takes a continuous line of boulders directly to the small waterfall up and right of South Buttress. This is the recommended approach to the next crags.

From the small waterfall traverse right, staying close beneath the band of cliffs, until an easy break is reached. This is the An Stac [41] bypass route that leads up to Sgùrr Dearg. Continue rising diagonally right for a short distance to reach Bealach Coire Lagan (2hrs). Top Buttress and Summit Buttress on the West Face of Sgùrr MhicCoinnich [42] are more easily approached from here than from below. The long West Buttress routes start between the An Stac Screes and the Great Stone Shoot and are approached directly from the loch (1hr 30mins).

The Coire Lagan faces of Sgùrr Theàrlaich [43] and Sgùrr Alasdair [44] start halfway up the Great Stone Shoot. The best approach starts up large boulders on the right of this to reach the first rocks of Sgumain's North Ridge before being forced into the shoot.

COIRE LAGAN

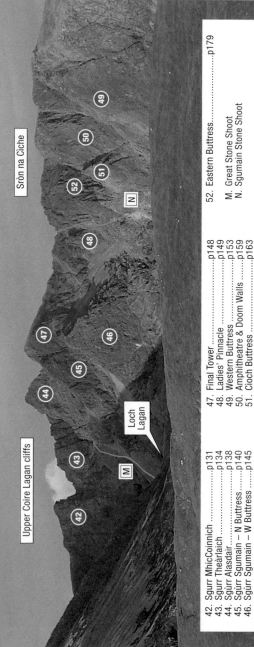

Upper Coire Lagan cliffs

Sròn na Ciche

Loch Lagan

The North Buttress of Sgumain [45] is approached from the loch by a broad scree slope to reach the left end of North-West Ramp (1hr 30mins). This ramp runs beneath the face giving access to all routes before joining the West Ridge of Sgùrr Sgumain below the top tier of the Final Tower [47].

Approach the West Buttress of Sgùrr Sgumain [46] from the loch over boiler plates of glaciated gabbro. Gain a prominent horizontal break by an awkward move (Moderate). A prominent white blaze above the break gives the best point of reference for most routes (1hr 30mins). This break can be used to approach the lower tier of the Final Tower [47] and Ladies' Pinnacle [48] but a more direct approach is by the Sgumain Stone Shoot beneath the walls of Sròn na Cìche (1hr 45mins).

The Round of Coire Lagan   10hrs   Grade 3/Very Difficult ★★★★
This corrie round packs in more classic climbs than any other in the Cuillin. Many harder variations, particularly on Sròn na Cìche, are possible but must be climbed speedily in order to complete the round. Individual climbs are described below and sections of the Ridge described in the Traverse chapter. The classic round starts with (and is timed for) Collie's Route onto the Cioch, continues by Eastern Gully, tackles The Bad Step (crux) onto Alasdair, climbs King's Chimney then crescendos with An Stac Direct and the East Ridge of the Inaccessible Pinnacle for the sunset.

SGÙRR DEARG

(NG 444 216)

39. PRACTICE CRAG

(NG 442 208)   Alt 450m   South Facing   Maps p98, 124

Approach: Continue past the Matterhorn Boulder for 300m. The crag lies on the left, a minute or two above the path. It is split into two distinct sections.

Practice Slab

The western section is a slabby crag of sound gabbro some 50m long and about 25m high. It has been exhaustively climbed in the lower grades and serves its purpose well. **Central Crack Direct** (VS 4c) is the only recorded route. Low and high-level traverses are popular. Descent is easiest on the left.

Practice Buttress

To the immediate right of the short slabs lies a much more impressive buttress split by a narrow gully. Continuing above the climb to Sgùrr Dearg is very loose and not recommended.

Descent: This is not obvious. Traverse east to gain an easy-angled gully. Descend it by a series of corners and ledges.

Western Drainpipe Direct 150m Severe   *(1952)*
The narrow gully. Climb past the initial overhangs by parallel cracks on the right, which later merge into a smooth groove. "Socks may be required."

Western Drainpipe Ridge 120m Hard Severe 4b ★★   *(1952)*
A good climb for a short day.
1. 10m Climb the ridge easily to a spacious ledge.
2. 40m 4b Follow the crack that splits the right side of the ridge. Climb past a large perched flake to the steepening. A fierce move leads to a delicate section up the groove above. The next steep overlap gives a well protected crux leading to a small recessed belay.
3. 20m Easier ground leads back left to a ledge overlooking the Drainpipe once more.
4. 50m Follow the broad rib in an excellent position to where the angle eases.

COIRE LAGAN

Western Drainpipe Ridge, Hard Severe 4b, Practice Buttress, Sgùrr Dearg.
Climber John Kingdom

Breakfast Wall

A recessed bay lies 60m up and right of the last route. The next routes follow cracks in the steep back wall.

Heinz Beans 15m VS 4c * *(2010)*
Reach then climb the obvious curving flake in the centre of the wall.

Sausage Sandwich 15m E2 5b * *(2010)*
Climb the steep straight crack in the right edge of the wall.

A winter route has been recorded on the southern flank of Sgùrr Dearg probably somewhere above the Practice Crag. It is described as the central chimney on the west shoulder of Sgùrr Dearg exiting via mixed ground on the right (IV, 1995).

40. SGÙRR DEARG - SOUTH BUTTRESS

(NG 444 213)   Alt 650m   South-East facing   Maps p98, 124

This impressive buttress of sound gabbro lies low in upper Coire Lagan and catches a lot of early sunshine. The main pitches are concentrated in the lower half. Above here lines merge and meander to reach the top. The continuation ridge to Sgùrr Dearg is disappointingly loose.

Approach: Atop the screes is a small band of rock. Climb it direct or turn it more easily on the right to the foot of the cliff.

Descent: Take broken ground and screes keeping well left (south) of the buttress edge. Routes are described from left to right.

These routes start up the gully on the left edge of the buttress avoiding the Great Cave at its foot by slabs on the left.

1 Mistaken Crack   50m   Hard Severe   *(1955)*
There are two obvious chimney-lines high in the left-hand corner of the West Face. This route takes the right-hand one.
1. 20m Ascend the chimney to an overhanging block and pass this on the left wall.
2. 20m Climb the wall close to and left of the crack, pass a chockstone and belay on a stance above.
3. 10m Pass another chockstone to reach a small cave, then climb its left wall.
Variation: **Oedipus   Severe and A2**   *(1958)*
A partly aided variation to the third pitch takes the overhang on the right.

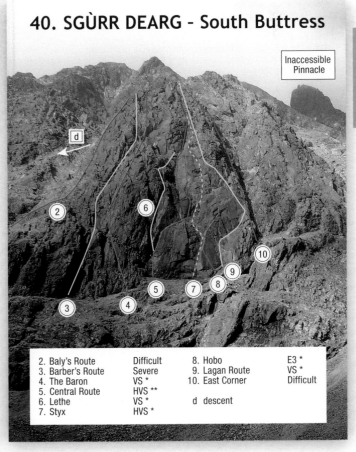

40. SGÙRR DEARG - South Buttress

Inaccessible Pinnacle

COIRE LAGAN

2. Baly's Route	Difficult	8. Hobo	E3 *
3. Barber's Route	Severe	9. Lagan Route	VS *
4. The Baron	VS *	10. East Corner	Difficult
5. Central Route	HVS **		
6. Lethe	VS *	d descent	
7. Styx	HVS *		

2 Baly's Route   150m   Difficult   *(1909)*
Ascend the gully on the left edge of the buttress for 45m and then climb the buttress on the right.

Main (South-East) Face

The following routes start from a central grassy bay, the Terrace, which can be reached by a variety of scrambling lines.

3 Barber's Route   110m   Severe   *(1937)*
Start at the lowest point of the buttress below a sentry box.
1. 20m Climb to the sentry box, then go up the chimney to a sloping ledge on the right. Awkwardly gain a groove and continue to a small stance.
2. 20m Ascend the left wall to a flake and cross this to the right wall of the groove. Climb up to a large platform on the right.
3. 20m Follow the groove to belays.
4. 50m Follow a line of choice to the top of the buttress.

4 The Baron   120m   VS *   *(1966)*
Start 6m right from the lowest point of the buttress.
1. 20m Up a shallow gully to a good stance and belay.
2. 20m Move left and up the obvious groove to a good stance and belay immediately above.
3. 40m Move right a short distance then ascend to beneath a small overhang. Swing right and mantelshelf, traverse right to a line of trap. Up this for about 6m then go left onto the rib.
4. 40m Up this to a large stance and belay. Continue up broken rocks above or traverse easily off left.

5 Central Route   120m   HVS **   *(1950)*
Start at the foot of the impressive steep central fault.
1. 20m 5a Climb the corner for 5m then go up a steep slab on the right to where it forms a corner.
2. 45m 4b Zigzag up slabs and climb a chimney and a groove to a broken recess, which is followed by a corner and an overhanging chimney.
3. 25m Climb the prominent chimney above, which rises to the right.
4. 30m Easier rocks lead to the arete connecting the buttress to the main mass of the mountain.

6 Lethe   105m   VS *   *(1965)*
1. 35m 4c Follow Central Route for 10m, then step left into the prominent right branch of the Y-shaped crack on the left wall. Climb on an overhang with a peg belay.
2. 35m Move right to a crack, then climb it to the top of a corner.
3. 35m Finish up the chimney of Central Route.

7 Styx   120m   HVS 5b *   *(1957/1979)*
Start 15m right of Central Route at a moss patch where a hidden stream runs behind the rock. The first and last pitches are good.
1. 15m 5b Climb the strenuous V-crack to a small ledge.
2. 20m Climb the crack to a platform on the left, then continue up the corner-groove to the foot of a chimney.
3. 30m The original line takes the chimney. However, it is better to go up right and climb a corner followed by slabs to a steepening and belays below a chimney.
4. 25m Climb the chimney to a grass ledge.
5. 30m 4c Climb directly to an overhung alcove, traverse right to the edge, then go up and back left to ledge. Above, 60m of scrambling leads to the rather shattered arete, which rises to the summit.

8 Hobo   65m   E3 *   *(2003)*
This route climbs the obvious slabby arete right of Styx.

1. 25m 5c Start at a small basalt dyke 3m right of an undercut rib and follow it over a ledge to a resting point at 8m. Make thin moves left to the arete and follow it to its apex.

2. 35m 5a Step off the pinnacle and make a thin traverse rightwards to gain a niched crack, then direct up slabs to a large ledge. Finish by either Styx or Lagan Route.

9 Lagan Route   90m   VS 4b *   *(1947)*

A red wall in a raised alcove lies 20m right of Styx. On its left wall is a dyke and a crack. Follow the crack, then step across the dyke once above the huge flake which leads to a belay (20m). Continue up an easy crack on the left. Move left, then climb slabs above (left of an inverted flake) to a grassy recess. Climb the groove above to a ledge, then bear right to climb steep slabs. From the top of the easy crack it is possible to climb straight up the slabs (VS 4c).

0 East Corner   150m   Difficult   *(1912)*

This climb takes the right edge of the buttress overlooking the bounding gully.

200m beyond South Buttress the screes dropping from the Inaccessible Pinnacle terminate in a minor waterfall. This was climbed in two pitches to give **In Pinn Fall** (IV, 1997).

41. AN STAC

(NG 445 215)   Alt 825m   South facing   Maps p98, 124   Diagram p133

This impressive peak supports the Inaccessible Pinnacle and prevents it from slipping down the slabs to Coire Lagan. It is often bypassed via an orange coloured rake that slants around the south side starting some 100m below Bealach Coire Lagan at the top of the screes. This leads directly to the summit of Sgùrr Dearg via the base of the Inaccessible Pinnacle.

1 An Stac Chimney   70m   Moderate   *(1908)*

Ascend the bypass rake until directly below the impressive south face of An Stac. Screes lead back up right to the prominent chimney that is best seen from Sgùrr MhicCoinnich. The trap dyke is narrow in places and chockstones are passed both inside and outside. Join An Stac Direct to finish.

2 An Stac Direct   250m   Grade 3 *   *(1898)*

The fine steep skyline gives the most continuous upward climbing along the whole length of the Ridge, 30mins. The reputation for loose rock is unjustified but care must still be exercised. Start by a sloping ramp that lies 10m left (south) of the crest at Bealach Coire Lagan. Easy ground then rises to a prominent U shaped notch in the skyline. A chimney, again just left of the crest, leads up to another scree filled notch. The ridge above narrows and steepens. Traverse left to gain the crest which is followed directly on good holds for 80m. An Stac Chimney joins from the left and is followed until it levels out. Traverse left across the face and climb easy corners to the summit. Continuing right beneath the overhung wall at the top of the chimney bypasses the summit by a few metres but gives a fitting finale with the sudden appearance of the Inaccessible beyond. A descent is not recommended.

Bealach Coire Lagan is a broad hump between An Stac and Sgùrr MhicCoinnich. The lowest point is the top of Rotten Gully which is the commonest approach to the superb north facing cliffs of Sgùrr MhicCoinnich [71, 72]. These are described in the Coruisk chapter.

42. SGÙRR MHICCOINNICH

(NG 450 211)   948m   Maps p98, p124   Diagrams p126, 133

Sgùrr MhicCoinnich has a broad open face between the An Stac Screes and the

Great Stone Shoot that only steepens near the top. Top Buttress is short but composed of good clean gabbro with a very sunny aspect lying just below the crest immediately west of Collie's Ledge. Collie's Ledge and King's Chimney are the two routes used to traverse the peak and lie high on the Summit Buttress overlooking Bealach MhicCoinnich. Long routes on West Buttress start low in the corrie on the right side of the face.

Top Buttress - West Face

(NG 449 213)   Alt 825m   South facing

This is an obvious clean wall just below the North Ridge of Sgùrr MhicCoinnich. The routes were all first climbed in a single day which makes a good project after all the effort of reaching the crag. There are three right-slanting corners starting from a narrow ledge – the east-most can be easily descended once located.

Approach: From Bealach Coire Lagan ascend the North Ridge. At just one point the crest becomes unusually broad and simple for 40m, shortly before Collie's Ledge. The cliff top lies 30m directly below and can be reached by a simple scramble where a good abseil is easily set up.

Approaching from below, starting by Jeffrey's Dyke followed by a rambling leftward traverse, is also possible. Routes are described from right to left.

1 Vanishing Beads   50m   VS 4b *   (1994)
Start immediately above a grassy bay at the right end of the crag Take a short, bulging, wide crack and the slab above to reach twin cracks. Follow these to a large ledge and climb the cracked buttress above.

2 Raven's Rib   30m   E1 5b *   (1994)
Start at the left side of the rib. Move up right and climb it to the large ledge.

3 Descent Corner   30m   Moderate   (1994)
The right-hand of the three most prominent corners.

4 Mud Wrestler   30m   Very Difficult *   (1994)
Climb the corner left of the descent, above the chockstone.

5 Huffy Messiah   30m   Severe *   (1994)
The next corner to the left. Avoid the large overhang by stepping left and climbing the corner-crack.

6 Up the Down Stoneshoot   30m   Severe *   (1994)
Start below the jutting overhang and climb the right-hand corner-crack leftwards past hollow flakes. Trend left and climb flake-cracks to the top.

7 Starless Bay   40m   VS 4c   (1994)
Climb the bay by a series of corners.

8 Flap Cracker   60m   HVS 5a   (1994)
Approach from the base of the previous route by Very Difficult climbing. Start up a dyke, then climb the obvious left-slanting corner-crack. Step left and finish up a corner. It should be possible to extend the route by adding a pitch below the start.

Summit Buttress - West Face

Approach: From either Bealach MhicCoinnich or Bealach Coire Lagan

9 Collie's Ledge   150m   Grade 3/Moderate ***   (1887)
The ledge is seen clearly from Sgùrr Alasdair with climbers appearing to walk in space. In reality the ledge is mostly wide enough to walk along but via three

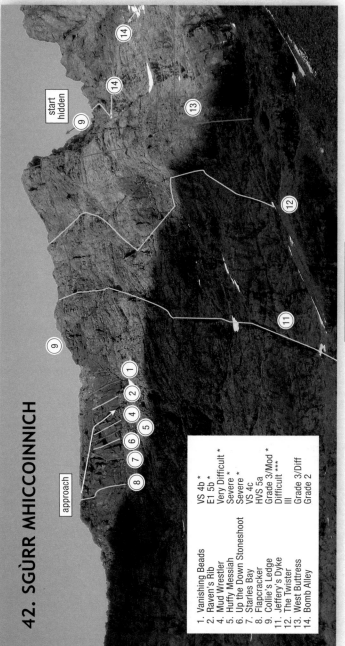

42. SGÙRR MHICCOINNICH

COIRE LAGAN

start hidden

9

approach

1. Vanishing Beads   VS 4b *
2. Raven's Rib   E1 5b *
4. Mud Wrestler   Very Difficult *
5. Huffy Messiah   Severe *
6. Up the Down Stoneshoot   Severe *
7. Starles Bay   VS 4c
8. Flapcracker   HVS 5a
9. Collie's Ledge   Grade 3/Mod *
11. Jeffery's Dyke   Difficult ***
12. The Twister   III
13. West Buttress   Grade 3/Diff
14. Bomb Alley   Grade 2

exposed sections of scrambling. From Bealach MhicCoinnich gain the east end of the ledge by smooth slabs and a small corner. Rise easily to the exposed nose at the highest point. Descend a slab and small narrow section to a horizontal scree path, traverse another small nose and then tip toe delicately across a steep band of rock to the easy final section.

10 King's Chimney   25m   Very Difficult ***   *(1898)*
A steeper ramp runs up right from the east end of Collie's Ledge after just 15m. Belay at the top of this below the prominent open book chimney. Ascend the corner on clean rock passing wedged chockstones with some trepidation. The slab below the roof has spaced but positive holds that lead right to an easy finish and a block belay overlooking Coruisk. The summit lies 60m to the north, up and along the narrow crest.

West Buttress

Approach: By screes left of the Great Stone Shoot.

11 Jeffrey's Dyke   300m   Difficult ***   *(1948)*
The conspicuous dyke 100m left of the long West Buttress gives a superb mountaineering route straight up the south face. The dyke starts as a shallow rocky recess (20m) and is briefly broken by a grassy terrace. The next section of the dyke is narrower, steeper and recessed (50m). Scramble 50m to the foot of the next steepening. The dyke now sits proud of the face. Move right to gain a groove on the right side of the dyke that rises almost unbroken to Collie's Ledge. The rock is generally solid and clean giving continuously good climbing. A couple of moves are particularly steep and can be avoided by short detours to the right. Cross Collie's Ledge and climb a wall to the summit ridge.
Winter: **III**   *(1970)*
In good winter conditions the line holds a mix of snow and ice but conditions can degenerate rapidly in sunlight.

12 The Twister   300m   III   *(1978)*
This follows the wide shallow gully immediately left of and parallel to West Buttress. Turn a vertical step at mid-height on the left.

13 West Buttress   300m   Grade 3/Difficult   *(1907)*
This broad buttress rises directly to the summit block and is just a scramble until 50m below Collie's Ledge. Gain the buttress by loose chimneys from the left or slabs from the narrowest section of the Great Stone Shoot. Ascend more or less directly with caution in many loose areas. Where the buttress steepens aim for a distinct chimney that leads to Collie's Ledge. Above here the central chimney is climbed on excellent rock to the summit.

14 Bomb Alley   250m   Grade 2
This shoot is more of a loose gully, christened because of frequent rocks sent down by parties descending from Theàrlaich. It can be descended easily but care is needed. The line is not easy to identify but gives rapid access to the Bealach MhicCoinnich. Cross the Great Stone Shoot at the first narrow neck, scramble up good rock for 60m and continue in the same line on small boulders to the small bay beneath the gully. No particular difficulties are encountered until the final rocks below the bealach that give good scrambling on rough peridotite. Grade I in winter.

43. SGÙRR THEÀRLAICH

(NG 451 208)   984m   Map p124   Diagrams p126, 135

A long narrow peak with complex descents; north to Bealach MhicCoinnich is described in the Traverse chapter or continue south towards the TD Gap for 50m past the summit before climbing down into the Great Stone Shoot.

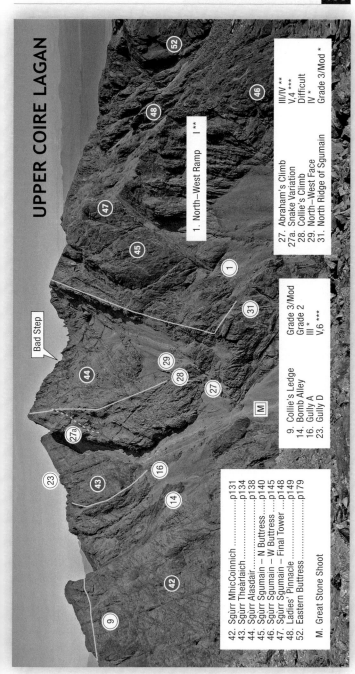

UPPER COIRE LAGAN

COIRE LAGAN

Bad Step

1. North—West Ramp   I **

27. Abraham's Climb .... III/IV **
27a. Snake Variation .... V,4 ***
28. Collie's Climb .... Difficult
29. North—West Face .... IV *
31. North Ridge of Sgumain .... Grade 3/Mod *

9. Collie's Ledge .... Grade 3/Mod
14. Bomb Alley .... Grade 2
16. Gully A .... III *
23. Gully D .... V,6 ***

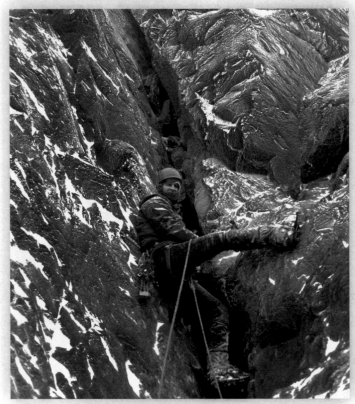

Gully D, V,6, Stone Shoot Face, Sgùrr Thearlaich. Climber Dave Ritchie

Stone Shoot Face

(NG 450 209)   Alt 825m   South-West facing

This face is not particularly popular in summer but has given some superb mixed winter routes that are in condition quite often because of their altitude. There are five gullies which run down into the Stone Shoot which have been climbed. They are imaginatively named A to E from the lowest to the highest. Approach is easy by the Great Stone Shoot.

15 Lower Rib   90m   Hard Severe 4b   *(1960)*
This is the furthest left and best defined of the ribs and buttresses on the Stone Shoot face. After a promising start up the conspicuous crack running up the right side of the buttress, the climb degenerates into an undignified scramble.

16 Gully A   130m   Difficult   *(1913)*
Ascend a narrow cave pitch on the left wall, through a tunnel into an enclosed chimney. Climb the chimney, then a chockstone pitch and finish up a narrow chimney.
Winter: **III** *   *(1970)*
The gully contains three short ice pitches and gives an interesting climb.

17 Gully B 120m Difficult (1908)

There are three easy pitches followed by a good one up a 20m chimney which is just 50cm wide.

Winter: **120m VI,6 ***   (2001)

Fine climbing following the summer route. The deep chimney obvious from below provided the crux and proved considerably harder than the summer description would suggest.

18 BC Buttress 110m IV,5 ** (2004)

Good icy mixed climbing taking the buttress between Gully B and Gully C. Start below a prominent groove mid-way between the gullies.

1. 25m Climb the icy groove and move up to below a corner.

2. 35m Climb the short corner above, step right then follow left-trending grooves to a point where a right traverse can be made to gain a prominent jutting block.

3. 50m Climb straight up reaching easier ground and the main ridge crest.

19 Vent Du Nord 80m V,6 * (2005)

This route follows the obvious open groove on the right side of the buttress situated between Gully B and Gully C. Start right of the original route at the point where the base of the buttress turns into the foot of Gully C.

1. 15m Climb the fault overlooking Gully C to gain a small ledge.

2. 30m Continue up the open groove above stepping left at a small bulge to gain easier ground. A good pitch.

3. 35m Move up and left, then back right climbing a short corner directly above the belay to finish up easier ground to the main ridge.

20 Gully C 100m Difficult (1908)

The highlight of this route is a deep fissure with jammed blocks at the top, followed by a cave with a through route.

Winter: **100m III,4 **   (2001)

Good climbing following the summer route.

21 Happy Returns 110m Very Difficult (1956)

This buttress looks like a sharp pinnacle when seen from the base of the Great Stone Shoot. Climb easy rocks up the arete for 15m to a steep 15m wall, climbed by its right side. A succession of small pitches follows, staying right of the sharp pinnacle face to finish on the crest.

22 CD Buttress 110m V,6 ** (2004)

A fine route taking the buttress between Gully C and Gully D. Start at the lowest rocks.

1. 40m Climb broken rocks to gain the foot of an obvious off-width corner-crack. Climb this followed by a second similar corner-crack.

2. 40m Move straight up for a few metres, then step right to gain a rightwards-rising snow ramp. Follow this to a point overlooking Gully D. Climb a short groove on the left followed by a traverse back right to below the obvious fault splitting the upper wall.

3. 30m Follow the fine left-slanting crack-line to finish on the main ridge.

23 Gully D 100m Very Difficult ** (1908)

A good climb with the piece de resistance being a 30m pitch near the top.

Winter: **100m V,6 ***   (2002)

An excellent climb with sustained interest following the summer route.

24 Gully E 90m Difficult (1887)

Lies 50m higher still and faces the top of the Great Stone Shoot. The gully is open for 20m, narrows somewhat for 15m then opens into a large bay. Climb slabby rocks on the right near the top.

Winter: **80m III,4**   (2011)

The gully proper was largely avoided because of deep powder snow. Climb

COIRE LAGAN

diagonally to the left edge and belay (35m). Follow the left edge until forced into the gully just below the open bay. Swim to belay just below the ridge (45m).

44. SGÙRR ALASDAIR

(NG 450 208)   993m   Maps p98, p124   Diagrams p126, 135

The highest peak in the Cuillin is actually at the head of a long south-west spur that includes Sgùrr Sgumain and Sròn na Ciche. It is separated from the Main Ridge by the Great Stone Shoot. Routes on the Lagan Face are very alpine in nature and scale with route finding presenting the major challenge. Better rock climbs lie on the South Face [57] in Coire a' Ghrunnda. The normal descent is down the Great Stone Shoot.

Stone Shoot Face

The walls above the shoot are steep and usually damp. The first route reached is an obvious clean line level with the lowest rocks of Sgùrr Theàrlaich.

25 Curving Corner   50m   VS 4c *   *(2009)*
A good pitch when dry. Pass a broad crevassed block at 20m before the corner steepens at 30m (crux). Belay in a left slanting break. Descend easily by traversing horizontally left to rejoin the Stone Shoot.

The next route lies on the steep walls immediately before the top of the Stone Shoot is reached.

26 Early Bird   130m   IV   *(1988)*
Start 50m below the top of the stone shoot by a short chimney. Traverse a broad steep angled slab for 30m then climb the steep wall above (crux). Easier ground leads to the summit.

Coire Lagan Face

(NG 448 208)   Alt 750m   West facing   Diagram p135

This face is thankfully sunnier and less intimidating then the Stone Shoot Face. It throws out a broad buttress that forms a prominent rib of Collie's Route. The routes start on the right side of the widest part of the Stone Shoot.

27 Abraham's Climb   300m   Difficult *   *(1907)*
This classic takes a line that stays left of the more prominent rib of Collie's Route and is best treated with care. The Stone Shoot passes through a narrow neck about 90m above the floor of the corrie. Above this, a short wall faces the corrie and the climb starts at a left-slanting chimney from the right end of this wall. Follow the chimney and its left retaining wall, then continue on this line over broken rocks to the crest of the wall overlooking the Stone Shoot where the face above becomes a steep headwall. A traverse right for 70m to gain a prominent rib that bounds the top bay gives the key to tackling the top section. Head back left and climb the steep ridge with minor deviations to finish on the summit.
Variation: **Stone Shoot Face Variation   120m   VS**   *(1937)*
This takes a direct line through the steep section avoided by the original route.
1. 15m Climb over a 'trap' and follow an awkward corner to a sloping ledge or slab.
2. 15m Go to the left and up a wall on small holds to a small belay.
3. 90m Follow a sloping shelf up to a sloping ledge and round an overhanging corner; undercut hold for left-hand. The step around the corner is extremely difficult, the hold for the right-hand is undercut and difficult to reach, the stance or small ledge slopes at an angle. A 4m high greasy chimney, with splayed out walls and partly overhanging leads to a good stance above.
About 30m of moderate climbing leads to the north arete, followed to just under the summit cairn.

Abraham's Climb, Snake Variation, V,4, Sgùrr Alasdair. Climber Mike Lates

COIRE LAGAN

Winter: **III/IV** ** (1952)
Follow the original line throughout; a sustained climb of quality.
Variation: **Snake Variation   180m   V,4 ***** (2006)
Takes the amazing snaking fault in the steep west wall of the summit tower. It is prominent when viewed from across the corrie rising rightwards for 120m until it breaks the western rib of Collie's Climb. Start at a bay at the top left end of the easy terrain.
1. 50m From the back of the bay climb a 5m crack to gain the enclosed fault (not obvious from below). Follow this for 35m to a snow cone that gives access to a bay above.
2. 50m Continue diagonally right up the fault on ice then snow.
3. and 4. 80m The fault continues for 20m to reach a rib. Cross this to an open scoop which leads to the South-West Ridge 20m below the summit.

28 Collie's Climb   270m   Difficult   *(1896)*

This climb is easier than Abraham's but is looser. It follows the ridge to the right. Climb to the base of the ridge. In poor visibility it is better to approach the ridge by climbing a further 120m up scree towards Bealach Sgumain, to a short wall facing the corrie. Start at the left-hand end of the wall and climb left to join the ridge. Pleasant climbing leads up the ridge with the upper sections more broken and rather loose. Finish close to the summit.

29 North-West Face   270m   IV *   *(1980)*

This climb follows snow and ice falls in a weakness to the right of Collie's Climb and finishes on the summit.

30 South-West Ridge/Bad Step   200m   Very Difficult **

The ascent of this popular ridge from Bealach Sgumain has one short Very Difficult move, the Bad Step, near the start. This can be avoided by the South-West Flank route. Both routes are described in detail on page 198.

SGÙRR SGUMAIN

(NG 448 207)   947m

To the south-west of Sgùrr Alasdair lies Sgùrr Sgumain. Bealach Sgumain is easily recognised by the prominent pinnacles in the gap between the peaks. The narrow ridge linking Sgùrr Sgumain to the Bealach is good when dry but best turned on the west side in the wet. In summer a descent to Coire Lagan from the Bealach is possible by skirting the upper tiers of rock on the north side. In winter the ascent is grade I and a good option when snow has formed runnels of neve. The western flanks have two major facets, North Buttress [45] and West Buttress [46], that merge at 800m to form the Final Tower [47].

31 North Ridge   350m   Grade 3/Moderate *   *(1887)*

This is the ridge which runs directly to the summit from the first narrowing in the Great Stone Shoot. An enjoyable scramble with some complex route finding in the lower sections and one steep band at mid-height. Care should be taken with the rock in places.

45. SGÙRR SGUMAIN - NORTH BUTTRESS

(NG 447 208)   Alt 750m   South-West facing   Map p124   Diagrams p126, 135, 142

This buttress is an imposing steep face above Loch Coire Lagan. The crest forms a steep ridge rising parallel to North Ridge with a small summit at the apex of the face. The face is separated from West Buttress [46] by the slabby North-West Ramp which rises to the Final Tower [47]. All routes start from this ramp. Two higher terraces traverse across the buttress, rising to the right. The upper one is a useful finish for several climbs, avoiding the top pitches which are decidedly loose.

Descent: Routes ending on the summit of North Buttress have to descend broken ground to reach a small col where Prometheus ends. Traversing the upper terrace below the final pitches leads easily to the same point. Beyond is a ramp line leading rightwards to the broad shoulder of Sgumain about 100m below the summit. Descend easily south-west to Bealach Coire a' Ghrunnda then down the Sgumain Stone Shoot. Descending to the foot of the climbs by the North-West Ramp is possible but often greasy and loose. **Heathcote's Gully** (80m Moderate 1892) is one of the indefinite gullies lying to the right of North-West Ramp, joining it at half height.

1 North-West Ramp   250m   Grade 3   *(1896)*

This route gives access to all of the North Buttress routes.

Gain the ramp at its lowest point. Pass a couple of steeper steps until below the chimney of Prometheus. Zigzag across the loose slabs above to reach the terrace

below the Final Tower. The terrace leads horizontally to the shoulder of Sgumain.
Winter: **I** **

A good line amongst very impressive scenery with a couple of icy steps. It often gives a better approach to Sgùrr Sgumain than the Sgumain Stone Shoot.

A prominent bib of green moss flows out of Frankland's Gully near the start of the North-West Ramp.

**2 Grannie Clark's Wynd   140m   E1 5b * **   *(1971)*
This route makes a direct start to join Frankland's Gully and then a direct line up the north-western nose of the buttress.
1. 45m 5a Start left of the mossy bib. Gain Frankland's Gully via a choice of direct starts and then follow it to an obvious roof on the right.
2. 10m 4b Make a rising traverse below the roof, then climb over it and go past a large block to a platform.
3. 35m 5b Climb a shallow corner passing a loose flake on the right. Trend up left to a small ledge and good belay.
4. 50m 5b Climb up and left to a bulge and go through it at the easiest point, crux, then continue up loose rock to the top.

**3 Frankland's Gully   300m   Hard Severe * **   *(1925)*
This route bounds the lower left edge of the buttress (120m). Above this it climbs a long section of easy ground to a final corner (180m). About 15m above the green mossy bib a ledge traverses left into the gully. Start along this to reach a triangular niche. Overcome a short sharp wall by a tricky mantelshelf. Scramble 50m to a cave belay. Traverse up on the left wall to a recess at 7m (possible belay), then traverse back to the bed of the gully on a rising ledge which gradually diminishes to a final awkward move. Finish by a steep but not difficult crack that finishes just north of the summit.
Winter: **V** **   *(1981)*
An excellent and technical expedition. Climb the gully direct to the end of a left traverse. Climb the rib above to finish at the top of the summer route. Continue up the now much easier gully, crossing the upper part of Prometheus, and then climb the narrow gully via a through route to the ridge.

**4 Wood-Johnson's Route   180m   VS * **   *(1932)*
A prominent corner-crack with a small green cave at its base starts 5m further up the ramp.
1. 30m Climb the corner to a large ledge.
2. 15m 4b Step round a corner on the left and climb an open chimney, trending back right, then left through an overhang.
3. 10m 4b Traverse right for a few metres, then climb to the left-hand end of the lower terrace.
4. 50m Traverse along the terrace to a belay below a steep crack at its end.
5. 30m Climb the steep crack on good holds and move right, continuing to the second terrace.
6. 45m It is safer to follow the second terrace rightwards to finish, as the summit rocks are loose. Otherwise ascend directly to the top of the buttress.

**5 Direct Route   180m   VS 4c * **   *(1957)*
This route provides some good climbing. Climb the first three pitches of Wood-Johnson's Route, then branch up a wide open groove to a rake sloping steeply to the right. Climb the rake for 25m, then climb a prominent slab on the left to below the final pitch. Climb an overhanging wall on good holds, crux, and move left to a steep slab which ends on top of the buttress.

The ramp narrows above before a recess is reached. In the centre of the face above is an overhanging wall turned on either side by the next two routes. Raynaud's takes the left of two prominent corners 30m up and Frostbite takes a line of corners and chimneys to the right.

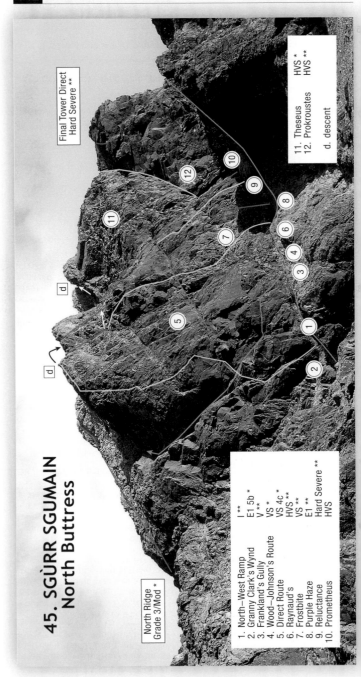

45. SGÙRR SGUMAIN
North Buttress

North Ridge
Grade 3/Mod *

Final Tower Direct
Hard Severe **

1. North–West Ramp — I **
2. Granny Clark's Wynd — E1 5b *
3. Frankland's Gully — V **
4. Wood–Johnson's Route — VS *
5. Direct Route — VS 4c *
6. Raynaud's — HVS **
7. Frostbite — VS **
8. Purple Haze — E1 **
9. Reluctance — Hard Severe **
10. Prometheus — HVS

11. Theseus — HVS *
12. Prokroustes — HVS **

d. descent

Raynaud's 110m HVS ** *(1994)*
1. 45m 4c Climb to the left-hand of the two corners. Follow the corner, moving left at the top to belay on the slanting fault.
2. 40m 5a Gain the corner left of a bay above, via a bulge. Climb the corner and, after mounting a shelf at the top of the corner, move out left and continue to a belay.
3. 25m Climb easily up right, and traverse off right to finish.

Frostbite 140m VS 4c ** *(1968)*
This good sustained climb takes the right-hand of the two corners. It is well protected after the initial 20m.
1. 25m 4b Climb up to a ledge below the right-hand corner; poor belay. It may be wise to continue.
2. 35m 4c Go up the corner on good holds to a ledge and climb a short wall to a grass ledge.
3. 40m 4c An easy diagonal break leads up right (part of Wood-Johnson's Route) to a big corner. Belay below the corner to avoid rope drag. Climb the corner, which is capped by a large overhang. Avoid this on the left to reach the arete; a good pitch.
4. 20m 4a Continue to a big rocky terrace and move up to the prominent final groove.
5. 20m 4c Climb a layback crack to a good ledge, surmount an overhang on dubious holds, then continue to the top.

Purple Haze 110m E1 ** *(1968)*
Low in the grade. Start where a small orange slab leads to a break in the overhangs.
1. 30m 4b Climb up through the break and continue diagonally rightward until able to cut back left up a clean slab to a small square ledge (some suspect rock and poor protection).
2. 35m 5b Follow a right-trending ramp-line and groove to a horizontal dyke (much better rock now all the way to the top). Make steep moves up an undercut wall to a good ledge. Climb a steep corner above (crux) to a large sloping ledge.
3. 45m 5a Climb a steep chimney at the back of the ledge and another corner above (possible belay). Follow a dyke line into a deep corner which was originally climbed. Instead traverse left near the top along a small ledge and climb a bold arete to finish.

A small steepening in the ramp above here is usually wet. The following routes start in a recessed bay just above here.

Reluctance 150m Hard Severe ** *(1970)*
This pleasant route gives some exposed climbing through a break in the wall 12m left of Prometheus. Climb a fault leading up left to a ledge. Move right and continue to the second terrace, as for Wood-Johnson's Route. Follow the terrace right to finish.

Prometheus 110m HVS *(1957)*
This climb takes the prominent gully on the right-hand side of the face.
1. 20m 4c The initial pitch is an unpleasant overhang. Climb left through the overhang to a block belay. The chimney of Prokroustes bears right from here.
2. and 3. 90m Continue up the main gully, passing a large chockstone on the left.

Theseus 120m HVS * *(1958)*
This climb is about Hard Severe after the initial pitch.
1. 30m 4c Climb the first pitch of Prometheus, then go 6m beyond the junction with Prokroustes to climb an open corner on the right. Follow an obvious line parallel to Prokroustes to a large block belay. (It is possible to continue right along the fault to rejoin Prokroustes below the last two pitches).
2. 30m Climb a steep wall to an exposed 20m traverse left.
3. 30m Easier climbing leads to a terrace. Go right to the foot of some open corners.

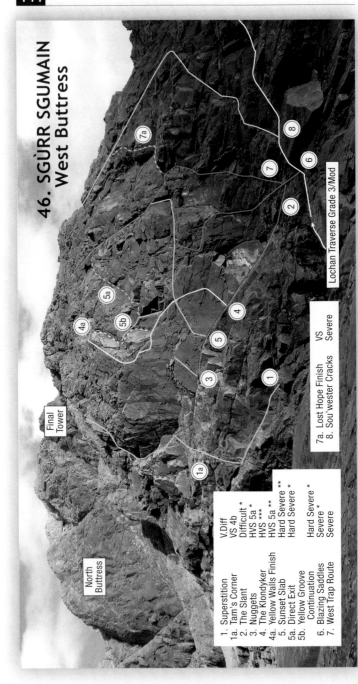

46. SGÙRR SGUMAIN
West Buttress

North Buttress

Final Tower

1. Superstition — V.Diff
1a. Tam's Corner — VS 4b
2. The Slant — Difficult *
3. Nuggets — HVS 5a *
4. The Klondyker — HVS ***
4a. Yellow Walls Finish — HVS 5a **
5. Sunset Slab — Hard Severe **
5a. Direct Exit — Hard Severe *
5b. Yellow Groove Continuation — Hard Severe *
6. Blazing Saddles — Severe *
7. West Trap Route — Severe

7a. Lost Hope Finish — VS
8. Sou'wester Cracks — Severe

Lochan Traverse Grade 3/Mod

4. 30m Climb the corners and continue to the summit ridge above a line of red basalt.

**2 Prokroustes   120m   HVS 4c ** **   (1957)
A classic traditional route.
1. 20m 4c Climb Prometheus, pitch 1.
2. 20m 4c Climb the chimney on the right on greasy rock, past a bolt and a peg, to a good belay above a pointed chockstone.
3. and 4. 80m 4b Scramble up for 20m, then climb a narrow chimney to a steeper top section. Climb an overhang on large blocks, then crawl under a chockstone to ascend a thin crack to another chockstone.
Two pitches lead to the top of the Final Tower. Alternatively, climb easier cracks on the right to the second terrace.

46. SGÙRR SGUMAIN - WEST BUTTRESS

(NG 444 206)   Alt 550m   West facing   Maps p98, 124   Diagrams p126, 135, 144

This slabby crag stands between Upper Coire Lagan and the Sgumain Stone Shoot. An entertaining rake **Lochan Traverse**, (Grade 3/Moderate) crosses the lower part of the buttress, passing under a prominent blaze of white rock and provides a good way from the lochan to Eastern Buttress of Sròn na Cìche for an evening climb. The start is the crux and often wet. The rock on West Buttress is generally very good quality. Two prominent yellow walls have led to some confusion: The groove below the lower, more obvious yellow wall is a variation pitch on the Klondyker. Yellow Groove Continuation to Sunset Slab runs below the upper yellow wall. Any combination is worthy of at least one star.

Descent: Many parties continue with a route on the Final Tower but it is possible to traverse into the Sgumain Stone Shoot on the right from the top of the difficult climbing sections.

1 Superstition   85m   Very Difficult *   (1951)
Start at the foot of a left-slanting gully, directly under the left edge of the obvious clean vertical wall.
Traverse diagonally left to a large sloping ledge (25m) then easy slabs to a grassy terrace. Climb a wall and go over slabs to the foot of a chimney in the left corner of the vertical wall (20m). Climb slabs to the immediate left of the chimney (10m). Traverse into the chimney and climb to large ledge and belay (10m). Move right along a sloping ledge and go up a steep corner. Traverse left across a steep slab and finish up another corner (20m).
Variation: **Tam's Corner   45m   VS 4b**   (2005)
Traverse down left from below the vertical wall for 15m. Climb a corner system on the undercut buttress left of the original finish. Finish up rough rock to join the final rocks of Superstition.

2 The Slant   100m   Difficult *   (1958)
Gain the slabby rocks left of the white blaze. Climb diagonally left under a large vertical wall to a chimney. Climb the open chimney and finish up a wall of very rough rock, probably as for Superstition.

3 Nuggets   15m   HVS 5a *   (2006)
A short wall immediately below the clean vertical wall holds a striking diagonal crack. Gain the start by ascending the Slant. Climb it, pulling out right at the top on good holds. Traverse down right to join the third pitch of Sunset Slab on the easy traverse ledge.

4 The Klondyker   135m   HVS * **   (1988)
A recommended route with fine climbing. Start about 8m below the white blaze.
1. 30m 4b Climb diagonally left up a slab to a corner left of the chimney on The

Sunset Slab, Yellow Groove Continuation, Hard Severe, West Buttress, Sgùrr Sgumain.
Climber Karen Latter

Slant. Layback up the corner until it is possible to move right to a cracked slab which leads to a belay at the foot of a steep impressive wall.

2. 30m 5a Climb a small corner and cracks to gain the left side of a large sloping ledge about halfway up the steep wall. Gain the indistinct crack-line above from a perched block on the left, then follow this and the wider crack above through an overhang to a large ledge on Sunset Slab. An improbable pitch for the grade.

3. 20m 4a Climb the groove above the peg until an easy left traverse leads to a ledge at the foot of an obvious groove with a yellow left wall.

4. 30m 4c Move left around an edge into an exposed position and climb up left past an overhang to a basalt recess. Climb to a small well positioned ledge, then up a short wall to belay.

5. 25m Move right and finish up the painfully rough arete.

Variation: **Yellow Walls Finish**   **60m**   **HVS 5a** **   (2005)
Instead of moving left on pitch 4 take the obvious groove with a yellow left wall, breaking left at the top to reach a second yellow wall (30m 5a). Follow the yellow groove beneath this wall to a large ledge and easier ground (30m 4c). This pitch includes at least part of the Yellow Groove Continuation to Sunset Slab.

5 Sunset Slab   160m   Hard Severe **   (1951)
Scramble to a belay below the white blaze.

1. 45m Follow The Slant, to the base of a steep crack on the right wall.
2. 10m Climb the steep crack
3. 45m Make a long easy traverse right to foot of deep-cut crack.
4. 30m Climb the steep, strenuous crack.
5. 30m Continue up the crack to a junction with West Trap Route. Follow this for 45m.

Variation: **Direct Exit   65m   Hard Severe** *   *(1958)*
Break off original route 10m along the easy traverse on pitch 3.
1. 10m Climb a groove to a corner below an overhanging crack.
2. 10m Climb the wall on the left of the crack then traverse back across the crack to a shelf and flake belay.
3. 10m Climb the overhanging crack (8m) to good finishing holds.
4. 35m A short crack now leads to easier climbing diagonally to the middle of the buttress. Join the easy finish of West Trap Route to finish.

Variation: **Direct Exit-Yellow Groove Continuation   65m   Hard Severe** *   *(1964)*
Gains the upper yellow groove to give a more continuous finish.
4. 15m Climb a slab, then round a corner, climb a steep groove (piton) and move left beneath an overhang to a stance and belays below a big corner with vertical, yellow tinted left wall.
5. 12m Climb rightwards to a stance and spike belays on the arete.
6. 30m Climb the arete until, beneath the top, move rightwards for 6m until a slab can be climbed to a scree ledge beneath another corner; belay.
7. 8m Climb the corner to reach easy scrambling.

6 Blazing Saddles   185m   Severe *   *(1996)*
Follows a line between West Trap Route and Sunset Slab to the right of the white blaze, aiming for a conspicuous groove near the top. Start up the West Trap Route. Climb the small chimney at 25m until below the open slabs on the right (passing two old pegs). Pull on to a narrow ledge on the left wall and follow this round to a wide ledge above the vertical section of the buttress (45m). Climb grooves and walls to the base of the conspicuous groove (45m). Struggle up the back of the groove, then move out and up a slabby wall to reach and obvious trap dyke (45m). Finish up the dyke and broken rocks above (50m).

7 West Trap Route   240m   Severe   *(1924)*
Start from the rake about 15m right of the white blaze. Climb broken rocks to join a fault-line rising to the right. Make for a small broken chimney at 25m and climb it. Continue in the same line, with one deviation onto open slabs on the left, to a dark chimney. Climb the strenuous chimney, crux, to a ledge. Climb a crack behind a flake on the left, continue up the slabs, then traverse left to join the dyke 30m above the ledge. Follow the dyke to finish.

Variation: **Lost Hope Finish   100m   VS**   *(1959)*
Follow West Trap Route to the large flake above the crux chimney. Move over to the large grassy ledge on the right to a right-angled corner with a crack in the back, 45m. Climb the thin crack in the right wall, then traverse right into a steep and difficult groove which leads to a belay, 20m. Continue up the buttress, parallel with West Trap Route, by short pitches and grassy ledges.

8 Sou'wester Cracks   190m   Severe   *(1959)*
Start about 5m to the right of the start of the West Trap Route. For about 100m the route principally followed cracks trending towards the right-hand arete of the buttress: a line of trap dyke was then followed diagonally left to the finish on the crest of the buttress.

West Buttress Route (480m Difficult 1907) climbs broken slabs direct to the narrow section of the fine West Ridge of Sgùrr Sgumain by slabs and grooves.

0 West Ridge of Sgùrr Sgumain   Grade 3/Moderate *
Most of the routes on West Buttress finish by this ridge. It can be joined above the climbs by an easy traverse across the Sgumain Stone Shoot from the foot of Eastern

Gully. The upper reaches have some fine narrow sections to ascend and descend. Traverse easily off right below the Final Tower, 30mins.

47. FINAL TOWER

(NG 448 206) Alt 825m South facing Map p124 Diagrams p126, 135, 149

This is a sunny cliff overlooking the Sgumain Stone Shoot. A prominent terrace at half-height divides the face into two tiers.

Approach: The Lower Tier is approached as for Sròn na Cìche up the Sgumain Stone Shoot to just below the level of Vulcan Wall. The crag lies 200m up left across scree and boulders.

Descent: Climbing a route on West Buttress leads to the terrace between the tiers with upper tier climbs giving good continuations. Descent is down the south-west flanks to Bealach Coire a' Ghrunnda and the Sgumain Stone Shoot again.

Lower Tier

1 Introduction   60m   Very Difficult *   (1958)
This route takes the left of three prominent groove lines on the lower tier.
1. 30m Climb the groove to a sloping shelf to a chockstone belay.
2. 30m Continue up a delicate slab above and finish on the terrace near the start of Final Tower Direct, which makes a good continuation.

2 Laceration   65m   Severe *   (1965)
This climb makes a fine prelude to Penitentiary Grooves. Start 15m right of Introduction.
1. 25m Follow the left-slanting groove line to a stance and belay.
2. 40m Move right into another groove with a large flake. Climb this, then traverse left into a broken groove which leads to the top.

3 Hermaphra and Ditus   95m   Severe   (1958)
Takes the line directly beneath Penitentiary Grooves.
1. 20m Climb a chimney to a sentry box and chockstone belay.
2. 35m Follow the chimney to a ledge.
3. 10m Continue easily to the terrace.
4. 30m Above and right lies a chimney (Ditus). Climb up, then go right to the chimney which is often wet. Climb it on the right to the top.

4 Priam   60m   Severe   (1958)
A variation start to Hermaphra. Start 10m to its right at a companion chimney. Climb this direct to a left traverse to reach the sentry box stance at the top of the first pitch of Hermaphra.

Upper Tier

5 Final Tower Direct   60m   Hard Severe 4a **   (1920)
This classic climb takes a line just left of the nose on a steep north-west facing wall. Start at the north-west corner of the Final Tower. Follow a crack up the face, trending back right on easier rocks near the top. The route is considered harder than Crack of Doom.

6 Penitentiary Grooves   45m   E1 5b **   (1971)
A very fine route in the middle of the upper face, forming a big diedre capped by a triangular roof. A curiosity is the jammed bolt at the top of the crack.
1. 15m Climb the diedre to a stance.
2. 20m Surmount an overhang and continue up the diedre over two small overhangs to below the top roof. Avoid this by the right wall to gain a ledge.
3. 10m Finish up a groove.

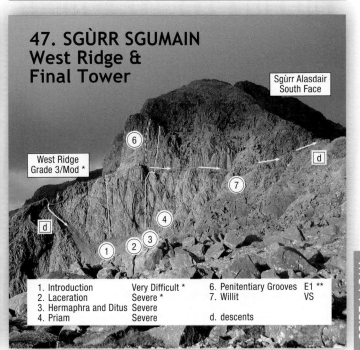

47. SGÙRR SGUMAIN
West Ridge &
Final Tower

Sgùrr Alasdair
South Face

West Ridge
Grade 3/Mod *

1. Introduction	Very Difficult *	6. Penitentiary Grooves	E1 **
2. Laceration	Severe *	7. Willit	VS
3. Hermaphra and Ditus	Severe		
4. Priam	Severe	d. descents	

COIRE LAGAN

7 Willit   45m   VS   (1959)

Further right the terrace is broken by a watercourse emerging from a gully with an enormous block in it. This climb follows the sharp arete on the left.

1. 25m 4c Climb the overhanging arete, then follow the ridge crest to a belay.
2. 20m Traverse 12m left, then climb the cracked wall on the left.

48. LADIES' PINNACLE

(NG 447 205)   Alt 750m   Diagrams p126, 135, 150

This large pinnacle lies opposite the uppermost walls of Sròn na Cìche. The lowest rocks are level with Vulcan Wall. The rock is very rough but care must be exercised with loose rock.

1 West Ridge   100m   Very Difficult

Follow the crest with numerous deviations to turn steep small walls.

2 East Ridge   20m   Moderate   (1908)

From the shoulder above the pinnacle cross large boulders to reach a small, 5m, wall. Climb this on large holds to the summit cairn.

SRÒN NA CÌCHE - COIRE LAGAN FACE

Map p124

This face is over a kilometre long and exceeds 300m in height in places. The connoisseur's choice is a long outing reaching the top by a combination of routes or one of the huge Western Buttress alpine expeditions. Equally popular are the many hard

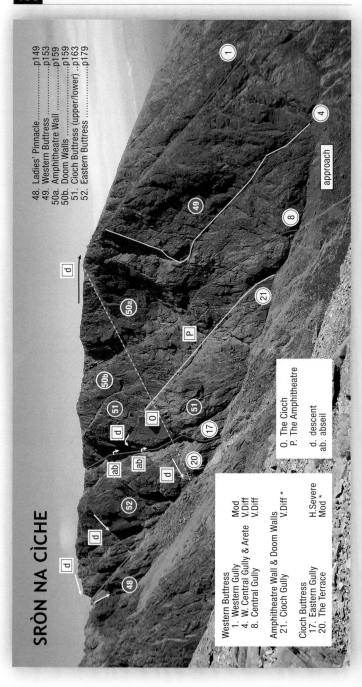

SRÒN NA CÌCHE

approach

Western Buttress		
1. Western Gully	Mod	
4. W. Central Gully & Arete	V.Diff	
8. Central Gully	V.Diff	
Amphitheatre Wall & Doom Walls		
21. Cioch Gully	V.Diff	*
Cioch Buttress		
17. Eastern Gully	H.Severe	
20. The Terrace	Mod	*

O. The Cioch
P. The Amphitheatre

d. descent
ab. abseil

routes that tend to be one or two pitches in length, generally on very high quality rock. There is the additional attraction of a relatively short approach from Glen Brittle.

The face can be a cold hole compared to some of its close neighbours with the north and east winds, that tend to give the Cuillin dry weather, blowing straight onto the crag. It begins to get the sun after about 2pm when the character of the cliff can change completely. Good route finding and clever rope work will be needed on almost all routes. Escape, either up or down, is complicated for most routes and the face gives infinite possibilities for getting lost. There is no substitute for a reconnaissance on a clear evening to identify key features of the face as morning shadows can cause most features to merge and the face appear as a dark two dimensional wall.

The face is divided into three main sections: Western Buttress on the right, Eastern Buttress on the left and Cioch Buttress in the middle. The recessed area between Western Buttress and Cioch Buttress is The Amphitheatre above which lie Amphitheatre Wall and the Doom Walls.

Western Gully, Central Gully and Eastern Gully are prominent features when viewed on the approach, stretching the full height of the cliff and all rising from right to left. West Central Gully starts on the right of Western Buttress, rises diagonally across the buttress then breaks directly upward, bounded by Amphitheatre Arete and West Central Arete. Central Gully starts 100m farther left, rises through the Amphitheatre and splits Amphitheatre Wall from the Doom Walls. Cioch Gully starts 50m left of Central Gully, crosses the base of the Amphitheatre and terminates behind the Cioch itself. The continuation of the fault forms The Shelf that runs beneath the Upper Cioch Buttress to join Eastern Gully.

The Terrace is the one prominent feature that rises in the opposite direction, from left to right. It starts at Eastern Buttress, passes below the Cioch and is then broken as it crosses the rifts of Cioch Gully and Central Gully. Many other significant features are described in the text accompanying each buttress.

Approaches: The finer details of approaches for many climbs are included with the route descriptions. Take the Coire Lagan footpath for 2km to a fork at NG 433 207. Here a horizontal path, indistinct at the start, leads south across lower Coire Lagan. Cross the two large branches of the Allt Coire Lagan then pass close to the lowest of the famous Coire Lagan boulders. The best approach for all buttresses is then by the grassy slopes directly below the Western Buttress [49], 45mins.

Make a rising traverse for 15mins beneath the cliffs to a ledge at the foot of Cioch Buttress [51] and the easiest access to the Amphitheatre Wall and Doom Walls [50]. Continue the easy rising traverse for a further 10mins, passing Eastern Gully, to reach a narrowing formed by huge boulders abutting the toe of Eastern Buttress [52]. The Terrace breaks right from this point giving access to the Middle and Upper Cioch Buttresses as well as the West Wall of Eastern Buttress. Routes on the East Wall of the Eastern Buttress lie above the huge boulders.

Allow 90mins to reach the foot of most climbs that start beyond the Lower Cioch Buttress. Bealach Coire a' Ghrunnda is reached in 2hrs giving easy access to the Alasdair-Theàrlaich crags which are often a lot sunnier and warmer to climb on.

Descents: Escape from most of the face will involve some abseiling with signs of epic retreats being commonplace. Suggestions are made in more detail for each separate buttress. There are two main choices of descent for climbs finishing on the shoulder of Sròn na Cìche which is a broad boulder field that can be very disorientating in the mist.

Turning left to reach the summit then descending by the Sgumain Stone Shoot is the best choice for parties returning to rucsacs at the foot of the face. Ascend the boulder field in a north-easterly direction to the cairned summit taking care around the top of Eastern Gully. Some 50m north-east of the summit a 5m wall creates an impasse that is turned slightly to the east before reaching a large cairn at the top of the Sgumain Stone Shoot.

The alternative descent, for those who carry all of their equipment, is to turn right and head south-west by the broad shoulder of Sròn na Cìche. Initially stay close to the face just ascended. The long boulder fields finally lead to soft grass. Continue descending south-westerly to the Coire a' Ghrunnda footpath before returning to Glen Brittle.

49. SRÒN NA CÌCHE
Western Buttress

1. Western Gully	Mod	12. Parallel Cracks Route	V.Diff **
2. Apex Route	Severe	13. Coronation	Severe
3. Cooper's Gangway	VS	14. Engineers' Slant	V.Diff *
4. West Central Gully	V.Diff	15. Chimney & Crack Climb	Severe
4a. West Central Arete	V.Diff	16. Zigzag	Difficult
5. Boomerang	Severe	17. Central Slabs	Severe
6. A.B. Route	Severe *	18. Trap Face Route	VS *
7. Median	V.Diff **	20. Central Route	H.Severe **
8. Central Gully	V.Diff		
10. Diamond Slab	VS		
11. Mallory's Slab & Groove	V.Diff *	P. The Amphitheatre	

The entire descent of Eastern Gully, using two abseils then a traverse out by the Terrace, is possible. It is very loose and more commonly used in sections by parties escaping from below the Upper Cioch Buttress.

49. WESTERN BUTTRESS

(NG 441 202) Alt 450m North-West facing Maps p98, 124 Diagram p126, 150, 152

The buttress is bound on the left in the upper half quite distinctly by Amphitheatre Arete. Western Gully forms the right boundary. The whole buttress is on a vast scale. To help with route finding key features must be recognised before and during the ascent. Only three routes independently run the full length of the Western Buttress: Western Gully, West Central Gully and Median.

The line of Engineers' Slant is also worthy of note as it traverses below a fairly continuous band of steep rock that forms the crux of many routes. Routes and variations have been recorded with varying degrees of detail and accuracy over the years. Many descriptions start some way up the face with an approach by a different route initially needed.

Every attempt has been made to add some clarity but there will always remain a need to use judgement and experience to pick the best line. The fine details may often be more misleading than just keeping to the general line. The essence of this cliff is exploration. Climbers should be capable of leading a full grade above their chosen route especially on the lower technically graded expeditions. An alpine mentality of carrying lightweight rucsacs is advised.

Routes are described from right to left. Climbs starting from the cliff base are described first, then routes starting from West Central Gully and finally routes starting from Central Gully.

Descent: For parties wanting to escape the face low down descending the lower reaches of Central and West Central Gullies is possible but not entirely simple. Descend from the top of the buttress as described above.

Routes From The Cliff Base

1 Western Gully 200m Moderate   *(1906)*
Numerous starts are possible to reach the gully proper which starts 60m above the screes. The slabby rocks right of Parallel Cracks route give the best climbing with dry rock. Traversing in from the west side by scree and grass gives the easiest approach in damp conditions. The gully contains numerous minor pitches and finishes at the apex of West Central Arete.
Winter: **III**   *(1973)*
Difficulties vary with depth of snow in particular.

Two routes start right of West Central Gully taking lines on the rocks below and parallel to Western Gully.

2 Apex Route 240m Severe   *(1946)*
This climb takes a line on the buttress between West Central Route and Western Gully. When seen from the corrie, it lies directly up the centre of the narrow pointed buttress, crossing Parallel Cracks and appearing to keep right of Cooper's Gangway. Start at a crack at the lowest point of the slabs forming the base of the buttress. At 60m, cross a rake and climb above this, always trending left across a number of slabs and over several steep ribs. Above, there are a number of more difficult pitches, including a vertical chimney, a crack in an overhanging wall, a strenuous slanting chimney and two steep narrow slabs flanked on the right by vertical walls. Finish at the apex of the buttress.

3 Cooper's Gangway 240m VS   *(1932)*
Start at a steep slab 15m right of the foot of West Central Gully and just right of

two small overhangs. Climb the slab until forced to the left edge; stance and belay a little higher (25m). More easy climbing up and right leads to a large grass platform, which is above and between two grass patches (45m). A brief traverse up left leads to a ledge at the foot of a steep wall. Climb up left towards a wide dyke at 15m, cross this and traverse left across the slab above, climbing over a short wall to a belay. The exposed wall above is not as rotten as it appears, and is easily climbed by a short steep crack. Easy rocks now lead to a steep wall of light coloured rock. The crux follows, a steep sloping gangway which leads to a stance on the left edge of the wall. Climb the easy rocks above to the top.

4 West Central Gully and Arete   400m   Very Difficult   (1908)
West Central Gully is important as it gives access to a number of routes that start on the walls above it. West Central Arete looks very fine from below but is actually broad, broken and very loose. Finishing by the open gully is not too difficult but usually damp and unattractive. Amphitheatre Arete gives the best quality climbing to finish by.

Climb the gully, which is more of an easy angled rake, to where it terminates in a corner with a conspicuous overhanging roof above. The crux section passes this overhang by slabs on the left. The gully now breaks vertically upward bounded by two aretes, Amphitheatre on the left and West Central on the right. To gain West Central Arete follow the gully for 30m then cross to the right of the arete by a prominent crack passing a huge block visible from the screes. Keep to the general line of the Arete, bearing slightly left of the crest where necessary.

5 Boomerang   210m   Severe   (1952)
Start on the screes, 30m east of West Central Gully.
Climb up and left over slabs and a water worn slab corner into West Central Gully, just below where Median crosses it. Take an easy line up right, crossing Engineers' Slant, into a conspicuous fault below a light coloured wall. The fault runs up and right to a grassy finish high in western Gully.

6 A.B. Route   400m   Severe *   (1936)
This climb starts halfway between the foot of Central Gully and West Central Gully, well to the right of Median. It runs parallel to the gullies, crossing Median and routes on the Diamond slab. Climb 100m of easy slabs, then traverse 20m left on a grassy ledge. Above, climb steeper slabs for 60m to a point level with a dyke. Traverse for 30m in an exposed position, crossing the dyke to a grass ledge. Climb 75m of very steep and exposed slabs on good holds to where West Central Gully meets Trap Face Route. Finish either up Trap Face Route or West Central Gully Arete.

7 Median   355m   Very Difficult **   (1909)
This excellent climb is serious for the grade and needs good route finding ability in order to avoid considerably harder variation. Normally 4hrs.
Start 40m west of Central Gully at the foot of a long crack-line.
1. 40m Climb the crack.
2. 50m Continue easily to West Central Gully.
3. 40m Go up the gully for just 5m to the foot of a deep chimney cutting rightwards through slabs. Climb the chimney to its end. Above is a big overhanging wall.
4. 45m Follow the chimney-line leftwards beneath the wall and belay on the more open crag above.
5. 40m Start up a wall some 5m to the right through some steep ground before making a traverse right and up to a belay at the foot of an easy angled slab. (This leads left to the base of the big fan shaped corners which form such a noticeable feature from the corrie floor).
6. 30m Avoid the corners by an easy but hidden ramp 5m to the right, climb easily to belay below a basalt groove that heads off rightwards.
7. 60m Follow the groove until the line turns more steeply left up a chimney. This pitch is very poorly protected.

8. and 9. 60m A further two pitches follow either the chimney, or the buttress on its left, to the terminal arete.

Many variations are possible, particularly from the base of the fan shaped corners (about 4c or 5a). An escape is possible at the start of pitch 6 by traversing to the right onto Moderate slabs which lead to Western Gully (90m).

8 Central Gully   400m   Very Difficult   *(1907)*

A fairly straightforward but long climb crossing the Amphitheatre to finish above the Cioch Buttress. Useful for understanding the layout of the western half of Sròn na Ciche. Starting by the first pitch of Median gives the best climbing. Follow the gully easily to The Amphitheatre. Some steeper pitches ensue, including one best turned on the left. Above, the gully forks and the left branch gives the better finish.

9 Eastern Wall of Central Gully   200m   Very Difficult   *(1909)*

This is a variation to the upper part of Central Gully. From above The Amphitheatre, follow the left wall of the gully to the Terrace, and climb the interesting arete to the summit plateau.

0 Diamond Slab   180m   VS   *(1946)*

A good route that terminates at West Central Gully. Descend this or continue by one of the many routes above. Start at a small overhang 15m right of Mallory's Slab and Groove.

1. 30m Climb the overhang, traverse right, then go up a crack to a slab below an overhang; belay in the crack.

2. 25m Traverse left and climb a crack to a grass platform and a boulder belay in Central Gully.

3. 35m Cross the gully onto a steep slab. Climb this direct on large sloping holds, then trend left to a knob belay in a shallow corner.

4. 20m Traverse up right, then climb straight up to a grass ledge with small flake belays.

5. 30m Traverse up right on a good ledge broken by sloping slabs to a small flake belay.

6. 40m Continue the traverse to a vertical dyke; follow this to West Central Gully.

Variation: **Direct Finish   70m   VS 4c** *   *(1964)*

A more logical but harder finish.

4. 35m From the belay at the top of pitch 3, continue directly up the slab instead of traversing right. At 25m, traverse under an overhang and across a wall on its right, crux, to a grass ledge.

5. 35m 4c Continue 5m along the ledge to a dyke, then follow this to a junction with West Central Gully.

1 Mallory's Slab and Groove   200m   Very Difficult *   *(1918)*

A good route finishing at West Central Gully but commonly used to start Trap Face or Central Routes . Start just before reaching the foot of Cioch Gully at a prominent crack immediately right of a large overhang.

1. 25m Climb the superb crack.

2. 25m Climb the exposed slab above that angles rightwards to reach Central Gully.

3. 25m Follow the gully up and left for roughly 25m (depending on where one joins the gully) to a prominent crack going up to the right. The start of this pitch is common with the start of Trap Dyke Route.

4. 25m Climb the crack to a large block, 3m higher an awkward traverse is made left to a perch.

5. 20m Climb a crack on the left then follow the groove above and a difficult corner to belays.

6. 30m A 5m crack leads to a sloping shelf which is traversed right before climbing steeply for 15m until level and left of the huge overhangs. A difficult crack is followed for 10m up and right to gain the easier open section of West Central Gully. Continue by the gully or by the aretes, West Central or Amphitheatre on either side.

COIRE LAGAN

Routes Starting From West Central Gully

**12 Parallel Cracks Route   150m   Very Difficult ** *(1920)*

This route is one of those more easily identified on this area of rock giving an interesting climb. Start at the foot of the tongue of West Central Gully where a steep rib bounds a large slabby depression on the right. Two parallel cracks go up the rib; climb the rib right of the right-hand crack, then step left to join it or climb directly from below at Severe. Follow the line of cracks, which give interesting short pitches. Where the walls above begin to steepen a chimney is gained by bearing distinctly to the right. Easier ground leads to the edge of Western Gully, which provides a scrambling descent route with minor Moderate pitches.

Variation: **60m   Difficult** *(1953)*

A crack further to the right can be climbed in place of pitch 2 to rejoining the original route.

A seemingly bizarre coincidence has led to two routes being climbed and given the same name in close proximity to each other and quite possibly on much of the same ground. The first was climbed four days after King George VI ascended to the throne on May 8th 1937. The second was climbed 16 years later in July 1953 one month after Elizabeth became Queen!

13 Coronation   150m   Severe *(1953)*

Start 20m left of Parallel Cracks at the entrance to West Central Gully. Start by an overhung recess in the upper wall. Climb the recess by the right, then trend left to a layback crack. A long groove now leads more easily up to a patch of grass. Climb an undercut bulge, then a short leftward trend. Turn the formidable wall above by a fine crack on the left; easier than it looks. Climb the next overhang by the wall on the left, crux; this leads to an easier crack to finish.

Coronation Route   **150m   Severe** *(1937)*

"We made what appears to be a new route approximately 25 to 30m to the left of the Parallel Cracks Route on Sròn na Cìche. Some exposed situations. Time forbade fuller description. Suggest name Coronation Route."

14 Engineers' Slant   390m   Very Difficult * *(1931)*

A more interesting and continuous climb than West Central Gully running above and parallel to it. The first part of the climb is the better with Amphitheatre Arete giving the best finish. Start from the foot of West Central Gully and climb this until the gully becomes a crack (50m). Branch to the right, following a line that crosses Median just below the prominent overhanging corners. An easy angled traverse left now leads beneath these corners, which has occasional steep pitches and reaches West Central Arete by a grassy chimney. Continue in the same line, crossing the Arete and West Central Gully to Amphitheatre Arete. Climb this and finish up a shallow chimney which leads to the plateau.

15 Chimney and Crack Climb   300m   VS *(1911)*

A hard variation of Median. At the top it appears to take the left-hand of the fanned corners where Median avoids them. This is reported as about 5a difficulty. Follow West Central Gully for about 75m, 10m beyond the deep chimney where Median crosses. Slabs on the right are climbed to a long vertical cave. Climb the cave by its left wall and continue direct to a deep-cut chimney. Gain a steep sloping ledge and follow it for a few metres until it is possible to traverse back right, past a steep corner to a platform. Above is a long crack. Climb this in two pitches, finishing over a bulge, crux.

16 Zigzag   300m   Difficult *(1911)*

Climb West Central Gully for about 90m then gain a vertical dyke and follow it for 30m, "nearly perpendicular at the top". Climb two chimneys above to a grass platform. Follow two ledge systems, the first to the left, the second to the right. A grassy chimney now leads a long distance left to West Central Arete which is followed to the top.

Routes Starting From Central Gully

17 Central Slabs   90m   Severe   *(1932)*
This route takes a direct line from low in Central Gully to the right side of the huge
overhangs at the elbow of West Central Gully. Start at a grassy patch some 50m up
Central Gully, just above where the gully becomes almost horizontal.
1. 45m Climb steep slabs to a sloping grass stance and belay on A.B. Route below
a small prominent overhang.
2. 15m Turn the loose overhang by a crack and belay just up and left.
3. 30m Follow easier angled slabs to finish in West Central Gully, just under the
crack in the upper overhangs. A variety of routes can now be followed to the top.

8 Trap Face Route   260m   VS *   *(1914)*
The Trap Face routes are possibly the most confusing of all the Western Buttress
routes with numerous variations recorded through the ages. The original route
starts as a chimney and cracks between Central Gully and West Central Gully and
continues by an obvious groove containing the trap that runs up parallel with West
Central Arete. Approach by Central Gully or, better, the first two pitches of Mallory's
Slab and Groove. Start 150m up Central Gully where a well marked chimney leads
up to the right below the line of the West Central Arete. The start is common with
this section of Mallory's route before taking a steeper line to the right.
1. 35m Climb the chimney-crack for 20m then move out right for 5m below a
small nose of rock and10m up a groove to a corner.
2. 25m 4b Climb a series of very steep and awkward cracks directly above (crux).
This pitch is unrelenting and very severe.
3. 30m Where the angle eases above it is possible to make a rightward line across
slabs to reach West Central Gully at a point below and just to the right of the
prominent overhangs.
Descriptions and distances blur above here as the climb becomes slightly easier
and the line more logical.
4. 70m Follow the prominent fault which snakes up the face just to the right of
these overhangs, passing a bridged block halfway, and reaching easier ground at
the rake on Zigzag.
5. 30m The trap depression continues above this then loses itself in a small
amphitheatre of trap rock.
6. 70m From here a variety of lines may be followed, to the summit of the
Western Buttress with any difficult pitches optional.
Variation: **Start   45m   VS 4c** *   *(1950)*
After rounding the corner from Mallory's Slab and Groove, climb a short layback
crack in the corner. Ascend the right wall of the corner, then move diagonally right
to an undercut ledge which is right of a shallow chimney. Climb this and move right
to a difficult shallow groove. At its top, move back left into the corner and climb
to a stance and belay.
   Recommended finishes from the small amphitheatre:
Variation: **Pitch 6   70m   Severe** *
Climb easy slabs up right to gain a very fine 30m left-trending crack. The crack
leads easily back right to a ridge shortly below and right of the summit of Western
Buttress.
Variation: **Pitch 6   70m   Very Difficult** *
Climb directly up a short way, then follow a diagonal fault up and left to a huge
detached flake with a fine crack separating it from the buttress. Finish by the crest
of the West Central Arete, or just right of it.

9 Trap Face Route Direct   300m   VS 4c *   *(1976)*
The name of this route is misleading as it only touches the original route for a few
metres above West Central Gully. There is some seriously steep climbing through
the overhangs above Engineers' Slant. The original description is reproduced here:
Start up Diamond Slab route. Climb the overhang, then follow easier slabs to
Central Gully. Go 5m up the gully, then climb straight up to cracks in the middle of
the slab, belaying 10m below them. Climb the cracks through an overlap and belay

50. SRÒN NA CÌCHE
Amphitheatre Wall & Doom Walls

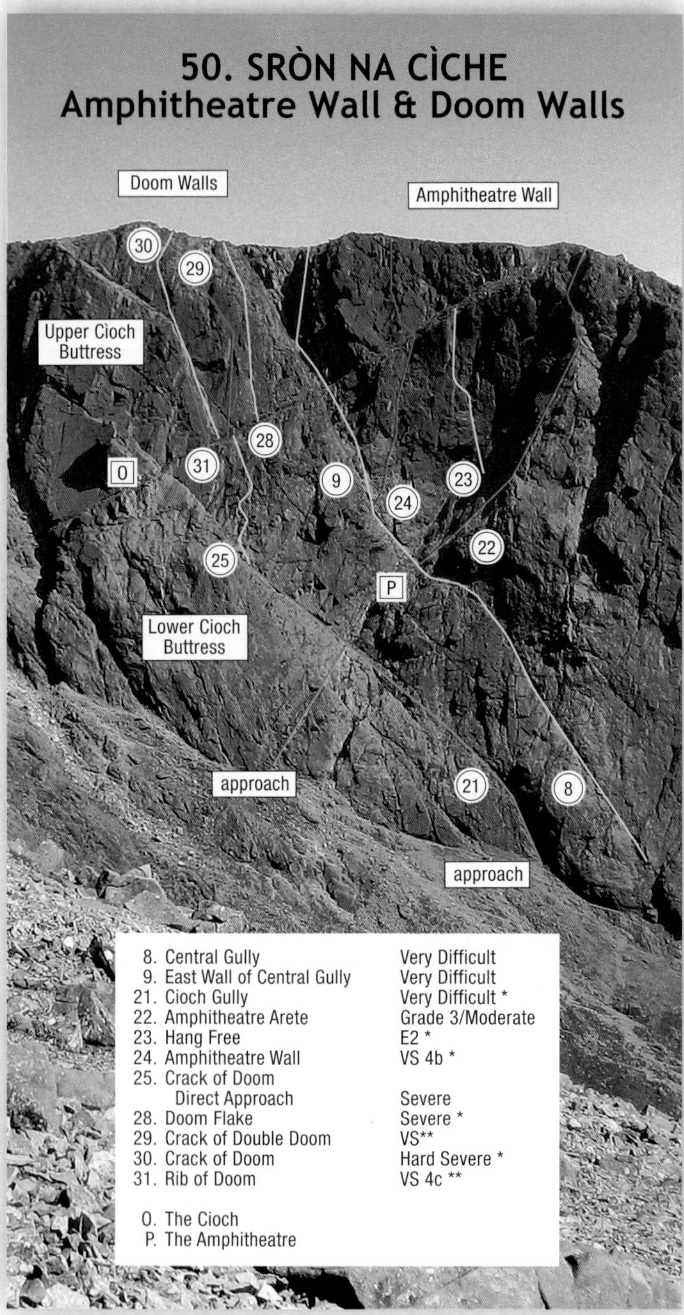

Doom Walls

Amphitheatre Wall

Upper Cioch Buttress

Lower Cioch Buttress

approach

approach

8.	Central Gully	Very Difficult
9.	East Wall of Central Gully	Very Difficult
21.	Cioch Gully	Very Difficult *
22.	Amphitheatre Arete	Grade 3/Moderate
23.	Hang Free	E2 *
24.	Amphitheatre Wall	VS 4b *
25.	Crack of Doom	
	Direct Approach	Severe
28.	Doom Flake	Severe *
29.	Crack of Double Doom	VS**
30.	Crack of Doom	Hard Severe *
31.	Rib of Doom	VS 4c **

O. The Cioch
P. The Amphitheatre

in the basalt dyke 3m above and right. Climb the slab above to a large overhang, then pull onto a glacis under the overhang via the left-hand corner of a brown wall; belay. Turn the overhang by the right-hand of two grooves and 5m up, layback the finger-crack right of the groove to exit from the overhang; belay. The next two pitches take the large overhang above, followed by a chimney, then go up left and belay on top. Continue straight up and follow the dyke to join West Central Arete. Finish up this, or keep to its right.

**0 Central Route   255m   Hard Severe ** *(1957)*

A superb expedition taking the cleaner rock left of Mallory's Slab and Groove then joining Amphitheatre Arete before moving right to finish up the buttress overlooking the top of West Central Gully. The best approach is by the first pitches of Mallory's Slab and Groove (90m). The description starts from below a steep wall just left of where Mallory's Slab and Groove leaves Central Gully.

1. 25m Climb steep broken rock to a sloping platform with a huge hollow block belay. Less worrying is to belay on the smaller ledge above.

2. 35m The next pitch takes a fairly direct upward line, breaking through small bulges whilst being drawn left along sloping gangways. The climbing is never difficult but a good eye is needed to follow the easiest line and to find protection. The walls on the left gradually steepen. Bear right to take a flake belay at the edge of a shallow vertical gully on Mallory's route.

3. 45m Climb steep rock directly above to the base of the left-facing corner. This is followed to an obvious break rightward through the bulge. Easier slabs above lead to a sketchy belay overlooking West Central Gully.

4. 40m Bear leftward across slabs to a steep break through the next overlap. Bear left to belay beneath a steep wall that bounds the right side of Amphitheatre Arete.

5. 30m Surmount the bulge above the belay. A choice of two corners lies above with the left being dry more often. Belay on Amphitheatre Arete.

6. 25m Go easily along the arete. A cairn marks a rightward horizontal traverse to the obvious triangular grass patch below the final tower.

7. 25m A very broken chimney leads to a perched block. More broken rock leads to a belay on the edge of the gully at the right-hand side of the tower.

8. 30m 4b An exposed crux follows. Traverse left on small holds to a break in the overhang above. Climb the break back right and belay on the final blocks of the narrow arete.

Variation: **Direct Finish   25m   E1 5c ** *(2006)*

A wake up call for those who have found their climbing prowess underused to this point. The obvious direct finish appears to originally have been aided. Good protection can be (strenuously) arranged in the main crack-line before a committing sequence up steep rock. Finish more easily above.

50. AMPHITHEATRE WALL & DOOM WALLS

(NG 444 204)   Alt 650m   North-West facing   Maps p98, 124   Diagram p126, 150, 158

This is a complex section of the face. The steep rocks of Amphitheatre Wall are bounded by Amphitheatre Arete on the right and Central Gully on the left. It is split at half-height by the upper most section of the Terrace. The Doom Walls lie between Central Gully and Cioch Gully above the left side of the Amphitheatre. A route on Lower Doom Wall must be used to approach the Terrace before reaching the Doom routes.

Approaches: Gain a small lower bowl of the Amphitheatre by awkward water worn grooves (80m) from the ledge beneath the Cioch Buttress or the lowest section of Cioch Gully. Doom Walls lie up left from here. Climb more smooth grooves to gain the larger bowl below Amphitheatre Wall. This can also be gained by Central Gully.

Descents: Most routes terminate on the shoulder of Sròn na Cìche. Descents from here are described at the start of the chapter.

COIRE LAGAN

21 Cioch Gully   200m   Very Difficult * (1906)

Start immediately left of Mallory's Slab and Groove or by an easier parallel gully line 20m further left (east). Alternatively gain the Amphitheatre by grooves leading in from the foot of Cioch Buttress. Beyond the Amphitheatre, Cioch Gully rises sharply leftward from the bowl. Long sections of easy climbing lead to two final pitches. The first of these involves strenuous backing up through a tunnel formed by a large fallen block, whilst the second is a short sharp layback that finishes on the Shelf behind the Cioch.

Winter: **III ***

Quite a good climb, but the last pitch needs a reasonable build-up.

Amphitheatre Wall

The main wall is criss crossed by cracks and overlaps, becoming very steep as it rises right. Numerous variations were climbed in the era of heavy pegging and descriptions were dismissed as too extensive to warrant recording but this may now change with digital photography allowing more precise recording of individual lines. Routes are described from right to left.

22 Amphitheatre Arete   270m   Grade 3/Moderate ** (1907)

A good route which is mostly a scramble when the slabby rocks are dry. The crux lies shortly before the top of the climb. It gains and then climbs the right arete, 1hr. Cross The Amphitheatre by a choice of exposed lines. Continue up and right across water worn slabs to the nose of the Arete. Follow this for 100m to where it narrows dramatically. A 15m steep wall on the right forms an exposed crux, leading to a small loose bay. Exit with care.

Winter: **III** (1989)

The route was climbed under verglas and powder conditions.

23 Hang Free   90m   E2 * (1980)

This good route lies up and right of Amphitheatre Wall. In the right half of the wall is a line of cracks. Originally, it may have been aid climbed as Prolepsis (200m VS, 1957).

1. 20m 5b Climb the thin crack past an old peg until it is possible to rest on the right.
2. 30m 5b Move up the overhanging crack and a slab to make a hard move left to a nest belay.
3. 20m 5b Reverse the slab, moving right to regain the crack and groove. Jam and bridge up the groove to pull into a niche.
4. 20m 5a Follow the groove to the headwall, climb this using twin cracks and follow easier ground to the Terrace.

24 Amphitheatre Wall   180m   VS 4b * (1932)

A good long route. The key feature is an obvious chimney system rising vertically right of Central Gully. A large rock fall makes the original approach pitches unpleasant. Instead climb Central Gully for 50m before making a 7m rightward traverse to the foot of the route. Follow the embryonic chimneys with three jammed blocks to a belay above. A bridging pitch now leads to a stance (7m). Continue up the easier angled crack to a spike belay (25m) and the Terrace above.

The upper wall starts at a cairn 5m right of the Flake. Gain a large corner and a huge poised block then traverse right to a spike belay. Turn an overhang above to a 5m groove and a stance. Go straight up for 3m then move obliquely up right across a steep rake and so to a stance. Climb the pinnacle on the right then step up to a hand-traverse left which leads to a belay. Continue up left over jammed blocks to the top.

Variation: **Variation finishes**

The Flake (1906) overlooks the right wall of Central Gully, while The Finger (1904) is a superb 20m monolith standing 70m further west. Both have been ascended and continued by the walls behind. The Finger is the oldest climb on the entire face, predating the first ascent of the Cioch by two years.

Crack of Double Doom, VS 4b, Doom Wall. Climber unknown.

Lower Doom Wall

The routes here make the crucial link between the Amphitheatre and the Terrace below Doom Wall (approaching from behind the Cioch by the Girdle Traverse, is more complicated). Routes are described as they are reached ascending Cioch Gully from the Amphitheatre.

5 Crack of Doom Direct Approach   60m   Severe   *(1936)*
Start 10m above a grass terrace in Cioch Gully which leads rightward from below a large chockstone. Climb a square corner to a short slab and hence to a line of holds leading diagonally right to an open V. Climb this by its left side to a small stance and belay by a detached block (20m). Descend again to the foot of the V, climb right around another slab, then go up a steep corner to a narrow ledge (20m). Traverse briefly right from the ledge then ascend a steep shallow groove which joins the lower section of Crack of Doom about 15m below the Terrace.

A far simpler approach to Doom Routes is possible.

26 Quick Doom 45m Severe *

Climb Cioch Gully easily to a point 20m below the large chockstone in the steep, narrow upper section. Two crack-lines split the slabby right wall of the gully before it narrows. Both give good climbing on solid rock at Severe leading to the Terrace directly below Crack of Doom.

27 Vaughan's Rake 40m Severe   *(pre 1965)*

An overhanging wall runs right from the point at which Cioch Gully becomes a chimney. This route takes slabby rocks beneath the wall leading to the base of Rib of Doom.

Doom Wall

Routes are described from right to left, all starting from the Terrace between Central and Cioch Gully.

28 Doom Flake 90m Severe *   *(1947)*

Start 25m up the Terrace from Crack of Doom, where a large fallen flake forms a right-angled corner with the main face. Climb a thin crack in the wall from the left-hand side of the flake, then climb a basalt jigsaw with an awkward mantel into a corner above on the right. Climb the crack above, then a wall above a large flake. Go right over perched blocks and climb a corner to finish.

29 Crack of Double Doom 120m VS 4b **   *(1947)*

This is an excellent classic climb. A clean-cut fault rises right of Crack of Doom. Start immediately right of Crack of Doom and follow the fault to an exposed (to rockfall) belay at 45m. Continue with more difficulty and the crux in the last 10m below the apex of the slab. Above the apex a worrying block should be treated with care. The climbing continues by a right-angled corner running up left to a perched belay. Finish up the corner above and easy scrambling to the plateau.

30 Crack of Doom (The Hanging Chimney) 80m Hard Severe 4b *   *(1918)*

This famous and historic climb is still a test piece of traditional climbing. The actual crack is an insecure thrutch, memorable for its polish. The route can be seen clearly from the corrie as a prominent curving crack leading to a long sloping shelf (the Glacis). Climb the crack easily to a chockstone. Above, the crack steepens and narrows, forming the crux. This is strenuous and can be hard if greasy . It is possible to avoid the crux on the left wall at Severe. The original climb finishes at the foot of the sloping Glacis and is improved greatly by the direct finish.
Variation: **Direct Finish 60m Hard Severe** **   *(1921)*
This is immediately above the Crack of Doom at the right-hand end of the sloping Glacis. Good climbing leads straight up a steep corner, taking the more prominent left fork at half-height, to the plateau. It also makes a very good finish for parties that have climbed Wallwork's Route, Integrity etc.

31 Rib of Doom 75m VS 4c **   *(1949)*

This is the fine rib to the left of Crack of Doom. Traverse towards the rib from Crack of Doom via a subsidiary groove. Follow the rib in a tremendous position to the top.

32 Sternum 80m HVS **   *(1979)*

The route lies on the narrow buttress left of Crack of Doom (climbed in error for Rib of Doom). Start from the terrace at the foot of Rib of Doom.
1. 40m 5a Go up this for 6m, then move out left round an edge and follow a thin crack, at first near the edge but trending increasingly leftwards, to reach a platform under a steep wall.
2. 20m 5b Climb the wall, swing left to gain a dyke and continue to a small niche. Move out right and climb cracks up and right to a ledge.
3. 20m 4b Step right and climb a cracked wall to the glacis. Traverse right to the top of Crack of Doom.

51. CIOCH BUTTRESS

(NG 444 203)   Alt 600m   North-West facing   Maps p98, 124   Diagram p126, 150, 164, 170

Cioch Buttress is the area of rock between Cioch Gully and Eastern Gully. The buttress sees more traffic than the rest of the Cuillin crags combined and rocks dislodged by other parties can be a hazard. A classic day includes a route on each section, but is often curtailed because of the number of pitches and relative ease of escape.

The buttress is divided distinctly into three tiers. Two major horizontal breaks separate the Lower, Middle (Cioch and the Cioch Slab) and Upper Buttresses with route descriptions listed in this order. The lower break is The Terrace. The higher break running above the Cioch Slab is referred to as The Shelf and is a continuation of the Cioch Gully fault. The Neck is a polished rib that links the Cioch to the main face. A less pronounced sloping ledge, the Glacis, runs across the top of the Upper Buttress below the Final Tier.

Lower Cioch Buttress

This is the longest and most complex of the three tiers. Time consumed here frequently prevents parties from tackling routes higher on the face. Routes are described from right to left.

Descent: Most routes end on the Terrace which is easily descended eastward beneath Cioch Slab and across Eastern Gully. Escape from the upper reaches by abseil is complex and continuing to the Terrace by the simplest route is recommended if caught out by bad weather.

The first three routes lie above the Amphitheatre on the left wall of Cioch Gully. Approach up awkward water worn grooves and slabs immediately right of the toe of Cioch Buttress. Routes are described as they are reached ascending from the Amphitheatre.

West Ridge of the Cioch   140m   Severe *   (1924)
This climb practically keeps to the crest of the West Ridge. It is formed into three well defined sections the last of which is the Cioch Nose route. Start by an easy horizontal traverse from the base of Cioch Gully. The lowest section is easy for two-thirds of the way. There are then two mantelshelf problems, the upper being difficult. Above this a subsidiary branch of Cioch Gully coming up from the right is reached. A 5m vertical pitch above this gives access to an easy slab which leads to the Terrace. The Cioch Nose route takes the obvious corner above.

Banana   40m   Hard Severe 4b   (1992)
This pitch takes a line on the wall right of the second pitch on the West Ridge route. From the Amphitheatre scramble halfway up the gully until a small subsidiary gully appears on the left. Follow this gully to the foot of a short steep corner above a chockstone (80m).The corner contains two cracks; climb the one on the left awkwardly to the top of the corner. Trend right around a bulge, then follow a rising traverse across a slab to a corner. Continue rightwards around this corner to a second slab which leads to the Terrace.

Slanting Crack of Cioch Gully   55m   VS   (1989)
Not to be confused with Slanting Crack on the Cioch itself. This route starts beyond the subsidiary gully and finishes at the Neck behind the Cioch.
1. 40m Climb the wall on good holds to a rightward slanting crack. Follow this to its end, then up the wall to an overhanging corner-crack. Climb this, then scramble up to a good ledge (the Terrace) on the right-hand side.
2. 15m Climb a short steep wall above the ledge. Scrambling now leads to where a chimney from Cioch Gully is met behind the Neck connecting the Cioch to the face.

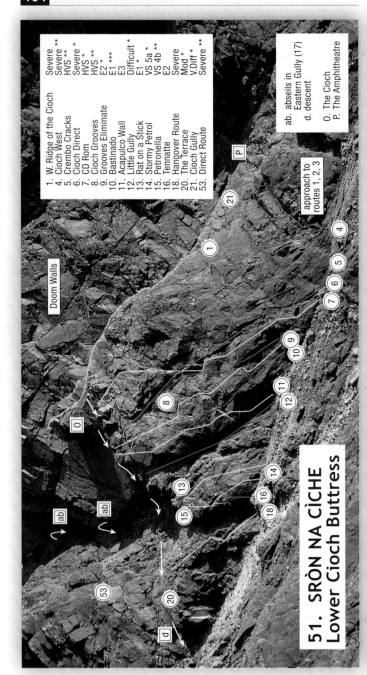

1. W. Ridge of the Cioch — Severe
4. Cioch West — Severe **
5. Crembo Cracks — HVS *
6. Cioch Direct — Severe *
7. CD Rom — HVS *
8. Cioch Grooves — HVS **
9. Grooves Eliminate — E2 *
10. Bastinado — E1 ***
11. Acapulco Wall — E3
12. Little Gully — Difficult *
13. Rat on a Stick — E1 *
14. Stormy Petrol — VS 5a *
15. Petronella — VS 4b **
16. Tennatte — E2
18. Hangover Route — Severe
20. The Terrace — Mod *
21. Cioch Gully — V.Diff *
53. Direct Route — Severe **

ab. abseils in Eastern Gully (17)
d. descent

O. The Cioch
P. The Amphitheatre

approach to routes 1, 2, 3

Doom Walls

51. SRÒN NA CÌCHE
Lower Cioch Buttress

The next routes start from the wide grassy terrace at the lowest point of Cioch Buttress.

4 Cioch West   215m   Severe ** (1919)

A fine climb giving constantly interesting climbing with a splendidly exposed crux. Start at the right end of the Terrace where cracks rise left to a notched chimney.

1. 50m Climb polished grooves into the strenuous chimney. Above, easier grooves lead to a sloping ledge on the left with a medium sized spike belay.

2. 35m The easy grooves continue to a recess below an off-width crack which is often climbed by mistake. Instead pull right and climb up right across a steep slab on polished incut holds to reach a crevasse. Easy rocks lead 10m right to the start of a grassy ledge.

3. 25m In the wall above a break heads diagonally right on good rock as far as an open groove which is reached before the right edge of the buttress.

4. 15m The open groove leads up left to the crux. A hand-traverse up and then left above a huge void, gains a narrow ledge. Memorable!

5. 25m The steep wall above is best climbed by a small corner immediately above the ledge giving the best climbing to reach easy ground and a block belay above. The original route traverses left along the ledge for 7m passing an old peg before breaking onto the easy slab above. This slab heads back right to the block belay. Beware of rope drag.

6. 30m Climb easier rocks to the west end of a large crevassed ledge that runs parallel to the Terrace. The subsidiary gully from Cioch Gully joins from the right.

7. 35m Climb the small vertical wall above the subsidiary gully on polished holds and continue to the Terrace, as for the middle tier of West Ridge route.

Variation: **Pitches 3 & 4   35m   Hard Severe 4b** (1951)

Gain the diagonal break and follow this for 8m. Climb a prominent crack in the steep wall above to meet the left end of the hand-traverse pitch.

Variation: **Pitch 7**

An easier finish is to walk 20m along the ledge to a spike belay below a broad shallow recess. Climb the recess over large slabby boulders to reach a short corner leading to the Terrace.

5 Crembo Cracks   190m   HVS ** (1958)

A superb but serious climb easily identified by a pair of cracks at the base.

1. 40m Either climb the right-hand crack (which has an inverted V 10m from the base) and follow the dyke up left to a ledge (4b) or, far better, climb the left-hand jamming crack to step up left on a nose and follow a slabby corner past flakes to the same ledge (4c).

2. 35m Continue up a very pleasant chimney and cracks to the base of a steeper slab. Traverse right to a ledge and climb the steep corner-crack (the off-width crack mentioned in Cioch West). Traverse cracked slabs right for 10m then ascend easily to the foot of an undercut square corner at the base of the steep wall. Belay beside a large loose flake.

3. 40m 5a The route attacks the unlikely wall above, often identified by signs of retreat. The corner is undercut by loose rock that can be avoided. Gain the corner and solid rock with some relief. Pull out left onto a slabby wall then climb steadily to the steepening groove above. The climbing now involves a series of poorly protected steps passing an old peg (crux) to a large but broken spike runner. Climb the bulge above by undercut flakes, taking care with a cuddly jug above. Step up right to a fine ledge on Cioch West. A serious pitch with numerous options for protection but few are above suspicion.

4. and 5. etc 75m Continue much more easily by Cioch West to the Terrace.

6 Cioch Direct   150m   Severe * (1907)

This classic line has a number of areas of unstable rock that must be treated with extreme caution. It follows the obvious main fault splitting the Lower Buttress starting at the bottom left edge of the face.

1. 25m Climb the open chimney-gully which is often damp in the back.

2. 40m Follow a long easy groove then two chimneys to a large sloping ledge at the base of an overhanging chimney. Try to avoid belaying immediately below.

3. 20m Loose rock at the start of this pitch requires care. The tight chimney gives an awkward crux which is best climbed without a rucsac. Continue up the cracks above until just below a small overhung nose.

4. 35m Follow a sloping shelf up and left passing a jumble of boulders (care; the protruding Yardarm fell off in 2000) and a slab to twin cracks.

5. 30m Climb the twin cracks then easy climbing to the Terrace.

Winter: **150m V**   *(1974)*

A remarkable feat achieved on the shortest day of the year with the benefit of only one ice axe. Few details have emerged but this was certainly very serious mixed climbing way ahead of its time.

7 CD ROM 160m . VS/HVS *   *(2002)*

An eliminate line, some of which has been climbed before. Start at the stone shelter left of Cioch Direct.

1. 20m 4b Step on to a rib and climb through an overlap by a crack on the left. Follow the edge to a large ledge.

2. 40m 4b Follow cracks up the rib and slabs to belay in Cioch Direct.

3. 30m 4b Follow Cioch Direct for a few metres and go left to climb the corner-crack of Cioch Grooves until it is possible to break back right across Cioch Direct to a bay right of a steep prow.

4. 25m 5a/4b Either climb the scoop and pull left on to the rib (HVS) or go left up the ramp on to the top of blocks and up the rib to slabs (easier).

5. 45m 4a Follow slabs straight up to the base of The Cioch.

8 Cioch Grooves 150m HVS **   *(1951)*

A superb climb, varied and exciting, the only drawback being the possible escapes into Cioch Direct. A prominent crack lies parallel to Cioch Direct. Left of Cioch Direct a grass ledge runs rightwards onto the buttress. Start at the right end of this at a crack near the corner.

1. 30m 4c Climb the crack to where it steepens, then step left to a parallel crack which is followed to easier slabs. Traverse right to belay near the crux chimney of Cioch Direct.

2. 25m 5a Traverse back left below a steep wall and go up this on the left to a block. A thin traverse right, crux, enables a delicate step onto the slab above. Belay below a fine crack which lies immediately left of Cioch Direct.

3. 25m 4b Climb the crack to easier slabs and belays.

4. and 5. 70m Continue up the left-hand crack, then follow easier slabs to the Terrace.

Variation: **Pitch 2   E1 5a**

An alternative to the crux pitch is to continue straight up from the step onto the slab and climb this via a mental mantel which leads to the top of the fine crack.

9 Grooves Eliminate 125m E2 *   *(pre 1966)*

This route takes a direct line between Cioch Grooves and Bastinado. Originally VS with aid and renamed The Nipple (1977). Start at a thin crack 6m left of Cioch Grooves.

1. 45m 5b Follow the crack, avoiding a steepening on the left, to reach easier angled slabby rock.

2. 35m 5c Move up diagonally left past an ancient peg runner towards a prominent groove with a smooth left wall. Step across the top of the groove to enter a deeper groove which leads to a stance on the left.

3. 45m Follow the slab between Cioch Grooves and Bastinado to the Terrace.

10 Bastinado 115m E1 ***   *(1956)*

A good, well protected climb needing a positive approach. Start 8m right of Little Gully.

1. 35m 4c Ascend to an obvious crack, which slopes slightly left, then climb it to a broad grassy ledge.

2. 10m 5b Climb the corner direct, then trend left to a sloping ledge.

3. 10m 5c Step left to below a groove which overhangs at its lower end. Climb this strenuously until good holds allow a move right to a triangular corner and belay.

4. 35m 4b Climb a crack immediately behind the corner to a small rock ledge.

5. 25m Continue up a crack to the Terrace.

Variation: **Pitch 3 10m E1 5b ***   *(1983)*

Climb a groove and jam crack right of the normal crux; a good alternative.

Acapulco Wall 110m E3 *   *(1980)*

This serious route takes a direct line up the buttress 6m left of Bastinado. Start just right of Little Gully.

1. 25m 5b Climb a ramp and a short wall to a ledge. Gain and climb a short steep crack to the large block belay of Bastinado.

2. 35m 5c Climb awkwardly left until it is possible to pull right into a very thin crack. Climb this and a bulge to a small ledge 5m left of the crux of Bastinado. Continue up the wall above to a niche with an overhang, then climb this to a tiny spike runner. Trend up right and go up a wide crack to block belays.

3. 50m 4b Climb slabs and cracks to ledges and the Terrace.

Little Gully 70m Difficult *   *(1908)*

This is the small but worthwhile gully to the west of Eastern Gully. Care should be taken with occasional loose rock. Easily follow either of the two branches until they converge below a cave. Climb this by backing up and out through a window above the entrance. The next pitch can be climbed direct or turned on the left. Above, the climb deteriorates into a groove, so traverse left onto the face where scrambling leads to the Terrace.

Winter: **III/IV**   *(1970)*

A good low-level route requiring cold conditions. Steep ice bosses lead to the easy entrance of a cave chockstone. Exit from this via a funnel, sometimes awkward. Above this, snow with short ice walls lead to the Terrace.

Rat on a Stick 50m E1 *   *(2002)*

1. 20m 5b Climb the crack just right of Stormy Petrel until near its top, then step delicately right and go boldly up to the big diagonal crack which is followed to below a steep wall.

2. 30m 5b Move a short way right and climb a tricky corner up the steep wall, then go easily to the top.

Stormy Petrel 50m VS 5a *   *(1985)*

Climb the crack right of Petronella, move left as the crack fades and climb to a stance. Continue direct to the top.

Petronella 55m VS 4b **   *(1952)*

This fine little climb is on the small buttress between Eastern Gully and Little Gully. From the screes, climb an awkward prominent crack which curves leftwards up the centre of the buttress. The overhangs above are turned by a shelf followed by an airy pull up.

Tennatte 40m E2   *(1990)*

Start 10m up the left wall of Petronella and follow a steep layback crack to an obvious down-sloping spike. Use this to gain holds on the right, then climb straight up to the in-situ thread on Petronella.

Two routes **Protect and Survive** (E2 5b 1990) and **Hindsight** (E1 5c 1990) are recorded on a slabby crag identified in the description as having MMS scratched on the rock. The only other clue gleaned is that they lie well down from Petronella.

Eastern Gully 250m Hard Severe   *(1938)*

Not a recommended route but details of the difficulties are significant for parties

COIRE LAGAN

Stormy Petrel, VS, Lower Cioch Buttress. Climber Alex Wheeldon

using the gully to approach or retreat. Three climbing pitches are separated by long sections of loose easy terrain. A waterfall is usually running down the first pitch where it reaches the Sgumain Stone Shoot. Avoid this on descent by traversing east along the Terrace (route 20). East Wall Route takes cleaner rock on the left wall giving a more recommended ascent route.

The Cave Pitch is formed by an enormous wedged boulder completely blocking the gully about 70m above the line of the Terrace. The left wall gives an awkward pitch to turn the blockage but Collie's Route on the Cioch Slab is a better climbing bypass. The final obstacle is another wedged boulder just above the level where the Shelf leads off right to the Cioch. A tight squeeze through a narrow window gives a memorable passage to the upper reaches. The right fork higher in the gully is slightly easier. In descent the top two pitches are passed with 20m abseils before traversing off east along the Terrace.

Winter: **150m   V**   *(2005)*
The lower two pitches of the gully were climbed with some aid necessary.

The next two routes start immediately left of Eastern Gully. They are technically on Eastern Buttress but are listed here to avoid confusion.

18 Hangover Route   60m   Severe   *(1947)*
Start at a corner 10m left of Eastern Gully. Climb easily trending left towards a ledge below a scooped slab. Traverse right into a short chimney like groove with a loose overhanging chockstone. Move up right to easy ground and the Terrace.

19 East Wall Route   270m   Severe *   *(1947)*
The first pitches give a good start to routes above the Terrace. Above here the route appears to stay east of Direct Route and cross it not far beneath the crux wall.
Start as for Hangover to the scooped slab. Traverse left across the slab and trend left across an open corner. Cross slabs to a good ledge. Continue easily up a gully going left to the Terrace.

Cross this, then climb diagonally up left across a slab to an overhung ledge. From here, an awkward left traverse leads to a small stance. Continue the difficult left traverse below the overhang (near scree), then go up the edge of a groove left by a decaying basalt dyke. Climb the dyke and over a slab used on the Girdle Traverse, then move left and up a prominent fault going round the corner of the amphitheatre then steeply up a crack to an airy perch. Struggle up and left over perched blocks to reach Orient Wall on the left. From below a thin flake, traverse up right to a steep crack in the wall left of a large rough, low angle slab, then follow a crack on the right to a good stance. Step left to split blocks and traverse up right to a good ledge. Step up right to a shelf to finish above. This last pitch is just right of the final wall on Direct Route.

The next route is the prominent left to right fault that gives the quickest and easiest access (and egress) to the base of the Cioch Slab. The Continuation Finish is rudely broken by Cioch Gully and Central Gully before reaching the shoulder of Sròn na Ciche above Amphitheatre Arete. Start 100m beyond the foot of Eastern Gully.

0 The Terrace (to Cioch Slab)   150m   Moderate * *(1906)*
Start on rock shattered by the 1997 rockfall where huge boulders abut the toe of Eastern Buttress. Polished rocks lead up and right to a broad section. After 25m the Terrace narrows alarmingly. Polished basalt leads around two noses of rock above steep ground before the fault broadens into Eastern Gully. These moves can be avoided by descending for 25m to the bed of Eastern Gully and a scrambling re-ascent. Gaining the Terrace below the Cioch Slab from Eastern Gully is, again, basalt, delicate and usually wet.
Variation: **Continuation Finish   500m   Very Difficult**
The continuation of the route is hard 20m after crossing Cioch Gully and a very exposed hand-traverse is needed to exit Central Gully.

Cioch Slab & The Cioch

This massive slab steepens at the top, is pockmarked with weathered augite crystals and is composed of the finest gabbro available. At its west end lies one of the Cuillin's most famous landmarks, the Cioch. It rests somewhat implausibly on the slab, cracked around the base, but is presumably very stable. It is a superb viewpoint and should be visited by every climber in the area. The traditional ascent is described in full by the original Collie's Route but direct approaches to the Neck are more commonly used. The Cioch is also a playground for short but hard technical test pieces. Approach by the Terrace as described above.

Descents: Descending from the Cioch is not a simple affair. Slither down the chimney and return to the Neck where there are usually plenty of old threaded slings. Abseiling from these is common but cramped and awkward to set up. It is better to continue climbing up the broadening Neck to the grass patch below Trophy Crack. Gain the Shelf and follow it across into Eastern Gully. Scramble down the gully bed for 50m until an abseil (20m) is needed to pass the Cave Pitch. Large blocks are often adorned with slings on either side of the gully. Escape is then by the Terrace some 70m below. Continuing up by Eastern Gully, (route 17), is often used by parties aiming to do the full round of Coire Lagan. A notoriously narrow squeeze lies 20m above the end of the Shelf and is highly entertaining.

Cioch Slab

Climbers with high levels of confidence in the friction will find this fantastic slab of rock can be climbed by virtually any line and variations are not now recorded. Routes are described from left to right.

1 Collie's Route   200m   Moderate ** *(1906)*
This historic route gives easy climbing but modern climbers usually opt for more

COIRE LAGAN

51. SRÒN NA CÌCHE - The Cioch
& Upper Cioch Buttress

46.	Left Edge Route	Severe
47.	Temerity	E4 **
48.	Slabby Wall Crack	VS
50.	Box–King Route	VS 4c *
51.	Ajax	HS 4b
52.	Yanks	Severe *
53.	Direct Route	Severe **

20.	The Terrace	Mod *
21.	Collie´s Route	Mod **
22.	Arrow Route	Diff ***
23.	Slab Corner	Diff *
27.	Overhanging Crack	E2 5c *
28.	The Highlander	E6 6b **
29.	Erotica	E3 6b **
30.	The Prize	E2 5c *
32.	Cioch Nose	V.Diff **
35.	Archer Thomson's Rte	V.Diff **
36.	Wallwork's Route	V.Diff ***
38.	Krugerrand	E3 *
39.	Trophy Crack	E1 ***
40.	Integrity	VS ****
41.	Atropos	E1**
42.	Vanity	E2
44.	Piety	VS **

ab. abseil
d. descent

Arrow Route, Difficult, Cioch Slab. Climbers unknown

direct ways to approach the Cioch. Start 15m down and left of Slab Corner. Gain a line of deep cracks that follow the left edge and follow these for 50m to ledges. Easy blocks now continue up and across into Eastern Gully which is ascended to the Shelf, a horizontal fault which runs across the top of the Cioch Slab. Traverse this easily to reach a large grassy ledge before descending to the Cioch itself by a highly polished arete, the Neck. Climb to the top either by a bold step across the nape of the Neck or by a more secure chimney 3m left (west). Descend by the same route. A recommended but bold Very Difficult variation (1911) breaks right up a recessed chimney then climbs steep blank slabs up right instead of entering Eastern Gully. It is one of the pitches on the Girdle Traverse.

2 Arrow Route   60m   Difficult *** (1944)

Justifiably the most popular route on the slab. Camming devices now offer protection but the route still requires a confident lead.

Cioch Nose, Very Difficult, The Cioch. Climbers unknown

From the base of Slab Corner easily follow the diagonal crack left across the slab for 25m to belay in a triangular recess on good nuts. Climb directly upward with minor deviations to place protection in slanting faults. Aim for the left end of the Neck above, directly below Trophy Crack. There are more direct and harder lines nearer Slab Corner which also capture the bold flavour of this magnificent slab.

23 Slab Corner 50m Difficult * (1921)
This is the big polished corner to the left of the Cioch. Possible belay at 25m. From the Neck either step boldly straight onto the Cioch or traverse 3m left and ascend the more secure chimney.

The Cioch

This unique rock feature deserves all of the climbing attention it has received because of its audacious position and the obvious challenge to surmount it. Routes are described from left to right beginning with routes starting out of Slab Corner. The Terrace continues right below the Cioch with one awkward move to reach an open bay. The western nose of the Cioch lies to the right beyond which the Terrace continues and narrows to Cioch Gully where it ends abruptly.

24 Slanting Crack (Cioch) 20m Severe * (1954)
Girdles the Cioch in a stunning position. Follow Slab Corner to 6m below the Neck, belay. Gain the slanting crack in the wall of the Cioch via jammed flakes. Hand-traverse diagonally up right to a platform, then follow an easy crack to the top; often greasy.

25 Oxytocin 20m E2 5c * (1987)
Follow the traverse of Slanting Crack for 10m to beneath an obvious jam crack splitting the overhang. Layback this to gain the upper slab and top of the Cioch. A strenuous route in a fine position.

6 The Gathering   30m   E8 6b ** ★★   *(2004)*

A spectacular but very serious line climbing the dark underside of the Cioch. The line follows a faint seam leading to an obvious spike in the middle of the wall. Belay on large friends halfway up Slab Corner, at the base of the seam. Hard technical moves lead to a good crimp. Follow the seam for a few moves then break out right on pock marks with a tenuous sequence leading to good edges and the spike (good rest and first protection). Continue rightwards past a diagonal crack to gain the easy upper slabs.

7 Overhanging Crack   35m   E2 5c ** ★★   *(1978)*

Follow Slab Corner for 25m then traverse easily right to the foot of the obvious over-hanging crack. Climb it with difficulty, past a hollow flake at 5m, to finally finish by open slabs. High in the grade.

The next routes start from the Terrace.

8 The Highlander   35m   E6 6b ** ★★   *(1989)*

A stunning pitch up the frontal arete of the Cioch. Climb easily up slabs to the arete. Climb boldly up the right side of the arete to an obvious hole (runners in the flake to the right). Continue via a thin diagonal crack to a resting ledge (crucial Friend runners). Move up to a large flat hold on the arete (poor micro nuts) and

The Gathering, E8 6b, The Cioch. Climber Dave Macleod

attempt to stand on it. A tricky mantelshelf gains the upper slabs and easy ground; belay on top of the Cioch.

29 Erotica   35m   E3 6b ＊＊   *(1983)*
Climbs the obvious thin crack-line 5m right of The Highlander.
Start up easy slabs then climb the crack with a rest out left on a ledge. A hard but well protected crux follows. Finish by easy slabs.

30 The Prize   35m   E2 5c ＊＊   *(2003)*
Located at the right end of the frontal face is an obvious right angled corner. Climb the easy angled slab from the Terrace to gain the corner. Climb the crack making use of a small stance on the left arête at half height then continue more easily to gain the upper section of Cioch Nose.

31 Lowlander   35m   E2 5c ＊   *(2005)*
Takes the wall right of The Prize and left of Cioch Nose by a faint crack-line. Climb the faint crack-line to a slab. Follow the crack left below an overlap on the slab. Join and finish up Cioch Nose.

32 Cioch Nose   45m   Very Difficult ＊＊   *(1907)*
An airy climb up the western edge of the Cioch. Start from the right end of the Terrace, beyond the delicate foot traverse. Climb a groove to a belay in a corner (20m). Traverse left and pull onto the slab and crack above. Follow this for 10m before pulling up right. A choice of lines gain and climb the easy knife edge to the top. A superb little climb, but nasty in the wet.

33 South-West Face   50m   Moderate ＊
The easiest route to the top of the Cioch avoids any queues but still leaves the complexities of descent. Make a delicate foot traverse to the point at which the Terrace turns abruptly towards Cioch Gully.
Start at the slab that forms the western nose of the Cioch.
1. 20m   Rise leftward to a recess then climb right by a sharp edged crack. Step down and right to belay below a prominent slanting crack on the west face.
2. 40m   Gain the crack (crux) and follow this to the ledge immediately below the final chimney which leads to the top.
Variation: **Hard Severe   50m**
A highly recommended line starts similarly before taking exposed slabs on the right to directly gain the knife-edge at the top of the Cioch Nose.

Upper Cioch Buttress

This high quality wall of rock has, for the Cuillin, an unusually large number of straight and obvious lines. Approach by any of the Cioch Slab routes. The routes are described from right to left starting at the grass patch where the Shelf first becomes enclosed.

Descent: All routes finish on the Glacis. Follow this left or climb a route on the Final Tier to reach the shoulder of Sròn na Ciche. Descents from here are described in the general introduction to Sròn na Ciche, (before Western Buttress [49]).

34 Fidelity   70m   VS 4c   *(1970)*
This climb takes an obvious line starting 6m right of the Wallwork's Route. Climb the large crack behind a big loose block, surmount a bulge directly (crux) at 15m and belay at a small block on the right-sloping ramp of Archer Thomson's Route. Climb up and left to a loose block, turning the overhang on the left, and follow the crack to finish at the bottom of the glacis.

35 Archer Thomson's Route   55m   Very Difficult ＊＊   *(1911)*
Start on the grassy patch behind the Cioch. Scramble right easily to a prominent basalt dyke forming a narrow ledge with a small nut belay.

Trophy Crack, E1, Upper Cioch Buttress. Climber Jonny Baird

1. 25m Climb up and right over well worn blocks until below a roof (15m). Take the obvious right-slanting gangway to belay below an imposing corner.
2. 30m The crux moves up the steep corner are well protected by a large hex. Continue out right to a steep wall overlooking the Crack of Doom. Climb this to the Glacis and a large flat block belay.

Wallwork's Route   50m   Very Difficult *** (1915)

A superb route on rough rock that can be climbed in one pitch with careful rope work. Start as for Archer Thompson's Route from the basalt dyke. Climb up and right over well worn blocks until below a roof. Traverse left for 5m beneath the blocky roof then surmount it to gain a small overhung recess and good belay (25m). The overhanging crack is avoided by a step round right into a right-angled corner. The corner is tricky but well protected and leads to a stance and possible belay (10m). Follow a wide crack through a slab and outflank a roof by a traverse

right to a ledge and small nut belay (15m).
Variation: **Faux Pas   90m   VS**   *(1978)*
Continue the traverse left beneath the roof across the line of Trophy Crack to reach Integrity which is followed to the Glacis.

37 Ghost Riders   85m   E2 *   *(1981)*
This line is directly behind the Cioch on the wall left of Wallwork's Route. Follow an arching dyke until an obvious hold can be used to surmount the overlap. Gain a ledge by a long reach and follow the wall up left for 10m to ledges, which lead back right to a jammed block recess beneath an overhang (5b). Gain the pinnacle up on the right and surmount the overhang slightly right of this. Continue to a sloping ledge, then move right around a corner. Follow the arete directly to the Glacis (5b).

38 Krugerrand   80m   E3 *   *(1980)*
This climb sports a difficult but well protected crux. Start 5m right of Trophy Crack.
1. 25m 6a Climb the slab to a large roof and surmount this using finger jams. Climb the crack above, crux, to a hanging stance.
2. 25m 5a Go up slightly left and over the next roof, then traverse back right to a crack and follow it to the Trophy Crack belay.
3. 30m Climb the slab parallel to Trophy Crack and cross the roof by a small ledge. Finish straight up the slab above.
Variation: **The Venus Transit   55m   E3 5c ***   *(2006)*
The hanging belay at the end of Pitch 1 was gained by a traverse from Wallwork's Route.
Climb the huge roof flake (crux) and then rock over on good holds onto the slab to a small stance (10m). Follow the wide crack above and finish by smaller cracks, zigzagging to the top.

39 Trophy Crack   80m   E1 ***   *(1956)*
This well protected classic takes the fine straight crack directly above the grass patch.
1. 40m 5b Go over the initial steepness, then follow a groove and a short overhang. A layback above is followed by the crux and a step left to a good ledge and belays.
2. 40m 4b Climb the much easier crack above. Step left through a narrow sentry box and climb the slab or, popular, climb the big overlap direct (5a). Step back right to the main crack, which widens before finishing on the glacis.

40 Integrity   75m   VS ****   *(1949)*
A magnificent classic that breaks through intimidating overlaps by an arrow straight line. Climb up inside the fault beside the grass patch to gain the start of the Shelf. Start immediately above here.
1. 45m 4b Climb the right-hand of two steep chimneys (left-hand variation slightly harder) to beneath the first overlap at 5m. Surmount this on good rough holds to arrive on the slab above. Continue up the crack in a superb position, passing a large roof on the left to reach a little block overhang. Strenuous moves lead to a welcome overhung niche with thread belay.
2. 30m 4c Continue in the same line which remains steep to the top. An inferior variation at 15m sidesteps right then back left or gains easier terrain at the top of Trophy Crack.
Variation: **15m   Severe**   *(1962)*
Where the crack-line of pitch 1 enters a corner and is then blocked by an overhang pull out left on to a triangular ledge on the left arete and climb to the normal stance. Similar in standard to the normal route.

41 Atropos   100m   E1 **   *(1978)*
A good route but with some loose rock.
Start 20m left of Integrity at the left side of the prominent damp streak. Climb a steep wall onto a slab. Go up this, trending slightly left before making a diagonal traverse up right across a slab to belay below an overhang (5b). Climb the over-

Direct Route, Severe, Eastern Buttress, West Wall. Climber Michael Johnston

hang on the left, then go up to a belay below roofs (4b). Traverse left and up through the overhangs (loose blocks), then move up right to a belay (5a). Finish straight up.

2 Vanity   90m   E2   (1980)
Start at the overhanging sentry-box just right of Depravity.
1. 20m 4c Climb rightwards round the sentry box and go up into a corner. Belay on a small stance.
2. 35m 5b Climb the corner, and halfway up it move left onto the upper slab. Climb this to below overhangs, then climb the double overlap above, move right and go straight up to belays.
3. 35m 4a Finish directly above.

3 Depravity   90m   VS 4c *   (1958)
Start about 10m right of Left Edge and just left of an overhanging sentry box. An awkward start leads left to an overhang with a tiny stance just above (4c). Climb a rib on the right for a short distance, then cross a groove on the left and climb to a platform and belay (4b). Continue to the top, keeping slightly to the right of Left Edge. Hard for the grade.

44 Piety   90m   VS ** (1985)
Climb an inviting corner between Left Edge and Depravity to its top, then move left to Depravity's belay (4c). Go back right to a hanging arete and climb this and slabs to the Glacis (4b).

45 Desire   100m   Severe (1963)
A recently unearthed route with this original description being the only information available. Start in shallow gully near Left Edge Route.
Climb the right side of the gully 40m, belay. Go up a short distance to a ledge; traverse this to the right, round an easy corner just beyond which a steep slab is climbed direct to a tiny recess. At 30m move left a little to a flake belay. Climb the rib for 2m where the gully forks then traverse left (crux) over loose rocks into the left fork, then straight up to the top at 30m.

46 Left Edge Route   75m   Severe (1937)
This route starts in the innermost corner of the deep recess on the left extension of the Shelf, left of the face of the buttress. The recess is well seen from below. Ascend the recess to a belay (20m). Traverse up and right to the buttress edge to belays. From there, climb directly up the edge to the Glacis.

47 Temerity   90m   E4 ** (2008)
The spectacular square-cut arete at the left end of the buttress. Start right of the arete in the deep recess of Left Edge Route.
1. 20m 6a Climb up via some large blocks until able to pull leftwards into a scoop. From the top of the scoop make a long move left, then continue hand-traversing to a sloping ledge on the arete and an awkward belay below an ancient retreat peg. Keep a Friend half for the belay.
2. 35m 5c Step left and climb the left wall via a bold section until able to move right to the arete. Follow the arete more or less directly to the top. A finely positioned pitch.
3. 35m Easy to the top.

48 Slabby Wall Crack   80m   VS (1994)
This quite good but slow drying route climbs the true left wall of Temerity, just above the exit of the Shelf from the Cioch. The wall is bounded on the left by a corner.
1. 5m 4c Pull through the initial bulge and belay at the foot of the corner.
2. 50m 5a Move up the corner until it is possible to step right into the obvious crack which splits the wall, then climb the crack to its top; less deceptive than it appears.
3. 25m Climb a short crack to easier ground.

49 Pearly Gates   170m   VS (1964)
This is the girdle traverse of Cioch Upper Buttress that has some good climbing in fine positions. Start 10m along the Shelf from Eastern Gully and 5m left of Left Edge Route.
1. 30m Traverse right and cross a diedre to a ledge and peg belay.
2. 20m 4c Continue 10m right, with some difficulty, then pull over the overlap before descending to a ledge.
3. 40m 4c Traverse right to a large slab and make an ascending traverse across the slab to belay on Integrity.
4. 30m 4b Move right across Trophy Crack to belay on Wallwork's Route.
5. 30m Move across and up Archer Thomson's Route to belay in the niche.
6. 20m 4c Finish by going right and continuing up the Rib of Doom.

Final Tier

The Glacis runs easily off to the left. Instead, one final pitch from the following options can be used to end a classic day. **The Direct Finish to Crack of Doom** (40m HS **) is a good climb that starts from the lowest point of the Glacis. Routes are described from right to left.

● **Box-King Route   30m   VS 4c *** (2005)
Climb parallel cracks above the overhang 5m right of Ajax.

◀ **Ajax   30m   Hard Severe 4b**
Climb the crack on the right side of the block directly above Integrity. Beware of an alarmingly loose rock in the upper section.

2 Yanks   40m   Severe * (2009)
Start on the left side of the block directly above Integrity and finish at the highest point of the tier. Step right to gain a short steep crack that leads to an open groove. Follow this to the foot of a straight jamming crack. Climb this until forced left to avoid a large bulge.

52. EASTERN BUTTRESS

(NG 445 204)   Alt 675m   Maps p98, 124   Diagrams p126, 135, 150, 180, 183, 186

Eastern Buttress is bounded on the left by the Sgumain Stone Shoot and on the right by Eastern Gully giving two distinct faces separated by the nose of Direct Route. The West Wall has some very attractive climbs on sound rock, and gets the sun earlier than many other parts of the face. The East Wall starts above the huge wedged boulders in the Sgumain Stone Shoot and is split by a wide rake, Zigzag Route, starting beneath Vulcan Wall. The Magic Buttress lies below the rake. The Vulcan Wall area above has the highest concentration of hard routes in the Cuillin.

Eastern Buttress, West Wall

West Facing   Diagram p180

Approaches: The Terrace gives access to all routes on the West Wall. Higher routes on the wall start from the bed of Eastern Gully above the level of the Terrace.

Descents: For all routes on the West Wall continue by Direct Route to the shoulder of Sròn na Cìche and descend as described at the start of the chapter.

The west wall of Eastern Buttress has some very attractive climbs on sound rock, overlooking Eastern Gully. Routes are described from left to right as they are reached

3 Direct Route   180m   Severe ** (1912)
This is the classic low grade route, climbing from the toe of the buttress to the top. It is anything but direct in the lower reaches with many variations possible. The wall above the first broad section on the Terrace contains a number of steep cracks. Start up the easy gully that bounds the right side of the wall to a small bay. Break horizontally left and around a corner to a sloping ledge before breaking right to gain the Girdle Traverse. The slabby bay above is bounded by two huge oblong blocks. The chimneys formed by them give good traditional squeezes or the blocks can be turned by slabs below and left. Easy rocks above lead back right to overlook the top of Trojan Groove and a narrow neck. A steep wall above is turned by an exposed edge overlooking Eastern Gully. Large boulders and easy rocks lead to the crux wall with a prominent central crack. Difficulties are fairly short and well protected but can be avoided on the right if the polished rocks are too wet. Continue more easily up and left to the top of the buttress which is only 100m from the summit of Sròn na Cìche.

4 Chimney Route   180m   Difficult * (1912)
Start from the Terrace where it first narrows down, about halfway to Eastern Gully. Follow a series of chimneys and corners. The most prominent rises from the Girdle Traverse ledge as a fine 20m chimney.

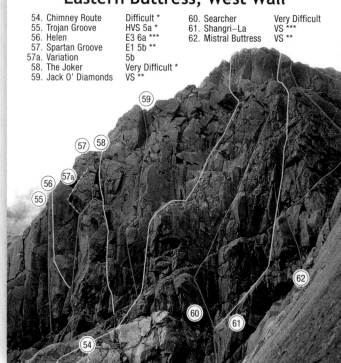

52. SRÒN NA CÌCHE
Eastern Buttress, West Wall

54. Chimney Route	Difficult *	60. Searcher	Very Difficult
55. Trojan Groove	HVS 5a *	61. Shangri–La	VS ***
56. Helen	E3 6a ***	62. Mistral Buttress	VS **
57. Spartan Groove	E1 5b **		
57a. Variation	5b		
58. The Joker	Very Difficult *		
59. Jack O' Diamonds	VS **		

The next routes start from the Girdle Traverse ledge, left of Chimney Route. Approach by the first pitches of Chimney Route or the Girdle Traverse.

55 Trojan Groove   25m   HVS 5a *   *(1965)*
Climb the left-hand of the two corners.

56 Helen   40m   E3 6a *   *(1994)*
This excellent route climbs the formidable looking arete between Trojan and Spartan Grooves. Climb the initial bulge of Spartan Groove, then move up left to a slanting crack which starts from a horizontal crack. Climb the slanting crack, crux, then the wall just right of the arete to a finish up the arete.

57 Spartan Groove   40m   E1 5b *   *(1965)*
Climb the right-hand of two corners, following it to a left-trending overhang. Traverse right with difficulty under this and continue to join Direct Route.
Variation: **E1 5b ***   *(1980)*
More logically, undercut 3m left to a small ledge then pull around the overhang to gain the slab above. Beware of rope drag.

58 The Joker   35m   Very Difficult *   *(1994)*
Start left of Jack O'Diamonds at a steep, undercut dyke-crack.

1. 30m Traverse left to gain the dyke and continue to belay in a big chimney.
2. 10m Back and foot the chimney to gain and finish up the right wall.

**9 Jack O'Diamonds   65m   Very Severe ** *(1953)*
A very good climb, well seen from the Cioch, named after the diamond shaped block left of the 20m chimney of Chimney Route.
1. 20m 5a Climb a steep wall left of the chimney and, after a mantelshelf at 5m, follow a steepening groove to the conspicuous diamond shaped block. Trend right across the top of the block, then follow a short crack to the top.
2. 35m Follow a line of blocks and grooves directly above to the foot of the final V-chimney.
3. 10m Climb the chimney to join Direct Route.

The next routes form a trilogy of long grooves rising from Eastern Gully to the top of the buttress.

0 Searcher   100m   Very Difficult *(1964)*
Start from Eastern Gully, 30m above the Terrace.
1. 40m Follow the left-hand of two lines of grooves to a ledge and large spike.

COIRE LAGAN

Shangri-La, VS, Eastern Buttress. Climber Pete Trudgill

Avoid the vertical groove above (this is VS 4c) on the left wall and return right by a ledge to a large block below the continuation of the groove.

2. 40m Follow the groove rightwards to a ledge near the corner of the fourth pitch of Shangri-La.

3. 20m The last pitch is the crux. Climb the fierce looking groove above, at first in the corner, then by a good crack on the left, to exit near the top of Chimney Route.

61 Shangri-La   130m   VS ***   (1964)

A classic climb which takes the fine series of corners right of Searcher. Start at the foot of Searcher, where a series of corners slants up right.

1. 40m 4b Easy grooves lead to a stance below a steep wide crack. Ascend this, or the wall on the left, to gain the grooves above via awkward cracks and flake belays.

2. 35m 4b Climb the excellent corner above and take the final overhang direct in a fine position.

3. 20m 4b Climb the deceptive groove to a wide platform.

4. 20m 5a Above are two corners; climb the strenuous left one past the pointed overhanging block (The Damoclean Sword!). Finish up easy rocks.

62 Mistral Buttress   105m   VS **   (1992)

This route gives good climbing up the buttress right of Shangri-La.

1. 45m 4c Start 15m right of Shangri-La and climb a cracked ramp up right. Step right and follow a corner to an overhang, moving right to a block belay. (The corner can be reached by moving left from the abseil point on Eastern Gully).

2. 45m 4b From the block, step left onto a slab, move left to a dyke which leads to the crest of the buttress and climb this to a ledge.

3. 15m 4c The left-hand corner above is taken by Shangri-La. Left of the right-hand corner are twin cracks. Climb the right-hand crack to an overhang, step left and follow both cracks to the top.

63 Boreas Grooves   90m   VS   (1958)

This final route starts above the Cave Pitch in Eastern Gully. Start 10m below where the Shelf reaches the Gully.

1. 20m Climb to the foot of an obvious corner and ascend this to a ledge.

2. 35m Climb a large groove to a terrace below an overhung corner.

3. 20m 4c Climb the left-hand corner, as for Shangri-La.

4. 15m Scramble over easy rocks to finish.

Eastern Buttress, East Wall

North-West Facing   Diagram p183

All the following routes start above the prominent boulders abutting Eastern Buttress.

Approach: For all routes on the East Wall clamber past the huge boulders to easier slopes above. A recessed slabby bay lies just beyond below Magic Buttress. Just beyond a short wall juts out into the Stone Shoot forcing the easiest line of ascent leftward for 30m. Above lies the superb clean face of Vulcan Wall.

Magic Buttress

The next routes all start at the slabby recess. The slab on the right is the start of the Girdle Traverse which gives a long and memorable outing.

64 The Girdle Traverse of Sròn na Cìche   900m   Very Difficult **   (1912)

This classic left to right traverse gives the longest rock climb in the Cuillin taking 3-6hrs on average. The route is well worn with very little loose rock. Descent pitches can appear terrifying and are abseiled by some parties. It is a major challenge of route finding, rope trickery and bold confident climbing. "The leader and last man should be expert climbers."

Start by ascending the slabby wall for 25m to reach the ledge system running below the first steepening. Traverse to the base of the 20m pitch on Chimney

52. SRÒN NA CÌCHE
Eastern Buttress, East Wall

		67. The Conjuror	E3 5c **
		68. Magic	E4 6a ***
53. Direct Route,		69. Magic Casement	HVS *
Eastern Buttress	Severe **	75. Zigzag Route	Grade 3/
65. Caravan Route	Hard Severe		Moderate
66. Prestidigitateur	HVS 5a	88. The Snake	HVS ***
		89. Schadenfreude	Severe

COIRE LAGAN

Route. Around the next corner ascend a slanting ledge on the gully wall over-looking Eastern Gully (30m). Descend an enclosed narrow 12m chimney with an undercut base to a lower ledge system. Continue past loose blocks before a deli-cate hand-traverse leads to Eastern Gully above the huge chockstone that forms its second climbing pitch.

Cross the gully then descend Collie's Route for 30m until a recessed chimney leads out onto the Cìoch Slab. An exposed traverse below the Shelf rises to the grassy ledge below Trophy Crack. Traverse below Archer Thompson Route to a prominent pinnacle. Cross behind this before descending an oblique chimney (30m) to the Terrace below the Rib of Doom. Follow this westward for 10m then descend a shallow diagonal gully until it steepens dramatically. Descend for 30m (crux) before gaining the mossy roof of the Hexagon Block.

Descend to the foot of Central Gully and the Amphitheatre. Traverse water worn slabs to the nose of Amphitheatre Arete and easily gain West Central Gully. Cross West Central Gully Arete below its steepest section before taking a rising line above the overhanging fan shaped corners to the left of Median. Easier climbing leads to a point beyond Western Gully, at the same approximate level as the starting point.
Variation: **300m   Severe**   *(1928)*
A finish more in keeping with the rest of the climb.

From the Amphitheatre the traverse is continued below Collie's cairn (on

Amphitheatre Arete) and continued across Slab and Groove to West Central Route. Median Route is crossed and a finish made 30m above the finish of Parallel Cracks Route.

65 Caravan Route 90m Hard Severe *(1949)*
Start at a bulging corner 10m along a flat ledge, at the top of the first pitch of the Girdle Traverse of Sròn na Cìche.
1. 35m Climb the corner, then trend right up a wall and slab (30m) until it is possible to cross right across a wall, via a break, to belays close to eastern variations of Direct Route.
2. 30m Blocks above and left of the stance lead to a corner. Climb slightly left above the corner to a wall split by slanting cracks. Climb the cracks to a belay.
3. 25m Easier slabs on the right lead to Direct Route below its penultimate pitch. Finish on the shoulder of Sròn na Cìche.

The back wall has three routes on good rock that all finish on Zigzag Route. Descend by reversing this to below Vulcan Wall.

66 Prestidigitateur 45m HVS 5a *(1987)*
This route takes a crack starting just right of The Conjuror. Climb the right-leaning crack to a ledge beneath a roof, pull over this and climb the groove to the top.

67 The Conjuror 45m E3 5c ** *(1983)*
This climbs the right-hand crack in the back of the bay. Follow the thin crack up the wall to gain a corner. Climb the corner to a roof and follow the crack to the top.

68 Magic 45m E4 6a *** *(1982)*
This climb takes the prominent left-hand crack 6m left of The Conjuror. It gives a superb and well protected pitch. Climb the flake and slab leading to a small overhang in a corner, move right and go up the crack to a corner which leads to the top.

69 Magic Casement 100m HVS * *(1953)*
A scrappy start leads to some quality climbing in the upper half. The left side of the slabby bay has a small squat buttress separating the Stone Shoot from the ledges of Zigzag Route. The squat buttress is split by a central crack.
Climb the crack to a scree ledge (12m). Climb the right-hand of two open grooves and slab above (8m). Gain an edge before stepping left under leaning flakes to belay on Zigzag Route (10m). An upper rake rises parallel but more steeply than Zigzag Route. Gain this by a choice of routes of which the best is a crack 10m right of the lowest point. Walk up the upper rake to an imposing vertical crack. Climb the crack, the top part of which was originally aided (20m). Continue by a difficult groove, through a cracked overhang and another steep groove to a large flat boulder (20m). Climb a left-slanting groove, return right to a ledge. Climb a steep crack right of a basalt dyke and cross it to finish leftward by a glacis (20m). Scramble to the top.

A number of Very Difficult routes can be followed left of here to approach the foot of Strappado, The Snake etc, effectively giving a direct approach to Zigzag Route. The trail is briefly forced left above here before reaching the foot of a magnificent clean wall.

Vulcan Wall Area

Alt 700m North-West Facing Diagram p186

This superb buttress of the finest Skye gabbro is best enjoyed in the afternoon and evening sun. A sustained mix of delicate slabs and fierce corner-cracks awaits the higher grade climber who makes the effort. The rake running below the routes is Zigzag Route. Routes are now described from left to right starting in the recess left of Vulcan Wall.

Descent: Traverse left to gain a loose slabby ramp that bounds Vulcan Wall on the left (east) side. Descend with this care.

0 Why   60m   VS 4c   *(1990)*
This climb takes the slabby buttress left of Kinloss Gully. Start by scrambling over a chockstone and climb a steep corner until it is possible to move right onto a slab under a basalt bulge. Follow a line of big flakes rightwards, then move back left to under the headwall, belay. Traverse down left along a crack, then finish up a corner.

1 Antonine Wall   E1 5b   40m   *(1978)*
This climbs the poorly protected buttress immediately left of Kinloss Gully with a technical crux. It joins pitch 2 of Kinloss Gully.

2 Kinloss Gully   55m   VS 4c   *(1957)*
The gully left of Vulcan Wall is often wet. Climb the large corner-crack to gully bed (20m). Climb an overhanging chockstone and the cracks above to a cave (25m). Traverse out on to the right wall and cross a bulge to a crack and flake which leads to a rake (10m).

3 The Team Machine   165m   E4 **   *(1982)*
A fine girdle of East Buttress. Start at Kinloss Gully.
1. 30m 4c Climb Kinloss Gully to a belay.
2. 25m 5c Follow a horizontal crack to belay on a slab under a roof, just beyond Confession; a well protected pitch.
3. 40m 5b Climb to the right end of the roof and follow a thin descending crack which leads into the corner of Creag Dhu Grooves; belay on the large ledge above.
4. 30m 5a Gain a small ledge on the arete and ascend to a thin horizontal break. Follow this to a junction with The Snake, which leads to a ledge and belay.
5. 40m 4a Finish up The Snake.

4 Confession   60m   E4 *   *(1982)*
A serious route with some dubious rock which takes an impressive line up the right wall of Kinloss Gully.
1. 15m 5a Climb a small groove, often wet, then continue up a corner to a cramped stance at the start of an obvious traverse.
2. 45m 5c Traverse right, then climb the crack to the top.

5 Zigzag Route   150m   Grade 3/Moderate *   *(1907)*
This route takes the easy rake that gives access to all the remaining routes. Start below Vulcan Wall, make a short descent below the Zephyr flake and ascend right to the crest overlooking the top part of Eastern Gully. It then trends back left to reach the apex of Eastern Buttress.

6 Spock   70m   E3 ***   *(1980)*
A very fine route with excellent bold climbing at the lower end of the grade. Start 5m left of Vulcan Wall.
1. 40m 5c Climb overhanging cracks on the arete, then continue up the arete on small holds through a shallow groove to belays above an obvious roof.
2. 30m 5a Go diagonally right to finish up the steep crack left of Vulcan Wall.

7 Vulcan Wall   70m   HVS ***   *(1957)*
A good route in a magnificent position. It takes the narrowing line of cracks toward the left side of the wall.
1. 20m 5a Climb to a ledge and block belay.
2. 40m 5a Move up to a ledge to the left of the block, then continue by a line of cracks. One short bold section leads to a small ledge on the right with a possible belay. Make a rising traverse left to bigger holds; a sustained pitch.

COIRE LAGAN

52. SRÒN NA CÌCHE – Eastern Buttress
East Wall, Vulcan Wall Area

72. Kinloss Gully   VS ***
76. Spock   E3 ***
77. Vulcan Wall   HVS ***
77a. Chambre Finish   E2 5c ***

78. Uhuru   E3 ***
79. Clinging On   E4 ***
80. Dilemma   E3 ***
82. Creag Dhu Grooves   E3 ***
83. Zephyr   E5 **
85. Enigma   E3 **
86. Strappado   HVS *
87. Strappado Direct   E2 **
88. The Snake   HVS ***

3. 10m Traverse left to the edge of the wall and climb to a glacis. Belay well back.
Variation: **The Chambre Finish   25m   E2 5c** *** *(1982)*
A very fine purist's finish giving a taste of some of the thinner wall climbing and a logical direct finish. Where the normal route goes left onto easier ground, ascend the thinner and left-hand of two parallel cracks above. The right-hand crack is taken by Uhuru.

B Uhuru   70m   E3 *** *(1990)*
Excellent climbing up the fine crack-line in the silver streaked wall between Vulcan Wall and Clinging On. Start at cracks just left of the vertical crack of Dilemma.
1. 25m 5c Climb to a small overlap and follow the crack above to a hard move right to the Vulcan Wall ledge. Traverse left to a flake block belay.
2. 45m 5c Step right off the block, climb cracks and go right over a curving overlap. Move up and right to pull into the main crack, then follow it with difficulty to better holds. Continue up the excellent crack to finish right of the large precarious block.

9 Clinging On   65m   E4 *** *(2001)*
Climbs the purist line on Vulcan Wall. Start as for Dilemma.
1. 55m 6a A long and sustained pitch. Climb the initial crack of Dilemma to its end. Where Dilemma climbs diagonally right across the wall, make a move up then gain the obvious vertical crack just on the left. Follow this to where it fades into tiny cracks and gain an obvious small protruding block above. Step on to the block and step left to a foot ledge on Uhuru. Step back right and gain a thin crack and follow it with difficulty to gain better holds. Follow these up right into a final crack to under the roofs. Traverse 2m left past the roofs to a vertical crack.
2. 10m 5a Climb up and left to beneath a projecting block. Take a hand-traverse out left to the top.

D Dilemma   80m   E3 *** *(1977)*
This route climbs the delicate slab and strenuous overhang between Vulcan Wall and Creag Dhu Grooves and is quite straightforward for the grade. Start at a thin vertical crack in the slab between these two routes.
1. 45m 5c Climb the crack until level with the stance of Vulcan Wall. Continue up the crack to its finish and then up right to a hanging corner at the left end of the overlap. Go up the corner and pull out rightwards to gain a descending traverse line to a small niche just left of the large stance on Creag Dhu Grooves.
2. 35m 5c Follow the crack diagonally left up the slab, then struggle up its continuation through the impressive overlaps.

I Pocks   85m   E3 *** *(1988/92)*
A very fine and varied route.
1. 35m 5b Start up Creag Dhu Grooves, then climb the crack on the left to where Dilemma crosses the overlap. Move right under the overlap to a ledge, step right, then climb the overlap and move up right to the belay on Creag Dhu Grooves. A superb pitch.
2. 50m 5c Climb a steep crack, just right of Creag Dubh Grooves, to a slab and follow this rightwards to an arete. Continue up right to finish up the crack on Enigma.

2 Creag Dhu Grooves   95m   E3 *** *(1957)*
Another superb climb which follows the chimney between Vulcan Wall and the huge flake on the right. Start on the ledge below Vulcan Wall at the corner of the wall and great flake.
1. 40m 4b Climb the chimney behind the flake to a chockstone, then continue to a large ledge above the flake.
2. 10m 5c Climb the superb technical corner.
3. 20m 5c Continue up the equally good corner to a good ledge.
4. 25m Continue to the top.

COIRE LAGAN

Vulcan Wall, HVS, Vulcan Wall Area. Climber Scott Kirkhope

**3 Zephyr   85m   E5 ** *(1982)*
This fine climb follows the arete right of Creag Dhu Grooves. The first pitch climbs a huge flake that is key feature of the next few routes. Start just right of that route at a slab leading to a small roof.
1. 40m 5b Turn the roof on the left, then follow flakes and grooves to the large ledge.
2. 20m 6a Gain a small ledge on the arete, ascend to a horizontal break, then move left around the arete into a slim bottomless groove. Climb this and the slab above to a small ledge.
3. 25m 4c Move left and continue up the wall to the top.

4 The Plunge   100m   VS 5a *(1962)*
An old aid route that traverses the steep headwall of Strappado. Start 3m right of Creag Dhu Grooves.
1. 25m Traverse right for 5m then straight up past a bulge to peg belay.
2. 20m Move up a corner to a sloping ledge below an overhang. Surmount this then continue to a block belay at the top of the flake.
3. 10m Traverse right round an overhanging wall, 5m, then climb to a peg belay near the arete.
4. 30m 5a Climb up to a small ledge then traverse right for 10m, originally finished by using aid for a further 3m and a hard move to a large platform (pitch 4 of the Team Machine girdle traverse).
5. 15m Finish up a thin flake to easy ground.

**5 Enigma   135m   E3 ** *(1979)*
The main pitch of this fine climb follows the crack in the steep upper wall, well left of The Snake. Start about 12m right of Creag Dubh Grooves at the right-hand end of a large flat ledge with a deep crevasse at the back.
1. 35m 5a Climb the wall above, first by a left-slanting groove then slightly rightwards by cracks; belay over on the left.
2. 25m 5b Climb easily right and up, crossing the right side of the prominent flake, to reach a thin right-slanting corner-crack. Climb this until below a large overlap, and then traverse right to nut belays on a well situated ledge.
3. 35m 5c Above and left is a thin crack splitting the wall. Gain and climb the crack to a belay beyond the final overhang.
4. 40m Continue up the crack.

6 Strappado   105m   HVS * *(1957)*
This climb follows the right side of the prominent flake to the right of Creag Dhu Grooves. Start below the broken rocks which lead to the top of the flake.
1. 45m 4a Climb the right side of the flake to a belay 5m from its top.
2. 10m 5a Traverse horizontally right to an exposed ledge on a steep wall, then follow a small dyke.
3. 20m 5a Where the dyke joins a small fissure on a slight overhang, make a hard right traverse to a ledge, followed by another difficult descending traverse to belay on a further ledge.
4. 30m 4c Cross The Snake and climb a wall on the right on small holds to easier ground.

**7 Strappado Direct   90m   E2 ** *(1980/88)*
This worthwhile climb takes a direct line to the right of the normal route, giving some fine climbing.
1. 25m 5a Start up Strappado or The Snake to reach a crack in a slab just left of The Snake. Climb the poorly protected crack to a ledge.
2. 30m 5b/c Climb Strappado for 10m, and where the original route makes a descending traverse right, continue straight up the crack above to a niche.
3. 35m 5a Go up the arete on the left to easy ground.

The Snake, HVS, Vulcan Wall Area.
Climber Mark Francis

88 The Snake   110m   HVS * **   (1965)

This is the classic medium grade route of the crag, but there are long run outs on vertical ground. The route follows the most striking trap fault in the steepest section of the wall. Start 3m right of Strappado.

1. 35m 4b Follow the vague fault to belay at the foot of the vertical chimney on a selection of poor gear.
2. 35m 4c A good nut runner is reached after 2m. Continue up the vertical basalt staircase to a horizontal break (10m) and spike runner. More steep moves lead to another horizontal break and spike runner to protect the easier final section and good belay. An outrageous pitch.
3. 40m 4a Follow the trap to the crest of the buttress

Some 5m right of The Snake an upper rake starts to rise at a steeper incline than the Zigzag rake. Gain this by a choice of short lines as for Magic Casement.

89 Schadenfreude   85m   Severe   (1957)

Start on the upper rake, 6m right of the prominent Magic Casement crack.

1. 30m Climb an awkward crack followed by easier rocks to the large flat topped stone on Magic Casement.
2. 20m Climb a fault on the right wall that faces the belay (12m) then trend leftwards on a sloping ledge to a dyke which is followed to a ledge.
3. 15m Climb the sharp arete to finish.

COIRE A' GHRUNNDA & COIRE NAN LAOGH

Maps p98, p124   Diagram p193

The rock scenery of Coire a' Ghrunnda is probably the most impressive in the whole Cuillin. On the moors below, the terminal moraine forms an almost unbroken line of boulders in the shape of a gigantic horseshoe. The corrie floor has been scraped smooth by glacial erosion and is enclosed by sheer compact rock and a bulging headwall. Above this lies Loch Coire a' Ghrunnda, the largest and highest of the Cuillin lochs. A mixture of deep turquoise pools and sandy beaches are set into a boulder field of strangely sculpted peridotite overlooked by steep rock faces.

The climbing is divided into two distinct areas. In the lower corrie lies the broad south face of Sròn na Cìche. With a sunny aspect it is generally set at an easy angle with many long lower grade routes on good rock. High above the loch the south facing cliffs of Sgùrr Alasdair and Sgùrr Theàrlaich provide a concentrated series of excellent climbs following well defined lines. Here the rock is unusually compact and fine grained but compensates with very positive holds.

In winter these higher cliffs can rapidly come into condition when they are blasted by fierce south-westerly snow storms producing some very high quality mixed climbing. Coire nan Laogh is a remote minor climbing area that uses the same initial approach.

General Approach: Start from Glen Brittle campsite. Take the Coire Lagan path for 1km then the right fork at NG 420 203. The path fords a small river immediately, crosses the Allt Coire Lagan after a kilometre and then rises across the Sròn na Cìche spur to a fork (NG 434 197). The lower fork gives access to Coire nan Laogh [61] and Gars-bheinn (described below). For Coire a' Ghrunnda follow the higher path for a further 1km. It now finishes by rising abruptly to reach a high terrace rather than continuing to the slabs at the mouth of the corrie as it traditionally used to.

Approach for Coire a' Ghrunnda, Bealach Coire an Lochain and Bealach a' Garbh-choire: The high terrace runs parallel to the corrie floor and the path remains obvious as it stays high above the glaciated walls. South Crag [53] is the broad sweep of cliffs lying immediately above the path on the south-east flank of Sròn na Cìche (1hr). An open gully bounds South Crag on the right. North Crag [54] is the smaller area immediately north (1hr 15mins).

Cross huge boulders for 100m below this face then an open gully and broken ground to reach the main water course, turning the final waterfall by corners on the left. Vagabond Buttress [55] is immediately above the path as it reaches the loch (1hr 45mins). Head up hill north from the loch beside the stream to reach the Alasdair-Theàrlaich crags [56-58] (2hrs 30mins).

Ascend the massive boulder field directly above the east side of the loch to reach the Bealach and Caisteal a' Garbh-choire [59] (2hrs 15mins). The West Flank of Sgùrr nan Eag [60] starts below the level of the loch and is approached by the slabby corrie floor. Below the steep final rise off the moorland break right and follow the old path for 200m to the mouth of the corrie, a spectacular viewpoint.

Approach for Coire nan Laogh [61] and Gars-bheinn: Take the lower, right fork on the spur of Sròn na Cìche (NG 434 197). Beyond Allt Coire a' Ghrunnda the path becomes rough and very boggy before reaching the Allt Coire nan Laogh. The slabby headwall above is reached in 2hrs from the beach. Beyond the mouth of Coire nan Laogh rises the southern flank of Gars-bheinn. Take a rising diagonal line right of the obvious cliff bands, following as much grass as possible, to join the Ridge close to the summit (3 hrs).

Round of Coire a' Ghrunnda   7 or 8hrs   Grade 2 or 3/Severe **

An important section for Ridge aspirants to research and difficult to achieve in poor visibility. The route is generally climbed anti-clockwise starting by ascending Sgùrr nan Eag from Loch Coire a' Ghrunnda. There are options to bypass Caisteal a Garbh-choire and the TD (Theàrlaich-Dubh) Gap for those not wanting to carry a rope. Descend by the Great Stone Shoot. Individual climbs are described below and sections of the Ridge described in the Cuillin Ridge Traverses chapter.

South End of The Cuillin Ridge   2km   Grade 1 ***

This route gives a fine easy scramble out to Gars-bheinn, one of the best view points on Skye. It remains one hour is usually enough to reach Gars-bheinn from Sgùrr nan Eag with only minor route choice needed in good visibility. Descend south rapidly from the small col immediately west of Gars-bheinn to gain the path back across the moor to Glen Brittle.

SRÒN NA CÌCHE - SOUTH-EAST FACE

53. SOUTH CRAG

(NG 447 198)   Alt 540m   South-East facing   Maps p98, 124   Diagrams p193, 195

South Crag is a broad sweep of slabby cliffs with a high concentration of lower grade routes. It remains in the sun well into the afternoon giving a relaxed atmosphere. The cliff topography is not all clear from below. The White Slab, set just above half height, gives the best point of reference but can be difficult to recognise in some light. An open gully bounds South Crag on the right separating it from North Crag. Other features seen in good light include Stony Rake, a narrow shelf which starts from the centre of the lowest rocks and runs diagonally left beneath the main face and Pinnacle Rake, which runs across the face at three-quarter height dropping right to the open gully. The left-hand end of the cliff is climbable more or less anywhere and the routes can be mixed at will. The face above Pinnacle Rake is complex and has some steep terrain.

Descents: Finish climbs at Pinnacle Rake if a quick return to the base of the crag is required. Descend rightwards to the open gully which has sections of water worn rock to negotiate. Many parties will continue their day by ascending to Sròn na Cìche or further. The descent to Coire a' Ghrunnda from Bealach Coire a' Ghrunnda is easy if required.

Lower Buttress

A small buttress of steep rocks lies just left of the path before the final scree ascent up to South Crag. Descend right by the Stony Rake

1 Intermediate Traverse   95m   Severe   (1957)

This route girdles the Lower Buttress. Start at the left edge of the buttress; just left of a large overhang 30m up.
1. 25m Climb an easy foot-wide dyke to a diagonal fault.
2. 40m Climb the fault for 6m then traverse right and around the base of an overhang on undercut holds.
3. 30m Climb the rib on the right to a ledge then continue easily to Stony Rake.

2 Cuckoo Groove   60m   VS   (1980)

The buttress is marked by a slabby ramp on the left and a deep chimney on the right. It has a lower tier of slabs and a steeper upper tier with a conspicuous two stepped groove near the middle. Start at a grass topped pedestal near the middle.
1. 35m Climb up for 6m, then work right towards a break at the top of the slabs. Step right to an overhung stance and belay.
2. 25m 4c Work left under the overhang until it is possible to pull over it into the groove. Take the first step of this direct, then turn the second by a rib on the right which leads to the top.

3 Rapid Progress   40m   HVS 5a **   (1998)

An obvious crack-line 15m to the right of Cuckoo Groove and 5m left of a short deep chimney. A small white blaze in the shape of India is passed at 5m. Constantly interesting climbing with a steep move to finish. Finish up the 5m continuation to the Stony Rake.

COIRE A' GHRUNNDA

high terrace approach

corrie floor approach

COIRE A' GHRUNNDA

Main Cliff

Far South Buttress   150m   Moderate   *(1920)*
This is the left-bounding buttress of Green Recess Chimneys. Start 80m up Stony
Rake, avoiding the obvious direct start. Ascend slabby rocks for about 75m to the
foot of a tower. Climb this by its left edge to Pinnacle Rake. Above here a difficult
pitch leads to a second tower which is climbed on the left.

Green Recess Chimneys   180m   Very Difficult *   *(1920)*
This is quite a good sheltered climb, suitable for wet or windy weather. The chimneys form the first continuous break at the south-west end of the crag. Start about
75m up Stony Rake avoiding the obvious entry pitch. Entertaining chimneys lead
to a small grassy recess below Pinnacle Rake. Take care with some loose blocks just
below the rake. The top section of the crag is confusing, and various ways are
possible, both left and right of one of the large pinnacles. In wet weather it is
possible to take the corner right of the pinnacle (as for White Slab), and then quit
this for an easy leftward line to rejoin the top of Green Recess Chimneys.
Variation: **Direct Start   Very Difficult**
This starts halfway up the slanting rake which leads to the horizontal ledge via the
corner of a pinnacle.
Winter: **260m   IV,5** **   *(2010)*
A winter line based on the summer route formed ice in exceptional conditions. Gain
the Stony Rake by icy grooves and thereafter follow it to the base of the chimney-
line (70m). More icy grooves lead to mixed chimneys and the Pinnacle Rake
(120m). Thereafter a rising traverse on snow ledges leads leftwards to the top of
the crag (90m).

Central Buttress   210m   Difficult **   *(1920)*
A good route. From Stony Rake, a horizontal ledge runs across the central part of
the face. Climb the smooth rocks below the horizontal ledge by a narrow curving

White Slab, Very Difficult. Main Cliff, Sròn na Cìche South East Face.
Climber Richard Hewson

dyke. Now attack the buttress on the left side of a projecting rib. After this, climb the centre of the buttress as closely as possible, with a traverse to the left edge below Pinnacle Rake. The tower above the Pinnacle Rake provides fine climbing to finish.

7 Trap Dyke Route   180m   Difficult   *(1920)*
The long dyke right of Central Buttress gives an interesting but not particularly difficult climb. The route crosses Pinnacle Rake at a lofty pinnacle which is loose.

8 White Slab   180m   Very Difficult *   *(1920)*
A good climb but the white slab is avoided. The start lies 10m up the Stony Terrace and is identified by 'White Slab' emblazoned on the rock. Climb 5m, move right then take a difficult crack to a platform (12m). Above here trend left by a dyke to the horizontal ledge (30m). Much variation from here is possible. Trend right by a series of shallow grooves and corners to the base of the slab (60m). Turn rocks above the grassy bay on the left to reach Pinnacle Rake(50m). Climb the corner to the right of the pinnacle up to a fine 12m chimney and scramble to the top (40m).
Variation: **Direct Finish   40m   Severe**   *(1970)*
An optional finish above Pinnacle Rake. Start 12m left of the final chimney of the normal route. Climb a prominent crack for 5m, then traverse right onto a steep loose wall, which is climbed direct.

9 White Slab Direct   170m   Severe **   *(1950)*
A good climb that takes on the challenge of the white slab. Start at an obvious open groove in centre of the wall and directly below the white slab.
1. 40m   Climb the groove or slabby rocks on the right to a spike belay below a steep section of the groove.
2. 15m 4b   Follow a crack in the steep wall above for 5m then step back left to rejoin the groove. Belay in the corner.

53. SOUTH CRAG & 54. NORTH CRAG

4. Far South Buttress	Mod	
5. Green Recess Chims	V.Diff *	
6. Central Buttress	Diff **	
7. Trap Dyke Route	Diff	

8. White Slab	V.Diff *	
9. White Slab Direct	Severe **	
10. Mega Route	VS	
11. South Crag Gully	V.Diff	
13. Owl Buttress Left	V.Diff *	
14. Owl Buttress Right	VS 4b *	
15. Owl Wall	HVS **	

16. Owl Chimney	Diff *	
17. Stack Buttress Direct	Diff **	
17a. Red Wall Variant	Diff	
18. Stormwatch	E3 *	
19. Gonzo Jamming	E1 *	
20. North Crag Gully &		
Black Knight's Wall	Diff	

d. descents

COIRE A' GHRUNNDA

Owl Wall, HVS, Sròn na Cìche South Face.
Climber Mike Lates on the first ascent

3. 50m Continue straight up to the base of the white slab.
4. 25m 4a From the middle of the lower edge of the slab delightful moves lead up and rightward to a small spike runner on the outer edge. Straight up good rock to a block belay above. Finish as for the original route (40m).

Variation: **Oxford Start 50m VS 4b** * (1950)
This tackles the right hand of two cracks rising to an obvious horizontal ledge at 50m. Climb for 12m to a stance and belay at the foot of a small scoop. Climb this then trend left then right to gain the foot of a slab, the lower edge of which overhangs. Climb the overhanging right-hand crack to a small platform at 20m before gaining the outer and lower part of the horizontal ledge. Head up left to rejoin the parent route.

10 Mega Route   125m   VS (1968)
This climb follows the left edge of South Crag Gully.
1. 35m 4c Climb the crack left of the gully, past an overhang, to a spike belay.
2. 15m Continue up the crack to the horizontal ledge.
3. 25m Climb a depression and the corner above then exit left to easier ground.

4. 50m Scramble up to Pinnacle Rake and finish by the corner above.

South Crag Gully   150m   Very Difficult   (1920)
This is the gully which forms near the right end of South Crag. Climb the shallow
trenches on the right for 60m, followed by a short mossy pitch, then a chockstone
pitch and a chimney. Above, climb a cave pitch and a flake of rock, then several
smaller pitches lead to Pinnacle Rake. Beyond, the gully diminishes to a crack and
the climb continues up the rocks to the right.

Girdle Traverse of South Crag   180m   Severe   (1947)
Start at the left end of the crag on a large mossy ledge. Traverse into Green Recess
Chimneys at about the foot of the first chimney proper, then keep as near as
possible to a level of about 12m below the foot of the white slab. A delicate crack
traverses past the white slab to a groove, 12m, followed by 10m of ascent to a
large ledge. From the right-hand edge of the ledge, climb a steep broken corner for
6m, followed by a delicate traverse across the South Crag Gully to finish.

At the right end of Pinnacle Rake stands a very fine owl shaped pinnacle complete
with ears. It is only clear when the rake is viewed in profile from the north. The
buttress below the pinnacle is significantly steeper than other parts of the cliff.

Owl Buttress Left   55m   Very Difficult *   (1924)
Start right of South Crag Gully and trend gradually right up a series of slabs. From
a horizontal shelf, a V-shaped chimney leads to Pinnacle Rake, just left of Owl
Pinnacle. The rocks above are easy but pleasant.

Owl Buttress Right   55m   VS 4b *   (1932)
Start 30m below and left of Owl Chimney at the left edge of Owl Wall. Climb
diagonally right to a belay above the steep section. Climb the slab above slightly
to the right, avoiding easier rocks to the left. The final pitch is a steep little wall
ending on rotten rock at the top of Owl Pinnacle.

Owl Wall   60m   HVS **   (2008)
A good route that climbs the obvious rising crack in the steep wall overlooking Owl
Chimney. Start at the foot of Owl Chimney.
1. 45m 5a Climb the chimney for 5m. Pull blindly round left on large sloping holds
to reach the base of the crack. Climb steeply to reach the small triangular roof then
right to a good rest (15m). The crack is well protected and continues in a good
position to a ledge below a huge hanging boulder.
2. 20m 4b Climb the recessed corner until it is possible to pull right onto the slab.
Step back left above the recess and continue to block belay right of the hanging
boulder.

Owl Chimney   45m   Difficult *   (1920)
At the extreme right end of the crag is a clean chimney. The lower part is
constricted, the middle part V-shaped and the upper part overhangs, but is easily
climbed on the right.

54. NORTH CRAG

**(NG 448 200)   Alt 645m   South-East facing   Maps p98, 124   Diagrams
p193, 195**

North Crag is a smaller area split by North Crag Gully. It lies immediately north of
the open gully bounding South Crag. The striking clean corner of Gonzo Jamming
is the most obvious feature from directly below. The Stack is a pinnacle overlooking
this corner.

Descent: From the top of the crag traverse north-east until it is possible to
descend into the upper part of Coire a' Ghrunnda. The open gully beside south
crag is also reasonable in dry conditions.

COIRE A' GHRUNNDA

**17 Stack Buttress Direct 150m Difficult ** *(1920)*
A good climb with sensational exposure at the top. Start at the foot of North Crag Gully. Climb the right-hand side of the buttress, overlooking the gully and on rough rock, to a rake below the Stack (60m). Ascend a steep slab on the right edge of the rake to a corner. Climb this to an edge overhanging the clean corners below. Reach the top of the Stack by a short wall (40m). The rocks to the top are easy (50m).
Variation: **Red Wall Variant Difficult** *(1920)*
Start 25m left of the parent route. Climb a wall of reddish basalt, a broken rib of gabbro, then a long chimney to the rake beneath the Stack.

18 Stormwatch 50m E3 * *(1988)*
This climbs a steep groove wall below the last route to join it near the top.
A good climb at the lower limit of its grade. Start from a belay 5m up the slab from the terrace, below a niche.
1. 25m 5a Step left to a short crack, climb this and step left to another corner. Climb to a large terrace and belay on the left at the foot of the groove proper.
2. 25m 6a Climb the groove and the steep slab by strenuous fingerlocks in the right-slanting crack, crux. Pull into a pod, swing back out left to a crack, then break into the steep corner to emerge on the notched arete.

19 Gonzo Jamming 50m E1 5b * *(1988)*
This is the obvious clean corner. Scrambling and easy climbing lead to a left-rising terrace at the base of the Stack. Belay 20m up the slab in the rightmost corner. Step left and continue up to the base of the second corner. Climb the lower corner to a large stance and belay. Climb the upper corner direct via a slippery jam.

20 North Crag Gully and Black Knight's Wall 165m Difficult *(1920)*
The lower part of the gully is avoided by the rocks of Slab Buttress. The upper part widens out with an overhanging cave pitch on the right. The centre of the wall is climbed past a large upright block, The Black Knight.

21 Slab Buttress 240m Grade 3 * *(1920)*
A good scramble in the sun. The buttress is in three sections divided by rakes. Start beside the footpath just left of the lowest point and follow the buttress as directly as possible. The rock is rough, clean and reliable throughout.

UPPER COIRE A' GHRUNNDA

The loch, beaches and cliffs of the upper corrie remain hidden on the approach. The skyline is dominated by Sgùrr Alasdair with three prominent pinnacles in Bealach Sgumain immediately to the left. A path runs right from this bealach beneath the Alasdair-Theàrlaich crags [56-58] which give the best quality south facing climbs in the Cuillin. These are split by the deep rift of the Theàrlaich-Dubh Gap shortly before the path rejoins the Ridge at Bealach Coire an Lochain.

Approach: In addition to the approaches already described a quicker route to the upper corrie in good visibility is to ascend the Sgumain Stone Shoot from Coire Lagan. At Bealach Coire a' Ghrunnda turn north and traverse Sgùrr Sgumain (Grade 2) to the Alasdair-Theàrlaich crags (2hrs 15mins) or descend easily to the loch for Vagabond Buttress.

55. VAGABOND BUTTRESS

(NG 449 202) Alt 700m South-East facing Maps p98, p124 Diagram p193

This is the prominent buttress left of the path just below the level of the loch. On the left side of the slab is a crack which bounds the right edge of the buttress. Left again is an overlap and a wide flared groove with a crack in the corner, a large horizontal flake at its foot and two large flakes at the top. The following climb takes this crack.

Vagabond Crack 130m HVS * *(1984)*
1. 30m Easy slab climbing leads to the horizontal fault.
2. 10m Step left to a ledge and make an awkward move up onto a ledge with a large flake.
3. 40m 5b The crack above is initially difficult. Finish steeply over doubtful flakes to belay on a slab; an excellent pitch.
4. 50m Step left to the arete and climb easily to the top.

A Walk On Part In The War 50m E3 ** *(2002)*
A direct line up the front face of the buttress. A little dubious rock on the first pitch, but excellent rock and protection where needed. The most obvious feature of the lower part of the buttress is a large, pale, right-facing and leaning corner. Start on the rake about 8m left of the corner's foot.
1. 30m 5c Gain the steep right-trending broken crack-line from the left and follow it, with difficult moves at a small cracked roof and at the bulge above, to a broken ledge.
2. 20m 5c Move the belay about 8m right along the ledge. Above and on the left is an overhanging nose and a final cracked bulge above. Climb a short wall to a break below the nose. Pull onto the wall right of the nose and climb steeply left-wards to the final bulge. Cross this rightwards via the crack with difficulty and finish leftwards.

56. SGÙRR ALASDAIR - SOUTH FACE

(NG 451 207) Alt 900m South facing Maps p98, 124 Diagrams p193, 201

A magnificent wall with over 100m of steep climbing below the highest peak on the island.

Descent: Most of the climbs finish near the top of the Great Stone Shoot, which provides the quickest descent to Coire Lagan. To return to the foot of the climbs descend directly from the summit of Sgùrr Alasdair by the South-West Flank route. This is a shallow scoop that descends parallel to the South-West Ridge leading to a chimney that avoids the Bad Step. Routes are described from left to right starting at Bealach Sgumain.

South-West Ridge by the Bad Step (Mauvais Pas) Very Difficult **
Above the pinnacles in Bealach Sgumain the ridge soon narrows. All options are bold and difficult for a few crucial moves. The tempting line on the Coire Lagan side is very loose. Turning the scooped wall on the right is the easiest and involves a crucial one finger swap with a small spike belay above. The blocky narrow ridge continues and requires caution but rewards with great scrambling in a fantastic position to the highest point on the island.

To avoid the Bad Step drop 20m into Coire a' Ghrunnda from the lowest point of the bealach and traverse right to reach the foot of the next route. It is commonly used but not very easy to spot.

South-West Flank 150m Grade 2 **
Starting 20m below the level of the bealach and 50m to the east is a 25m polished chimney that provides the normal route onto Sgùrr Alasdair. A shallow scoop above leads directly to the summit. Cutting back left to enjoy the South-West Ridge above the chimney is highly recommended.
Winter: **II ****
Easier if the bottom chimney is banked out.

A footpath descends from Bealach Sgumain into Coire a' Ghrunnda, keeping close below the line of cliffs. After 100m the path levels off briefly across an open bay containing the following routes. All finish by scrambling broken ground to the head of the Great Stone Shoot.

3 West Gully   105m   Very Difficult ** (1912)

This is the first definite gully at the west end of the cliffs. It is narrow and steep giving good climbing on clean, solid rock for the first 60m. Steep slabs above lead to easier ground and the head of the Stone Shoot.

Winter: **180m   V,6 ** (2009)

Fine, sustained and well protected climbing in the lower section. The steep wall was turned by a short dog-leg to the left. Mixed ground bearing left finished at the summit of Alasdair.

4 W.C. Route   105m   Very Difficult * (1965)

Between West Gully and Central Route is a big obvious corner. Climb the corner to a belay shortly before the overhang. Move diagonally right over slabs then horizontally left across a wall to climb the corner-crack to a stance and belay. Climb the steep cracks above to the top.

A recessed bay lies right again beneath an array of vertical faults. There is a prominent cave in the left wall about 5m up.

5 Central Route   105m   Severe * (1921)

Start up the buttress immediately left of the cave. Follow the left edge to a smooth wall. Trend right towards a chimney and climb this to an overhang, where it is possible to climb the left wall. The climbing above is easier.

6 Commando Crack   105m   Hard Severe **** (1950)

One of the best climbs in the Cuillin. The pitches can be run together (recommended, two pitches 40m and 35m) but each of the shorter sections has its own distinctive character. It follows the prominent chimney in the left corner of the bay, turning the initial overhangs by the narrow right fork.

1. 10m Climb the rib right of the crack for 3m, traverse left into the chimney, then climb to where the chimney forks.
2. 20m 4b Ascend the right wall for a few metres until forced into the tight chimney. Pass the awkward narrowing to an airy position then gain a block belay on the left.
3. 10m Continue up the crack on the right to belay in a sentry box below an overhanging chockstone.
4. 10m Thread the chockstone, climb the nose on the left and climb to a stance and belay.
5. 25m 4b Boldly layback the right-hand crack, then cross to the left-hand jamming crack, which is followed by a short scramble.
6. 30m Easier climbing leads rightwards to the top of the Stone Shoot.

7 The Asp   105m   E2 5b/c *** (1965)

An excellent well protected climb which takes the steep off-width crack 7m right of Commando Crack.

1. 30m 5b Climb the crack, largely by chimneying, to an overhang, then pull out onto an inclined ledge beneath the overhang.
2. 35m 5b/c Move up to the overhang (large Friend protection) where a difficult move left (made easier if hidden holds are found) gains the upper crack. Climb the crack to easier ground.
3. 40m Scramble to the top.

8 Oneshotbang   130m   VS (1977)

Climb the large (usually wet) gully cleft 5m to the right of the Asp.

Follow the path down right for 30m to the lowest point of the buttress.

56. SGÙRR ALASDAIR - South Face
57. THEÀRLAICH-DUBH WALLS

Theàrlaich–Dubh Buttress

3. West Gully — Very Difficult **
4. W.C. Route — Very Difficult *
5. Central Route — Severe *
6. Commando Crack — Hard Severe ****
7. The Asp — E2 ***

8. Oneshotbang — VS
9. Con's Cleft — E1 ***
10. Atlantis — HVS *

11. TD Gap Gully — Grade 2
12. Bower's Climb — Very Difficult
13. Eilidh's on the Lash — HVS **
14. Eilidh's Ceilidh — V,7 **

COIRE A' GHRUNNDA

Sgùrr Alasdair from Sgùrr Sgumain. Climber Mike Lates

9 Con's Cleft 60m E1 *** (1965)

A very good climb up the cliff's most prominent diedre (corner-line). Start just up from the lowest point of the buttress. A loose block mentioned in previous guides appears to have fallen off leaving the first pitch significantly harder.
1. 15m 5c Climb with increasing difficulty to an overhang, then gain the crack above (crux) and belay on a ledge.
2. 10m 4b Climb the crack to another good ledge.
3. 35m 4c Continue up the crack directly, then finish with 50m of loose scrambling.

10 Atlantis 90m HVS * (1980)

This bold steep route climbs the wall and groove just right of Con's Cleft. Climb the lower wall by a series of left-trending cracks to gain the shallow upper groove. Climb this to the top of the buttress.

57. THEÀRLAICH-DUBH GAP WALLS

(NG 452 207) Alt 900m South-East facing Map p124 Diagram p201

The TD (Theàrlaich-Dubh) Gap is very often a frustrating bottle neck for climbers attempting a Ridge Traverse. New routes here give some alternatives to queuing or great climbing in their own right. Routes are listed from the bottom to top of the Theàrlaich-Dubh Gap Gully.

Descent: Make a short easy traverse right to the top of the TD Gap then abseil

Photo Rob Lawson

from a selection of in-situ sling placements. Take care not to annoy climbers in the Gap. The gully is very loose in descent and can be abseiled.

Theàrlaich-Dubh Gap Gully   65m   Grade 2
This is the deep gully that leads up to the Theàrlaich-Dubh Gap. It is mostly loose above the steep entry rocks.

Bower's Climb   90m   Very Difficult   (1919)
A broad recess goes up left from the base of Theàrlaich-Dubh Gap Gully and leads into the scree which lies on the eastern side of the Great Stone Shoot. Climb the first rocks of Theàrlaich-Dubh Gap Gully until it is possible to break out onto the left wall by a slab. Climb the right face of the recess to finish near the bottom of the scree. Useful in boots as an alternative to queuing for the classic TD Gap route.

Eilidh's on the Lash   65m   HVS **   (2008)
This is a left-hand variation of Eilidhs' Ceilidh with just the first 3m common to both routes.
Start 25m up the Theàrlaich-Dubh Gap Gully at the first continuous vertical fault in the left (west) wall.
1. 15m 4c Step left into the crack to start. After a couple of steep moves step left out of the crack and reach a pedestal (8m). A thin crack just to the left protects a hard move to enter a shallow groove which is climbed to a belay beneath the large roof.

58. THEÀRLAICH-DUBH BUTTRESS

20. West Face	Very Difficult *	
21. Swamp Fox	HVS 5a *	
22. Sundance	HVS	
23. Grand Diedre	VS ***	
24. Quiver	Severe	
25. Domesday	E3 5c **	
26. Spear of Destiny	E1 5b **	
27. The Whet	HVS	
28. Victoria Buttress	Very Difficult **	
29. Victoria Sponge	HVS 5a **	

d. descent

Theàrlaich-Dubh Gap, Sgùrr Alasdair

2. 50m 5a A thin sequence of moves lead horizontally (5m) left below the roof to reach a ramp come groove. This gives delightful climbing with a steep exit (40m). Carefully climb the tower of balanced blocks above to a spike belay (10m).

4 Eilidh's Ceilidh   50m   V,7 ** *(2008)*
A short route but high quality with sustained technical moves.
Start 25m up the Theàrlaich-Dubh Gap Gully at the first continuous vertical fault in the left wall.
1. 35m Sustained moves with good protection lead to a ledge below the large roof at 15m. Turn the roof on the right by fierce but well protected moves. The groove above is harder than it appears. Belay below the final slabby corner.
2. 15m Easy climbing leads to broken ground level with the top of the .
Summer: **Hard Severe **** *(2009)*
A fine climb with the crux also just above the roof.

**15 Ruari's Rammy   55m   E1 ** **   (2008)

Start 8m up and right of Eilidh's Ceilidh at the foot of a clean steep crack-line. The top pitch takes the broad rib above.

1. 25m 5c Good climbing leads to a small square foothold on the left edge of the crack-line (6m). Protection in the crack above is in dubious rock but good small gear can be found in the right wall. The crux above is steep and technical for 5m. Reach an area of large hollow blocks above and delicately pass these to a small grass ledge.

2. 30m 4c Steep moves start up the crack above. Break leftward up clean slabs to avoid the overhangs above. Finish immediately right of the top groove on Eilidh's Ceilidh

**16 Theàrlaich-Dubh Gap, Original Route   20m   Severe ** * **   (1889)

A strenuous classic route that uses most parts of the anatomy to make upward progress at the crux. There are at least four thread runners and 240cm slings are useful. Rucsacs make the effort greater but the wedging easier. Delicate bridging in rock shoes is also possible. Start from the jammed blocks that form the top of the gully. The key to the crux groove is a large polished break in the left wall (8m). Ascend more easily to a small cave containing a good thread (16m). Step left immediately above the cave to reach a block belay at the foot of the Great Stone Shoot (east side!).

Winter: **20m   Grade unknown**   (1903)

After much discussion about a modern ascent and possible grade it turns out that Raeburn had led SMC parties in both 1903 and 1905 in full winter conditions! "It was very cold here and the snow was being blown through the Gap, plastering the rocks and obscuring the holds. The climb was thoroughly interesting, and took the party just one hour" W.W.Ling.

**17 CL Route   25m   HVS 4c *   (2008)

Start from the base of the original route taking care not to block the way for other parties. Follows the obvious crack-line in the right side of the original TD Gap route before breaking onto the slabby wall above. A sustained 10m section of good but thin slab climbing follows. Protection is small and sparse. Continue more easily above to good belays.

**18 Crib Route   30m   VS 4b ** * **   (2008)

A fine route gained by the ludicrous bridge of blocks on the outside edge of the Gap. From the foot of the abseil traverse out past perched flakes (good belay possible) before crossing the bridge and a step onto the sloping ledge. A crack-line rises parallel to the outside arete. In combination they give good climbing in an amazing position. Steep moves at the start form the crux and care should be taken with blocks near the top.

**19 Short (east) side of the TD Gap   10m   Very Difficult *

Normally abseiled but climbed by parties traversing the Ridge from north to south. Compact, steep polished rock with one awkward move at half-height.

Winter: **IV,6**   (pre 1963 with aid)

This is the hardest move on a Winter Traverse and is often bypassed by abseiling into Coire a' Ghrunnda. Has been aided by lassoing the top blocks.

58. THEÀRLAICH-DUBH BUTTRESS

(NG 452 206)   Alt 850m   South facing   Map p124   Diagram p204

This is the buttress immediately right of the TD Gap. Descent is down the east ridge by a steep exposed 10m wall, best done whilst still roped. Alternatively, abseil from the in-situ slings into Theàrlaich-Dubh Gap Gully as far as possible and descend this.

Crib Route, VS, Theàrlaich-Dubh Gap Walls. Climber Mike Lates

0 West Face 90m Very Difficult * (1955)
Start under a small overhang near the left edge of the buttress and make a short traverse right, then follow a shallow groove until a corner leads onto a terrace. At the left end of the terrace is a steep slab topped by two overhangs. Climb a crack in the slab and take the first overhang direct. From under the second overhang, step left onto the edge of the buttress, and follow it to a stance and belay. Continue up easier rocks until progress is barred by another series of overhangs. Traverse across the left wall of the buttress to a projecting nose then finish by a steep shattered groove. A better finish turns these overhangs on the right and continues more directly.

1 Swamp Fox 80m HVS 5a * (2010)
Start at the lowest point of the buttress just left of the overhanging recess forming the start of Sundance.

Grand Diedre Direct, VS, Theàrlaich-Dubh Buttress. Climber Dan Moore

1. 30m Climb a steep wall then move left into the shallow groove of West Face climb to the terrace.
2. 50m Climb a short left facing corner just right of the crack. At the top pull steeply out right around a block onto the steep slab. Follow a crack running up the left side of the slab joining Sundance to reach the arête which is followed to the top.

22 Sundance 95m HVS   (1976)

1. 35m Start up an overhanging recess immediately left of Grand Diedre and exit left. Trend up and right into a small corner which leads to easier ground.
2. 35m Climb the steep slab above, which is split by a higher crack, and continue to a ledge.
3. 25m Climb up steeply on a left-slanting slab, move out right to gain the arete,

then continue to the top.

3 Grand Diedre Direct   70m   VS *** (1958)

This excellent, popular and well protected climb takes the prominent diedre running up the buttress.

1. 20m 5a Climb directly up the corner with one hard move after 15m.
2. 30m 4c Continue up the diedre across an overhang to a small ledge.
3. 20m Follow the diedre directly to the top.

Winter: **VI,6 ***** (2008)

Climb the first pitch on perfect tool placements. The second pitch gives a steep and sustained crux. The Original Start to Grand Diedre (4c) was by cracks 5m right. It gives good but inferior climbing to the Direct variation which was climbed on the same day by the same party. It transpires that this Original Start had been climbed seven years earlier, on the first ascent of Quiver. Confusingly the line was omitted in previous editions of the guidebook and the name wrongly given to West Face route. The proper line climbs the steep wall right of Grand Diedre making it a very bold lead for the era.

4 Quiver   80m   Severe (1951)

Almost certain to be under graded (see above). The route is on the Ghrunnda face of the south wall of the TD Gap. Climb steep cracks 3m right of prominent right-angled corner before climbing a steep and severe wall on small holds. Easier but less reliable rocks lead to the top of the pinnacle by its left edge.

Grand Diedre Direct, VI,6, Theàrlaich-Dubh Buttress. Climber Pete MacPherson

25 Domesday   60m   E3 5c ** *(2010)*

A fine bold route, climbed in one long pitch that could be split at 30m. Start at a thin crack in the right wall of the recess 6m right of Grand Diedre. Climb the crack then move right of a prominent pale coloured area to the right edge of the slab. Climb this with difficulty using two parallel thin cracks and small holds (crux) then continue slightly rightwards until below the upper and largest roof (possible belay). Move right below the roof then step back left above and climb a short groove leading to a smaller roof which is passed at its right end. Move left and climb easier slabs to finish up a shallow left facing corner.

26 Spear of Destiny   60m   E1 5b ** *(2010)*

Another excellent, well protected route which can be climbed in one long pitch. Takes the obvious shallow corner 4m right of Domesday. Climb the corner to a small overhang where the corner peters out. Move up left then climb a corner and flake crack. Continue up and slightly right onto an exposed edge to the foot of a small corner (45m). Step right and finish up steep slabs and easier broken ground.

27 The Whet   65m   HVS * *(1970)*

This route takes a line that rises from right to left across the whole buttress. Start by the broad crack at the right side of the Buttress.
1. 40m 5a Climb diagonally to a recess at 5m. Pull left onto the front of the buttress then straight up for 10m. Move left for 3m. Make bold moves up the groove above and left around a minor overhang to belay on a small ledge.
2. 25m 4c Finish up steep walls near Grand Diedre.

Victoria Buttress

This small buttress of rough gabbro is immediately beyond the gully on the right side of the Theàrlaich-Dubh Buttress.

28 Victoria Buttress   45m   Very Difficult ** *(1992)*

Climb the corner in the left side of the buttress.

29 Victoria Sponge   45m   HVS 5a ** *(1992)*

Climb directly up the smooth wall to the right of Victoria Buttress.

The southern flank of Dubh na Dà Bheinn lies to the right of Bealach Coire an Lochain. It is formed into short tiers of solid rough peridotite giving numerous scrambling and bouldering possibilities. Icefalls form centrally in good conditions and one line has been climbed at grade III.

59. CAISTEAL A' GARBH-CHOIRE

(NG 454 203)   Alt 800m   Maps p98, p124

This fierce looking castle stands athwart the main ridge between Sgùrr Dubh na Dà Bheinn and Sgùrr nan Eag in Bealach a' Garbh-choire. It is composed of exceptionally rough gabbro and peridotite.

Approach: Traverse the loch in either direction until a diagonal approach over huge peridotite boulders leads north-east to the castle (2hrs 15mins).

Descent: The easiest scrambling descent leads back almost to the foot of the South Ridge. Descend the west face from immediately north of the summit cairn. Many parties abseil from a large boulder above the overhanging north wall.

South Ridge   50m   Grade 3/Difficult **

A quality climb up improbably steep rocks.

North Ridge   20m   Very Difficult *

Climb a narrow rib immediately left of the huge wedged block. A steep move gives access to the abseil ledge on the right.

Lumps 45m Very Difficult * (1963)
This climb takes a direct line up the south-east face, via curious lumps of rock protruding from the wall.

60. SGÙRR NAN EAG - WEST FLANK

(NG 450 196) Alt 480m West facing Maps p98, 124

Approach: From the mouth of the corrie ascend the slabs for 500m, virtually to the headwall, until it is possible to break up right to a scree covered terrace. Antler Buttress is the cliff band that stretches back right from here (1hr 30mins). Western Buttress lies 200m above, reached by broken ground.

Antler Buttress

This steep gabbro buttress lies across the corrie and level with South Crag (53). The easiest way off is to descend a gully to the right of the crag. Alternatively continue by Western Buttress.

The Stag 80m VS 4c (1979)
Start 15m right of a shattered gully by a crack.
1. 40m Climb the crack and the slabs above to a stance.
2. 40m Continue up the crack above.

Western Buttress

Western Buttress 180m Very Difficult (1948)
This follows a prominent curving ridge high up in the centre of the west flank. Start at the foot of the steep lower section and follow a line of short cracks and chimneys up the centre of the ridge. The final steep section gives 30m of climbing to a broad terrace. A short traverse to the right leads to a steep little groove in the right-hand corner of the ridge. A few minutes' walk leads to the northern top of Sgùrr nan Eag.

The next route lies on a prominent triangular buttress high up on Sgùrr nan Eag's west flank. It lies immediately right of Western Buttress, but starts at a higher level. Approach by ascending broken ground right of Western Buttress or by following the first part of that route and then escaping by an obvious ledge on its right-hand side.

Triple Whammy 75m Very Severe (2011)
1. 35m 4c Start in the centre of the buttress at a slight recess. Tricky moves gain the wall above some steep leftward-leaning slabby rocks. Take a fairly direct line on the wall above to reach a small stance near the foot of a leftward-leaning groove.
2. 40m Start up the corner-groove, then ascend further left to a ledge. Climb a steep wall direct to a large ledge.
3. 15m Easier climbing with some loose rock leads to another good ledge and a scramble to finish at the same place as Western Buttress.

COIRE NAN LAOGH

This is the most southerly and open corrie in the Cuillin with a sunny aspect and feeling of solitude. Descent into the corrie is not recommended. The outflow is the last place to gather water for a Ridge Traverse on this approach.

61. COIRE NAN LAOGH - SOUTH FACE

(NG 461192) Alt 600m South facing Map p98 Diagram p212

The climbing consists of a back wall of slabs around 150m in height cut by gullies.

COIRE A' GHRUNNDA

61. COIRE NAN LAOGH

1. Coire nan Laogh Slabs	Grade 3 *	4. Lambda	Difficult
2. Mu	Severe *	5. Central Gully	Difficult *
3. West Gully	Easy	6. East Gully	Difficult

Descent: Descending into the corrie or the southern flank of Sgùrr nan Eag is not recommended. Traverse the Ridge east to Gars-bheinn or west to Coire a' Ghrunnda before descending.

1 Coire nan Laogh Slabs 200m Grade 3 *
A very pleasant long scramble that takes a line well left of West Gully bearing west towards the summit of Sgùrr nan Eag.

2 Mu 65m Severe *   (1958)
This climb takes the buttress left of West Gully, and is worthwhile if you happen to be in the vicinity. Start in the gully below a chockstone and 3m below a square-cut overhang in the left wall.
1. 20m Climb the wall and follow the edge of the slab to below an overhang.
2. 25m Traverse 10m left until the wall steepens, then climb it direct. Go right, then climb a left-sloping crack in the slabs above to belay in a crack.
3. 20m Climb two short walls to the left of the crack to finish.

3 West Gully 150m Moderate   (1912)
The furthest left gully. Pass the first chockstone by a through route. Turn a sec-ond major chockstone by a hard move on the ramp on the left side to reach easy ground. Grade II in winter (2004).

4 Lambda 120m Difficult   (1958)
Start 30m left of Central Gully and 15m above a grassy terrace just left of a recess. Climb a chimney formed by the recess and go up the slabs above; unfortunately the climb becomes a scramble soon after.

5 Central Gully 150m Difficult *   (1912)
A good route passing a square chockstone on the left followed by an undercut pitch, turned by a slab on the left, then a traverse back to the left. Above this, a long dyke chimney leads to a pitch of bridged boulders.

6 East Gully 150m Difficult   (1912)
Considered a less interesting option than Central Gully. A lower 30m corner gives good climbing before reaching the main feature. Grade II in winter (2004).

COIR'-UISG (CORUISK) BASIN
Map p214   Diagrams p216, 227, 241

The Coruisk (Coir'-uisg) Basin is a huge rocky arena overlooking the dark waters of Loch Coruisk. Crags are dissipated over more than ten different mountains and through half a dozen corries from sea-level to the summits. There are acres of continuous slabby rock lying between the established climbing areas. To a climber with plenty of time and good weather the possibilities are close to infinite but few are privileged enough to fully explore the intricacies because of the isolation. The corrie is like the inner sanctum of a castle, with huge walls encircling it and entrances defended by the sea or long rough approaches. Brief raids from Glen Brittle or by boat are more normal but require early starts, complex logistics, good navigation and a high level of self sufficiency. Overall a sense of remoteness is felt here far more greatly than in the rest of the Cuillin with no easy escape possible. The scale of this area is vast and many routes remain unchecked.

The Dubh Ridge is the classic mountaineering route, ascending continuous rock from sea-level to the summit to give one of the best easy climbs in the country. The Upper Cliff on Sgùrr MhicCoinnich is the longest steep face in the Cuillin providing a concentrated selection of long hard routes, supplemented by others on Bealach Buttress on the walls opposite. Coir'-uisg Buttress has gained the recognition it deserves following the addition of Skye Wall (E7/8) to its steep solid walls. Difficulty of access means that only 11 winter routes have been recorded in the entire basin but the potential is undoubtedly immense.

Access to Coruisk: There is a thriving business of boat tours from Elgol providing the easiest way to reach the eastern end of the Coruisk Basin for day trips or parties wanting to base themselves in this magical arena. The major crags all take well over an hour to reach from the jetty and for many parties access is quickest from Glen Brittle. Cross the spine of the Main Ridge (750m+) by a choice of passes and descend to the foot of the climbs (2-4 hrs). The traditional approach from Sligachan is long but worth knowing about. Walking through Glen Sligachan and over Druim Hain reaches the wrong end of the loch for all of the major Coruisk crags. Instead cross the Druim nan Ràmh from Harta Corrie at **Bealach Mac an t-Soair** NG 467 227 (not marked). The ascent is by an open grassy gully but the descent is more intricate. It starts by a major horizontal terrace just a minute above where the crest has been gained. Descend westward, zigzagging occasionally and losing as little height as possible towards Coir'-uisg Buttress (3hrs 30mins).

Approaching from Kilmarie or Elgol involves tackling the infamous Bad Step at the end of the walk. A problem more likely to trouble climbers in wet weather is encountering high water levels at Camasunary (also tidal) or the final stepping stones at Coruisk. Allow 2hrs 30min.

Topography: Cliffs are described in a clockwise direction around the Coruisk Basin starting from the jetty by the JMCS Memorial Hut and finishing with the lowest flanks of Sgùrr na Strì at the east end of Loch Coruisk. The shortest non-tidal river in Britain connects Loch Coruisk to the sea and a well constructed path takes hundreds of tourists from the jetty to the world famous viewpoint every year.

An Garbh-choire is the first major corrie lying beneath the southern peaks of the Ridge. Traverse around the bay for routes on Gars-bheinn. It is better to follow the south shore of Loch Coruisk for 1km then make an easy rise below the east flank of the Dubh Ridge [68] for routes on Sgùrr a' Coire Bhig and Sgùrr nan Eag. The Dubh Ridge dominates the view from the east end of Loch Coruisk, obscuring Coireachan Rhuadha and the important peaks surrounding it. West of the Dubh Ridge continuous sweeps of slabs rise from the shore of Loch Coruisk for over 2km across the mouths of two minor climbing corries, Coire a' Chaoruinn and Coire an Lochain.

The basin opens out beyond the flood plain into an open bowl of scree and grass. Coireachan Rhuadha is a huge corrie holding the majority of classic routes in the area. The corrie is bound by the towering north face of Sgùrr a' Coire an Lochain [70] on the left and the long South-east Ridge of Sgùrr a' Ghreadaidh to the right.

The head of the Basin is dominated by Coir'-uisg faces of Sgùrr a' Ghreadaidh [76] and Sgùrr a' Mhadaidh [77]. Glac Mhòr is an easy open corrie further north

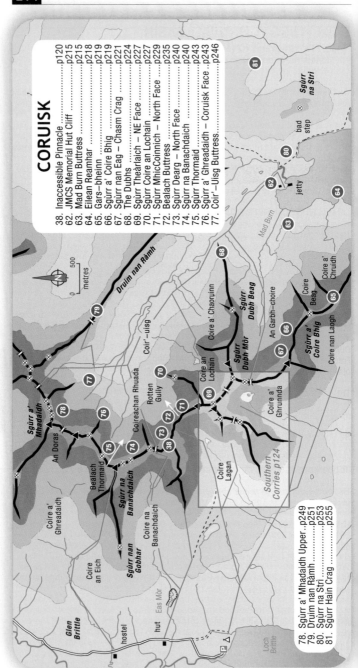

214

that gives one of the simplest passages to Glen Brittle. It is bounded to the north by Druim nan Ràmh [79], the ridge that bisects the heart of the Cuillin Bowl between Coruisk and Harta Corrie. The cliffs on its south flank are over 300m high and stretch for more 3km. Sgùrr na Strì [80] overlooks Coruisk from the east. It is a magnificent viewpoint sitting boldly between Coruisk and Camasunary. Sgùrr Hain Crag [81] overlooks Camasunary and is reached from Coruisk via the bealach north of Sgùrr na Strì in about 1hr.

Approaches: The most logical and useful routes are described in detail at the start of each crag description. Most have an approach from both Glen Brittle and Coruisk described. Timings from Coruisk are given for parties departing the jetty in Loch Scavaig and the passes from Glen Brittle are page referenced to their full descriptions.

LOCH NA CUILCE

The innermost part of Loch Scavaig is called Loch na Cuilce.

62. JMCS MEMORIAL HUT CLIFF

(NG 487 197)   Alt 15m   West facing

Extensive sections of rock lie immediately north of the hut with several routes from Very Difficult upwards. By linking pitches, as much as 100m of good climbing on excellent rock is possible. The crag just outside the hut is an obvious attraction with the following routes recorded. Routes are described from left to right starting directly behind the hut door.

Thurman's Request   20m   Severe *   (1976)
Start in shallow groove & go up 5m onto sloping ledge. Traverse left 5m and ascend a shallow groove, finishing up a short slab, one runner.
Duffy Variation: **25m   Severe ***   (1976)
From the ledge step just left then climb thin cracks rising up and left (piton placement at 6m). Ascend a wider crack left up to the top.

The Minke   20m   E2 5b *   (1997)
Start directly behind the hut door. Climb the basalt dyke which slants rightwards up the wall.

Beached Whale   20m   E3 5c *   (1994)
A good route which is protected by small Friends. Start 5m right of the hut and climb directly to the big horizontal break. Follow the break leftwards with difficulty to finish.

The next climb lies up left of the hut on the cliff above the descent path from the previous routes.

Half Century Crack   30m   E1 5c   (1999)
On the right side of the crag is a very prominent groove with a crack which peters out just below the top. Start up a grassy rake on the right and traverse left into the crack at one-quarter height. Climb the crack to a well protected crux at the top.

Meall na Cuilce between the Mad Burn and Loch Coruisk has a broad south face which also provides some fine exploratory climbing.

63. MAD BURN BUTTRESS

(NG 479 195)   Alt 150m   South-East facing   Map p214   Diagrams p216, 217

This is an excellent, quick drying diamond shaped crag of perfect gabbro, giving

COIR'-UISG

CORUISK - South

Q. Bealach Coire a' Ghrunnda
U. Coire a' Chaoruinn
V. An Garbh–choire
W. Sgurr Dubh Beag
X. Sgurr Dubh Mòr

d. descent

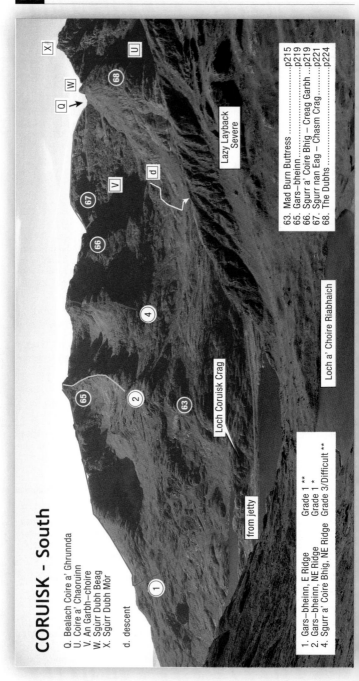

Loch Coruisk Crag

from jetty

Loch a' Choire Riabhaich

Lazy Layback   Severe

1. Gars–bheinn, E Ridge   Grade 1 **
2. Gars–bheinn, NE Ridge   Grade 1 *
4. Sgurr a' Coire Bhig, NE Ridge Grade 3/Difficult **

attractive climbing in the middle grades. It is a good choice when cloud is low over the tops. Descend easily by either flank.

Approach: From the jetty traverse the bay with some awkward steps unless the tide is very low. Cross the Mad Burn not far above the shore then strike uphill to the obvious large buttress (30mins).

Widdle   120m   Severe   *(1984)*
At the left extreme a small buttress forms a squat pinnacle with a chimney-line above. This route appears to climb these features: "Climb easy angle to an old iron spike. Climb a chimney on the left for 6m then exit on right to a slab. Ledge. Continue up chimney to top."

Midge-a-mad-tosis   105m   HVS **   *(1999)*
Dries much faster than Mayday. Start 7m left of Mayday below a hanging block.
1. 20m 5a Mantelshelf on to the block and go up to a left-trending ramp-line. Move left using a thin crack, then right to belay on Mayday.
2. 45m 4b Go up the corner for 3m, then strike leftwards up a slab. Continue trending leftward on slabs and go up a gangway to a large grassy ledge.
3. 40m 5a Step left into a groove and cross Mayday. Continue direct towards a shallow right-facing corner. From the base of the corner, step right to gain and finish up cracks.

Mayday   90m   Severe *   *(1961)*
On the left-hand side of the face is a conspicuous left-sloping diedre, starting 25m up the face.
1. 25m Start 15m left of the lowest rocks where a line of weakness on a steep smooth wall leads to the diedre via a mantelshelf and a left-trending crack.
2. 30m Climb the diedre by delightful climbing on small holds to a small stance.
3. 35m Move left, then climb a crack, walls and ledges to easy ground.

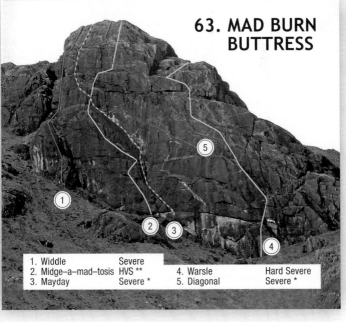

63. MAD BURN BUTTRESS

COIR'-UISG

1. Widdle	Severe	
2. Midge–a–mad–tosis	HVS **	
3. Mayday	Severe *	
4. Warsle		Hard Severe
5. Diagonal		Severe *

4 Warsle   90m   Hard Severe *   (1962)
The lowest point of the buttress is formed by a 6m pulpit, above which a deep crack cleaves the rock.
1. Either gain the pulpit from the right, or better from directly from below.
2. Climb the crack above the pulpit, then an easy looking corner on the left to reach a broad grass ledge. The face above is seamed by two left-slanting ledge crack systems.
3. 35m 4a Climb the obvious crack system towards the right of the grassy ledge, past the obvious left-bending crack, to a point about 3m above, where a ledge is followed leftwards until it is possible to climb to a thin crack (wires). Then, move right onto an easy slab and climb on this holds to a grassy terrace.
4. 4b   From the terrace, take the crack slightly to the right of where pitch 3 finished (beware loose blocks at top). Then, move up and right to a ledge, and make an awkward move back left to a larger ledge. Climb a short wall to another grassy terrace.
5. 4b/c Climb the obvious crack on the right (crux) at the top of which an easy angled slab leads to the top.

5 Diagonal   135m   Severe *   (1962)
This is the longest possible climb on the crag. Start as for Warsle and gain the broad grass ledge. Ascend 6m of the next pitch of Warsle to reach the lower of the two diagonal crack systems, and climb it to a stance (15m). Continue along the ledge crack system until below the south end of the first terrace and under an overhang. Regain the ledge system 3m higher by climbing a steep nose to a stance (30m). About 50m of interesting climbing by the easiest line leads to the top.

64. EILEAN REAMHAR

(NG 487 187)   Tidal   Map p214

The islet of Eilean Reamhar lies on the shore 1km south of the JMCS hut. It is home to the large colony of common seal that forms the main attraction of the boat tours from Elgol and should not be climbed on between April and October. Despite close inspection by boat no climbs or faces resembling those described have been identified.

Approach: Follow the coastal path around the bay and descend easily when directly above the islet which is only accessible at low tide. The routes are on south-east facing gabbro sea-cliffs and are described from left to right as approached from the mainland. The first route is on a barrel shaped buttress.

No Gain Without Pain   E2 6a   (1990)
Start centrally and follow a line of very small sharp holds. Go up to a corner, move left and follow a basalt intrusion leftwards through a bulge. Unprotected.

Slabsville   VS 4b   (1990)
This route takes a slab right of the previous route. Start at low tide 6m from the right arete in a small corner with a square block. Climb the slab on the left to a horizontal crack. Move left slightly, then go straight up the white streak in the slab above, passing two pockets. Unprotected.

There are two Severes further right. The first climbs the slab and the second goes up the right arete on a hanging ramp, then over a bulge and roof to finish up the headwall centrally.

Half Crack   Hard Severe   (1990)
This route is on the east face of the crag, taking the top half of a prominent crack. Start centrally and climb the wall on good holds to a big ledge. Go up and left, then ascend the superb crack to a block. Move left and follow the slab to the top.

The next crag is a 30m slab with overhangs at the bottom left and top right.

Nettie   Difficult   (1990)
Climb the left edge of the slab.

Sealsville   VS 4c   (1990)
Start at a large spike at the bottom of the slabs. Go up to a V-notch. Pull through
this rightwards, then move left a metre and follow the left-hand of two thin cracks.
Move leftwards to belay on a grass ledge just below the top.

Short Spurt   E2 5b   (1990)
There is an obvious protruding block 10m up and just right of the previous route.
The route goes through the overhang to the right of this. The rope can be flicked
over the block as a runner. Bridge up a short corner on the right and surmount the
roof by a good hold on its lip. Easier climbing leads to the top.

65. GARS-BHEINN

(NG 468 187)   895m   Map p214   Diagram p216

Gars-bheinn is a worthy peak from which to start the Cuillin Ridge with the
magnificent summit dome standing out proudly above the Atlantic Ocean. Only the
East and North-east Ridges form any worthy routes although the vegetated north
faces may reward the winter explorer. The approach from Glen Brittle is described
in the Coire a' Ghrunnda chapter.

Descent: Coire Beag can be descended towards Coruisk by unpleasantly loose
ground from either of the two tiny cols west of Gars-bheinn. A rapid descent west
to Glen Brittle is by scree slopes to gain the boggy path at 240m.

**East Ridge   4km   Grade 1 ** **
The purists start to a Traverse is both aesthetically and physically attractive saving
over an hour of effort compared to the Glen Brittle approach. Two plateaus lie
halfway up the south-eastern flank of Gars-bheinn, visible on the skyline from the
jetty. Follow the coastal path which is discontinuous. A series of steep rises followed
by leftward traverses have to be made to reach the upper plateau at NG 477 181
(1hr 30mins). A short steep rise above ends through some small bluffs of loose
basalt to reach the start of the Ridge proper (Pt 686). Enjoy the gently rising crest
to the summit, finishing with some simple scrambling (2hrs 30mins).

North-East Ridge   3km   Grade 1 *
Pass close by Mad Burn Buttress before gaining the small nose of rock that forms
the base of the route at the lower left side of Coire Beag. Scramble easily to a large
moss covered pinnacle which is bypassed on the right before regaining the line.
The steep summit rocks are bypassed on the right by a narrow shelf (2hrs 15mins).

66. SGÙRR A' COIRE BHIG

(NG 466 192)   875m   Map p214   Diagrams p216, 220

Approach: The Coire Beag routes are only worth approaching from Coruisk via
the flood plain of An Garbh-choire. The upper cliff is best approached from Glen
Brittle via Coire a' Ghrunnda, as described below for Chasm Crag [67]. From the
unnamed dip between Sgùrr nan Eag and Sgùrr a' Coire Bhig descend and traverse
east beneath the upper cliffs.

Descent: Coire nan Laogh and the south flanks of Sgùrr nan Eag are very slabby
and not recommended. Following the Ridge north to Bealach a' Garbh-choire via
Sgùrr nan Eag and descending Coire a' Ghrunnda is the most conventional return
to Glen Brittle.

66. SGÙRR A' COIRE BHIG
Creag Garbh

67. SGÙRR NAN EAG
Chasm Crag

1. The Yorkshireman's Debut   HVS 5b **
2. Rough Stuff   E2 5b **
3. The Romp   Severe
4. West Gully   Difficult
5. East Gully   Difficult

6. Ladders   VS 4c *
7. Leviathan   E1 *
8. Left Edge   E1 **
9. The Chasm   III **
10. Reverse Thrust   VS 5a *

Coire Beag Face

Dwindle Wall   120m   Severe   *(1968)*
This route starts at an altitude of 600m, high on the right side of Coire Beag.
Left of the North-East Ridge is a buttress with a spring at its foot. Climb a chimney
above to a glacis (30m). Continue leftwards up broken slabs to a broken ledge.
Continue to a grassy rake and belays (25m). Climb much steeper rock up a tapering
wall, overcome a small overhang and then traverse left at 25m on a gangway to
belay on a small flake. Continue directly to a steep exit on a grass ledge.

North-East Ridge   600m   Grade 3/Difficult ★★   *(1896)*
This is a shorter but similar excursion to the Dubh Ridge with far less traffic giving
a superb scramble. Start at the lowest slabs of the ridge at an altitude of 500m.
The route is open to much variation and this freedom of choice remains higher up
where the ridge narrows. Near the summit a steeper section of rock is turned on
the right (1hr 30mins).

Creag Garbh

(NG 463 195)   Alt 700m   North facing   Map p214, Diagrams p216, 220

Routes are described as they are reached from the col when descending eastwards.
The first climb takes the rightmost corner of the crag

The Yorkshireman's Debut   25m   HVS 5b ★★   *(2008)*
After a tricky start up the short slabby corner on the right, the main corner gives
delightful bridging on excellent rock.

On the steep wall left of the largest and leftmost corner are three striking crack
lines. Scramble up and right via a series of ledges and short walls to belay at the
foot of a corner, directly beneath the cracks.

Rough Stuff   45m   E2 5b ★★   *(2008)*
The righthand crack. Climb easily up the corner and follow the rib above for a few
metres before a traverse can be made to gain the foot of the crack. Climb this past
a ledge to reach an obvious left-slanting dyke, which is followed with continued
interest to the top.

The Romp   65m   Severe   *(2010)*
1. 35m 4a Climb the corner as for the above and continue leftwards up a ramp to
its top. Step down into a gully on the left and climb the lefthand corner.
2. 30m Finish easily up the slab on the right.

Continuing the diagonal descent two large gullies lie either side of the lowest point
of the buttress.

West Gully   100m   Difficult   *(1921)*
The gully is split by a rib of rock. Climb the right fork to a large cave and a through
route. Climb slabs on the left to another fine cave which is also climbed by an
aperture in the roof. One smaller pitch leads to easier rocks.

East Gully   100m   Difficult   *(1921)*
Pass numerous large chockstones of which the second is Difficult. Finish by a clean
rake to the Ridge.

67. SGÙRR NAN EAG - CHASM CRAG

(NG 459 196)   Alt 780m   North facing   Map p214 Diagrams p216, 220

A large north facing crag of compact rock with some very good routes. It lies just
north of the unnamed bealach between Sgùrr nan Eag and Sgùrr a' Coire Bhig.

Approaches: From Coruisk ascend An Garbh-choire to beyond the first narrowing then climb south-west over boulders and scree directly to the cliffs (2hrs). From Glen Brittle gain Bealach a' Garbh-choire via Coire a' Ghrunnda as described in the Coire a' Ghrunnda chapter (2hrs 15mins). The cliff lies 600m to the south-east, beyond the summit of Sgùrr nan Eag. The most direct approach is a horizontal traverse across the boulder field running below the slabby crest. Easier but longer is to traverse the long summit ridge and descend to the unnamed bealach beyond. Descend for 50m before traversing 100m back west to the foot of the cliffs (3hrs). Routes are described from left to right.

Descent: Return by the appropriate route of approach.

6 Ladders 110m VS 4c *   (1957)
This is a good, sustained and pleasant route giving varied and, at times, steep climbing. It starts in the second corner 25m left of The Chasm. Gain a line of holds on the left wall of the corner; a shoulder is traditional but not essential. Go up and swing left to a jutting platform. Climb the steep wall above to join the corner-crack at a nose projecting from the right wall, then follow the crack to a broken terrace and block belays on the right (30m). From just left of the start of the second pitch of Left Edge, traverse 10m left then go up to the base of the shallower of two dykes. Follow this back up right to come out near a small ledge on the edge. Traverse 5m left to a narrow dyke-chimney and climb this to the top.

7 Leviathan 115m E1 *   (1968)
A rather serious route with areas of loose rock, albeit in good positions. Start at a corner 15m left of The Chasm.
1. 35m 5a Climb a crack to a sloping ledge at 10m, then continue up the wall by a basalt dyke to a large ledge with jammed boulder thread belay.
2. 40m 5a Step left from the belay and climb a short wall to gain a left-rising ramp. Follow the ramp to an area of rotten rock. Where the ramp ends under a small overhang (small wire runner beneath the overhang), move down a little and step left into a bottomless groove. Climb the groove until a traverse can be made left to a large basalt boulder jammed in the bottom of the crack system.
3. 40m 4b Climb the crack directly, passing a small overhang without difficulty; belay on the summit ridge.

8 Left Edge 90m E1 **   (1957)
Takes the clean-cut edge above the left wall of The Chasm. Fine climbing with only just adequate protection.
1. 30m 4a Climb the edge to broken rocks and belays on the left.
2. 40m 5a Climb just left of the edge in a fine position to a small ledge (25m). The original route traversed from here for 5m to an overhung nook which only contains an ancient peg. Instead, continue up the edge until small cams form a reasonable belay
3. 20m 5a Continue up the edge to reach easier rocks.

9 The Chasm 120m Very Difficult **   (1919)
A popular route often holding late snow. There are four pitches of which the topmost is the hardest. Highly recommended for the rock scenery.
Winter: **III **   *(1919)*
An excellent route but hard if the snow is unconsolidated.

10 Reverse Thrust 80m VS 5a *   (1997)
Well right of The Chasm is a recessed area. This route follows a big corner bounding the right side of the recessed area and finishes just right of a prominent white scar. Climb the corner over a basalt bulge at 10m and continue into a recess (30m). Continue up a crack-line, climb a bulge into a V-groove (crux) and go up to a glacis (20m). Climb slabs, then trend left below a monster block to easy ground.

The final route remains unidentified and may well be elsewhere!

The Chasm, III, Chasm Crag, Sgùrr Nan Eag. Climber Charlie Hill

Micawber 70m Severe *(1972)*
On the right-hand half of this crag two westward facing slabs abut the main wall. The route starts on the slabs on the right from a wide terrace.
1. 35m Climb cracks and small holds sometimes fragile to the second of two wide shelves at the top of the slab.

Mrs Beaton, HVS, Loch Coruisk Crag, The Dubhs. Climber Graeme Johnson

2. 30m Make an exposed traverse to the right for 7m, at first out of balance but on good footholds, then upwards for 3m. Make a leftward traverse for 5m and an awkward upward move on the right of a trap dyke. Cross this then up leftwards to emerge suddenly on perfect rock on top of the ridge.

68. THE DUBHS

(NG 476 208)   Map p214   Diagrams p216, 241

The northern boundary of An Garbh-choire is the long ridge which comprises the three summits of 'The Dubhs', namely Sgùrr Dubh Beag (733m), Sgùrr Dubh Mòr (944m) and Sgùrr Dubh na Dà Bheinn (938m).

Loch Coruisk Crag

(NG 485 200)   Alt 15m   North-East facing

This crag is 10mins walk from the JMCS hut on the approach to the Dubh Ridge. There are two buttresses with a huge boulder between them. This is the right-hand buttress that is divided into two prominent slabs by an overlap running the length of the crag.

**Mrs Beaton 45m HVS ** **   (2008)
Start at the base of the left-hand slab.
1. 30m 5a Climb thin crack up immaculate slab for 20m then follow a right-slanting crack to a block belay.
2. 15m Climb an easy corner and slab to finish.

Double Zero 55m E4 ***   (2010)
Climbs left edge of right hand slab. Bold.
1. 20m 4b Climb rib on left edge of slab to obvious diagonal fault line & roof (easier to belay at right end of fault)
2. 35m 5c Traverse left along fault to pull through roof at triangular niche. Step right & follow left edge of upper slab to finish up the vague crack (crux).

Fanny Cradock 55m VS 4c *   (2010)
1. 20m Climb easy corner to belay at right end of diagonal fault line.
2. 35m Traverse left along fault to pull through roof at triangular niche. Step left & follow slab & corner to top.

Ginger Nut 55m E1 *   (2010)
1. 20m Climb corner & slab right of Fanny Cradock to shared belay.
2. 35m 5b Climb crack in upper slab above through bulge (crux). When crack peters out, move right to finish up slab.

Dubh Slabs

Approaches: The shore path is forced close to the water by the lowest rocks of the Dubh Ridge 1.5km from the jetty. Some very good quality pitches can be climbed in the steeper lowest tier but make for a long day with a heavy sack if combined with an ascent of the ridge. Approaches from Glen Brittle by Coire a' Ghrunnda or Bealach na Banachdaich or down the glen from Sligachan all take at least 3 hours.

Descents: There are no quick or easy descents from the Dubhs. From Dubh na Dà Bheinn the quickest escape is by Coire a' Ghrunnda to Glen Brittle (2hrs). Return to Coruisk is conventionally by An Garbh-choire which is spectacular but painfully slow to descend starting from the south side of Caisteal a' Garbh-choire (2hrs 30mins). Descending into Coire an Lochain then reversing the slabby approach route via Coire a' Chaoruinn (described immediately below) to the west end of Loch Coruisk is more pleasant, but not at all recommended in poor visibility (2hrs).

Two climbs have been recorded on the buttress immediately left of the starting gully for the Dubh Ridge. Traverse right and descend this if not continuing.

Firkin 95m Hard Severe   (2008)
A variation start from below a large overlap 40m left of the starting gully for the Dubh Ridge.
1. 20m Follow easy slab to belay below a corner.
2. 30m 4b Pull over a bulge and follow a wide crack to belay at a large boulder.
3. 45m Continue up a fault for 15m then follow a right-curving line across the slab to the top.

Old Mortality 100m HVS **   (2008)
Another variation start 15m left of Firkin at toe of buttress
1. 35m Climb thin cracks on left edge of slab until it is possible to move right to an overlap. Follow this to belay below a crack.
2. 25m 5a Climb a fine crack to top in superb position.
3. 40m Follow a fault-line and the left edge of an easy slabs to top.

The Dubh Ridge 2.5km Grade 3/Moderate ****
The Dubh Ridge is very committing for such a technically easy route with escape down the steep flanks uninviting. Once started there are no easy or quick ways back to civilisation adding a tension not often felt on other Cuillin Classics, 4hrs 30mins to Sgùrr Dubh na Dà Bheinn.
    Start by a straight vegetated gully rising from the loch that is hidden on the approach to gain a short level shoulder at 75m. Above here the ridge is very broad but generally the left side is followed. Bypasses of almost any difficulties are possible right to the summit of Sgùrr Dubh Beag. Those tackling the blank slabs will find they have a habit of steepening unexpectedly and testing the nerve of the formerly confident climber.
    Pass two small terraces with tiny pools before reaching a grassy hollow at 470m (possible escape to the east). Above here the strata become more vertical forming a selection of slabby corner-lines. At 650m a horizontal area lies on the left edge

The Dubh Ridge, Grade 3/Moderate. Climbers Ray Lee, Lou Kass and Mel Nicoll

of the ridge giving access to a south facing short and open scree gully. This is the quick bypass of Sgùrr Dubh Beag that avoids the need to abseil and is recommended for parties not carrying a rope or behind schedule (2hrs 30mins from JMCS hut to here). The summit of Dubh Beag is reached 10mins above.

From the summit a short scramble leads down to a very steep edge and a spiked block usually adorned with abseil tat. Down-climbing is at least Severe and most parties make a 20m abseil. Awkward to start, it drops to the south side of the promontory passing through a small roof before reaching a grass ledge below. Down-climb a final nose to reach the col at the head of Coire a' Chaoruinn which gives a possible escape. The bypass rejoins here, having followed below the south wall for 200m.

From the col a long section of good easy scrambling, descending initially, is followed directly until steep rocks are encountered below the summit ridge of Sgùrr Dubh Mòr (944m). Care should be exercised with loose rock if these are tackled directly. Diagonal grassy rakes on the south flank bypass these and lead left to the crest. All but the left most have a steep rock pitch to finish. The summit lies at the far western end of the narrow ridge. Zigzag down the steep south-west spur to a rocky col. Difficulties here are bypassed on either flank before regaining the ridge to Sgùrr Dubh na Dà Bheinn.

Winter: **IV** *

A serious winter expedition. Conditions vary hugely and can be very time consuming under heavy snow.

COIRE A' CHAORUINN & COIRE AN LOCHAIN

These two corries are minor in climbing terms but very worthy of exploration. They initially share a common approach by highly enjoyable slabs. Coire a' Chaoruinn empties down slabs and waterslides to the west end of Loch Coruisk. It is bounded on all sides by the steep walls of Dubh Beag and Dubh Mòr giving access to the col. Only one route has been recorded high on the west wall of Dubh Beag just to the right of the biggest overhang. **Paddy and Mick's Route** (Moderate 1983) traverses horizontally above the overhang then zigzags up water worn slabs to a grassy gully and easy terrace. Coire an Lochain is a beautiful spot that is rarely visited with fairly easy access from Glen Brittle. It has one broken face best viewed from Sgùrr Dubh Mòr.

Approaches: From the west end of Loch Coruisk start up the slabs of Coire a' Chaoruinn which are continuous to the Dubh Ridge. Occasional cairns mark a westward rising traverse line towards Coire an Lochain. At 360m a prominent grass rake, identified by a large flake at the bottom which forms a natural arch, slants right across the North-East Flank (Grade 3) of Sgùrr Dubh Mòr. Rise more steeply up delightful slabs to reach the gem like lochan nestling in upper Coire an Lochain (2hrs). From Glen Brittle it is easy to descend from Bealach Coire an Lochain if approaching from Coire a' Ghrunnda and steeper but more direct from Coire Lagan via Bomb Alley (see Sgùrr MhicCoinnich [42], route 14), and Bealach MhicCoinnich, (2hrs 30mins).

69. SGÙRR THEÀRLAICH - NORTH-EAST FACE

(NG 452 207)   Alt 825m   North-East facing   Map p214

Aladdin's Route   80m   Difficult   *(1950)*
This is the intriguing cleft that forms the chimney on the north-east side of the Theàrlaich-Dubh Gap. There are several entertaining problems finishing by a through route.
Winter: **80m   IV,6 ***   *(2005)*
By the summer route, found to be disappointingly short but worthwhile nevertheless. Start below and left of the chimney in a snowy alcove.
1. 35m Climb an easy angled snowy slab and cross a snow ledge to gain a cave below the main difficulties.
2. 35m Climb the chimney above with interest to below a huge chockstone.
3. 10m Surmount the chockstone using the left wall (crux) and climb steeply to finish in the TD Gap.

North-East Ridge of Sgùrr Theàrlaich   200m   Moderate   *(1913)*
A wall bounds the right side of the screes below Aladdin's Route and forms a ridge leading directly towards the summit. Start at the lowest rocks. A broad terrace is crossed at half height. A number of breaks through the steeper rocks above can be used to reach the summit as directly as possible. A winter ascent has also been made at grade II (2009).

70. SGÙRR COIRE AN LOCHAIN

(NG 455 216)   Alt 500m   North facing   Map p214   Diagram p241

"Sgùrr Coire an Lochain was the last unclimbed mountain summit in the British Isles and, though of no great height, an ascent of one of the most magnificent and forbidding rock faces in the Cuillin exudes a truly mountaineering atmosphere with plenty of route finding problems plus lots of solitude." Stuart Pedlar, Cuillin Historian.

Approaches: The South Ridge is approached easily from Coire an Lochain. Climbs are on the broad north-east face. Technically easiest is to continue to the head of the Coruisk Basin past the slabs for an awe inspiring view of the peak. Take a direct line up peridotite blocks and buttresses to reach the toe of the north-east face (2hrs). More fun in dry weather is to approach as for Coire an Lochain to the end of the slanting rake. A gradual rising traverse of the slabs, crossing the outflow from the lochan, is then needed to reach the toe of the north-east face (2hrs).

From Glen Brittle cross Bealach Coire na Banachdaich, (see opening diagram Coire na Banachdaich chapter), descend scree and boulders then follow the cairned trail

COIR'-UISG

down until level with the base of the face (3hrs). Escape from the peak is made by the South Ridge route which leads to Bealach MhicCoinnich for the simplest return to Glen Brittle. For Coruisk descend via Coire an Lochain.

South Ridge

This is the short ridge above Coire an Lochain linking the peak to the Main Ridge below Bealach MhicCoinnich. It gives the easiest approach and only escape. The summit is accepted as the most northerly top which is actually lower than parts of the South Ridge.

South Ridge   300m   Grade 3/Difficult *   (1896)
The ridge soon narrows and a level section leads to the higher south top. A Difficult move is required descending into a prominent gap that cuts across the ridge. A short scramble then leads to the small rocky summit and great viewpoint that lies below the level of the approach. The gullies either side of the prominent gap have been climbed. Both are scrappy with the western gully holding a through route near the top (1960).

North-East Face

This is the steep tiered face overlooking Coir'-uisg and hidden from the Main Ridge. It consists of overlapping slabs and walls which steepen as they swing west. The rock is of a reasonable quality, but lines of weakness are few. An eye for the best line and the ability to climb with a grade or two in hand is advisable here. Descriptions should be used only as an indication of the lines to climb.

Original Route   300m   Difficult   (1896)
"The ascent gave over 300m of rock climbing, most of it across steeply inclined slabs of wet and rather slippery rock. Though no part was especially difficult, nearly every step required care, and good anchorages were few and far between."

Raeburn's Route   300m   Very Difficult   (1913)
Start below the overhang of the very steep edge facing Bidein. After 100m a traverse is forced on steep slabs round to the east. There does not appear to be any way through the overhang until right on the other corner of the tower facing the head of Coruisk. **Rum Doodle** (1984) was recorded as a variation as a result of getting "a little lost."

Shelf Route   150m   Severe **   (1949)
An interesting and enjoyable mountaineering route on the north face. It follows the 100m right-sloping shelf above the overhanging section of the north face, some 75m above the lowest rocks. Start either by a traverse from the right, or directly from below by a left-slanting line of weakness which continues beyond the shelf; the shelf is 45m from the start of the traverse or at 75m when approached from below. The shelf is initially 1m wide ledge, widening to a 12m sweep of slabs. There are three 35m pitches along the shelf, with the difficulties concentrated at the slabs. From the top of the slabs, an easy traverse leads to broken rocks at the right end of the shelf. Climb steep rocks for 12m to a ledge and block belay. A short wall of slabs on the right leads to easier ground.

COIREACHAN RUADHA

Although far quieter than more accessible regions, many of the climbs in this corrie have become justifiably famous for their quality and epitomising the big mountain atmosphere. The Upper Cliff of Sgùrr MhicCoinnich is considered by many as the best crag in the Cuillin but complex approaches ensure a secluded experience. The first cliffs are in close proximity to each other and share a variety of approach choices.

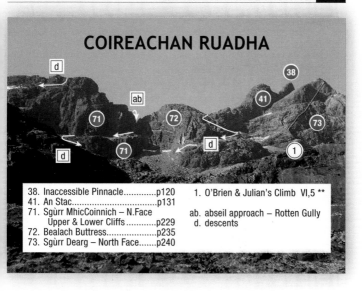

COIREACHAN RUADHA

71. SGÙRR MHICCOINNICH - NORTH FACE

**(NG 449 215)   Alt 630m   North-East facing   Maps p98, 124, 214
Diagrams p229, 232, 241**

The Lower Cliff is a large and significant face but is overshadowed by the magnificent steep climbs of the Upper Cliff. A settled period of good weather should always bring climbs on this cliff into consideration for strong teams.

Approach from Coruisk: This is simple. Follow the faint cairned trail from the head of the Coruisk flood plains. It leads to Bealach na Banachdaich staying on the south side of the main watercourse with stunning views of Sgùrr Coire an Lochain. Above the level of a slabby waterfall (c.600m) follow a left tributary to reach the lower slopes of Rotten Gully (2hrs). Bypass the Lower Cliff most easily on the east to reach the Upper Cliff.

Approaches from Glen Brittle: There are three choices. Most popular is to climb the An Stac Screes from Coire Lagan then make a 50m abseil descent of Rotten Gully. This is the lowest point between Sgùrr MhicCoinnich and An Stac easily identified by an ideally situated huge flake just on the Coruisk side. The gully is very loose but leads to the terrace running below the Upper Cliff (2hrs 30mins). A second abseil from a spike at 30m leads to the foot of the Lower Cliff and Lower Wall of Bealach Buttress. Longer (3hr) approaches by Bealach MhicChoinnich or Bealach na Banachdaich are also possible but mean climbing with boots and rucksacks.

Lower Cliff

This lies below the terrace that supports the Upper Cliff. Approach from Rotten Gully by traversing east for 200m below the Upper Cliff to where an easy scrambling descent can be made. A large raised slabby terrace lies beneath J Buttress to the left of the central Great Gully. The gully itself is still unclimbed and the St Andrew's U.M.C. party of 1958 found it 'unclimbable'. St Andrew's Crack lies immediately right of Great Gully. A pronounced bowl starting halfway up the crag is The Amphitheatre. Right again more steep crags separated by gullies and clefts stretch up towards Rotten Gully. The routes are described from left to right.

1 Magpie Cracks   65m   VS   *(1968)*
Left of Great Gully and 30m up lies a huge sloping terrace. Start on the terrace immediately left of a smooth overhanging wall.
1. 35m 4c Make a rising traverse left across slabs to reach and climb a corner-crack.
2. 30m 4b Move left and climb to the top by cracks and walls.

2 St Andrew's Crack   105m   HVS   *(1958)*
Definitely a climb for lovers of wide cracks! The route follows the left-hand of two cracks which run up the lower cliffs just to the right of Great Gully. It is slow to dry as it acts as a drain. Start 10m right of Great Gully at the foot of the crack.
1. 30m 4c Climb the right side of the crack, traverse left, then go up right over a small slab to a stance.
2. 25m 5a Climb the left-hand crack which overhangs in two places.
3. 20m Follow the crack over two jammed blocks, then easier rocks lead to a pinnacle with a stance at its crest.
4. 30m Climb the harder crack, then continue under and over jammed blocks to the terrace.

3 Chemist's Constitutional   120m   Very Difficult   *(1958)*
Start 30m right of Great Gully at the lowest rocks, and just right of another gully. Climb a buttress for 60m to The Amphitheatre. Traverse left across its mouth, then go over the left wall to the first gully; climb this to the terrace.
Variation: **Sue's Chimney   35m   Very Difficult**   *(1959)*
Start at the foot of a gully on the left side of The Amphitheatre, halfway up J Buttress. Climb the gully, then its right wall to the terrace.

Upper Cliff

All routes start at least 100m east of Rotten Gully with the huge recessed North-East Gully the first prominent feature recognisable. Fluted Buttress lies to the left with the prominent cleft of Cocoa Cracks on its front face before the cliff turns to face south-east. The south-east wall contains a prominent crack that forms the starts of both Crack of Dawn and Dawn Grooves. Mongoose Direct tackles the great cleft to the left and King Cobra tackles the buttress left again. Left of the 235uous gully is the Hanging Slab high above some huge overhangs.

Descents: All routes end on the summit ridge towards its north end. Descend this north by a series of steps on the Coire Lagan side to the head of Rotten Gully. One obscure descent to the base of the cliffs, other than by Rotten Gully, is by the East Face Rake (route 15), an eastward slanting rake towards Sgùrr Coire an Lochain. The descent starts left (south) from the top of all routes by a notch immediately below the only broad easy (40m) section of the North Ridge. Routes are described from right to left as approached from Rotten Gully.

4 North-East Buttress   120m   Very Difficult *   *(1950)*
This is the broad buttress between North-East Gully and Rotten Gully. Start near North-East Gully by climbing a series of broken walls and corners. At 60m there is a short steep pitch to a shelf with an awkward wall at the back. Climb this and then a steep clean 15m crack. Easier ground above leads to the neck of the buttress with North-East Gully on the left and a small gully on the right. Climb the steep final wall by starting on the left and trending right to reach the Ridge.

5 North-East Gully   120m   VS *   *(1912)*
The climb is unchecked and the grade likely to be considerably higher. The second ascent in 1951 took 2 attempts by the same climber who put up Crack of Dawn. It was by far the hardest route in Skye when first ascended and done in bare feet. Climb the deep gully easily for 60m. A large flake on the right is gained by holds on the left followed by an exposed right traverse across its top to a stance. Take the right-hand crack until it merges into a slabby corner. A difficult pull up onto a small and steeply sloping shelf with minute finger holds gives the crux. Above, an

overhang with good holds is passed to a recess. Step right before traversing back to the crack where the angle eases and leads to the broad shoulder of North-East Buttress. Finish by easy scrambling.

6 Populace   180m   HVS   *(1977)*
On the left wall of North-East Gully is a very obvious corner system. This climb follows the corners for 105m to where the system splits into a very steep V-groove on the right and a steep chimney on the left. Climb the chimney to exit onto slabs (45m). Above, climb an obvious fault that splits the final buttress (30m).

7 Fluted Buttress   210m   HVS 4c **   *(1950)*
This classic route tackles the broad buttress left of North-East Gully. It is bold and gives the full mountain route experience. About 60m up on the right-hand section are three flutes (square cut towers) which give the climb its name. Start just right of the corner of Cocoa Cracks.

Climb a little rib for 7m, then traverse up under overhangs for 20m (good protection half way along) to where the overlap can be climbed to a ledge above (30m). Follow the ledge to the right, then go up an easy angled chimney. Climb this to where it steepens under the flutes, then traverse out right to a slab (The Gangway) below a huge overhang. Follow the slab rightwards until the slab steepens. Traverse out to the wall on the right (that drops into North-East Gully) where 10m of delicate and exposed climbing, crux, leads right and up to an easement above the overhangs. Follow a broken groove, trending back left to the centre of the buttress, then climb a short groove to a small terrace and a cairn at its left end (junction with Crack of Dawn). The Escape Route continues up Difficult slabs on the right-hand edge or, better, continue up the Direct Finish.
Variation: **Direct Finish   90m   HVS *   *(1950)*
Climb the clean rib to the left of the cairn by a crack on its crest to where it steepens and ends at a ledge below a 'stupendous overhanging nose' split by a crack. Climb its right wall by a hard crack in a groove, step left to a ledge, then go back right to an easy groove. From the recess at the top of the groove, traverse right to a ledge, go along it, moving up and right over two little corners, and finish at a cairn on the ridge.

8 Cocoa Cracks   165m   E2 **   *(1969)*
A very fine route which follows the huge right-angled corner in the very front of Fluted Buttress, mid-way between Crack of Dawn and the flutes. Takes a while to dry unfortunately. Scramble up a slab at the foot of the corner.
1. 25m Climb the corner, often wet, to a stance on the ledge to the right.
2. 20m Climb a chimney above to a peg belay below an overhang.
3. 15m 5c Climb the overhang, often wet and the crux, then continue up a wide chimney to belay in a nook.
4. 15m Climb the narrowing, often wet chimney above by its right arete to reach easy ground; belay at the next steepening.
5. etc. 90m Easier rocks lead to the Escape Route.

9 Crack of Dawn   180m   HVS **   *(1951)*
This is a very good climb especially if the Direct Finish is taken. The route follows a prominent slanting crack up the south-east wall of Fluted Buttress, then the continuation crack across the buttress. It originally finished by easier rocks (The Escape Route), but the Direct takes the true line. Start at a crack-line in the wall which forms a chimney after 45m.
1. 25m 4c Climb the crack to a niche and belay.
2. 15m 4b Climb out of the niche, go up the overhanging crack for a few metres, then traverse onto the exposed wall on the right to reach a platform.
3. etc. 135m Climb the steep chimney in the wall directly above to the top of the south-east wall. Follow the easier angled crack which slants across the face to where it becomes indefinite; cairn. Climb the short steep crack immediately left of a little rib of clean rough rock, moving across the rib at the top and passing a big

COIR'-UISG

71. SGÙRR MHICCOINNICH
North Face, Upper Cliff

7.	Fluted Buttress, Escape Route Finish	HVS 4c **	9. Crack of Dawn	HVS **
8.	Cocoa Cracks	E2 **	10. Dawn Grooves	HVS **
			11. Mongoose Direct	E1 ***
			12. King Cobra	E1 ****
			12a. King Cobra Direct	E3 5c *
			13. Exiguous Gully	VI,6 **

flake. Climb to the left end of the terrace and the cairn at the junction with Fluted Buttress. The Escape Route continues up Difficult slabs on the right-hand edge or continue by the Direct Finish of Fluted Buttress.

0 Dawn Grooves   175m   HVS *** _(1958)_

An excellent line which takes a series of grooves right of the central cleft of Mongoose Direct and forms the left-hand boundary of Fluted Buttress where the south-east and front walls meet.

1. and 2. 45m 4c Climb the first two pitches of Crack of Dawn.

3. 25m 4a Climb the corner on the left to a grassy ledge.

4. 45m 4b Continue by the corner-groove, 3m below the point at which the main groove becomes Mongoose Direct traverse right (unprotected) for 5m to a crack in the right wall. Climb the crack to the slabby edge of the buttress. Follow this (15m) to a good ledge.

5. 15m 4b A steep 15m wall leads to a ledge girdling the upper part of Fluted Buttress route which lies 15m to the right (possible escape).

6. 35m 4c Traverse 12m left to a chimney marking the line of the grooves. Climb the chimney to an overhang and exit left to a flake by a ledge. Climb the steep slabs above, trending right to regain the grooves; belay at the foot of a narrow chimney topped by a 5m V-corner.

7. 15m 4c Climb the chimney and the corner to the summit ridge.

Winter: **VIII, 8 *****   _(2008)_

The summer route was followed for four pitches until below the steep 15m wall. From here a short pitch traversed right to the rib, then up to below the split over-hanging nose. A long final pitch (in the dark) approximated the Direct Finish to Crack of Dawn, trending right up a right-facing groove with a wide crack in the back. A superb, sustained and well protected winter adventure in a magnificent setting – every pitch apart from pitch 5 has considerable difficulty. The first pitch is probably the crux of the route. There was some useful ice on the first ascent.

1 Mongoose Direct   195m   E1 ***   _(1974/7)_

This fine climb takes the great cleft in the buttress directly. It is a drainage line and is often wet. The original route bypassed the crux groove by joining the drier Dawn Grooves for 20m. Start at a corner-crack 5m left of Crack of Dawn.

1. 25m 5a Climb the crack to a sloping ledge.

2. 20m 5a Continue up a similar crack, then move up a slab to a belay beneath the deep groove of the main cleft.

3. 35m 5b Climb a crack in the right wall, then the groove itself. Where it splits in two at a junction with Dawn Grooves, climb into the prominent clean-cut V-groove of the left-hand branch, crux, to a stance in a niche on the left.

4. 35m 5a Continue up the chimney-groove to a spacious ledge.

5. and 6. 80m Step up left across the overhang in the chimney-line, then continue up the fault to easy ground.

2 King Cobra   210m   E1 ***   _(1960)_

This is one of Skye's great routes. Towards the north end of the face is an impressive buttress which can appear cobra like in shape from the east. From the large bay on the left, an exiguous gully goes to the top of the cliff. The climb follows the buttress on its immediate right, but left of the cleft of Mongoose Direct.

1. 45m Scramble up the gully for 40m. Just below where it steepens, traverse easily right to a large flake at the foot of the 25m corner.

2. 25m 4c Climb the right wall of the corner to a big ledge.

3. 25m 5b Traverse 4m right. A bold swing of the leg across a bottomless corner and a few moves between the blank walls above form the crux of the route. Easier climbing leads to belays.

4. 15m 4b Climb easily up a loose rib on the right to a comfortable shelf (poor belay).

5. 35m 5a From the right end of the ledge climb a steep thin crack that overlooks Mongoose Direct. Hard moves lead to a slab below the large overhangs. Climb out on the left wall of the groove, swing across to jammed spikes on the left, then climb

Dawn Grooves, VIII,8, Sgùrr MhicCoinnich North Face. Climber Guy Robertson

a short chimney on good holds to a small airy perch.

6. 40m 4c Traverse left across a slab into a chimney which leads to a good ledge. Take a chimney on the right which becomes an open groove.

7. 25m Climb a chimney set in the left wall of a narrow buttress to the top.

Variation: **Pitch 3 Direct   20m   E1 5b**

The continuation of the corner system above pitch 2 was seen ascended in dry conditions, rejoining the original route above. The grade is not confirmed.

Variation: **King Cobra Direct   190m   E3 ***   (1992)

1., 2. and 3. 95m 5b Climb the first pitches of King Cobra.

4. 45m 5c Follow pitch 4 to the shelf at the left end of the big overhang. Go through the left end of the overhang into a groove, crux, and follow this to a ledge with a chockstone in a wide corner-crack.

5. 50m 4c Climb the corner and a chimney to a large ledge, then climb a corner behind the ledge to belay on easy ground a short way from the top.

**13 Exiguous Gully   145m   VI,6 **   (1995)

This impressive line gives fine climbing up the obvious gully left of King Cobra. Start at the foot of the gully.

1. 40m Climb the left-hand corner of the gully until about 10m below a marked steepening. Transfer to the right-hand corner and belay 5m below an obvious

groove line forming the right-hand corner of the steep section ahead.
2. 25m Steep strenuous climbing in the groove-corner leads to a good belay at a slight easing in the angle.
3. 45m Continue up the groove line by more fine climbing, which eventually eases at a broad snowy ramp.
4. 35m Follow the ramp up left and break out right to join the ridge at the first opportunity.

4 Hanging Slab   235m   HVS   (1971)
This route takes the slab above the overhangs left of Exiguous Gully.
1. 45m Climb the left wall of the gully to a stance.
2. 45m Traverse 35m across an undercut slab on the left to a line of vertical cracks. Climb these then make a short traverse left to a small stance and high flake belay.
3. 15m Move up and left again to climb a steep little rib to a large ledge (easy walk off possible).
4. 30m Climb steep cracks behind the ledge.
5. and 6. 100m Follow cracks and chimneys more easily to the top.

The next routes lie 400m to the south, overlooking Sgùrr a' Coire an Lochain. From Glen Brittle they are best approached by Bealach MhicCoinnich. Descend to the neck that leads out to Sgùrr Coire an Lochain.

5 East Face Rake   200m   Moderate   (1903)
An obvious diagonal fault leads up west to the top of the North Face routes by a series of grassy ledges and rock steps and can be used as a descent.

From the start of the East Face Rake a long groove runs directly towards the summit, with a large slabby expanse to the left.

6 Forgotten Groove   75m   Very Difficult *   (1951)
Scramble up to the foot by easy rocks. Enter the groove directly or by a traverse from a slab on the left. Very steep to start, the angle eases and the groove finishes after 60m. From here, awkward climbing over friable rock leads to the summit.

7 Raeburn's Route   200m   III   (1903)
A winter line above the East Face Rake was made direct to the summit by Harold Raeburn and party at Easter 1903.

72. BEALACH BUTTRESS

(NG 448 215)   Alt 690m   East facing   Maps p124, 214   Diagrams p229, 236

This very fine cliff compliments its close neighbour superbly and keeps the sunshine a bit longer in the height of summer. Climbs are in two distinct sections with a large vertical wall of sound gabbro lying above Thunder Shelf accessible by a single long abseil. Below and right of this wall, the angle is more amenable with several long medium grade routes.

Approaches: In addition to using approaches described for the Sgùrr MhicCoinnich cliffs, the Top and Lower Walls have specific possibilities described below.

Top Wall

Approach: A long abseil (up to 80m) directly to Thunderbolt Shelf for the steep pitches on the Top Wall is possible but allows pre-inspection. Directions for setting up in the right line can be given from the opposite side of Rotten Gully. Alternatively gain Thunderbolt Shelf by the first pitch of Tinn Lamh Crack. Routes are described from left to right.

COIR'-UISG

72. BEALACH BUTTRESS

1. Tinn Lamh Crack   E1 **
2. Lightfoot   E3 **
3. Rainman   E5 ***

Sgùrr MhicCoinnich Upper Cliff

4. Thunderbolt Shelf	Severe *
5. Black Cleft	VS
6. Pinnacle Face	H.Severe *
7. Central Groove	V.Diff
9. Hourglass Crack	VS 4b *
10. Lost Arrow	VS
11. The Bow	VS *

d. descent ending on lower terrace from Bealach Coire Lagan

Sgùrr MhicCoinnich Lower Cliff

1 Tinn Lamh Crack   105m   E1 **   *(1969)*

This is the striking vertical crack left of centre on the vertical wall. The first two pitches give a loose approach to Thunderbolt Shelf that are avoided by an abseil approach. Start at the foot of the first steep section (25m) in Rotten Gully.

1. 45m 4c Traverse right along a prominent fault, surmount a shattered overlap and climb loose slabs to a grass landing. Go right and through a break to reach Thunderbolt Shelf some 12m right of the crack.
2. 15m Follow the shelf to belay left of the crack.
3. 45m 5b Traverse right into the crack and climb it to a horizontal break. Continue up the crack to the final steep wall. Where it narrows, the crux move brings good holds within reach near the top of the wall.

2 Lightfoot   80m   E3 **   *(1983)*

This finds a way up the vertical wall to the right of Tinn Lamh Crack, cutting through a pronounced right-trending corner. It is a good steep route amidst impressive surroundings. Start from Thunderbolt Shelf.

1. 40m 6a Climb the obvious leaning corner in the middle of the face over a small roof and continue until moves left can be made below a roof. Surmount this, then move up right above the roof, overlooking the corner, until hard moves enable a small ledge to be gained.
2. 40m 5c Climb the splendid crack-line above to the top.

3 Rainman   70m   E5 ***   *(2007)*

A tremendous route up the smooth right side of the big vertical wall. Start below the prominent overlap on the bottom right of the wall.

1. 20m 5b Climb up left to enter and climb the obvious groove at the left end of the overlap, then continue directly for a few metres to a semihanging belay at a

small sloping ledge.

2. 30m 6a Step left then climb directly up passing just left of a large niche to gain an obvious sloping ledge. Continue up, then trend right to follow a vague crackline over a small overhang to a good rest. Continue up the crack to below a bigger overhang, then traverse horizontally left below this and pull up through its left-hand end. Make some thin moves up and leftwards (bold) to gain a line of flakes leading back right and up to a ledge below a short crack.

3. 20m 5a Climb the crack and then escape out right to avoid a loose finish.

Lower Wall

Three converging cracks form a down-pointing arrowhead marking the starts of Hourglass Crack, Lost Arrow and The Bow. A pale rock scar left of Hourglass Crack decorates the central part of this area of crag. Two terraces run across the face, making the climbs somewhat disjointed but less daunting than many neighbouring routes.

Approach: Another possibility to those already described is useful for approaching routes on the Lower Wall. Scramble down from the broadest part of Bealach Coire Lagan on loose grass and boulder slopes passing many outcropping basalt dykes. Head first right then back left and finally down a 2m wall to a scree fan. From here traverse back right across scree below broken rocky slopes, descending gradually until on a terrace which sweeps around the buttress. From here climb down to the foot of the Arrowhead. Routes are described from left to right.

Thunderbolt Shelf   150m   Severe * (1953)

This is the shelf running across the foot of the Top Wall. Despite rather broken climbing, the great position makes the route worthwhile. The lower part consists of three short vertical walls, each about 20m high. Turn the first by climbing the initial pitch of Black Cleft, the huge chimney that borders the right side of the vertical wall. From the chimney, traverse 10m left along a ledge and climb the wall to another ledge. Now move 25m left and climb the third tier to another ledge below the vertical wall. The route now slants up to the left, keeping close to the wall, one pitch going over a huge semidetached flake on the wall itself. Higher up, take a direct line and finish by a prominent vertical chimney.

Black Cleft   120m   VS (1954)

The deep chimney-crack right of the vertical wall gives a strenuous and good climb. The first 25m gives scrambling with a little chockstone pitch leading to a platform. Climb the steep narrow chimney above, passing a chockstone, to a ledge at 15m. Turn the chimney above on the immediate left, then steep and delicate climbing on loose rock for about 15m leads to an easier section. After 12m, the climbing steepens, going over an awkward slab in the chimney to the foot of a small chockstone overhang. Climb the overhang to a jammed block belay, then surmount another short strenuous overhang. Continue over a large and doubtful jammed block to a chockstone in the recesses of the cleft. A final 20m pitch goes up the chimney ahead until it is possible to climb out on the left wall and so up to the top.

Winter: **VI,7 *** (1992)

A superb, sustained and well-protected route following the summer line.

Pinnacle Face   135m   Hard Severe * (1954)

A very pleasant climb on sound clean rock. The route starts halfway between Black Cleft and the foot of the arrowhead, aiming for a prominent pinnacle on the face of the buttress. Climb an easy shallow crack for 30m to the lower terrace. Climb the clean crack in the face above, then traverse right across the foot of the pinnacle to a stance in its right corner. From the top of the pinnacle, step back left into the crack and go up to a ledge. Easier climbing up the face of the buttress leads across a grass patch and up a short steep wall behind, climbing to the right of a basalt fault. From the upper terrace, about 60m above the pinnacle, climb up and right over pleasant rock to the summit slopes.

7 Central Groove   75m   Very Difficult   (1960)

Start from the lower terrace a short distance right of Pinnacle Face. Climb vertically for 5m into a groove, initially shallow but soon deepening, avoiding loose blocks at the top. Easy climbing now leads to a junction with Pinnacle Face and Gemini below the upper rocks. The final slopes are enlivened by climbing a remarkable flying buttress, more difficult and exposed than it appears from below.

8 Gemini   155m   VS *   (1954)

A good route on clean rough rock despite some loose sections. Start immediately right of a shallow broken groove on the flat face, and left of the arrowhead recess.
1. 45m Pleasant climbing up the slabby face to the right of the groove leads to the lower terrace. Cross this to a chockstone belay in a corner-crack left of the fresh broken rock.
2. 30m Climb 5m to the right of the crack, following an obvious right-rising traverse, then trend back left to a small terrace.
3. 30m 4c From a pair of shaky pinnacles, step onto the face and climb to the foot of a steep groove. Traverse right to twin cracks on the steep section of the face, then climb the right-hand crack, crux, to an easing. Now follow the left-hand crack to a belay on the left.
4. 20m A good pitch now follows; climb the pinnacle immediately above the belay to its top, then climb the face beyond to the top of the right-hand of twin pinnacles. Go up and over another pinnacle to the upper terrace.
5. 30m Easy climbing up the buttress above leads to the summit slopes.

9 Hourglass Crack   150m   VS 4b *   (1950)

Start from the scree where the three downward pointing cracks form the arrowhead. Climb the left crack to the lower terrace. Take the left-hand crack that runs up right of the fresh broken rock to a steep wall. Climb the tight crack, crux, to where it deepens to an impressive cleft. Follow this easily over a few small pitches to a huge overhanging cave. Climb the right wall of the cave on smallish holds, or back up between the walls to pass the cave; an enjoyable and unusual pitch with fine views to Sgùrr Coire an Lochain. The wide crack continues to the final cave; back up out of this and cross to the left wall to reach the buttress left of the overhang. Scrambling above leads to the ridge.

10 Lost Arrow   160m   VS   (1954)

A dry weather route only, with vegetated sections. The grade assumes the usual damp conditions, if dry it is probably easier.
1. 45m Ascend the centre chimney of the arrowhead past awkward chockstones to finish up the left wall. Cross the lower terrace to belay below the continuation of the same.
2. 25m Climb the easy and broad grassy crack, then cross The Bow and belay in a wet cave in the steeper chimney.
3. 20m Climb the chimney, normally mossy and wet, to belay in a cave below a large pointed chockstone.
4. 10m Climb down, out and round the chockstone, then go over it to the foot of another overhanging section.
5. 15m Continue up the crack, surmounting the overhanging loose chockstone on huge holds, then scramble up the gully to the upper terrace.
6. 45m The fault-line finishes here; either climb the easy top crack of The Bow, or the face straight ahead, which gives good climbing on friable rock to end in a scramble to the summit slopes.

11 The Bow   165m   VS *   (1954)

A pleasant and enjoyable route with a short sharp crux. Start below the right-hand crack of the arrowhead.
1. 45m Climb the crack and the slab on the right. Walk across the lower terrace to the right-hand of two faults which cross the cliff above.
2. 10m Now climb a short greasy chimney and the fault which crosses Lost Arrow

Happy Go Lucky Route, VII,7, Bealach Buttress Lower Wall. Climber Francis Blunt

to where it becomes an overhanging crack.
3. 15m 4c Climb the overhanging crack, which splits higher up and leads to an isolated slab.
4. 20m Continue pleasantly up the slab by the crack in its right corner, which steepens near its top.
5. 30m Scramble to the upper terrace, with the deep-cut section of Hourglass Crack on the left, and pass a weird rock bridge on the left.
6. 45m Climb the broad and easy crack above the upper terrace to the top.

Happy Go Lucky Route   205m   VII,7 *   (2010)
1. 20m Ice flows out of a recess 20m below the tip of the arrowhead. Climb this to a spike belay.
2. 50m Climb an easy deep slot to reach a hidden ice-flow. Climb this for 30m to

the lower terrace.

3. 30m Traverse left to the steep corner, left of the prominent light coloured rock shield. (Hourglass Crack is the wider crack on its right side).

4. 35m Very sustained moves are well protected throughout. Loose rock beneath the higher roof add spice to the crux moves.

5. 25m Traverse left for 5m to an easy corner. Follow this until an easy break right leads to the Pinnacle Face Route.

6. 10m Gain a broad ledge above and behind.

7. 25m Descend to the foot of the gaping fault on the right (Hourglass Crack). Ascend this until beneath a huge roof.

8. 10m Break out by a fault in the right wall to reach easy ground above.

73. SGÙRR DEARG - NORTH FACE

(NG 445 217) Alt 700m Maps p98, 124, 214 Diagram p229

The Coireachan Ruadha faces of An Stac and Sgùrr Dearg are very steep and impressive but with few obvious lines.

Approaches: From the head of the Coruisk bowl follow the faint cairned trail south towards Bealach na Banachdaich (2hrs). From Glen Brittle cross the Main Ridge by Bealach na Banachdaich (see opening diagram Coire na Banachdaich chapter) and descend easily staying close beneath the face (2hrs 15mins).

1 O'Brien and Julian's Climb 150m Severe *   (1912)

A serious route but recommended for experienced climbers in a period of dry weather. Route finding is complex with few features identifiable from below. Near the foot of the north-east face is a well formed cave, not easily visible from the south and easily confused with a rib and damp recess 50m left. Climb the lowest slabs, initially steep for 20m, to the cave. Climb the left wall of the cave, then a further 20m of steep rock to a long slanting shelf. The climbing gradually eases above the shelf and trends right to an upper shelf and a prominent rock tower on the north-north-east ridge. The summit is easily gained from here.

Winter: **VI,5 ** **   (1996)

A fine climb up a big face. Climb to the cave (60m). A strenuous pull onto its left rib leads to sustained mixed climbing up the rib. Traverse left into a short cracked corner (40m) which leads to the slanting shelf. Climb another corner on the left to an obvious rising traverse (45m). Follow this right for 70m to an icy gully leading to a subsidiary crest. Climb to the Ridge.

2 Springbank Gully 170m III,4 *   (2010)

A good ice climb close to the crest of the Ridge. Descend 200m from Bealach na Banachdaich. A splendid easy gully (150m I) breaks back right to the Ridge. Ascend this for 80m to a broad ice sheet emptying from a well defined gully above.

1. 30m Traverse a thin snow ledge close below the overhang with good rock protection before stepping further left to gain the steep section, 10m. Belay 20m above, where the angle eases.

2. 40m Continue easily by ice bulges and a short corner to reach the headwall where an easy escape right to the Ridge is possible.

3. 50m Follow easy snow up left to block belay.

4. 50m Climb a short ice step before more ice and snow leads to the Ridge 100m from the summit of Sgùrr Dearg.

74. SGÙRR NA BANACHDAICH

South-East facing Maps p98, 214 Diagrams p229, 241

The north-east face of Sgùrr na Banachdaich presents extensive but broken areas of separate crags that lie below the various tops. The rock varies from quite loose to deplorable but the faces should be visited by connoisseurs of Cuillin backwaters.

Approaches: Approach Bealach na Banachdaich easily from the head of Coruisk

CORUISK - North

B. Bealach Mac an t–Soair approach from Sligachan
G. Bealach na Glaic Moire approach from Coire na Creiche
T. To Coireachan Rhuada
U. To Coire a' Chaoruinn
V. To An Garbh–choire

as described above with **Peridotite Buttress** (see below) a recommended addition. The Twins Buttress is on the north side of the Bealach and the Summit Buttresses lie 300m further north. From Glen Brittle reach Bealach na Banachdaich (see opening diagram Coire na Banachdaich chapter) in 2hrs. Descend screes for 50m to reach the foot of the Twins Buttress. Routes on the Summit Buttresses are approached more easily from the next bealach north, 200m along the Ridge (NG 443 220). Easy ground leads north to a level terrace below the summit cliffs (2hrs 15mins).

Sròn Buidhe

(NG 447 220)   Alt 650m

An outcrop of high quality peridotite gives a good scramble running parallel to the final rise to Bealach na Banachdaich. **Peridotite Buttress** (200m Grade 3 *) takes the centre of the face.

Summit Buttresses South

(NG 444 218)   Alt 800m

The first routes lie just north of Bealach Coire na Banachdaich under a minor top. The Twins form a pair of prominent steep buttresses separated by a dark gully.

1 South Twin   75m   Difficult   *(1953)*
At the foot of the buttress is a huge slab topped by an overhang. On the left flank is a chimney which marks the start of the route. Climb the right edge of the steep and pleasant chimney to a level crest. From here, trend left across a wall and go up the crest to the summit.

2 North Twin   105m   Severe   *(1953)*
From a recessed platform 6m up, climb a steep crack to a ledge on the left flank. From the far end of the ledge, climb the steep slabby left wall of the buttress until it is possible to traverse right to the crest. A vertical knife edge leads up on good holds to a level arete of solid rock ending at a neck. Finish up shattered rock.

Summit Buttresses North

(NG 442 224)   Alt 850m

The following climbs lie well to the north and are better approached by a terrace from the broad bealach 200m north of Bealach na Banachdaich. The first route takes a prominent narrow arete to the South Top and the second route lies 200m further north, right of a large gully, directly under the summit of the mountain.

3 Midget Ridge   120m   Moderate   *(1953)*
The narrow arete trends slightly right. Follow the edge exactly by very pleasant climbing. In time the arete narrows to a knife edge, and the climb finishes on the Central Top.
*Winter: IV,4 ***   *(2011)*
Gain the top of the initial slab from just inside the gully and follow the crest of the ridge to the top turning a steep wall on the right at mid height.

4 Clouded Buttress   180m   Severe   *(1953)*
The climb follows the main line of weakness. From the foot, trend first right, then left. Cross some steep slabs to the left until it is possible to climb up and right towards a slabby shelf. Traverse left along the slabs to a short shallow chimney, then continue left and up to a recess in the left-hand corner at a great white scar. Exit from this recess by the right-hand corner, crux, then go straight up for over 30m to a terrace. The final tower above may be avoided, but it gives a pleasant finish.

75. SGÙRR THORMAID

(NG 442 227) Alt 850m South facing Maps p98, 214 Diagram p241

This steep face has an attractive aspect, is composed of reasonable quality rock and is well viewed from the summit of Sgùrr na Banachdaich.

Approaches: From the head of the Coruisk bowl ascend due west, passing the Coruisk Face of Sgùrr a' Ghreadaidh [76] until 100m below Bealach Thormaid in 2hrs. From Glen Brittle Youth Hostel gain the summit of Sgùrr na Banachdaich, most easily by Coire an Eich (1hr 30mins). Head north along the Ridge for 150m to Bealach Thormaid and descend east for 100m (2hrs).

Peridot   215m   HVS *   *(1968)*
The most obvious line of weakness is a peridotite dyke overlooking the descent from Bealach Thormaid making a fine line to the summit. Start left of and above the lowest point of the buttress at some pale grey rock.
1. 40m 4b Climb slabs and a corner to a large sloping grass ledge.
2. 40m 5a Move 3m right to an obvious deep-cut trap dyke. The dyke is initially undercut and its entrance forms the crux; it can be tackled direct or traversed into from the left.
3. 100m Continue more easily to where the fault becomes a terrace.
4. 35m Break right towards the summit of Sgùrr Thormaid by short walls.

COIR'-UISG

The view from the flood plain west of Loch Coruisk is dominated by the eastern faces of Sgùrr a' Ghreadaidh and Sgùrr a' Mhadaidh above Coir'-uisg. Most climbs have a sunny aspect until well after midday.

76. SGÙRR A' GHREADAIDH - CORUISK FACE

(NG 541 225) Alt 375m South-East facing Map p214 Diagrams p241, 244

This face of Sgùrr a' Ghreadaidh is a huge mass of rock, broken into buttresses and gullies sweeping right down to just above the level of Loch Coruisk. The South-East Ridge is credited with being the longest (non-girdle) climb in Britain and forms the boundary between Correachan Ruadha and Coir'-uisg. Due south of the summit, at a height of 720m, is a large grass terrace. Below the terrace and facing south is a prominent rock mass cleft by two gullies; the steepest is Terrace Gully with East and West Buttresses flanking it. In general the rock below the level of the terrace is sound whilst above it is very loose. The face gives good traditional climbs which dry fairly quickly.

Approaches: From Coruisk follow scree slopes direct to the toe of the crags in about 1hr 30mins depending on the climb. From Glen Brittle approach by Bealach Thormaid as for the last crag. An easy diagonal descent leads to the end of the grassy terrace below Terrace Buttress. Continue the same line of descent to reach the start of the South-East Ridge (2hrs 30mins).

Descents: Traverse Sgùrr a' Ghreadaidh north to An Doras or south and on to Sgùrr na Banachdaich as described in the Cuillin Ridge Traverses chapter.

Terrace West Buttress   330m   Difficult *   *(1924)*
Start near the foot of Terrace Gully at some steep rocks. Climb these past a vertical section at 35m, which leads to a stretch of open slabs. Above the slabs, follow a left-sloping chimney-gully to a shelf at 120m. On the right, a fine 25m wall leads to a ledge of shattered rock. Climb a section of steep basalt, tricky in the wet, to an excellent wall of fine rough gabbro which leads to the terrace, 200m from the foot. Cross the terrace and gain a narrow ledge which runs up towards the Thormaid-Ghreadaidh gap. Follow this until it 'threatens to become non-existent'.

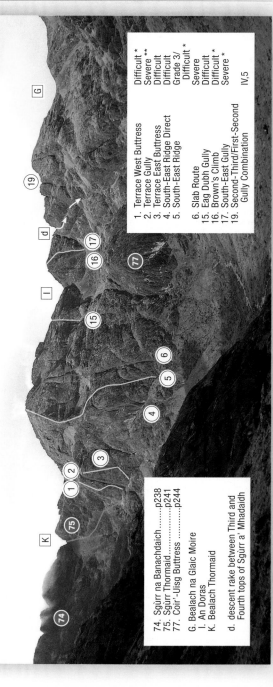

76. SGÙRR A' GHREADAIDH
Coruisk Face

78. SGÙRR A' MHADAIDH
Upper Cliffs

1.	Terrace West Buttress	Difficult *
2.	Terrace Gully	Severe **
3.	Terrace East Buttress	Difficult
4.	South-East Ridge Direct	Grade 3/
5.	South-East Ridge	Difficult *
6.	Slab Route	Severe
15.	Eag Dubh Gully	Difficult
16.	Brown's Climb	Difficult *
17.	South-East Gully	Severe *
19.	Second-Third/First-Second Gully Combination	IV,5

74. Sgùrr na Banachdaich p238
75. Sgùrr Thormaid p241
77. Coir'-Uisg Buttress p244

G. Bealach na Glaic Moire
I. An Doras
K. Bealach Thormaid

d. descent rake between Third and Fourth tops of Sgùrr a' Mhadaidh

Climb a dyke chimney, with a difficult exit, to open ground above. Reach the main ridge a short distance below the summit.

Terrace Gully 210m Severe ** (1920)

A natural route of drainage it is infrequently dry but gives a very good climb of its type. Start from a broad green ledge which runs along the foot of the cliff above a low vertical wall. The first pitch is a deeply-cut cave and then a ledge on the left leads to an enclosed chimney. Emerge from this by an aperture between the chockstones. Take the small obstacles above directly, and turn a wet chockstone pitch by the edge of the buttress to the left. A short distance higher, a fine unclimbed chimney rises to the right.

A wet and slippery pitch in the main gully leads to the Great Cave Pitch. Ascend water worn slabs then, at the start of a short scree slope, climb the right wall of the cave to a small ledge. Traverse up left to enter a recess beside the capstone. The recess is difficult to enter but easy to leave. Above, the gully forms a long chimney, usually wet, containing an arched block high up. This has not been climbed, so instead climb the narrow crack on the right, then traverse back left into the gully. Scrambling remains to the terrace. A suitable continuation is the distinct rib in the centre of the face to the south top of Sgùrr a' Ghreadaidh, giving 500m of climbing in all.

Terrace East Buttress 200m Difficult (1922)

This is the large rounded buttress to the east of Terrace Gully. Start by a large cairn near the east angle of the buttress at the right-hand end of the broad grass rake. A shelf and chimney lead to a large grass patch at 35m. From the top of the grass patch, follow a long left-slanting chimney-fault for 100m. Gain another grassy shelf and make an exposed left traverse across a vertical wall to a ledge above a long drop into Terrace Gully. Climb the steep wall above for 20m to a region of easy slabs and the terrace. Finish by the same rib as the previous route.

South-East Ridge Direct 400m Difficult (1920)

This route starts well left of Collie's original route, and 20m left of a deeply-cut gully marked by a rowan tree. Work up and left by a series of steep pitches connecting dyke lines to reach the terrace. Finish up the south-east ridge proper.

South-East Ridge 700m Grade 3/Difficult * (1896)

The true south-east ridge of the mountain starts from the terrace some 250m below the summit. Collie's original line is open to much variation below here. Start left of where two gullies meet higher up like an inverted U, well seen from Loch Coruisk. Either follow the left-hand gully or the rocks to its left, a mixture of climbing and scrambling, for over 400m, to where it is possible to traverse diagonally left by walking to the start of the south-east ridge proper. This is followed in an impressive position to easier slopes below the south summit.

Variation: **Difficult** (1938)

Above the terrace a more direct line takes a prominent buttress between two deep-cut watercourses. Begin up a steep overhang on the right corner and make your way up direct until forced by a steeper overhang to the left. The buttress rises in a series of steps, each of which overhangs and grows progressively more rotten and unsatisfactory.

Slab Route 350m Severe (1939)

This lies to the right of the prominent inverted U formed by the two gullies. Start 7m right of the right-hand gully at some red slabs. Climb the slabs for 30m to the gully and go up to a cave. A short steep wall on the right leads to about 45m of easy rocks. Cross the gully, then climb slabs for over 150m, making for a large perched block on the skyline. Pass this on easier ground either side. Walk up to the final crags, then climb a left-slanting slab that lies 15m right of a large black overhang. The slab is quite delicate at 13m; traverse across and at 45m climb a basalt wall to a large grass terrace. The final buttress is situated between two

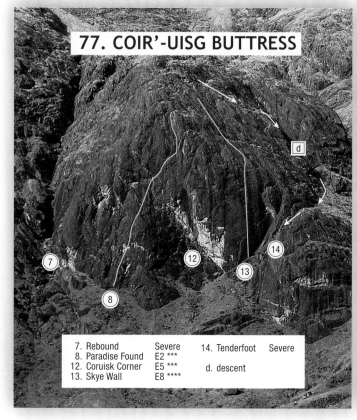

77. COIR'-UISG BUTTRESS

7. Rebound	Severe	14. Tenderfoot	Severe
8. Paradise Found	E2 ***		
12. Coruisk Corner	E5 ***	d. descent	
13. Skye Wall	E8 ****		

gullies and has an overhanging base. A steep start on the left leads to very loose rocks until the buttress steepens to a tower. Start by a mantelshelf on the left and either climb direct or by a traverse left to easy ground. The loose rock on the final tower requires great care.

77. COIR'-UISG BUTTRESS

(NG 454 228) Alt 240m South-East facing Map p214 Diagrams p241, 246

This very attractive crag lies below Coire an Uaigneis and is easily reached from Loch Coruisk. The initial 80m are steep and sound black gabbro with several overhangs. There is a prominent white scar in the centre of the buttress. Routes are described from left to right.

Approaches: An easy rise from the head of the Coruisk bowl reaches the foot of the buttress in 1hr 15mins. The quickest approach from Glen Brittle crosses the Main Ridge at Bealach na Glaic Moire (2hrs). Make a long easy descent to an altitude of 200m before contouring south for 250m to the foot of the Buttress (2hrs 30mins)

Descent: Take a grassy terrace sloping rightwards down the steep frontal face to the foot of the northern bounding gully. This avoids the gullies on either flank that both contain rock pitches.

Rebound 180m Severe   (1966)
This lies left of Original Route and follows the first feasible line round the corner to the left on the west gully wall. Start from the gully, just above the first waterfall.
1. 25m Climb diagonally right to a break in the overhang close to the right skyline. Gain a small slab and follow this to a grassy ramp.
2. 35m Follow the gangway rightwards, then go back left to an obvious chimney-groove with a small overhang at the top.
3. etc. 120m Escape directly or on the right wall. Continue to the top by easier climbing.

Paradise Found 200m E2 *   (2007)
A fine route with good rock and an outstanding outlook, taking the most obvious line up the centre of the larger, but slabbier left side of the buttress. The main difficulties are concentrated in the first half of the route; thereafter the angle eases. Start well up and left from a tongue of easy angled rock in the centre left of the buttress (left of the huge dirty groove).
1. 45m 5a Climb up onto a tiny shoulder of rock, pull over onto a slab, then trend up slightly rightwards aiming for a prominent crack-line cutting through overhangs. Belay in a small alcove left of the crack-line itself.
2. 40m 5c Traverse delicately right into the crack, then follow this with sustained interest to a ledge.
3. 45m 5a Continue directly up, then trend right across an unprotected slab to gain a stepped right-trending groove.
4. and 5. 70m 4c Follow the groove line to the top.

Original Route 240m Severe *   (1949)
A conspicuous line of weakness runs diagonally up from the bottom left of the buttress, forming the greater part of the climb. Start at the lowest tongue of rock and move diagonally up left into the groove until checked by a small overhang beneath a big black one at 60m. Escape right, crux, to gain a series of continuous grooves. Follow the grooves to a point about two-thirds of the way up the cliff where they form a vertical corner. Climb this, continuing on the same line. Above, the angle eases to slabs and an easy crack leads straight up to finish.

Rongwrong 210m VS   (1966)
Start as for Original Route. From the grass ledge below the main diagonal weakness, follow an obvious rising traverse line to below a prominent steep groove breaking through the left-hand end of the central overhangs. Continue on the traverse line to a gangway, then climb this rightwards to below a steep corner-crack in the centre of the left-bounding wall of the main groove. Climb this crux crack to a platform level with a big black roof on the right. Easier climbing leads to the top.

Rawhide 95m E1 5b *   (1985)
Start 20m right of Original Route at a vertical crack-line, just right of a white scarred overhang.
1. 30m Climb up to the white scarred overhang and belay.
2. 35m Climb the crack on the right to a belay on slabs.
3. 30m From the right-hand end of the slabs climb a shallow groove, then move left to join Original Route. Finish as for Original Route.

Coruisk Corner 135m E5 **   (2010)
Climbs the obvious hanging corner above the central vegetated bay. Scramble up this to the start.
1 20m 6b Climb the overhanging off width crack in the corner, often damp, to a hanging stance beneath a roof. (Friend and wires – good hanging belay).
2 20m 6a Continue leftwards up the overhanging corner to an exciting position on the nose. Move up with difficulty to belay at the bottom of the big corner.
3 25m 5c Climb the corner and up a wide crack to gain a blocky stance under the roof. Beware of loose blocks below the belay.
4 50m 5b Traverse left along the obvious handrail and then move up easy ground

Skye Wall, E7/8, Coir'-Uisg Buttress. Climber Dave Birkett

to belay anywhere in the ocean of rock.
5 20m 4c Easier until walk off right is possible.

13 Skye Wall   105m   E7/8 ****   *(2007)*
The obvious blank wall at the right side of the buttress. Start 10m right of the
obvious left-facing corner at a vertical white seam.
1. 20m 6b Follow finger cracks, protected by small wires (poor) to a good ledge.
2. 35m 6b/c Move up and right to a small ledge. Thin moves up the wall gain a
sloping hold and loose flakey sidepulls. Bold climbing leads to a crack which is
followed to a ledge.
3. 50m 5b Move up and left, then go straight up to easy ground.

4 Tenderfoot   195m   Severe *(1966)*
At the right-hand side of the main face is a prominent sloping corner topped by an inclined roof at 40m. Climb the corner to the roof, then traverse right across a slab to chimney-cracks (45m). Climb these to a platform, then head back up the wall on the left past a flake to reach a sloping ledge with a perched boulder (15m). A groove on the right leads to the grassy terrace, then easier rocks lead to the top.

COIRE AN UAIGNEIS

(NG 448 233)   Alt 700m   South facing

This is the shallow upper corrie encircled by the summit ridges of Sgùrr a' Ghreadaidh and Sgùrr a' Mhadaidh that are separated by An Doras.

Approaches: Turn Coruisk Buttress [77] well to the north of the bounding gully and ascend slabby rocks. Continue by boulders to the foot of the climbs in 2hrs. From Glen Brittle reach An Doras in under 2hrs (see approaches in Coire a' Ghreadaidh chapter).. Descend the east side for 200m with caution on steep moves in the initial 40m. An easy rake descends below the Third Top of Mhadaidh on the south side and may be of use to some parties.

5 Eag Dubh Gully   200m   Difficult *(1913)*
This gully leads up to the prominent notch of the Eag Dubh and is only likely to be approached from the Coruisk side. There are eight or nine pitches, the hardest being about mid-way.
Winter: **200m   III** *(2002)*
The gully was found to be disappointingly shallow, mostly banked out but with 2 or 3 interesting icy pitches over chockstones.

An Doras Gully (Moderate) is not the easy door expected with one steep, awkward section 30m below the Ridge.

78. SGÙRR A' MHADAIDH - UPPER CLIFFS

Map p214   Diagrams p241, 244

Sgùrr a' Mhadaidh has four tops numbered from north to south with the southern, Fourth Top being the summit. Access and escape from the routes is not simple but the southerly aspect and solitude should be enticing to the explorer. The rock is compact and rough but care is needed with loose debris.

Descents: Traverse the Ridge north to Bealach na Glaic Moire or south to An Doras for the simplest descents to Glen Brittle. Both options involve some complex route finding and exposed Grade 3 scrambling, as described in the Cuillin Ridge Traverses chapter. An easy rake descends to the Coruisk side of the Ridge between the Third and Fourth tops

6 Brown's Climb   240m   Difficult * *(1897)*
Takes the full length of the buttress left of South-East Gully.
Start on the left-hand side by the lowest rocks. The first 150m are on steep sound rock. As the angle eases the climbing gets harder.

7 South-East Gully   240m   Severe * *(1910)*
This is the prominent gully that splits the buttress below the summit (Fourth Top). Not a good route to carry rucksacks on. An awkward short step leads to a deep cave (25m). A very tight awkward 15m pitch leads to a smaller cave. Bridge out (crux) and reach another cave and a through route to escape. A very loose step leads to a belay at the foot of a buttress on the right (30m). Continue by the gully more easily to a steepening formed by worrying jammed blocks (45m). Delicately climb these and then escape the bay above by the first fork on the right to gain a left-slanting ramp (45m). Follow this up left to the crest or finish more directly to the summit.

South-East Gully, IV,6, Sgùrr a' Mhadaidh Upper Cliffs.
Climbers Mike Lates and Dave Turnbull

Winter: **IV,6** *(2009)*
The tight chimney involved ridiculous contortions and tension from a runner. The summer crux was more conventional and the through route avoided by good climbing out and round the lip of the overhang. Easier climbing led to the bay which was exited by the right fork and ramp-line to finish.

18 Third-Fourth Gully   150m   Moderate
This is the largely scree filled gully that lies east of the main or Fourth Top. It has one 15m pitch and it forks near the top.

19 Second-Third Gully   150m   Very Difficult * *(1913)*
This lies right of Third-Fourth Gully, starting near the foot of the easy descent rake. The steep lower section contains some fine pitches, including a large cave turned by a chimney a few metres to the left. Rejoin the main gully by traversing over an intervening rib. At half-height the gully turns to scree and it is usual to traverse over to the top half of First-Second Gully to get a more continuous climb.
Winter: **Second-Third Gully/First-Second Gully Combination   260m   IV,5** *(2004)*
1. 40m   Icy steps and chockstones lead under a huge chockstone followed by a short wall to a small cave .
2. 60m   The large cave avoided in summer was climbed direct (crux) followed by easy snow.
3. and 4. 80m   Traverse right over a rib and descend into First-Second Gully, following this to a narrowing.
5. 60m   Climb over several interesting chockstones until above the final difficulty.
6. 20m   Easy snow to the ridge.

20 First-Second Gully   150m   Difficult *(1913)*
This lies to the right of Second-Third Gully. The lower half is scree and easy ground but above half-height the gully narrows and deepens to give three fine pitches on continuous rock.

79. DRUIM NAN RÀMH

Map p214   Diagram p241

The south-west flank of the Druim nan Ràmh above the shore of Loch Coruisk contains large amounts of slabby rock with only a handful of recorded climbs. The Coruisk face of the ridge is very accessible and at low level. A major rockfall (200m wide) occurred in 1996 depositing huge boulders right into the loch.

Druim nan Ràmh   5km   Grade 3/Moderate *

The ridge is an obvious challenge with all major difficulties concentrated in the final 500m of its length unless a direct start is taken, 3hrs. Many climbers will find that gaining the ridge at **Bealach Mac an t-Soair** (not marked, NG 467 227) from Sligachan via Harta Corrie, as described in the approaches, logistically far simpler.

Start below the prominent nose dropping towards the east end of Loch Coruisk. This can be climbed directly at Difficult standard for 75m or turned more easily by a gully to the right. The long broad section beyond is frustratingly cut by rifts perpendicular to the line of ascent. A gradual grassy rise ends abruptly at a deep cleft and the restart of climbing. Descend the cleft for 20m before a horizontal traverse beneath the Druim Pinnacle is possible on the Coruisk side.

Far more exciting is the traverse of the **Druim Pinnacle** (Grade 3 1920). From the foot of the cleft climb loose rock to regain the ridge at a large block that was used to set up a Tyrolean traverse on a winter ascent. The ridge beyond narrows to a knife edge very rapidly. Traverse this until it ends at an overhung drop. Descend flakes and small ledges on the Coruisk side to the safety of the grass slopes below. The central peak rises sharply 50m beyond. The easiest line takes ledges on the south side before gaining the crest just 80m from the summit. Two more direct variations were recorded in 1945 by competent parties at Difficult standard.

Winter: **III** *

A long undertaking with the crux high on the mountain.

Descent: The descents from this route are technically harder than any of the ascent route and are described in the Cuillin Ridge Traverses chapter. Descend south from the Central Peak and then traverse the South-West Top to Bealach na Glaic Moire. Alternatively traverse north by two abseils initially and then crossing the North Top to reach Bealach Harta.

Dubh View Buttress

(NG 479 213)   Alt 75m   South facing

This is the biggest buttress on the northern shore of Loch Coruisk lying opposite the foot of the Dubh Ridge.

Approach: It is easiest underfoot to approach via the path along the south shores of Loch Coruisk, cross the river and then head back along the north shore for 400m. The descent follows slopes down to the south-west and requires care.

JMCS Buttress   270m   Hard Severe   *(1964)*

Follows the obvious right-facing fault above the white wall on the right side of the buttress. Start by gaining a large ledge below the white wall and a left traverse. Follow the arete and the gully, the crux is at the top corner. Easier rocks now lead to the half-height terrace, from where it is possible to escape to either side. Above the terrace, the climb degenerates, starting initially up the right edge from where a variety of lines lead to the ridge.

Variation: **40m   Severe**   *(1970)*

From the prominent white overhang on the original route climb the obvious corner above for 25m. From a ledge climb a vertical wall on the left (strenuous) to belay. Stomach traverse left along an eroded trap dyke to the top of buttress to rejoin the original line.

Swamp Donkey, Severe, Coruisk Slabs. Climber Colin McGregor

Coruisk Gully   300m   Very Difficult   *(1960)*
This route lies immediately to the right of the JMCS Buttress. There are three main pitches of which the final one overhung. Turn this by the wall on the right.

Coruisk Slabs

(NG 484 210)   Alt 75m   South facing

This is the general name for the huge area of slabs stretching east from Dubh View Buttress. It appears broken but the scale means that long sections of good climbing can be found. Most parties making scrambling descents after a few pitches rather than continuing to the ridge above. **Coruisk Slabs Route** (1962) appears to have been destroyed by the rockfall.

Swamp Donkey   265m   Severe 4a *   *(2007)*
This climb is halfway between the lowest area of slabs and the large area of the rockfall taking the cleanest section of slabs. Start on the clean sweep of slabs, to the left of the rockfall at a crack lying roughly 20m to the right of a dark roof. The route takes a direct line up the slabs aiming for an obvious corner forming a way through the overlapping roofs above.
1. 45m Climb the crack and slabs to the right of two detached looking dinner plate slabs to a steeper left-facing corner on the right which is exited on the left via some dubious blocks to reach a corner.
2. 50m Continue up the corner with some blank slab sections to a grass ledge. Continue up the easier slabs to reach a terrace below some steeper slabs.
3. 45m Climb directly up the bold slab above to find a way through the blank section via a welcome flake (crux). This leads to a ledge and overlap and continuation above on bold slabs to the corner.
4. 45m Continue up the easier slabs trending right to reach a grass terrace and the first tree at the base of the obvious corner.
5. 45m Climb the slab left of the corner trending left to climb the arete where it steepens. Move back right to blocks at the top of the corner.

6. 35m Move out left to climb the final slabs directly to where the angle lessens. To descend, continue by scrambling to the top of the buttress escaping right on grass ledges to reach the Druim nan Ràmh ridge.

One route is recorded on the north-east facing band of cliffs overlooking Loch a' Choire Riabhaich on the south-western end of the Druim nan Ràmh; **Lazy Layback** (90m Severe 1984). Follow an obvious banana shaped rightward trending lay back groove. Follow crack and then rib on right of greasy gully at 40m.

80. SGÙRR NA STRÌ

West facing   Map p214
This superb little pointed peak rises directly above Loch Scavaig blocking easy access to Coruisk from the east. It comprises of rock from bottom to top on the entire western flank but a direct ascent is broken by slanting slabby breaks and blocked by impenetrable compact bulges. Scrambling ascents tend to follow the rakes which lead out just south of the summit. An ascent is highly recommended for the best view of the Cuillin bowl and possibly the best view on the whole island. Recorded routes all lie within 20mins of the jetty and are currently confined to the lowest sections where the rock is most continuous.

Approach: Cross the Allt Coir'-uisg by the stepping stones just below Loch Coruisk.

Descent: Obvious descents exist between the areas of crag. The easiest descent from the summit is by the open rift that splits the summit. Follow this north for 1km until a direct descent is visible to the Sligachan path in Choire Riabhach to the west.

North Buttress

This small buttress remains unlocated being described as "The obvious rock band, running down from Sgùrr na Strì, on the north side of the Scavaig river and 20 mins walk from the hut."

Totie Lum   30m   Very Difficult   *(1975)*
On the left hand of the crag is an obvious chimney. Classic back and foot for 15m Awkward exit. Continue to top of crag.

Stair Heid   40m   Very Difficult   *(1975)*
About 6m right of Totie Lum a right-hand curving dyke is unusually hollowed out like a breaking wave. A steep awkward start for 7m leads to easier climbing inside dyke to top.

Coruisk Corner   80m   Difficult   *(1975)*
Climb the most obvious corner to the right of the above routes. Very pleasant. Easily distinguishable on the approach as the most obvious corner on the crag.

Stepping Stone Buttress

(NG 492 195)

This is a big sprawling mass of slabs above the stepping stones, interrupted by overlaps and with a steep right-bounding edge. Behind is a deep rift that separates the buttress from the steeper rocks above.

Bee Cee Crack   140m   VS   *(1965)*
The climb takes the fourth crack from the left on the prominent whalebacked buttress, seen clearly from Loch Coruisk. Start on the lower band of rock separated from the buttress by a grassy promenade.
1. 30m Climb a crack below and left of an obvious white overhang to a terrace. Move up the terrace to a large overhang.
2. 35m Go up easy rocks to a stance behind a flake. Now climb left via a hand-traverse (peg runner) to a belay below a crack.

3. and 4. 75m Follow the crack, steep at first, to the top of the buttress.

The Happy Wanderer   140m   VS 4c   *(1968)*
This route provides much easy slab padding separated by strenuous overlaps. Start at the foot of the prominent slabs that rise above the path, taking in an optional little slab to start. Climb the slabs easily to a large overlap. Traverse right to a shattered crack and ascend this, crux, to gain the slabs above. Follow another 60m of pleasant slabs to another overlap. Take this more easily on the right via a cracked bulge. Traverse right across the large rolling slab above towards a steepening and the right-hand edge. Climb the slab bordering the edge direct, including the overlap above (avoidable on the left) to easy slabs to finish.

Skye Ride   120m   Very Difficult   *(1968)*
Cross the gully behind Happy Wanderer on the left. This route takes the curving groove near the middle of the steeper rocks above. Start at a crack, taking either a dirty rake on the left or the better cracked slab to the right; belay on the ledge above. Mount the small overlap, then traverse right to the groove. Climb the groove in two loose pitches, then either climb an easy slab on the left or, better, climb up right over a bulge and continue easily over broken ground to finish.

The coastal path back to Elgol crosses the stepping stones then heads south through an easy open gully to reach the shore. 200m beyond it passes by a rocky bay with small trees before reaching the infamous Bad Step, a bulging slab that drops into the sea.

Scavaig Slabs

(NG 494 194)

The slabs are a big sheet, falling nearly to the waters edge, about 100m north of the Bad Step.

Phaeton   120m   Severe *   *(1968)*
Start at a small spring and climb the short slab above (15m). Step up left over the overhangs at their lowest point and continue for a further 12m to a flake belay. Traverse left and follow a curving groove up a steepening slab, then belay on the heather ledge above. The slabs above are roofed by overhangs. Climb the centre of the slabs, over a small overlap at 15m and go up boiler plate slabs. At 25m, traverse right to a broken rib and poor belays. Climb up left of the rib, near the edge of the roofs, to the top.

Mizzen Buttress

This is the area of rock above and to the left of the Scavaig Slabs, steep in its lower part with slabs higher up. The following route takes the obvious crack and corner system up the middle of the buttress. Approach by the broken rib directly below the corner.

Outhaul   120m   HVS 5a   *(1997)*
From the left-hand end of the terrace climb a steep slab left of the main roof to the foot of a series of cracks in the wall above. Follow these to a steep corner (crux, 45m). Follow the line of cracks in the slab above (50m). Further slabs lead to the top of the buttress (25m).

Bad Step Buttress

Lost Chord   180m   Very Difficult   *(1998)*
The climb takes the line of least resistance above the Bad Step. Climb from the middle of the traverse on the Bad Step in four pitches.

81. SGÙRR HAIN CRAG

1. Peterless Crack	E1
2. Brayantless Crack	HVS
5. James' Crack	HVS

CAMASUNARY

This is a very beautiful bay at the southern head of Glen Sligachan, on the path between Coruisk and Elgol. It can be easily reached in 1hr by the landrover track from Kilmarie. An open bothy run by the Mountain Bothies Association lies at the west end of the beach and makes a good base, but is due to close in 2012. Sgùrr Hain Crag lies 1km north of the bothy.

81. SGÙRR HAIN CRAG

(NG 508 201)   Alt 75m   South-East facing   Map p214   Diagram p255

This impressive crag faces south-east and consists of two main buttresses separated by a wide gully. The rock varies from perfect gabbro to looser sections requiring care.

Approach: From Camasunary cross the river and follow it north for just over 1km. When both the tide and river levels are low a good stepping stone crossing lies 100m up river from the sea. Other crossing points are possible further up stream but wading across is not unusual. From Coruisk cross the stepping stones and take the Sligachan track until level with Loch a' Choire Riabhaich. Head uphill, passing Captain Maryon's Monument to reach the lowest point of the broad saddle between Sgùrr na Strì and Sgùrr Hain (NG 502 206). Descend easily on the eastern side of the pass. The crag forms a wall on the north side of the open grassy corrie shortly before the river is reached (1hr).

Descent: Descend the south flank of the left-hand buttress.

Left-hand Buttress

1 Peterless Crack   120m   E1   *(1990)*
Start 4m left of a small bay, which is just left of the toe of the buttress.
1. 15m 5b Climb over initial bulges, moving right then left, to gain a crack-line in the slabs.
2. 20m 5b Continue up the crack-line through an overhang to block belays.
3. 20m 5a Climb directly above the belay, following the crack-line through overhangs. Go up to a grass ledge, then traverse left to the foot of a corner.
4. 35m Climb the corner-groove until steep heather leads to rowan trees.
5. 30m Move round to the right and follow slabs to the top.

2 Bryantless Crack   125m   HVS   *(1990)*
Start at the small bay.
1. 15m 4c Climb the overhanging corner to slabs.
2. 25m 4c Continue up the corner to a block. Make an awkward entry into a gangway up to the left, then continue up left to a block belay on Peterless Crack.
3., 4. and 5. 85m Climb Peterless Crack, pitches 3, 4 and 5.

The next three routes lie on the walls high in the wide central gully. The first two climbs are on the left wall, the third on the right.

**3 Assault Course Bimbo   20m   E4 6a ** **   *(1990)*
An excellent pitch on perfect rock, both very sustained and well protected. It takes the thin crack-line up the centre of a vertical wall high on the left-bounding wall. Scramble 10m to a block belay. Climb to the top of the blocks just left of the crack. Make a short traverse along a quartz band to the crack, then climb it to the top.

4 Witchless Corner   20m   VS 4c *   *(1990)*
This is the prominent corner several metres right of and slightly higher than Assault Course Bimbo. Another well protected pleasant route on good rock.

Right-hand Buttress

5 James' Crack   85m   HVS   *(1990)*
This is the prominent continuous vertical crack-line in the right-bounding wall of the gully. It lies at the same level as Witchless Corner. The crack starts about 12m beneath a large jammed block in the gully and is not the wider crack 5m below the boulder.
1. 25m 5a Climb the crack.
2. 25m 4c Continue in the same line.
3. 35m 4b Continue up the crack. This pitch is poorly protected and much loose rock was removed on the first ascent.

6 The Slabs   210m   Grade 3/Moderate
The broken slabs 100m north of the right-hand buttress provide a reasonable scramble with a tricky direct start and considerable exposure to the ridge of Sgùrr Hain.

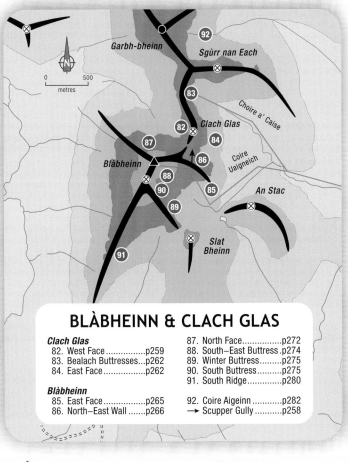

BLÀBHEINN & CLACH GLAS

BLÀBHEINN (BLAVEN) & CLACH GLAS

Glen Sligachan cuts a swathe through the Black Cuillin Bowl leaving these eastern peaks isolated from the Main Ridge but, comprising of the same geology, there is climbing and scrambling every bit as good. An added attraction is that the approach from the road is considerably shorter.

South Buttress has a good selection of lower grade routes with a sunny aspect. The Great Prow has over 100m of vertical rock and is home to Stairway to Heaven and Jib, two of the finest rock climbs in the Cuillin. The corrie round is considered by many as the best scramble in Britain. The area is a good option in a north-westerly wind, often being shielded by the Main Ridge. North facing cliffs tend to be steep with the southern faces more open and slabby. There is a large selection of high quality winter climbing and most routes can be studied from the road at the head of Loch Slapin. Sailaway forms ice quickly at 600m giving an indication of conditions.

General Approach: Approach from the shore of Loch Slapin is the shortest and most popular. The majority of climbs lie on this east side of the massif and even those on the western faces are more easily reached by crossing the ridge from here than by a long walk down Glen Sligachan. The easiest path up Blàbheinn is known as the Normal Route which is common to all approaches. Park in the forestry near the head of Loch Slapin (NG 560 215). Cross the road bridge back to the north bank of the Allt na Dunaiche. Follow this up past some beautiful waterfalls to a levelling at an altitude of 200m where the footpath first crosses the burn.

Approach for Clach Glas: For the Clach Glas-Blàbheinn Traverse take a direct line north to the East Ridge of Sgùrr nan Each. For Bealach Buttresses [83] and the West Face [82] aim for Bealach Clach Glas. Stay on the north bank of the Allt na Dunaiche taking the right fork into Choire a' Caise then bypass a gorge on either side. Grass and screes above end in a short stone shoot of gabbro boulders which lead pleasantly to the bealach. The Normal Route crosses the Allt Uaigneich (NG 542 216) before rising more steeply by a badly eroded path. The East Face [84] is best approached by a rising traverse after this crossing to reach the lowest rocks (1hr).

Approach for Blàbheinn: As the path rises the East Face [85] and Lower North-East Wall [86] are approached by a direct line (1hr). This is not recommended for the Upper North-East Walls [86]. Instead continue to the alpine-style meadow in Coire Uaigneich. A huge boulder is the most obvious feature ahead (450m, NG 535 212). 100m before reaching the boulder the Normal Route becomes fragmented; strike right sharply through a band of small crags to where the trail becomes obvious again. Head north-east, passing through an open boulder filled gully, until it suddenly overlooks the impressive North-East Wall at an altitude of 675m. The path continues easily to the top of **Scupper Gully** (750m; see p257, 263) which gives the only simple route through the Upper North-East Wall [86]. It is usually cairned and has a deep subsidiary gully 15m above. Descend Scupper Gully with caution to the toe of the Great Prow in 1hr 30mins. The North Face [87] is traditionally approached from Sligachan but it is quicker to cross by the Putting Green and make an easy descent (2hrs). The summit of Blàbheinn is an easy walk of less than 30mins from the top of Scupper Gully.

A more obvious trail from the huge boulder goes up scree to the South-East Ridge. This leads to the south top and an intimidating down-climb to reach the main summit. Other trails lead into the loose Great Gully that separates the two tops. South-East Buttress [88] is the broad face to the right of Great Gully. Bear right before reaching the huge boulder to reach the toe of the impressive face (1hr 15mins). From here traverse up and left across Great Gully to reach Winter Buttress [89] and South Buttress [90] in about 1hr 30mins.

The South Ridge of Blàbheinn [91] is approached from the car park at Kilmarie (NG 545 172) but routes on the upper section are reached more quickly by crossing the foot of the South-East Ridge from Coire Uaigneich.

Clach Glas-Blàbheinn Traverse   7hrs   Grade 3/Difficult ✱✱✱✱

This is one of the finest mountaineering routes in Britain. Clach Glas is known as The Matterhorn of Skye because of the similar profile it presents from the north to that of the Matterhorn when viewed from the west. The classic horseshoe ascends the South-East Ridge of Sgùrr nan Each, traverses Clach Glas, gives some Difficult climbing to gain the summit slopes of Blàbheinn, crosses to the South Top and descends the South-East Ridge before descending Coire Uaigneich. Starting at Bealach Clach Glas is a popular abbreviation and escape down the screes from the Putting Green is common.

Leave the path 100m above the waterfalls to gain the broad wet spur that starts the South-East Ridge of Sgùrr nan Each. In dry weather this ridge offers good scrambling on small steep buttresses to reach the east summit. Grass slopes above rise gently for 300m to gabbro slabs and the main summit (2hrs). The crest ahead narrows for 300m, (30mins) with one notable descent where a steep cracked slab can be avoided on the south side before reaching the gentle western slopes. Head south for 200m where a loose descent leads to Bealach Clach Glas.

The simplest directions for traversing Clach Glas (allow 2hrs) are to follow the crest wherever possible. On the ascent difficulties are turned on the west and in descent difficulties are turned on the east. Escape is only recommended by returning or continuing along the crest.

The route soon bares its teeth with narrow ribs rising and falling with amazing frequency. A 10m wall in particular gives a problematic descent early on. A major scree gully is reached immediately below the Final Tower. Start this by climbing the prominent slanting chimney or the rib on its right. From the neck above, climb the wall to a small overhang (10m) and exit by the slabby right wall. A short break left gains the top wall, above which easier rocks lead to the summit. Many more direct variations on the Final Tower are possible at about Very Difficult standard.

The descent lies down slabs to the east which end after 40m, now even more abruptly. A lightning strike in 2008 removed most of the rock that was traditionally used. The grade is similar but the rock quite loose. A more solid line descends 10m to the left (north). Continue south to fully appreciate the Impostor, the edge that has just been descended. A false gully leads down and right some 70m beyond the Impostor with a better line taking the crest then slabs on the left. The pattern of turning steps on the left then returning to the crest continues to the grassy bealach known as the Putting Green.

The ascent to Blàbheinn (1hr) finds breaks through the imposing North-East Wall. The first difficulty is hidden in a rift 100m beyond the Putting Green. A surprisingly hard 8m wall is taken left, right or centrally at Difficult standard. This leads to a large bib of scree beneath the Horn (Half Crown Pinnacle). Follow a trail west for 70m to an obvious elbow where a gully rises to the left. This opens out into a grassy bay with a prominent steep 25m chimney on the right. This is the easiest line and is frequently climbed in a single pitch (Moderate) with the polished start forming the crux.

From the top, traverse blocks to a large gully which leads to the Normal Route just 15mins from the summit of Blàbheinn. Crossing to the South Top has a delightful short rock step at the head of Great Gully and superb views down into Camasunary and Coruisk from the broad summit beyond. Descend by the South-East Ridge.

Winter: **IV ****

The route can be sublime in good conditions but frequently the lack of height and southern aspects can leave many sections of bare rock. Serious under deep powder snow, 8hrs.

CLACH GLAS

This superb pointed peak lies 600m north-east of Blàbheinn offering mostly long traditional routes.

Descent: Traverse Clach Glas, as described above, either south to the Putting Green or north to Bealach Clach Glas for routes finishing north of the summit tower.

82. WEST FACE

(NG 533 223)   Alt 600m   West facing   Map p257   Diagram p260

The West Face overlooks Coire Dubh and Glen Sligachan. It has more continuous rock than the east face and is also cleft by gullies, the two most prominent of which lie on either side of the summit tower. The left-hand, The Black Cleft corresponds to B Gully on the East Face and is unattractive and unclimbed. The right-hand is Pilkington's Gully, the line taken by the first ascensionists in 1888. Routes on the summit buttress can be used as harder finishes to the Naismith and Pilkington routes.

Approach: To reach the lower tier climb north out of Bealach Clach Glas then descend west on scree fairly easily and curve round leftwards to below Arch Gully (that leads to the bealach), at an altitude of 600m. The Summit Buttress is gained by traversing left (north-west) from just below the Impostor to the base of the routes. Descend north or south along the ridge as described above.

Routes are described from left to right.

82. CLACH GLAS
West Face

1. Arch Gully   IV,5
2. Consolation Gully   Moderate
3. Naismith's Route   Difficult *
4. Pilkington's Gully   Moderate
5. Penelope   V,6 *

Bealach Clach Glas

The Putting Green

87. BLÀBHEINN
North Face

1. Ledge Route   III
2. North Face Direct   IV,5 ***
3. Forked Pinnacle Ridge   Grade 3/Mod *
4. Pinnacle Gully/Summit Gully   II

Willink's Gully

Arch Gully, IV,5, West Face of Clach Ghlas. Climber Mark Shaw

Lower Tier

Arch Gully   190m   Moderate   *(1896)*
Below Bealach Clach Glas is a well pronounced deep gully. It has a big chockstone
pitch halfway up, a natural arch and a few interesting pitches before all these
obstacles.
Winter: **190m   IV,5**   *(1999)*
By the summer route in four pitches. The overhanging start was avoided on the left
with some thin mixed climbing. The second pitch was climbed round the huge
chockstone. The top two pitches under the arch were banked out and straightforward. Better conditions would ease the initial difficulties.

Midway between Arch Gully and the Black Cleft lies Athain Gully that is described
as being "without interest". The rocks either side both give good hard scrambles
called **Athain Slab Route** and **Athain Rib** (200m Grade 3 /Moderate 1967).

Consolation Gully   200m   Moderate   *(1907)*
Starts immediately left of the Black Cleft and gives three good pitches before
regaining it below the final tower.

Naismith's Route   Difficult   220m   *   *(1896)*
This is a good route on sound and clean rock. The original description is as good as
any available. "The route lay about mid-way between the two prominent gullies
which cleave the mountain face. The lower rocks were smooth slabs of the 'boiler-
plate' variety. About a third of the way up, a steep angle of good rock, 12m high,
was scaled (this steep corner pitch may be turned by a chimney on the right).
Reach the ridge at the final tower just north of the summit."

Pilkington's Gully   220m   Moderate   *(1888)*
The first ascent route follows the major right-hand gully. Scrambling above leads to

the crest of the south ridge just below the Impostor. The apparent knife-edge is merely the arete formed by the easy summit slab.

Summit Buttress

5 Penelope   70m   Very Difficult   *(1958)*
A chimney cuts vertically through the upper rocks. Climb the chimney direct.
Variation: **Odysseus   70m   Severe** *   *(1958)*
Climb the wall 3m right of the chimney.
Winter: **70m   V,6** *   *(1998)*
By the summer route. Although short, this route offered fine climbing, a superb outlook and a finish at the summit of Clach Glas.

83. BEALACH BUTTRESS (EAST FACE)

(NG 535 226)   Alt 550m   East facing   Map p257   Diagram p263

These crags lie on the East Face, either side of the stone shoot leading to Bealach Clach Glas. The summer routes lie right of the bealach, catch plenty of sun and can be used as a climbing start to a traverse of the Clach Glas-Blàbheinn ridge. The winter lines lie left of the bealach with a shady aspect and plenty of drainage.

Bealach Buttress Right

This section is clearly split into two prominent buttresses.

1 Trundle Buttress   120m   Very Difficult *   *(1968)*
Start at the left edge of the right-hand buttress and follow the crest. Two steep steps give good climbing, but after 120m only scrambling remains.

2 Left-Hand Buttress   135m   Very Difficult   *(1968)*
Climb pleasant slabs for 60m to a grass ledge below a bulge. Climb the bulge and continue to the top. There is an easier variation to the right.

Bealach Buttress Left

Situated immediately south of the Bealach Clach Glas is a prominent east facing buttress holding two parallel, left-slanting fault-lines.

3 Slighe a' Bhodaich   115m   IV,4 *   *(1998)*
This route climbs the right-hand fault, up the chimney in two pitches over several interesting chockstones. Finish left on easier ground to the summit ridge.

4 The Cailliach   130m   IV,4 *   *(1999)*
Climbs the left-hand fault. Avoid the initial rocks by starting up Slighe a' Bhodaich until below its initial steepening, then follow an obvious ledge left to gain the left-hand fault-line. Follow this over highly vegetated ground to easier climbing and a finish on the summit ridge.

84. EAST FACE

(NG 538 220)   Alt 200m   East facing   Map p257   Diagram p263

This presents a 600m face of steep broken rock mixed with frequent grass ledges. It holds good scrambling lines for those seeking a change from the classic round and some big traditional mountain routes that can be easily escaped. The face is split left and right by two long gullies A and B. Left of the main mass of Clach Glas and right of The Putting Green lies Bealach Tower. Descend as described above. Routes are described from right to left.

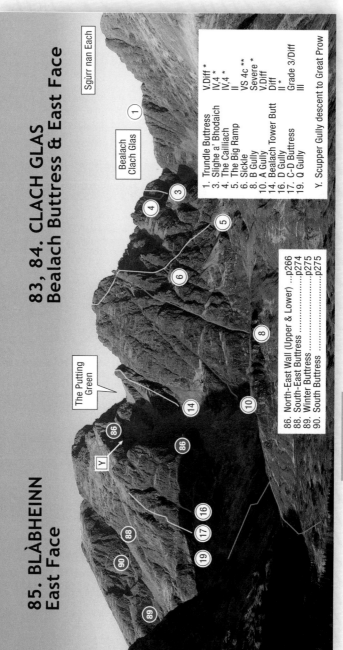

85. BLÀBHEINN
East Face

83, 84. CLACH GLAS
Bealach Buttress & East Face

Sgùrr nan Each

Bealach Clach Glas

The Putting Green

1. Trundle Buttress	V.Diff *
3. Slighe a' Bhodaich	IV,4 *
4. The Cailliach	IV,4 *
5. The Big Ramp	II
6. Sickle	VS 4c **
8. B Gully	Severe *
10. A Gully	V.Diff
14. Bealach Tower Butt	Diff
16. D Gully	II *
17. C-D Buttress	Grade 3/Diff
19. Q Gully	III

Y. Scupper Gully descent to Great Prow

86. North-East Wall (Upper & Lower)	...p266
88. South-East Buttress	...........p274
89. Winter Buttress	...............p275
90. South Buttress	...............p275

BLÀBHEINN

5 The Big Ramp   400m   II *(1995)*

Start by a left-rising traverse to gain the obvious big ramp on the right-hand side of the face that finishes 30m right of B Gully. From the top, follow a steep but simple snow line leftwards across the top of B Gully and go up ramps to finish at the summit cairn of Clach Glas. This avoids the Impostor but needs a good banking of snow.

**6 Sickle   85m   VS 4c ** *(1968)*

This fine route lies on the vertical north wall of the first pinnacle of Pinnacle Buttress most easily gained by a slabby glacis that runs from the north. A prominent chimney marks the start.

1. 30m   Climb the chimney to a belay.
2. 15m   The chimney continues above, but the route follows a tempting right-curving gangway to the foot of a steep corner.
3. 20m   Climb the corner with difficulty then exit onto a ledge on the crest below a steep wall.
4. 20m   Climb the wall on small holds at its exposed right edge to reach the summit of the tower. Continue up by easy climbing over another pinnacle, then scrambling leads to the summit ridge.

Variation: **Left-hand Finish   20m   E1 5b** *(2005)*

Described as technical and serious. From the belay, traverse left around a corner to reach a vague weakness (possible belay). Follow this firstly up to a small roof (protection). Traverse left on small holds (crux) to more positive holds on the left arete which is followed to the summit and belay.

7 Pinnacle Buttress   600m   Very Difficult *(1920)*

This buttress is right of B Gully with four detached pinnacles near the top. The steep wall of the first pinnacle can be turned on the left, regaining the ridge at the gap behind it.

8 B Gully   600m   Severe * *(1920)*

This is the long vertical deep-cut gully starting from the bottom of the face and ending just right of the summit tower. The initial section gives ten pitches with scant protection between the belays. The penultimate pitch is the crux. A mighty wedged boulder above forces a bypass on the right walls. Above, the gully is easy and it is best to gain Pinnacle Buttress on the right by a subsidiary grass gully. Climb the ridge, bypassing the prominent tower on the left, and reach the summit via slabs.

Winter: **IV ** *(1991)*

The gully requires the unfortunately uncommon conditions of heavy snowfall and a long freeze, and it is almost certainly harder under thin or powder conditions. Numerous short steps are interspersed by long easy sections. Short excursions out of the true line of the gully may be necessary at two points.

9 Central Buttress   600m   Difficult *(1915)*

This is the discontinuous buttress between the two main gullies, starting anywhere between them and taking the line of choice. The crux is a vertical wall at half-height which can be climbed direct or by a 20m chimney on the left overlooking A Gully. Above, the rocks are more broken.

10 A Gully   650m   Very Difficult

This is the left-hand of the two major gullies. Open in the lower reaches the gully becomes deeply set into the mountain higher up. There is only one long pitch at half-height which is climbed on the right wall. Above here the angle eases and the line slants right to join the ridge north of the summit tower.

11 Sids' Rake   600m   Grade 3 * *(1900)*

The original route up this face is an entertaining scramble. Start up the buttress left of A Gully until forced into a minor gully on the left. Regain the buttress on the right. Cross A Gully by an impressive bridge shortly before it merges with the left-hand gully. Follow this to the ridge north of the summit tower. Alternative routes are abundant.

South-East Route   300m   Difficult   *(1914)*
The gully right of Bealach Tower is deeply-cut with a very steep north wall. This route tackles the steep wall, starting just below where the gully emerges on to the screes. Start just left of a deep black chimney and climb up past some grass patches. Now follow a face and a chimney to broken ground some 60m below and south of the summit cairn. A landmark at three-quarters height is a transverse slab.

South-East Gully   250m   II   *(1994)*
This is the large gully between Bealach Tower and Clach Glas with one pitch at the top of the right-hand finish.
Summer: **Difficult**   *(2010)*
A 30m pitch leads to a large chockstone that gives the second protection from loose debris on the final 35m.

Bealach Tower Buttress   300m   Difficult   *(1926)*
This is the buttress immediately right of the Putting Green. Start from the toe of the buttress half-way up the scree slopes below the Putting Green.
Easy slabs lead to a broad terrace at half-height. The upper section is crossed by a diagonal gully low down. Climb the left side of this initially then cross to climb the steepest rocks overlooking South-East Gully.

BLÀBHEINN

85. EAST FACE

(NG 537 216)   Alt 450m   East facing   Map p257   Diagram p263

This is the complex series of buttresses and gullies in the lowest reaches of the East Ridge. The face runs parallel to the footpath up Coire Uaigneis and is cleft by three gully lines. Routes are described from right to left.

East Ridge   250m   Grade 3/Moderate   *(1900)*
The broad spur right of D Gully at the northern end of the East Face. The lower pinnacle is most easily climbed by a fault which runs straight to its top. Cross the right fork of D Gully to climb the second pinnacle. Complex route-finding.
Winter: **II/III** *   *(1960?)*
The lower chimney provides the key to the ridge.

D Gully   300m   Very Difficult
The furthest right gully on the East Face. This cleft cuts right through the cliffs and from a col drops down into Access Gully on the North-East Face. Ascend a short steep wall directly above the col to reach the top of the crag.
Winter: **II** *   *(1995)*
On the first ascent, the cleft was well filled with snow and it allowed a simple passage through its deep narrows up to the col. Above the col on the left, a point of aid was used on the short fierce wall barring access.

C-D Buttress   250m   Grade 3/Difficult   *(1914)*
This scramble lies left of the East Ridge proper between C Gully on the left and D Gully on the right. Climb centrally over glacier worn rocks to a protruding belt of rock. Keep left up cracks and steep grass and climb a deep narrow chimney. Above, the route crosses the left fork of D Gully to the right and joins the East Ridge at the second pinnacle.

C Gully   200m   *(2009)*
One recorded winter descent through some very impressive rock walls with two 15m abseils used to pass large chockstones.

The buttress left of C Gully gives some good open scrambling (Grade 3/Moderate).

19 Q Gully   160m   III   *(2009)*
This is the shallowest and most southern of the gullies splitting the face. Two pitches were climbed with the second giving 10m of good steep ice.

86. NORTH-EAST WALL

Map p257   Diagrams p263, p267
This creates an impressive barrier between the scree slopes below the Putting Green and the bulk of Blaven. It provides a very wide variety of climbing with superb steep rock on the Upper Wall and long winter routes on the Lower Wall. Descent is by Blàbheinn's Normal Route or descending Scupper Gully (see Blàbheinn approaches) and the screes below.

Lower North-East Wall

(NG 537 217)   Alt 500m   North-East facing
This is a huge steep sweep of largely damp and vegetated rocks criss-crossed by ramps and gullies suited far more to winter climbing than summer. Few of the finishes have been identified clearly. A continuous diagonal ramp (Serious Picnic) is the most prominent feature of the lower North-East wall. 200m further up screes towards the Putting Green is Access Gully, a deep gully that crosses Serious Picnic forming a crucifix, that then continues to the col at the top of D Gully.

1 Serious Picnic   240m   III *   *(1995)*
This route takes the prominent right-rising ramp-line low down on the wall. Easy ground leads to the foot of the first pitch. Climb up left, then go back right on turf to gain the ramp-line (40m). Climb this for several pitches to a col and continue past a short difficult step to the top.

2 Thrutcher's Groove   250m   III   *(1996)*
Start right of Serious Picnic taking easy ground to a very narrow chimney. Climb the chimney (crux) then head for well defined gullies higher up linking them by a short traverse.

The face above the scree becomes very steep for the next 100m as height is gained before reaching the obvious easy fault of Access Gully.

3 Hawse Pipe Chimney   130m   VS   *(1969)*
This is the prominent steep chimney on the buttress left of Access Gully. There is a cave to the right of its base and a series of caves and overhangs in the chimney itself. Climb the chimney direct, belaying in the various caves en route, and exit right of the chockstone.

4 Access Gully   100m   Moderate   *(1969)*
A chockstone suspended high above the head is a worrying landmark. Exit right by the transverse fault taken by Serious Picnic.
Winter: **200m   II ***   *(1994)*
Climb the gully over a short iced chockstone to reach Serious Picnic. Turn right and follow this until below a selection of 3 exit gullies. The first ascent took the right-hand most. A very tight through route behind a chockstone and two long easy pitches led to the top.
Variation: **Teddy Bears' Gulch   70m   III,4**   *(1997)*
An alternative finish, climb Access Gully to the 'X' junction; go right for 10m on to the ramp of Serious Picnic to a short step, then leave the ramp and climb directly up the obvious chockstoned gully in two interesting pitches, exiting right to the crest of the East Ridge.

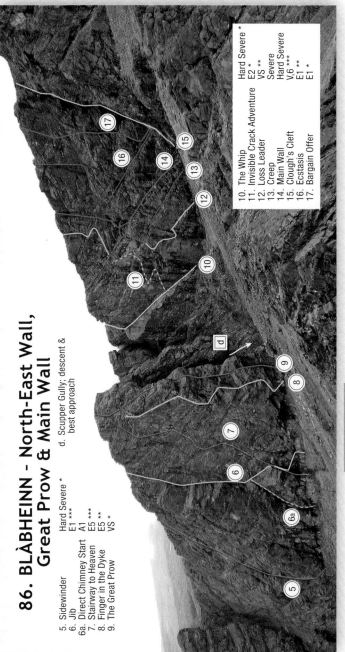

86. BLÀBHEINN - North-East Wall, Great Prow & Main Wall

5. Sidewinder — Hard Severe *
6. Jib — E1 ***
6a. Direct Chimney Start — A1
7. Stairway to Heaven — E5 ***
8. Finger in the Dyke — E5 **
9. The Great Prow — VS *

d. Scupper Gully; descent & best approach

10. The Whip — Hard Severe *
11. Invisible Crack Adventure — E2 *
12. Loss Leader — VS **
13. Creep — Severe
14. Main Wall — Hard Severe
15. Clough's Cleft — V,6 ***
16. Ecstasis — E1 **
17. Bargain Offer — E1 *

Upper North-East Wall - Great Prow Area

(NG 534 218)   Alt 700m   North-East facing

This is a significant climbing area with routes at all grades crossing some impressive territory, largely on good rock. Settled warm weather makes the cliff a very attractive proposition. The Great Prow is a jutting rib of gabbro that houses several classic climbs. The steep Main Wall lies above and is bounded on the right by Clough's Cleft. Right of this, Chock-a-Block Chimney separates The Horn (Naismith's Half Crown Pinnacle) from the main face.

Approaches: The upper reaches of the North-East Wall are quicker to reach by following the Normal Route to a height of 750m where rucksacks can be left before descending Scupper Gully (see Blàbheinn approaches). Ascending by the long scree slopes beneath the face is purgatorial. Routes are described from left to right (bottom to top).

Great Prow

5 Sidewinder   110m   Hard Severe * (1968)

This good climb follows the left extremity of the big left wall of The Great Prow. Start 40m left of the big corner of Jib where an open slabby groove leads left.
1. 30m 4c Climb the groove for 6m to a crack in its right wall. Climb the crack (crux) and its right fork to a stance.
2. 15m Continue up grooves to a ledge.
3. 35m Continue in the same line for 20m, then follow a fault diagonally right to a pedestal.
4. 30m Climb the wall to the top.

6 Jib   130m   E1 ***** (1969)

This excellent route follows the big corner left of the wall of Stairway to Heaven. After a hard and intimidating start the climbing is continuously challenging and in a stupendous position.
Start 30m below The Great Prow in an open cave. At the left edge an undercut gangway is just in reach.
1. 40m 5b Pull fiercely up left (crux) to the left-trending gangway. Traverse this for 15m before it crosses a welcome crack to eventually gain a broad ledge. Climb the crack for 5m above the ledge and then traverse left into the main line.
2. 40m 4c Climb the crack with ever increasing interest. Belay at the higher of two sloping ledges.
3. 15m 4c Climb the chimney above to a stance.
4. 35m 4b Step right to climb the fine groove in the top wall.
Variation: **St. Andrews Crack   15m**
15m below the cave a crack-line leads to the gangway. This is the first pitch of Stairway to Heaven which continues directly above.
Variation: **Direct Chimney Start   25m   E2 5b** (1977)
Climb the off-width corner 30m below the cave to join the original line at the base of the broad ledge. No unaided ascent has been recorded.

7 Stairway to Heaven   120m   E5 ***** (1977)

A great Skye classic, giving some impressive climbing. Start at the overhanging off-width corner 30m left of the start of Jib.
1. 30m 5b Climb the corner to the Jib traverse. Take the crack above then step left to a niche. This crack is often uninviting and can be avoided by taking the broad ledge on the left for 5m then climbing back right to gain the niche.
2. 20m 4c Follow the crack above to a further niche.
3. 30m 6a Move up to a fault-line and follow this leftwards until it is possible to climb the overhang by a short crack. Traverse right with difficulty to a narrow ledge, then climb diagonally up right to a short crack which leads to a stance and peg belay on a slanting gangway.
4. 40m 5b Follow the crack, climb an overlap, then move up in a tremendous

Stairway to Heaven, E5, Great Prow Area of Blàbheinn. Climber Tom Prentice

position to a flake covered wall which leads to a ledge. Finish up the wall and move right to the top.

**Finger in the Dyke 120m E5 ** **   (1997)
A serious and atmospheric route up the arete of The Great Prow. Start at a left-slanting dyke at the left-hand side of the cave below the arete. The dyke climbed by Jib is 10m down to the left.

1. 30m 6a Follow the dyke to a small right-facing corner (serious) and gain the shelf above. Move a short way up this ramp, swing right into an undercut groove and climb it until the line fades. Make a slightly descending traverse right across the lip of a roof to a curious hole, continue to the right-hand side of a slabby niche and climb the crack above. Take a hanging belay below a loose niche.
2. 30m 5c Follow the crack through the niche to climb a wall on hollow holds, moving right round the arete below a bulge. Gain the ramp above, move back left round the arete and step down to belay in a scoop.
3. 45m 5b Continue directly above the belay crossing a dyke, then follow good holds leading rightwards on to the arete. Continue more easily up a wide left-slanting crack and its continuation to belay on a broken terrace.
4. 15m Scramble up left to the top.

The Great Prow 105m VS *   (1968)
Despite its classic status and great position, the rock could be better in places. Start below an overhanging chimney-corner.
1. 35m 4c Climb the crack to an awkward exit onto a slab. Climb the slab to a

The Great Prow, Splinter Finish, E2.
Climber Chris Moore on the first ascent

belay at its top.

2. 40m 4c Continue up the crack above to belay below an obvious pedestal ledge.

3. 10m 4c Move back down from the pedestal, level with an orange coloured slab, then follow a pair of thin diagonal faults up the wall leftwards to the crest (poor belay).

4. 20m 4a Continue up a ramp until a crack on the right leads back to the crest and the summit.

Variation: **Twilight Slab   VS** *   (1975)*

From the cracks on pitch two, below the orange slab, traverse left across the prominent slab on the front of the Prow; belay on the edge. Continue up and right to a large block, then go straight up to join the original line for the final pitch.

Variation: **The Splinter Finish   25m   E2 5c (2 rests) ***   (2010)

Viewed from the footpath this takes the obvious diagonal crack rising right from the pedestal above the second belay on the original route. Well protected but care is needed with blocks at the end of the pitch. The crux sequence is very similar to Left Wall.

Winter: **VII,8**   *(2010)*

An exceptional snow fall brought this route into unusual winter condition. The summer line was followed throughout.

To the right of Scupper Gully is a narrow subsidiary prow, which gives a rather scrappy climb **The Gutter** (Severe 1977).

Main Wall

This is a big steep wall crossed by four prominent diagonal faults that rise with comparative ease to give impressive situations. The rock is largely of good quality but long run-outs on the traverses are a feature. The central bay at half-height is a useful landmark.

The Whip   55m   Hard Severe *   (2000)
Follows an obvious left-slanting hanging slab at the left side of the face.
1. 45m 4b Gain the ramp easily at the lowest point. Follow the top edge of the slab until it widens and thin moves up and left gain a basalt pavement. This leads to the top of the slab.
2. 10m Go straight up easy ground to the top.

The Invisible Crack Adventure   60m   E2 *   (2007)
A crack-line splits the wall above The Whip. This route zigzags across the crack through some very steep terrain.
1. 20m 4b Start up the Whip. The second steep section leads to a small belay ledge with an obvious break onto the right wall.
2. 20m 5c Traverse right, crossing the crack-line, then surmount a large pillar. Make a rising traverse back left across the crack and the steep wall beyond on positive holds (crux) to reach an overhung ledge. Two huge flakes sit on this ledge. Hand-traverse these carefully, passing the crack again to a cramped corner stance and good thread on the pillar above.
3. 20m 5a Hand-traverse 6m further right to easier ground. Step onto the slabby wall above the basalt break. Reach more large flakes which lead left to a loose finish and belay on the slab above. Scramble easily up the slab (Creep) to finish.

Loss Leader   110m   VS **   (1969)
This route may well be hard for its grade given the steepness of the rock it crosses on the first pitch and ascends on the final pitch. Start 35m right of the Whip where the lowest diagonal fault rises. Climb left along the gangway to where it narrows (belay). Move down to a lower gangway and continue across onto a smooth wall to gain the chimney beyond (this feature splits the wall from the bottom) and ascend this to the central bay. Move 5m left (Creep) then climb a wall and gangway rising right to a short steep wall. Climb this by a crack, go left on a basalt pavement to cracks on another steep wall and climb these to finish by a scoop.

Creep   90m   Severe   (1969)
This climb is recommended for the fine positions gained on the wall. It follows the next highest dyke to gain the main chimney (Loss Leader) and the recessed central bay. Exit diagonally more easily leftwards across slabs and broken walls to the top.

Main Wall   110m   Hard Severe   (1968)
The original line on this face follows the third, largest and most obvious, trap dyke from the bottom of the wall (Ecstasis takes a higher dyke from Clough's Cleft). Climb up directly to large detached flakes from the same starting point as Creep. Continue along the fault, passing under a jammed square block, to a sentry box. Continue the traverse to the central bay. Climb the steep chimney above on the right to finish.

To the right of Main Wall are two deep damp chimneys. The left-hand chimney is Clough's Cleft, the right-hand is Choc-a-Block Chimney.

Clough's Cleft   105m   VS   (1968)
The grade varies in proportion to the amount of seepage, but it is very rarely dry.
Winter: 105m   V,6 ***   (2000)
This natural winter route, although short, provided superb icy mixed climbing. Follow the summer route finishing directly by the continuation chimney at the top. Rucksacks are not recommended.

BLÀBHEINN

16 Ecstasis 95m E1 ** (1972)

The climb takes the highest diagonal fault, leading left out of Clough's Cleft.

1. 25m 5a Start up Clough's Cleft, then follow the pleasant slabby ramp leftwards to a stance.

2. 25m 4c Continue, easily at first, to a spike runner. Now climb poorly protected undercut slabs leftwards to a belay in the bay.

3. 15m 4b Climb the slab rightwards to a substantial ledge under a soaring crack.

4. 30m 5b Tackle the steep jamming crack. Sustained.

17 Bargain Offer 100m E1 5b * (1969)

Climbs the wall between Ecstasis and Clough's Cleft.

1. 40m Start up Clough's Cleft, move left on the highest diagonal fault as for Ecstasis and ascend the first crack above to the base of the prominent chimney.

2. 20m Climb the chimney to a good ledge with a large block belay.

3. 20m Take the wall above the blocks directly (crux) to a ramp (possible escape left).

4. 20m Climb the steep right wall direct to the top.

18 Chock-a-Block Chimney 105m Hard Severe (1961)

The right-hand chimney gives another route whose grade varies directly in proportion to the moisture content! Climb the bed of the gully, breaking out right to below the first overhang (15m). Go up steep rocks right of the chimney proper, then traverse back into the chimney above the first overhang. Just above is a small cave topped by a greasy chockstone (crux), best climbed by back and foot. The boulder bed above recedes into the misty depths; far back, a cave leads to a subterranean chimney. Above the chimney, continue easily up the scree channel to the col.

Winter: **105m V *** (1999)

1. 25m Climb easily up the bed of the gully.

2. 25m Climb steeply up rock on the right of the gully for 7m until it is possible to traverse a precarious slab to regain the gully fault. Climb up and exit awkwardly on to an easing.

3. 20m Tackle the next series of overhangs via a through route to a deep cave.

4. 35m Exit on the left, trend back right to regain the bed and continue on snow.

19 The Horn 120m Severe (1967)

This is the east face of Naismith's Half Crown Pinnacle. Start at the toe of the buttress and climb beside Chock-a-Block Chimney for 30m. Traverse right across a steep wall and then continue up the right (north) side of the buttress. Turn the final band of overhangs on the right by a steep and exposed wall above the north face of the pinnacle.

Variation: **The Horn Direct HVS 5b** (1968/1977)

This gives alternative start and finish pitches to the original route. Start 10m right of Chock-a-Block Chimney by a rib and a short smooth groove then moving left to join the original route. Climb the final belt of overhangs centrally, direct to the top of the pinnacle.

Naismith's Half Crown Pinnacle is most easily gained by a short detour from the normal Clach Glas-Blàbheinn Traverse, lying opposite the final chimney; 5m Difficult.

87. NORTH FACE

(NG 524 223) Alt 400m North facing Map p257 Diagram p260

This is a broad complex face overlooking Glen Sligachan with largely easy climbing amongst impressive rock scenery. Connecting a succession of features up the face gives a long mountaineering outing in guaranteed solitude. **Willink's Gully** (1873) is the huge gully separating the summits and blocked by a monstrous chock-stone low down. The following routes are on the steeper rocks well to the north starting at an altitude of about 400m and are described from left to right. Approach via the Putting Green (2hrs) or from Sligachan (2hrs 30mins).

North Face Direct, IV,5, North Face of Blàbheinn.
Climber Mark Shaw on the first ascent

Ledge Route   500m   III   (2009)
This route links left trending snow terraces left of and below North Face Direct
route. Generally easy climbing with two pitches of interest. Start in the very large
recess up left of Forked Pinnacle Ridge and 200m below the Putting Green.
Climb North Face Direct for 20m then follow the obvious easy snow terrace rising
to the left to an alcove. Traverse left to reach a short wall overlooking a gully on
the left. Climb the wall moving rightwards to gain another easy left trending terrace and follow this to gain a small coll. Descend 15m to a horizontal snow shelf
then follow the shallow gully slanting up leftwards, crux, to gain easier ground
overlooking a large snow bay. Climb to the top of the snow bay and finish by
steeper rocks to the summit.

North Face Direct   470m   IV,5 ***   (2009)
The main feature of this route is a rising hidden fault cutting deeply into the upper

section of the North Face. Traverse right across the recess then up to an easy open gully.

1. and 2. 100m Follow the easy gully trending left to gain a snow bay dominated by a steep rock wall. Left of this wall lies the start of the upper fault, access to which is barred by a large blunt rock buttress. There is an overhanging cave chimney on the right and a snow gully below an icy chimney on the left.

3. 60m Follow the gully to below the icy chimney.

4. 30m Back and foot the icy chimney to gain a small cave, bridge out right (crux) to gain easier ground and belay on the right.

5. 50m Climb easily up the open gully above to enter the depths of the upper fault.

6. 60m Continue up the chasm between impressive rock walls passing under two chockstones wedged high above.

7. 50m Reach the top of the gully at a notch right of a prominent pinnacle.

8. 60m Climb directly out of the notch to gain mixed grooves running up the left side of the steep summit buttress.

9. 60m Continue up grooves and easier ground to gain the summit.

Summer: **470m** **Difficult**   *(1923)*

The original description has the crux manoeuvres similarly just below chasm with combined tactics essential.

3 Forked Pinnacle Ridge   350m   Grade 3/Moderate *   *(1905)*

This is the most prominent feature of the north face as seen from Loch an Aithain. The route starts by a slabby buttress just right of the lowest rocks. The first 90m are quite steep and interesting, followed by much scrambling. Where the gullies meet cross to the right side of Summit Gully and follow a ridge to finish 100m south of the summit.

4 Pinnacle Gully/Summit Gully   350m   Grade 3/Moderate   *(1890)*

Ascend Pinnacle Gully for 100m until it is logical to join Forked Pinnacle Ridge on the left. Follow this for a further 100m, passing the Forked Pinnacles to the point at which Pinnacle and Summit Gully meet. Take slabs left of Summit Gully directly to the summit cairn.

Winter: **350m   II**   *(2000)*

Follow the summer line.

The remaining climbing areas all lie on the east side of Blaven above the upper section of Coire Uaigneich. They overlook **Great Gully** which splits the north and south summits giving an unpleasant loose route in summer. With good snow it is the best line to the summit, passing below impressive walls (grade I, **).

88. SOUTH-EAST BUTTRESS

(NG 533 214)   Alt 585m   South facing   Map p257   Diagram p263

Technically this is the south-east face of the northern top of Blàbheinn. It is the impressive rocky face lying right of Great Gully. The face is laid back giving an infinite number of scrambling routes. A beautiful pool that is always cold and clear lies at the lowest point. The slabs are very enjoyable with incut holds on good rock. Overlaps are formed by any less solid rock that remains and should be treated with care. The face has been climbed in winter; it forms ice rapidly in good conditions but is stripped even more quickly by a morning of continuous sunshine.

South-East Buttress   300m   Grade 3 **   *(1907)*

The best and longest line stays on the left edge of the buttress. Start left of the small pool, cross the obvious left-slanting chimney-line then pass three broad terraces with slabs gradually easing in angle to the summit slopes. Superb!

Eventide   60m   Severe   *(1983)*

This route is on the walls of Great Gully opposite the highest routes on South Buttress [90]. Start at a grassy bay below the chimney and about 15m above a large cave. Climb a wall to the chimney, then go up this and the continuation crack, which bears left to finish after a bulge.

Escape from Colditz, III, Winter Buttress. Climber Tony Rees

89. WINTER BUTTRESS

(NG 532 212) Alt 675m North-East facing Map p257 Diagram p263

On the south-west side of Coire Uaigneich, below South Buttress, is a buttress which can be clearly seen from the bridge at the head of Loch Slapin. Ice forms readily to give two excellent routes. Traverse right for 100m to an easy descent to Great Gully.

Where Eagles Dare 50m Severe *(2005)*

Climb the slabby buttress a few metres left of Escape from Colditz more or less directly. Although largely on good rock the climb is very bold with the unprotected crux above a poor belay. Climb 20m to a grassy ledge and poor friend belay. Climb awkwardly through the crux bulge above the ledge heading towards a left-slanting diagonal crack underneath an overlap, climb the crack to a dirty finish.

Escape from Colditz 65m III *** *(1994)*

The deep slanting gully running below the icefall is climbable in most conditions and gives a superb short adventure through a barred tunnel.

Birthday Breakout Finish **25m IV ****** *(2010)*

Break right to finish by steep ice 10m after escaping the tunnel.

Sailaway 50m IV **** *(1994)*

Unique in the Cuillin this route climbs water ice that forms quickly and can be seen from the road. Climb the icefall direct, via several vertical steps separated by terraces; ice screw protection.

90. SOUTH BUTTRESS

(NG 530 214) Alt 700m South facing Map p257 Diagrams p263, p278

The crag gives long lower grade climbs on mostly sound rock that get plenty of sun. The most obvious feature of the buttress is Central Pillar, an area of pale slabs on

BLÀBHEINN

Escape from Colditz, Birthday Breakout Finish, IV, Winter Buttress
Climber Mike Lates

the left-hand side. The long fault immediately right is Birthday Groove. Canopy takes the open book corner on the right edge of the face. Routes on the North-East Face overlook Great Gully and are significantly steeper.

Descent: The best descent to the foot of the climbs is by a diagonal terrace which starts about 30m above the top of the climbs. It slopes easily down right above the routes to Great Gully. The South-East Ridge gives an easy descent to the corrie floor. Continue above the routes before traversing left above South Buttress Gully to join the path.

South-East Face

Belinda   90m   Very Difficult   *(1968)*
This climb lies on the smaller buttress to the south of the main crag. Start centrally.
1. 25m Climb to a spike belay situated amidst blocks.
2. 30m Climb up for 10m, then traverse right to cross an overlap and continue left to a ledge and chock belay.
3. 35m Continue to a grassy terrace. Continue by a steep corner (crux) to gain the easy slabs above.

South Buttress Gully   210m   Difficult   *(1969)*
This is the large gully immediately to the left of Central Pillar. It gives several pitches separated by scree and culminates in a chimney with an overhanging chockstone.
Winter: **210m   II** **   *(2010)*
A good route with an easy 30m ice pitch leading to the main fault line. Three small steps gave well protected mixed climbing higher in the route.

Central Pillar   195m   Severe *   *(1968)*
This is the prominent light coloured pillar on the left of the face. Start from the base or from a chimney on its right. Climb up the right-hand side of the pillar to belays (45m). The crux pitch breaks through the overlap above by a steep corner through loose rock (15m). Continue up the left edge and climb to an open scree ledge. Climb the corner above to gain the left edge of the pillar, then ascend the corner on the right of the wall and exit left at the top. Scramble to finish.

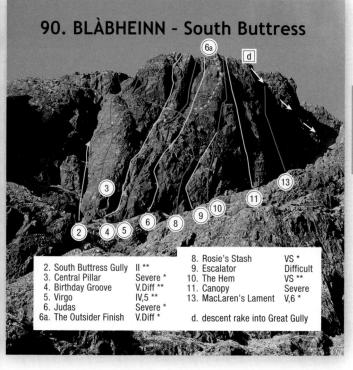

90. BLÀBHEINN - South Buttress

BLÀBHEINN

2. South Buttress Gully	II **	
3. Central Pillar	Severe *	
4. Birthday Groove	V.Diff **	
5. Virgo	IV,5 **	
6. Judas	Severe *	
6a. The Outsider Finish	V.Diff *	

8. Rosie's Stash	VS *	
9. Escalator	Difficult	
10. The Hem	VS **	
11. Canopy	Severe	
13. MacLaren's Lament	V,6 *	
d. descent rake into Great Gully		

4 Birthday Groove   195m   Very Difficult ★★   (1968)
A good line which follows the deep groove to the right of Central Pillar. Climb the groove for 120m to a large grassy ledge, the terrace. Above lie two big corner chimney-lines; climb directly to the top by the left-hand chimney.
Winter: **IV,5 ★★**   (1996)
Follow the summer line by good mixed climbing.

5 Virgo   195m   Difficult ★   (1968)
About 5m right of Birthday Groove lies another groove line. Climb the groove all the way, finishing by the right-hand of the two corner-chimneys.
Winter: **IV,5 ★★**   (1995)
Excellent mixed climbing throughout.

6 Judas   195m   Severe ★   (1968)
Start 12m right of Virgo below a large but shallow slabby corner which is guarded by a bulge. Climb past the bulge (crux), then follow the line of corners to the terrace. Follow a line of thin cracks up the great slab above, starting a few metres to the right of the chimney of Virgo, and finish by a small corner.
Variation: **The Outsider Finish   65m   Very Difficult ★**   (1968)
Traverse above the terrace to the right edge of the Judas slab. Belay on a grass ledge at 40m. Turn the steepening on the left and finish up the right arete.

7 Motown   80m   HVS   (1989)
Follows the prominent steep flake-crack just to the right of a small overhanging recess 6m right of the start of Judas. The route is always to the left of the wandering line of Rosie's Stash.
1. 40m 5a Climb the flake-crack to a roof and move right into a groove which is followed to a ledge.
2. 40m Climb a narrow ramp above before pulling out left onto more broken ground leading to the terrace below the upper corner of Virgo. Finish by Judas, Virgo or The Outsider.

8 Rosie's Stash   195m   VS ★   (1987)
A good line, probably easier if dry. Start to the left of Escalator. Climb cracks, then a narrow right-slanting ramp (above and parallel to Escalator), to a ledge. Move left and climb a bulge using a large block (4c). Continue up to the terrace, then climb the arete between Birthday Groove and Virgo, with a move right to avoid a bulge.

9 Escalator   120m   Difficult   (1968)
Start 20m right of Judas. Follow a rightward line of slanting grooves to finish at the large terrace below the crux pitch of The Hem. Finish by this (4c) or The Outsider to the left.
Variation: **Direct Start**   (1968)
Start 5m further right at a prominent groove. Follow a line of grooves then stay just right of the original route to finish at the same large terrace.

10 The Hem   180m   VS ★★   (1968)
A first class climb with three hard pitches. Start at the right edge of the buttress and scramble up to the bifurcation of two groove lines. Climb the steep left-hand groove to a ledge and belay then continue by another groove above. To the left of this second groove is a corner of white rock that is prominent from the ground. Continue more easily to a grass ledge and block belay on the rightward descending terrace. Climb a bulge to enter a slab corner. Follow this, keeping left, until a short slab on the right leads to a small ledge below an overhang. Climb the overhang on the left to another slab and follow this up right until another bulge (crux 4c) leads to a stance at the foot of a glacis (40m). Follow the glacis right to its end then back left into a trap fault and up to belay in a chimney on the right side of a huge flake. Finish up the chimney and arete above.

South Buttress Gully, II, South East Face of Blàbheinn.
Climber Sam Halligan

BLÀBHEINN

North-East Face

Canopy 130m Severe   *(1968)*

A good sustained climb tackling the prominent corner of overhanging chimneys on the apex of the East and North-East faces. Start 50m further up the Great Gully than the previous routes. Gain the foot of the chimney-line by a right-slanting groove and follow it, passing several bulges to a grass ledge. Now follow further chimneys on the left to the top.

12 Scorpion 110m Severe *(1968)*
This route follows a prominent crack-chimney 30m higher up Great Gully, just beyond a shallow cave that gives good shelter.
Joins Canopy at the grassy ledge.

13 MacLaren's Lament 60m V,6 * *(2007)*
A short and very entertaining route some 70m up the gully from Scorpion. Finishes on the huge terrace which gives an easy walk off.
1. 15m Take an obvious leftward rising break to a large flake belay. This is directly below a large deep chimney.
2. 25m An awkward step off the belay flake gives entry to the deep chimney. Fun moves lead behind two massive blocks to a confined ledge below the final impasse. Excellent gear protects some ridiculous contortions in a battle to the top.
3. 20m Break out of the cleft. Finish easily up to a broad terrace.

91. SOUTH RIDGE

Map p257

This classic ridge is approached from Kilmarie by the track to Camasunary. It is flanked by rock on either side for most of its length with infinite possibilities for scrambling. Two areas of more continuous rock are described here.

South-West Buttresses

(NG 522 203) Alt 300m South-West facing

South-West Buttress (250m Grade 3/Moderate) rises from Glen Sligachan above Loch na Creitheach to join the South Ridge at about half-height. Start from the lowest rock buttress by steep moves followed by slabs. Climb slabs and small buttresses in a weaving line to join the South Ridge.

Blàbheinn South Ridge Grade 2 ***

Stunning views into the heart of the Cuillin make this route special. The ascent is only a walk to the South Top (3hrs from Kilmarie) with some scrambling possibilities for those who want. The crux is a steep descent to the dip between the tops that stops many walkers from reaching the main summit. The direct line is not as difficult as it appears but many favour a slanting terrace on the east side of the crest. From the trig point on the summit descend the Normal Route. The South Top is easily descended by the South-East Ridge.

South-East Face

(NG 527 209) Alt 675m South-East facing

Approach: It is easiest to approach this area by crossing the South-East Ridge above Coire Uaigneich from the Normal Route but the scrambles could be added to an ascent of the South Ridge.

An area of four continuous buttresses lies on the south-east face of the South Ridge level with the broad col at the base of the South-East Ridge (Pt 583, NG 533 210). It is easy to scramble all of the routes in one trip with only minimal equipment required. Routes are described from right to left. The first two buttresses reached (D and C) give Difficult standard climbing for about 250m. There is a 50m Severe corner giving a good direct start to D buttress. The next two buttresses (B and A) are 130m long and Moderate with Difficult pitches possible. **Mistaken Identity** (135m Difficult 1994) probably took one of these lines.

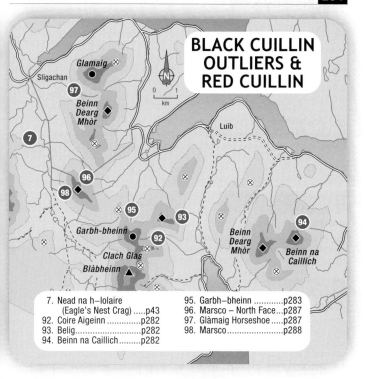

BLACK CUILLIN OUTLIERS & RED CUILLIN

Major intrusions of acidic magmas emerged through the north-east boundary of the Black Cuillin bowl about 57 million years ago resulting in the formation of some beautifully shaped hills that will always remain in the shadow of the Black Cuillin in terms of climbing significance. The Beinn na Caillich (732m) Horseshoe above Broadford, the Glàmaig (775m) Horseshoe above Sligachan and smaller shapely peaks between are all generally referred to as the Red Cuillin. The geological boundary is most distinct on Garbh-bheinn, historically christened a Cuillin Outlier, that deserves to be considered as a Black Cuillin peak. Here the black gabbro can be seen uplifted and resting directly on the rounded red granite. Marsco is an Outlier generally accepted as a Red Cuillin peak despite remnants of gabbro remaining on the summit crest.

Rock climbing is limited to two main venues. Rough Marsco granophyre on the South-West Buttress and the clean solid gabbro of Creag Druim Eadar da Choire on Garbh-bheinn both give high quality climbing. Other peaks, crags and faces in this chapter provide quality mountain days for the explorer and lover of solitude. Footpaths and clues to others passing are virtually non-existent. It is in winter that the size and latitude of these overlooked hills are brought to life for the climber with many obvious lines appearing. The area is bound by the Elgol road (B8083) to the south and by the A87 from Broadford to Sligachan to the north and east.

LOCH SLAPIN

West of Strath Mòr at the head of Loch Slapin lie the shapely peaks of Sgùrr nan Each, Garbh-bheinn and Belig. There are numerous areas of rock but they are generally broken and easy angled. Park at the head of the loch.

OUTLIERS

92. COIRE AIGEINN

(NG 540 233) Maps p257, 281

Approach: This quiet corrie is approached by boggy terrain beside the Allt Aigeinn. Pass the small gorge and beautiful marble pools by either bank and continue for another 1km until directly below Bealach na Beiste NG 541 234 (1hr). The bealach is gained easily and gives the best descent from Belig to Loch Slapin.

Sgùrr nan Each - North Face

Raeburn's Route (North Ridge of East Summit) 400m Grade 2 *   *(1898)*
This broken looking ridge lies opposite Bealach na Beiste. It is bounded on the right by a large open stone shoot which gives a fast descent. The route is far better than it appears and becomes well defined with height.

Garbh-bheinn

(NG 533 231)

The ridges on this mountain all give easy scrambling with some exposure near the summit. Tributaries to the Allt Aigeinn run up to a series of short gullies that line the North-east ridge of Garbh-bheinn. Some have been climbed in winter conditions.

93. BELIG

(NG 553 236) Map p281

About half a dozen gullies descend discontinuously from the eastern summit of Belig toward the floor of Strath Mòr. In winter they can be followed at about grade I or II throughout. The best descent is to traverse the main summit and follow the old boundary wall westward down to Bealach na Beiste. The South-East ridge gives a good simple route of ascent with a few sections of rock that can be scrambled in dry weather or avoided on the right (east).

EASTERN RED CUILLIN

94. BEINN NA CAILLICH

Map p281

This favourite mountain of local people is the Hill of the Old Woman, so named because she often wears a shawl of mist over her shoulders. There are two north facing corries split by a fine ridge. The horseshoe around Beinn Dearg Mhòr and Beinn na Caillich gives a very enjoyable walk best done from Strollamus.

Northern Faces

(NG 605 235) Alt 450m

Approach: Take the minor road that turns left 1km north of Broadford (known locally and signed as the Old Corry road). Park considerably close to the road end. The main trail leads north-west, directly to the summit of Beinn na Caillich. Follow the Allt a' Choire, skirting the worst of the rough boulder field, to reach Coire Fearchair (1hr).

Descent: Descend the steep south-east flank directly to the end of the Old Corry road.

North-East Face 250m Grade 2
Surprisingly solid rock forms the headwall of Coire Fearchair giving a pleasant scramble. Steeper in the lower reaches.

Winter: **II**
Old snows frequently form excellent lines direct to the summit.

The North Face above Coire Seamraig is far more broken and less steep. The shapely North Ridge is easy giving a pleasant route of ascent or descent.

Creag Strollamus

(NG 610 263) Alt 75m North facing
The small ice-fall overlooking the road has been climbed **Creag Strollamus Burn** (50m I 2010).

Creagan Dubh

(NG 590 244) Alt 300m North facing
An obscure outcrop on the north ridge of Beinn Dearg Mhòr. One winter climb is reported, taking a mixture of shallow gully and easy buttress on the longest section of crag (130m, II). The rock is fairly solid and positive but compact and difficult to protect.

Approach: Park in a lay-by beside the main A87 road just south of Strollamus where the river descends Strath Beag from the north. Follow the Strath Beag path then bear left to reach the foot of the broken buttresses (1hr).

LOCH AINORT

Strath Beag is the pass lying between Beinn Dearg Mhòr (709m) and Beinn na Cro (572m), a shapely peak with no recorded climbing. The deep glen of Strath Mòr lies west again staying virtually at sea-level between Luib and Torrin. The peaks overlooking Loch Ainort rise to the west with increasing ruggedness to the boundary between Red and Black Cuillin on Garbh-bheinn.

The Lesser Traverse 16km Grade 3/Difficult ***
Linking the peaks above Loch Ainort to the classic Clach Glas-Blàbheinn Traverse gives a superb circuit with just a hint of what the Main Ridge Traverse will involve. Park considerately in the village of Luib. A rough approach leads to the north ridge of Glas Bheinn Mhòr (570m). Follow the boundary wall and fence up over the summit, up onto Belig (702m) and down to Bealach na Beiste. A long easy rise up Garbh-bheinn (806m) finishes with the first scrambling of the route. Descend the south ridge of Garbh-bheinn to Bealach Clach Glas. Traverse Clach Glas (786m) to the summit of Blàbheinn (Grade 3/Difficult), and then descend to the shores of Loch Slapin. Return to Luib by the level footpath in Strath Mòr (5km) which turns boggy towards the end, 9hrs.

95. GARBH-BHEINN

Map p281 Diagram p285
This classically shaped mountain is the northern most peak of the eastern Black Cuillin, linking directly to Clach Glas. It is composed largely of gabbro above 400m.

Creag Druim Eadar da Choire

(NG 528 242) Alt 450m East facing
This is a morning crag with good routes on wonderful rough gabbro. It often has better weather than the main areas of the Cuillin due to its isolated position and the east facing routes are quick to dry. The cliff is bisected by Seilg Gully into Left and Right Flanks and routes are described from left to right.

OUTLIERS

Approach: Park in the large car park above the waterfall at the head of Loch Ainort. There are two approaches similar in length. Ascend Druim Eadar da Choire to a magnificent viewpoint on the grassy knoll Pt 489 where it forms the north ridge of Garbh-bheinn then traverse below the cliffs from Pt 429 just beyond (1hr). Alternatively follow the Abhainn Ceann Loch Ainort to below the cliff then approach by slabs or grass (1hr).

Descent: Climbs on the clean slab right of Seilg Gully can be descended by abseil as described below. From the top of the crag descend the north ridge to the col (Pt 429) and traverse slopes easily to the foot of the cliff.

Left Flank

The toe of the long eastern buttress ends in a short vertical wall. The first two routes lie left of this.

1 Far East Buttress 150m Difficult   (1980)
Left of the recessed slab of Cubs' Corner is a long, easy angled buttress which gives some delightful climbing. Take a line linking the best sections of rock.

2 Cubs' Corner 60m Severe   (1980)
Left of Skye Ride is the recessed slab. Climb this, then trend left and go up the blocky crack to finish up easy ground.

3 Skye Ride 100m VS *   (1988)
This climb is worthwhile for the rib pitches.
1. 25m 4c Climb the artificial, but fun, left-hand edge of the steep lower wall direct to easy blocky ground and a block belay.
2. 25m Continue in the same line to the base of the fine rib, well seen from below.
3. 25m 4c Climb the rib direct, following a thin crack left of a drainage groove, crux, then pull over onto a slab below an overhanging corner with a tiny stance below it.
4. 10m 4c Climb the corner on jams, then belay on the ledge above.
5. 15m 4b Step up to another ledge with flakes and climb a straight crack to big ledges. Another 20m of scrambling up and right avoids a loose wall to finish.

4 Cunning Stunts 100m E1 *   (1988)
A very varied first pitch makes this climb worth doing, though the line is artificial above. Start at the right-hand corner at the right end of the steep lower wall.
1. 40m 5b Climb a slab to reach the corner, then traverse right along flakes to a grass patch. Climb a crack right of perched flakes to an overhanging corner. Surmount this using a hidden hold, crux, then exit into a groove. Climb the bold slab on the right in a fine position, trending up left to belays.
2. 25m Climb pleasant rocks first right then left to belays below a cracked wall which lies right of the rib pitch of Skye Ride.
3. 35m 4b Climb a gangway slanting left below the vertical crack. Trend up right, then traverse right for a few metres until a scoop can be climbed to a narrow ledge below a steep friable wall. Traverse right to a grassy groove to finish and scramble to the top, as for Skye Ride.

5 Seilg Gully 150m Very Difficult   (1980)
This is the long broken gully that lies left of the big slab. Climb it direct, via some interesting pitches, one or two being much trickier than they appear.
Winter: **III/IV**
The gully gives four pitches with quality dependent on the degree of freezing.

Right Flank

The big slab right of Seilg Gully is the crags finest feature. To reach the base, approach either up Seilg Gully then traverse right, or scramble up heathery shelves and rock steps to the same point.

95. GARBH-BHEINN
Creag Druim
Eadar da Choire

3. Skye Ride	VS *	
4. Cunning Stunts	E1 *	
5. Selig Gully	III/IV	
6. Hand Jive	VS **	

7. Streetwise Dancer	HVS *	
8. Cuckoo Waltz	E1 5b ***	
9. Rites of Passage	E1 5b ***	
10. Alpha Groove	VS *	
11. Tapered Buttress	E1 **	
12. Black Magic	E2 *	
ab. abseil (50m)		
d. descent		

The next five routes all climb the clean slab. There is a large block at the top of the slab giving a good anchor for a 50m abseil back to the start of routes on this beautiful wall. It avoids re-scrambling the heathery terraces below. The wall above the routes is split by a 15m hanging chimney which can be climbed at Severe.

**Hand Jive 55m VS ** *(1981)*

A good introduction to the crag, taking the left-hand crack.
1. 20m 4b A lobed crack runs diagonally up left from the stance. Climb up to the lobe, step right onto the slab beneath it, then follow this trending left to a stance and belay overlooking Seilg Gully.
2. 35m 4c Step right and follow the crack through the overhanging corner. Climb the crack beyond in a fine position to the top.

**Streetwise Dancer 50m HVS ** *(1990)*

Start at the same point as Hand Jive.
1. 25m 4c Below the centre of the curved overlap is a niche; climb the steep slab directly below this, then follow a right-slanting crack until a line of holds trends up left before stepping back right into the niche itself. A bold, sparsely protected pitch on good rock.
2. 25m 5a Climb up above the niche to gain the overlap on the right, then pull

over this at its highest point, crux. Now trend left along little edges to join Hand Jive to finish. A well protected airy pitch.

8 Cuckoo Waltz   50m   E1 5b ***   (1990)

An excellent well protected line on excellent rock, which reveals the way only on close inspection. Start at the same point as Hand Jive. Climb Streetwise Dancer initially, aiming for the right end of the overlaps. The right-slanting crack then straightens out and breaks through the upper overlaps via a finger crack. Climb this (crux), then continue more easily to the top.

Direct start: **Flights of Fancy   E2 5b**   (1990)

A bold start that joins Cuckoo Waltz where the right-trending crack straightens out. Start up and right on a higher ledge, as for Rites of Passage, and step left onto the bald slab. Surmount a little overhang then trend up left to join the crack.

9 Rites of Passage   50m   E1 5b ***   (1990)

The best pitch on this section follows cleaned cracks up the wall left of the bounding arete. Approach as for the other routes but go further right to a commodious ledge and belays. Protection improves with height.

Climb up left to the corner then follow a diagonal crack right. A thin move gains the base of the main crack. Follow this in a great position to the top, where a step left onto a slab gives a fitting finish. The second sometimes has to move left from the belays to allow sufficient rope for the leader.

The North Face, to the right of the black arete, is very steep and can be slow to dry. It is characterised by grooves and a banana shaped corner.

10 Alpha Groove   60m   VS *   (1981)

A very good first pitch, in the classically strenuous style, provides the meat of the climb. Near the left end of the North Face is a very prominent groove.

1. 20m 4c Climb the increasingly awkward groove to a tight exit onto a fine eyrie stance.
2. 20m 4c The continuation groove to the right of the stance is usually wet, so step right to and climb a subsidiary groove. Move back left across the top of the main groove on wet underclings to belay below the upper wide grooves.
3. 20m Continue to the top.

Variation: **Direct Finish   45m   HVS**   (1990)

A much drier alternative to the top pitches.

2. 30m 5a From the stance, step right into and climb the subsidiary groove to a steep and awkward crack which ends at a large stance below the top pitch of Black Magic.
3. 15m Climb the cracks splitting the right wall. Finish by scrambling easily up a narrow gully with a bridged chockstone.

11 Tapered Buttress   60m   E1 **   (1981)

The fine tapered buttress between Alpha Groove and Black Magic. Start directly below the banana shaped groove of Black Magic.

1. 30m 5b Climb the steep buttress direct.
2. 30m 5b Continue in the same line to the top.

12 Black Magic   75m   E2 *   (1990)

This route takes the obvious banana shaped groove starting at 25m directly above a hanging bog. An excellent middle pitch makes the route worthwhile and small wires protect where it matters.

1. 25m Climb either the vegetated groove below the main line or the hanging gardens by a line of choice further right. Belay below the main groove.
2. 30m 5c Climb the groove, initially stepping left, then go back right to a small ledge. Climb the steep and sustained groove in a fine position to a precariously wedged block by a wet seep. Stand above the block (without using it) then traverse left to a rib and crack (the top few moves of Alpha Grooves Direct Finish) to avoid the wet final few metres up the groove. Belay on the large stance above.

3. 20m 5b Now climb the artificial but increasingly difficult corner direct. Numerous escapes are possible, but unsporting.

Garbh-bheinn - North Face

Highly recommended but only as a winter face. Snow runnels in the north face offer a variety of good approaches directly to the summit. Mainly grade I with occasional ice steps up to grade III possible. Approach directly and descend by either the north or east ridges. Both are narrow in the upper reaches but broaden out rapidly.

96. MARSCO - NORTH FACE

Map p281

Loch Ainort Waterfall - Eas a' Bhradain

(NG 534 265)   Alt 20m

The waterfall at the foot of the Allt Coire nam Bruadaran is a popular tourist attraction right beside the main A87 road. **Robber's Fall** (I 1994) gives a short easy ice scramble when frozen.

Coire nan Laogh

(NG 510 253)   Alt 550m   North facing

In full winter garb the North Face is very impressive but is not steep and provides an enjoyable, easy and direct ascent unless difficulties are sought out. A fence-line rises up the easy spur east of the corrie giving a walkers approach and the best line of descent. Some easy scrambling is possible on the steeper spur west of the corrie. A small corrie lies west again and easy ice lines form quite frequently and have been climbed (grade II 2005).

Approach: The obvious direct approach up Coire nam Bruadaran is not very pleasant. Instead park above the hairpin bends on the A87 (NG 531 279). A crafty crofters approach rises gently onto Bruach nam Bo then traverses to Mam a' Phobuill in 1hr.

Wooly Gully   150m   II,4 *   (2007)

Follows a right-slanting groove line in the centre of the face. Five short pitches are linked by the easy angled gully bed. Continue easily in the same line to the summit. Frozen turf, rock and wool, under thin snow, were used on the first ascent.

RED CUILLIN OVERLOOKING SLIGACHAN

More than half of the view from Sligachan is dominated by the wonderfully shaped mountains of the Red Cuillin often referred to as the Glàmaig Horseshoe. Marsco sits alone as an impressive bulky mountain blocking the view of Blàbheinn on the east side of the Glen Sligachan. It offers a good selection of long routes that catch a lot of sunshine.

97. GLÀMAIG HORSESHOE

Map p281

Along the outside of the horseshoe as the road heads towards Sligachan long runnels of snow are complete from very low-levels right to the tops most winters. A low band of cliffs overlooking Loch Sligachan has numerous icefalls that form easily but always thinly and no record has been made of any ascents. In exceptionally hard winter conditions a few streams have been climbed around Sligachan. The horseshoe is a technically easy walk with superb views into the Black Cuillin (4-5hrs).

OUTLIERS

Beinn Dearg Mhòr

(NG 515 286)

Coire na Sgairde is the large open corrie enclosed by the horseshoe. In 1997 two frozen watercourses gave easy angled climbs at grade II, both ending halfway up the west face.

Bunkhouse Gorge

(NG 498 298)

The rocky walls of the gorge have been used for practicing abseiling and some top-roped rock climbs. Swimming in the pools is a more popular pastime.

Allt an t-Sithein (NG 494 312) is the stream lying beyond the campsite at Sligachan giving a beautiful grade I (1997) in a hard winter.

98. MARSCO

Map p281   Diagram p290

The rough granophyre of the North-West and South-West buttresses offers excellent climbing and is frequently drier than on the Main Ridge. Although the rock is generally sound, care should be taken with loose blocks and on the darker rock, some of which is brittle.

Approaches: Follow the path up Glen Sligachan from the hotel for 4km until below the North-West Buttress (NG 496 260) and approach directly (1hr 30mins). The impressive South-West Buttress is seen in profile on the approach and lies 500m further south. Ascend grass directly beside the Allt Fiaclan Dearg from the path (1hr 30mins).

North-West Buttress

(NG 503 259)   Alt 350m

This buttress looks rather unimpressive on the approach but closer acquaintance gives a better impression. A cave lies in the centre of the crag, just left of the highest point. Descend by a grass filled gully (Harker's Gully), that runs parallel to the buttress 50m to the south.

The Boojum   115m   HVS *   *(1968)*
This is an interesting climb with a good top pitch. The initial pitch is a little loose but can be avoided by using the start of Teflon. Start below the highest point of the buttress where an overhang guards the base, with another overhang 10m right.
1. 40m 4c Climb a shallow groove through the lower overhang to reach a left traverse. Go across this until it is possible to climb straight up to the cave.
2. 40m 4a Move out of the cave on the right, then step back left onto the lip. Go up slightly left to the base of a clean ribbed buttress.
3. 35m 4a The buttress gives a fine pitch.

Teflon   125m   HVS   *(1976)*
Start left of The Boojum, below and left of the cave. Scramble 45m to a stance below the buttress left of the cave.
1. 40m 4a Climb the buttress until it is possible to traverse down and right into the cave.
2. 25m 4b Move out of the cave on the right and step back left onto the lip, then climb straight up to a ledge.
3. 35m 4a Climb up to the final wall.
4. 25m 4c Traverse left under an overhang then climb to the top.

South-West Buttress

(NG 502 254)   Alt 350m

This is the attractive buttress seen in profile from Sligachan, named Fiaclan Dearg on some maps. A prominent steep wall lies between the First and Second Terraces of Central Buttress and leads to The Shoulder. To the left a large amphitheatre has a steep headwall which Odell's Route turns on its right at The Shoulder. To the right of Central Buttress is an area of steep brown rock with a waterfall.

Descent: From the second terrace it is possible to scramble up over the shoulder and down the lower sections of Odell's Route. Descent from the top of the cliff is very complex with a huge detour needed to avoid the Allt Fiaclan Dearg. Most parties continue to the summit with rewarding views. From here descend the south-east ridge for 400m then head north down the easy spur that bounds Coire nan Laogh before returning to Sligachan. Routes are described from left to right.

Fiacaill Geal   150m   IV,3 *   *(1998)*
The Allt Fiaclan Dearg forms an impressive line of ice quite readily and is obvious from the hotel. A wide dyke starts just above the glen footpath but the initial sections are rarely frozen and usually avoided by grass slopes until the difficulties begin at an altitude of 375m. A steep 25m pitch (crux) out of the small gorge leads to easy angled ice above. After three more pitches, scramble up the frozen stream bed to the upper west slopes of Marsco. Rock belays are virtually non-existent and the ice often thin above the crux.

Odell's Route   300m   Difficult *   *(1943)*
The original route on the crag starts near the centre of the amphitheatre and follows easy left-slanting slabs for 75m to a scree patch. From here head for the Shoulder which is a long way off to the right. Now climb the best part of the route, the steep rock above for 100m to the top. Route finding is open to much variation.

Central Buttress   235m   Very Difficult *   *(1953)*
This route climbs the corner system which delineates the mass of Central Buttress from the amphitheatre. Start at the foot of the buttress to the right of the amphitheatre. Follow a line of corners passing close to the gangway of The Snark at 40m and First Terrace at 80m. Scramble up and left to the foot of a more vegetated corner. Climb this for 50m to the Second Terrace. Scramble onto The Shoulder to join Odell's Route and finish up this.

April Fools   130m   VS   *(1979)*
A hybrid route with little independent climbing. Climb Central Buttress for 80m until it debouches onto easy ground near First Terrace below the pedestal of The Snark. Gain the pedestal from the left and climb pitch 4 of The Snark to the pinnacle (20m 4c). Above, move right to the arete and go up this until it is possible to move right onto a wall. Continue up rightwards to the peg runner on Slow Riser and finish up the short wall above to Second Terrace (30m 4c).

The Snark   240m   VS **   *(1968)*
The original classic of the crag. The rock is superb and it is often dry when the Black Cuillin are wet. Though a little contrived in line, it takes in the best climbing and starts directly below the middle of Central Buttress.
1. 25m 4b Climb a wall and over a small overhang. Traverse left and go up a small corner to a ledge.
2. 45m 4c Continue up and slightly left until, at about 20m, an exposed gangway on the right can be gained. Follow this to a groove and climb to the first terrace.
3. 25m 4a Scramble up slabs to a crack right of a pedestal below a steep smooth wall. Climb the crack and belay on the far side of the pedestal.
4. 40m 4c Climb the undercut crack on the left to a groove with a large detached pinnacle. Move out onto the right wall, then go up to a crack leading to the second terrace.

98. MARSCO
South-West Buttress

2. Odell's Route — Difficult *
3. Central Buttress — Very Difficult *
5. The Snark — VS **
6. Slow Riser — HVS **
6a. Right–hand Finish — VS 5a
7. Zeke — HVS **
8. Heart But No Sole — Severe

d. descent (complex)

5. etc. 105m 4a Scramble up to the shoulder and go straight up to the final wall. Climb the wall and finish by a prominent V-cleft with two small overhangs.

Slow Riser   230m   HVS ** (1980)

An excellent route which takes the most direct line up the crag. Central Buttress is split by an obvious deep groove. Start directly below the groove, just right of the start to The Snark.

1. 20m 5a Climb directly up to the foot of the groove by a faint crack-line. Just left of the foot of the groove is a good stance and belays.
2. 25m 4c Move into the groove and climb this using the right wall to gain a ledge and belay on the right.
3. 25m 4b Step back into the groove and continue to a steepening. Turn this on the right and continue up the groove taking another steepening directly. Belay on easier ground below First Terrace.
4. 15m Scramble onto First Terrace and belay beneath a steep wall.
5. 40m 5a A vertical fault splits the steep wall at its centre. Climb the fault to a sentry box at 5m and a horizontal dyke. Hand-traverse left for 10m to an arete. Gain a crack above and climb it for a few metres until it is possible to move left into a groove. Go up the groove and a wall past a peg runner to finish on Second Terrace.
Variation: **Right-Hand Finish   VS** (1995)
5a. 30m 5a Climb the vertical fault past the sentry box at 5m and continue up until a diagonal fault leads off to the right. Traverse this past a hard move to gain a short crack leading to easier ground and a belay on Second Terrace.

Zeke   110m   HVS ** (1995)

This route climbs the steep brown rock between Central Buttress and the waterfall. Start 10m left of the waterfall.

1. 30m 5a/b Climb a wall for 8m and ascend diagonally leftwards over slabs to a niche. On the left is a steep wall. Cross this horizontally (crux) and move up over a hollow flake. Continue left to a mantelshelf onto easier ground, then climb directly to a large bay.
2. 25m 4b Leave the bay at its left end and ascend a deep groove passing a rowan sapling. Step right to a rib and groove and gain a stance in the main groove on the left.
3. 30m 4c Ascend the groove for 6m and make a rising traverse rightwards to gain a wet chimney. Escape from this on the left and continue up and left to the First Terrace.
4. 25m 4c Climb the right-hand edge of the steep wall above First Terrace and belay on Second Terrace. Descend via Odell's route or continue to the top as for Slow Riser.

Heart But No Sole   130m   Severe (1995)

Right of the waterfall is an area of slabs starting at a lower level. Start at the lowest point of the slabs at a cracked slab.

1. 50m Climb slabs pleasantly to a belay.
2. 30m Further walls and slabs lead to easier ground. Belay on the right.
3. 50m Step right and continue upwards until the angle eases.
A scrambling descent can be made diagonally rightwards about Difficult standard.

The Yellow Jersey   50m   E1 5b ** (2006)

100m right of the waterfall is a pronounced wet gully. This is a fine well protected route following a prominent crack-line on the small buttress a few metres right of the wet gully.

CUILLIN RIDGE TRAVERSES

The Black Cuillin Bowl forms a near perfect circle of mountains, remnants of the magma chamber at the base of a huge, long extinct volcano. Subsequent weathering and erosion has left the bowl split, down almost to sea-level, by Glen Sligachan that runs essentially north to south. The range is more extensive on the western side and forms the classic Main Cuillin Ridge Traverse. The Greater Cuillin Ridge Traverse continues by crossing Glen Sligachan then re-ascends the eastern Black Cuillin to finish over Clach Glas and Blàbheinn. It is over twice the distance and is not often undertaken. Such purity of shape and quality of climbing put the Traverses high on the list for many mountaineers, but they don't give themselves up easily.

The Main Ridge forms a cirque that provides a uniquely attractive challenge to the climber. It rises straight from the sea to 900m and does not drop below 750m for the entire 12km length. It involves a minimum of 3000m of ascent and descent between the end peaks in addition to the approach and descent and is accepted as the toughest mountaineering challenge in the British Isles. It is also a strong contender for the best climb when completed in good style.

The biggest attraction is undoubtedly the joy of so much continuous high quality climbing. Most is of the simplest, purest and most exhilarating form, following the crest of an obvious narrow ridge. A handful of harder, single pitch rock climbs along the route are used for a diretissima but the biggest challenge is always the scale. A time of 12 to 16hrs has been given between the start and finish peaks with an additional 5 to 6hrs for the approach and descent. One bivouac has now become favoured, a tactic that creates nearly as many problems as it solves. Clever bivvying is accepted as a good way to enhance chances of success for the majority of aspirants.

Traditionally and historically the complete line takes in all of the 22 summits and peaks along the crest between Gars-bheinn and Sgùrr nan Gillean with the addition of Sgùrr Alasdair, the highest Cuillin peak, which lies a short distance off the Main Ridge. A huge number of variations are possible with these traditionally recorded for clarification. The definition of a successful Traverse is up to the climbers involved. It is recommended that the first objective be to reach the summit of the route at Sgùrr nan Gillean. Following the crest as closely as possible is the next ideal but there are sections where this is just not feasible and the standard route takes many practical deviations. A pragmatic approach is needed for the vast majority of attempts if the Traverse is to be completed.

The Traverse sees a high failure rate largely due to underestimation and lack of familiarity with the challenge. Ascending and descending 4000m from sea-level is no mean feat but only tells half of the story. Mental fatigue from concentrating on footwork, unrelenting exposure and route finding is the real test. Route finding is incredibly complex for most of the 12km length and making an attempt in good conditions is essential.

The Traverse is a prize to be won through patient research, planning and practise more than rock climbing ability. In good conditions stamina and strength can carry an unprepared climber in a haphazard manner to the end but the problems of wet rock or poor visibility usually lead to a rapid retreat. Many years of planning precede a successful outcome for a great number of aspirants and their success is all the sweeter for the experiences that led to it. Six major corrie rounds are the ideal forum for practice. They provide a chance to learn the intricacies of individual sections and are all classic routes in their own rights. These are outlined at the start of each chapter with route details described more fully below.

Technical Advice

This is a climbing guide and not an instruction manual, but a few tactical pointers are warranted.

Route: A South to North Traverse is the classic route in summer conditions with the famous climbs being ascended instead of abseiled. The route is described in this direction. Full descriptions of the rock climbs are given in appropriate chapters easily found by using the index.

Climbs: Leaders should be comfortable leading Severe rock climbs in walking boots and rucksacks. At this level a minimal rack of equipment is required. Five sewn slings for spikes and threads should suffice on all standard routes but the addition of a small wire for the TD Gap and a large nut and friend for King's Chimney and Naismith's Route are useful. Abseil tat may be required in at least four situations especially if the rock becomes wet and 40m of rope is needed for abseils and climbs.

Weather: A Traverse is virtually impossible in the wet when rocks become very greasy and navigation a nightmare. The crest dries very quickly however and progress in showery weather can be made. Crossing wet rock takes almost twice as long as dry rock for confident climbers. Weather forecasts are now very accurate in the short term and allow a weather window to be anticipated with some confidence. Conversely, long term forecasts can be way off the mark as fronts move through faster or slower than anticipated.

Water: In the fortunate situation of hot dry weather, parties may find themselves needing to descend quite large distances to source water. More commonly there is water flowing out of numerous nooks and crannies. A mug or siphon can be used to collect extra supplies, and if used cleverly no more than two litres need be carried. There are two reliable springs involving small amounts of descent; 100m directly below the (Theàrlaich-Dubh) TD Gap in Coire a' Ghrunnda showing clearly as an incandescent green bed of moss and, at the opposite end of the Ridge, 100m below Bealach na Lice in Fionn Choire.

Two less reliable but useful sources involve hardly any height loss. Pools are clearly visible from the east end of Sgùrr nan Eag above the South Face of Coire nan Laogh. Diagonal Gully on the West Face of Sgùrr a' Ghreadaidh is approached from 100m up the South Ridge across very loose ground and is seen well from Sgùrr Thormaid. Both require use of a siphoning system the majority of the time. Parties pre-stashing water are asked to label the bottles with dates and make sure they are used or removed. Old bottles form a high percentage of litter in the Cuillin.

One Day Attempts: Only very fit and confident climbers should attempt this method. The rope should only be needed for the rock climbs which must be completed with an absolute minimum of effort and time in order to stay on schedule. Many using this approach in fine weather will find a queue at the TD Gap at about 5am along with all the others who have decided to "go for it".

MAIN RIDGE TRAVERSE

12km, 3000m ascent, Grade 3/Severe ✱✱✱✱ 11-16hrs, bivouac normal

Maps & Diagrams: The Ridge appears on the maps and many diagrams throughout the guidebook, see p5.

Approaches: 4-6km, 900m ascent, 2-3hrs

There are three common approaches: From Glen Brittle traverse beneath the Ridge for 7km then ascend 500m of scree to Gars-bheinn (3hrs). Approach via Coire a' Ghrunnda to keep dry feet, fill up from the loch only 100m below the crest then head out and back – not advised in the dark (3hrs to Gars-bheinn). For the purest start, which is significantly shorter, climb the East Ridge of Gars-bheinn from Loch Scavaig (2hrs). Some people choose to start from the first Munro or the TD Gap. Others start by the Dubh Ridge or even via the Cioch.

Descents: 6km, 1000m descent, 2-3hrs

The three ridges of Sgùrr nan Gillean give a choice of descents, none of which are simple. The South-East Ridge (Tourist Route, Grade 2) gives the easiest climbing but is complex in its upper reaches. The narrow crest soon steepens into a fine ridge The easiest line takes a broad rake that lies 50m down to the right (south). At 800m the ridge levels out and the boulder field to the north is descended. Many parties prefer to return over familiar terrain to Bealach a' Bhasteir by the West Ridge (Grade 3/Moderate) that has just been ascended. The classy finish is to descend Pinnacle Ridge (Grade 3/Difficult) to the north which is every bit as good in descent as it is in ascent.

*Abseil from Basteir Tooth on a winter traverse of the Ridge.
Climber Colin McGregor*

Descriptions: The route has been divided into five sections.

A. Gars-bheinn to Theàrlaich-Dubh Buttress

3km Grade 2, 2hrs 30mins

The first part of the ridge is straightforward to the summit of Sgùrr nan Eag. Complex route finding is now caused by the huge peridotite boulder field that stretches between Sgùrr nan Eag and Bealach Coire an Lochain. Turn the narrow North Ridge of Sgùrr nan Eag on the left to reach Bealach a' Garbh-choire. Caisteal a' Garbh-choire can either be bypassed on the right or climbed at Difficult standard descending by scrambling west or a short abseil from the north end. Dubh na Dà Bheinn is a good scramble ascended just left of the crest. Dubh Mòr can be added here with a 30min detour to the east. It is not traditionally or historically included on a Traverse. Descend by the broad boulder strewn North-West spur to Bealach Coire an Lochain. The Ridge narrows significantly 100m beyond as the TD Gap is approached.

B. Theàrlaich-Dubh Buttress to Inaccessible Pinnacle

1.5km Grade 3/Severe, 2 – 4hrs

The ridge dramatically steepens into a tower as the Gap nears and is climbed by very exposed moves on the left wall. Abseil into the Theàrlaich-Dubh Gap. Climb the Original Route, (Theàrlaich-Dubh Gap Walls [57]), with the minimum of fuss. Epic struggles are frequent causing a bottleneck effect. Queuing should be avoided by another route. This is usually by descent into Coire a' Ghrunnda and progress made by climbing the South-West Flank route to Sgùrr Alasdair.

From the Theàrlaich side of the Gap a detour to the highest Cuillin peak, Sgùrr Alasdair, is traditionally included with the summit reached in less than 5min from the top of the Stone Shoot. Regaining the Ridge from the head of the Stone Shoot requires a move of Difficult standard before reaching the summit of Sgùrr Thearlaich.

Descending Sgùrr Thearlaich (Grade 3/Moderate) to Bealach MhicCoinnich is a major cause of problems with a choice of two descents bypassing the steep northern end on either side. Two abseils are often used by teams unable to locate the scrambling descents. The eastern bypass traverses down diagonally right from a small shoulder immediately before the final promontory, 100m before the final steep nose. Two 10m sections of Moderate climbing have to be descended. On the Coire Lagan side a well trodden gully gives a false line 50m before the steep nose. The best line is just 10m left of the nose by a square-cut notch that leads to steep slabs. A delicate traverse beneath the nose leads to a loose gully, which is descended. When level with Bealach MhicCoinnich a final chimney leads down to broken ground which is crossed to the Bealach.

Gain Collies' Ledge by a short section of Moderate climbing at the start of Sgùrr MhicCoinnich. A steeper ledge breaks up right after a few metres giving access to the base of King's Chimney which is a far simpler climb than the Theàrlaich-Dubh Gap. Many parties choose to continue by Collie's Ledge instead, doubling back for 200m to the summit.

Descending the North Ridge of Sgùrr MhicCoinnich is Grade 2 with the final nose turned on the Coire Lagan side before an easy descent to the head of Rotten Gully. Cross the small rise above Bealach Buttress to gain the eastern toe of An Stac. An Stac Direct (Grade 3) is highly recommended, giving the longest section of continuous scrambling ascent along the whole Ridge. It starts by a groove 5m left of the crest, passes two scree filled rifts before taking a fine narrow rib directly. Many parties sacrifice this section and take a broad brown rake that passes An Stac on the south to reach the base of the Inaccessible Pinnacle. Climb this without fuss by the long East Ridge. See the Inaccessible Pinnacle [38] for alternative routes and tactics in busy periods.

C. Sgùrr Dearg to Sgùrr a' Mhadaidh
2.5km Grade 3/Moderate, 2hrs 30mins – 3hrs

A nick in the summit ridge of Sgùrr Dearg directly above the Inaccessible Pinnacle marks the start of the scree descent. The ridge narrows at 900m then heads north ending in a slabby descent to the narrow (2m) Bealach Coire na Banachdaich.

Traverse scree to regain the Ridge for a magnificent easy rise to Sgùrr na Banachdaich. The Central Top (Grade 2) has particularly good quality rock on its crest and is descended by a shallow gully on the Glen Brittle side before the final rise to the small summit cairn. The summit plateau is quite broad and a false gully is met before the correct gully descends northward to reach Bealach Thormaid. Climb Sgùrr Thormaid direct in two separate steps (Grade 2). A slabby descent leads to the Three Teeth which give good easy scrambling but are usually walked past on the Coruisk side to reach Bealach Coire a' Ghreadaidh.

The Traverse of Sgùrr a' Ghreadaidh (Grade 3/Moderate) is one of the classic sections. A long ascent is made turning all difficulties on the Glen Brittle side but returning to the crest whenever possible. There are few alternatives to the very narrow crest between the south and north summits. This is tackled "tightrope" style or a more ungainly "au cheval" depending on conditions. Descent from the summit is fairly direct with small detours to avoid drops from The Wart and into Eag Dubh. An Doras is gained by a short (3m) Moderate descent just on the Glen Brittle side. Easy ground leads to the summit of Sgùrr a' Mhadaidh. This peak is known as the fourth top with the tops numbered from north to south.

D. Sgùrr a' Mhadaidh to Bealach na Lice
3km Grade 3/Difficult, 3 – 4 hours

The Traverse of Sgùrr a' Mhadaidh (Grade 3/Difficult, 1hr) is the most complex and difficult section of the Ridge that cannot be bypassed. The crest is narrow immediately beyond the summit and is followed north to where the Thuilm ridge joins from the west. A short slabby descent on the Coruisk side leads to a boulder filled notch at the true top of Deep Gash Gully. The tower above is usually climbed by a steep wall and an easier descent but can also be turned by a smooth slab below when dry. A narrow ridge leads to the base of the third top which is gained by a zigzag route on the broad south wall, starting from 30m down the rake beneath the face. The second top is guarded by a steep tower which is easier than it looks but in a very sensational position. The first top is gained slightly more easily before making a long descent by scree slopes on the Coruisk side to reach Bealach na Glaic Moire.

The Traverse of Bidein Druim nan Ràmh (Grade 3/Difficult, 1hr 30mins) is the single most complex section of the Ridge with very exposed climbing. It is easily bypassed on the Glen Brittle side by scree and boulders (25mins). Gain the south-west peak by a prominent snaking fault. Descend very smooth rocks to the notch below the central peak. Take corners above directly to the summit.

The descent route takes the ludicrous looking narrow rib that runs north about 20m below the summit. Abseil or down-climb (Difficult) slabs slightly on the Coruisk side from the rib. Care must be taken with in-situ slings as they are frequently battered by the wind. A second abseil is normal to reach the gap below the north peak. Anchors are not great and care must be exercised. The direct line involves ropes passing over a sharp edge whilst the climber is suspended in space. On the same level, 5m towards Coruisk, a zigzag abseil is possible with care. Down-climbing this line is possible (Very Difficult) but hard for the short with a small jump involved. Take an obvious rising ledge on the Glen Brittle side to the nose of the north top which gives a pleasant finish. Descend slabs just right of the crest to reach Bealach Harta, the lowest point of the Ridge.

The Traverse of An Caisteal (Grade 3/Difficult, 30mins) is a short but serious section that finishes with an off balance descent of a Difficult wall. Two deep rifts have to be crossed by long steps or jumps before the summit is reached. A shoulder of ruddy rock leads out west just before the summit cairn and must be followed to avoid an abseil from the summit block (the Belly Crawl). Descend the narrow North Ridge directly to a final steep wall. This wall is often abseiled but can be down-climbed first left then right (when looking down) with the hardest move at the bottom. Ascending Sgùrr na Bhàirnich and the South Ridge of Bruach na Frithe (Grade 2, 30mins) gives a welcome break on the mental strain with easy ground broken by a few steeper steps. Descend the East Ridge of Bruach na Frithe easily to Bealach na Lice (5mins) with a simple detour over Sgùrr a' Fionn Choire for teams travelling well.

E. Bealach na Lice to Sgùrr nan Gillean

1km Grade 3/Severe (1hr 30mins – 2hrs 30mins)

A complex section with rock climbing and more exposed scrambling just to twist the knife.

Gain the Basteir Tooth by either Naismith's (Severe) or Collie's Lota Corrie Route (Grade 3/Moderate), the latter being longer but far quicker. A short descent from the Tooth leads to the Basteir Nick. Finding the ramp that rises to the final overhang below the summit often gives a problem. Breach this by a choice of routes described as the West Face of Am Basteir. Descend the East Ridge (Grade 2) directly, with the Bad Step giving just a pleasant scramble in this direction, to Bealach a' Bhasteir.

The West Ridge of Sgùrr nan Gillean (Grade 3/Moderate, 30mins) is a fitting climax to the expedition. The ridge narrows 200m beyond the bealach. Follow a ledge on the left (north) easily for 50m to a broadening with two large boulders. Easy Chimney (Grade 3/Moderate) lies directly above giving access to the very exposed pinnacles where The Gendarme used to stand. Tooth Chimney (Difficult) lies at the left side of the small bay immediately beyond the boulder ledge. (In descent it is common to abseil this lowest part of the ridge from the large block immediately west of Tooth Chimney). Welcome easy ground above leads to a final narrowing, squeezing through The Window and the tiny summit plinth.

Main Ridge Traverse - North to South

Traversing north to south in summer is only slightly inferior but does miss the classic climbs and is interrupted by more abseils. However it gets to the serious scrambling quicker, allowing climbers to make the most of a small weather window. It also leaves the long section south of the TD Gap as an easier finish. Popular with guided parties. Descriptions of key obstacles are given in the Winter Traverse section below.

Approach: This is conventionally started by the South-East Ridge (Tourist Route) of Sgùrr nan Gillean but a clever alternative leaves a vehicle at the head of Glen Brittle and approaches Bealach na Lice via Fionn Coire in 2hrs. Fill up with water 100m below the Ridge. Sacks are then deposited to allow a light weight traverse of the northern peaks before returning beneath Am Basteir to start heading south.

GREATER RIDGE TRAVERSE

20km, 4000m ascent, Grade 3/Severe ** 18-25hrs**

This challenge is a logical extension of the Main Ridge Traverse to complete the full circuit of the Black Cuillin Bowl. It includes the summits of Clach Glas and Blàbheinn and should technically include Sgùrr na h-Uamha and Garbh-bheinn to complete the geological boundary. Starting with the Main Ridge and sleeping at a provisioned tent in Glen Sligachan is a traditional tactic but starting with the eastern peaks and making serious inroads into the Main Ridge on the first day also makes sense.

Beyond Sgùrr nan Gillean descend An Ghlais-choire between Sgùrr na h-Uamha and Sgùrr Beag to reach the Lochan Dubha in the bottom of Glen Sligachan. A good line takes the open river bed in An Fraoch-choire before gaining the North Ridge of Garbh-bheinn at Pt 429 (NG 527 242). Traverse the mountain to join the Clach Glas – Blàbheinn Traverse (Grade 3/Difficult) at Bealach Clach Glas.

WINTER MAIN RIDGE TRAVERSE

12km, 3000m ascent, IV ** 2 or 3 days**

Equipment: One 50m rope, a small selection of pegs and nuts and plenty of abseil tat is needed. Take one ice hammer per climber, sharing both on just a couple of short sections. Bivvy gear will depend on many factors but remember that there are 14 hours of darkness in mid-January.

In good conditions this is probably the greatest single climb to be had in Britain. Good conditions are rare with one period a season possibly above average since it was first achieved. The good news is that frequency does not seem to be decreasing and the internet now gives aspirants unprecedented access to forecast and condition reports.

Anything but good quality neve on the crest makes progress very slow and physical. Tom Patey suggested that a heavy dump of snow with little wind, so that the crest isn't stripped, is the first stage. A minor thaw right to the summits followed by a sharp freeze and good weather (an easterly wind and high pressure) for the next few days is the ideal scenario. Often the thaw makes walls appear black from the glen with the perfect crust only apparent once on the crest. Opportunities must be grasped quickly before sun or rain strip the crest back to bare rock (see below). It is usual to travel from north to south because the major difficulties can be avoided in this direction by abseil. The hardest sections of the ridge will be no more than grade IV, but most of the ground is grade II and III in both ascent and descent with dire consequences for a simple slip.

Speed will vary hugely depending on snow conditions, daylight hours and whether a set of footprints shows the way. Given a good forecast parties would be well advised to pack provisions for three days unless they know the route very well, know of existing tracks or are highly competent alpinists. With all the prerequisite planning and conditions in place the climb is a thoroughly absorbing challenge involving at least 10 abseils.

A highly alpine Traverse can be made when the crest has been stripped but significant quantities of snow still lie on ledges and faces. That this style may not be a full winter Traverse is irrelevant as long as the climbing is enjoyable.

The major difficulties and abseils are as follows:

The West Ridge of Sgùrr nan Gillean
Abseil the lowest section down Tooth Chimney on the north side.

Am Basteir to the Tooth
Abseil towards Lota Corrie from the rift immediately west of the summit. Down-climb to the Basteir Nick.

Basteir Tooth
Return to the Basteir Nick and gain abseil slings in the cave at the top of King's Cave Chimney by dropping through a small hole on the Sligachan side. If blocked a peg belay in the wall of Am Basteir allows Coire a' Bhasteir to be reached by a 25m abseil.

Traverse of Bidein Druim nan Ràmh
Abseil from the north peak to the gap. The easiest line to the summit, in good conditions, follows snow covered slabs on the Harta Corrie side linked by short ice steps on the left (south) side of the face. Descend from the central peak and abseil into the next gap.

Traverse of Sgùrr a' Mhadaidh
An easy 20m abseil descends the second top. The only good abseil from the third top is approached by descending 50m down a twisting open gully at the western end of the south face. A good spike lies at the end of the fault above the final 15m wall.

The Inaccessible Pinnacle
The East Ridge (IV,4) is a heart stopping climb in full conditions. The south face is almost always dry rock but the crest can hide treacherous quantities of snow. The West Ridge is impossible if covered with snow unless the flake at 10m can be lassoed for aid.

King's Chimney
It can be hard to find the abseil point above the top of King's Chimney; follow the crest down eastward and slightly left from the summit for 60m. A 25m abseil from the large block above King's Chimney just reaches the upper ledge system that descends to Collie's Ledge. From the bealach below, the ascent of Sgùrr Theàrlaich can be awkward.

Theàrlaich-Dubh Gap
Climbing the short side of the Gap will be technical Grade 6 in all but the most banked out of conditions. The top has been lassoed for aid in the past but is not easy. Most parties abseil into Coir a' Ghrunnda to avoid the difficulties. Avoid the temptation to return to Glen Brittle and complete the Traverse with a joyous romp to the summit dome of Gars-bheinn as the snow turns red in the sunset.

Records
The first completed Main Ridge Traverse was made in 1911 by Shadbolt and MacLaren in a time of 12hrs 15mins from Gars-bheinn to Gillean. Their line included all of the major peaks and climbs along the Ridge with the addition of the highest Cuillin, Sgùrr Alasdair, which lies just off the continuous line. This remained as the accepted line well beyond the 1960s with any teams including Sgùrr Dubh Mòr, Sgùrr Sgumain and other outliers noting their routes as variations. A dramatic change occurred in the 1980s with runners competing for the record deciding on the inclusion of Sgùrr Dubh Mòr as part of the acceptable line. This is a contentious addition with the peak lying 300m off to the east of the Main Ridge. Bypasses of Sgùrr Dubh na Dà Bheinn are even used to make up time thus avoiding one of the major peaks on the Ridge.

This is just one of the many contentious points raised when "records" are discussed in the Cuillin. Inclusion of Sgùrr na h-Uamha and Garbh-bheinn into a Greater Traverse is logical and geologically correct but Clach Glas and Blàbheinn are the only two accepted peaks that need to be climbed for completion. Extensions to include more or less of the Red Cuillin have been completed by at least half a dozen runners.

The first Winter Traverse was completed in 1965 with the crest of the Ridge in full winter garb, setting a good precedent. Climbing the summer rock pitches would have been impossible and so north to south was the only way to achieve a direct traverse. One of the most aesthetically pleasing traverses possible is in spring

Descending the West Ridge of Sgùrr nan Gillean. Climber Mark Shaw

when the rock pitches are dry and snow slopes link the rocks. The first Greater Traverse in winter conditions was claimed by a party traversing south to north under these conditions and remains contentious. The current winter record was achieved solo when following a complete set of footprints laid the day before.

Being contentious does not undermine these achievements; indeed they are remarkable feats by top athletes in a very dangerous environment. It does, however, show that records are open to much variation and ultimately only matter to those directly involved. As a microcosm of mountaineering this seems particularly fitting.

CUILLIN RIDGE TRAVERSES

SKYE CUILLIN
Glen Sligachan & Harta Corrie
Glen Sligachan Buttress & Crags

S	1969 Jul 17	Sidetrack	Mr & Mrs Adams, I.S.Clough
S	1969 Jul 17	Blasphemy Chimneys	Mr & Mrs Adams, I.S.Clough
S	1980 Apr 10	Cheek of the Devil	P.Hunter, Miss S.Drummond
S	1980 May 3	Rat Trap	S.Drummond, P.Hunter
S	1980 May 4	Opal Creamer	P.Hunter, S.Drummond
S	2000 Apr 9	Luke's Climb, Post Mortem, Runaway Slabs, Slash and Burn	R.Simpson, D.Morrison
S	2002 Jun	Hartatak	S.Kennedy, D.Ritchie, M.Shaw

Sgùrr na h-Uamha & Harta Corrie

S	1871 Aug 28	Sgùrr na h-Uamha	J.Ponsonby Cundill, J.R.Hall
S	1887 Jun 5	North-East Face Original Route, Sgùrr na h-Uamha	C.Pilkington, H.Walker, J.Heelis
	The party thought their ascent was the first.		
S	1887 Jul 1	An Caisteal	H.C.Hart, J.Mackenzie
S	1890 Jul 30	South Ridge, Sgùrr na h-Uamha	W.E.Corlett, E.R.Kidson
S	1905 Apr 21	Raeburn's Route, An Caisteal	H.Raeburn, W.C.Slingsby, G.A.Solly, E.Ullen

The first route made on these impressive buttresses, with Raeburn as leader choosing Klettershuhe to climb the slabs before tackling snow and ice near the summit.

S	1911 Sep 11	Archer Thomson's Route, An Caisteal	J.M.A.Thomson, H.O.Jones
S	1911 Sep 11	South Buttress, An Caisteal	L.G.Shadbolt, A.C.MacLaren

Direct Start: 30 May 1946, E.L.Wigham, C.E.W.Johnson. Superdirect Start: 1998, W.Jeffrey, R.Milne.

S	1937 Jun 26	Murray's Climb	W.H.Murray, J.K.W.Dunn
	The only Cuillin contribution from the great W.H.Murray.		
S	1948 May 22	West Gully	D.H.B.Reynolds, G.W.Wrangham
S	1949 Jun	Smith's Climb	C.M.G.Smith, R.C.Putman
S	1953 May 10	North Buttress, An Caisteal	E.A.Wrangham
S	1964 Summer	Un-named Climb	A.Williams, C.Read
S	1965 Aug 19	Braehead Climb	H.M.Brown, J.Matyssek, J.R.Tomlinson
S	1968 May 27	Aslan's Tongue	H.M.Brown, D.P.M.McNabb
W	1983	White Wizard	K.Hopper, C.Rowland
W	1999 Feb 11	West Gully	M. Shaw
W	1999 Feb 22	Cuill Climb	M.Shaw
W	2000 Dec 30	Left Hand Route	M.Shaw, D.Paterson
S	2002 July 21	The Crescent (Sgùrr na h-Uamha)	S.Kennedy, D.Ritchie
S	2010 Jun 18	Holiday Bonus	M.Lates, M.Airey

Northern Cuillin
Nead na h-Iolaire

S	1897 May	Central Chimney	
	Recorded in Climbers book as 'had been climbed three or four times.'		
S	1918 Aug 7	Left Rib	R.W.Lamb, M.G.Bradley
S	1952 Aug 19	Nihilist's	A.J.D.Wyder, J.E.Holliday
S	1967 Aug	August Rib	C.J.Rumball, J.Rumball.
S	1993 Jun 4	Eagle's Eyrie	R.McLaughlin, P.Stone.
S	1994 May 15	Elizabeth	R.McLaughlin, P.Stone
S	1994 May 15	Raptor	P.Stone, R.McLaughlin
S	1994 May	One Flew Over the Cuillin Ridge	M.Lates, M.Francis

Low Crag

Oxford University discovered a broad area close to the Tourist Route with half a dozen unclimbed buttresses. All early routes were climbed by A.Baugh, S.Broadbent, H.Jenkins or K.Wigmore with contributions from R.Welford, A.Ross, A.Parker, J.Wakeman, G.Demerell, C.Atkinson.

S   2000 Apr 6/8   April Crack/Direct, I'd Rather be Wet than Sorry, Ground Control to Major Tom, Spaceman's Slab, Grand National, Electric Mainline, Iffley Dreams, Adrian's Wall, Apollo 13

S	2002 Jan 4	Escapist's Daydream, Oxford Blue, The Purple Turtle, The Groove, Kandahar, Small Slab, The Seamstress, East Ramp	
S	2002 Dec 30/31	Venus, Warmin Up, Mercury Rib, Varsity Crack, Coolin Off, Taliban Groove, Alison's Rib, Electra, Faithless	
S	2003 May 30	Journey Into Space, Pulse	S.Broadbent, K.Wigmore, A.Baugh
S	2005 Mar 27	Arrows of Desire	S&KBroadbent
S	2005 May	Frost Route	M.Lates, G.Frost
S	2006 Apr 14	The Flake Traverse, Silver Slab	S.Broadbent & K.Broadbent
S	2006 Nov 1	Spaced Out	M.Lewis, A.Ross

Northern Cuillin Peaks

S	1836 Jul 7	Sgùrr nan Gillean, South-east Ridge (Tourist Route)	
			J.D.Forbes, D.Macintyre

'...the extreme roughness of the rocks rendering the ascent safe where, with any other formation, it might have been considerably perilous. Indeed, I have never seen a rock so adapted for clambering.'

S	1845 May	Bruach na Frithe	J.D.Forbes, D.Macintyre
S	1865 Jun	Nicolson's Chimney	
		(First descent)	A.Nicolson, D.MacIntyre

First Ascent; A.Nicolson, D.Hepburn, Reverend Black, A.McPherson,18 August 1879.
'By means of the crook the plaid was hitched over an overhanging point and after considerable difficulty Angus McPherson succeeded in drawing himself up'.

W	1872 Feb 11	Sgùrr nan Gillean	A.Nicolson
S	1873 Aug 12	Knight's Peak	W.A.Knight, A.Macpherson

Only the tourist route had ever been guided and Macpherson was naturally reluctant; 'when I told him of much more difficult things which climbers do in the Alps and doubled the bribe, he yielded.'

W	1883 Jan	Bruach na Frithe	Anonymous recording in Temple Bar Magazine

Whoever it was took with him a local spaniel called 'Chunach'

S	1886 Aug 20	Knight's Peak, West Face	A.H.Stocker, A.G.Parker
S	1887 May 28	Pinnacle Ridge	C.Pilkington, H.Walker, J.Heelis
S	1887 Jul 1	West Ridge by Gendarme	H.C. Hart, J. Mackenzie
S	1887 Jul 1	Am Basteir (first recorded ascent)	H.C.Hart, J.Mackenzie
S	1887 Aug	Basteir Tooth, by descent from Am Basteir	J.N.Collie, W.W.King
S	1888 Sep	Doctor's Gully Left, Doctor's Gully Right	J.P & R.C.Gilson

Probably discovered and named after Doctor Norman Collie in 1887/88.

S	1889	Basteir Tooth, Lota Corrie Route	J.N.Collie, J.Mackenzie
S	1889	Second Pinnacle, Basteir Face	W.W.King
S	1890 May 29	Slingsby's Route	W.C.Slingsby, G.Hastings, E.Hopkinson
S	1893 Jul 13	First Pinnacle variation Chimney on Basteir Face	W.W.Naismith, W.Douglas
S	1893 Sep 16	Second – Third Gully	J.Collier, J.A.Parker, W.W.Naismith, W.Reid
S	1896 May 15	Original Route, Second Pinnacle	T.A.Falcon, E.Gray
S	1896 Jun	First Ascent by RH Chimney of Am Basteir from the Tooth	W.Inglis Clark, J.Gall Inglis, W.J.Shannon

A short corner above the overhung Mouth was used before this.

S	1896 Sep 4	Route I, Sgùrr a' Fionn Choire	J.A.Parker, W.W.Naismith
S	1896 Sep 7	Naismith's Route, Sligachan Face	W.W.Naismith, J.N.Collie, E.B.Howell

The first route on this face.

S	1897 Jun/Jul	Subsidiary Gully	E.A.Baker, J.Croft
S	1898 Aug 3	Maclay's Gully	J.Maclay, G.A.Solly, G.P.Baker, (Oscar Röhde?)

A winter ascent is mentioned in SMC guidebook 1968.

S	1898 Aug 15	Naismith's Route, Basteir Tooth	W.W.Naismith, A.M.Mackay

Naismith had pre-inspected the line on a rope from above which will hearten some modern climbers!

S	1898 Aug 12	Knight's Peak, North Face	W.W.King, W.W.Naismith
S	1898 Aug 15	Forked Chimney	W.W.Naismith, J.F.Dobson, A.M.Mackay

First descent by Pye, Shadbolt and Bartrum Aug 9th 1918.

S	1898 Aug 18	Deep Chimney	W.W.Naismith, G.B.Gibbs, W.W.King
S	1898 Aug 25	King's Cave Chimney	W.W.King, G.B.Gibbs, J.Mackenzie

'King thrust his head into a kind of rabbit burrow and gradually disappeared, all but his boots! He ultimately made a small hole, through which he wriggled into a funnel. Very few minutes after his total disappearance, we heard a joyful yodel.'

S	1898 Aug 27	First Traverse of Tooth (by Naismith's and King's Routes)	H.Raeburn, G.B.Gibbs
S	1898 Jun 16	Third – Fourth Gully	Robertson Lamb, W.Heap, W.Tattersall, H.E.Bowron

Had been climbed by Norman Collie prior to 1890 but subsequent rock fall had rendered a section dangerous and very loose.

S	1902 Jun 13	Gully Climb, Sgùrr a' Bhasteir	J.Mackenzie, T.E.Dalton

'John Mackenzie tried it directly up and after nearly getting to the top slipped and fell, luckily not hurting himself at all as he was well hitched.'

S	1906 27 Jul	Shadbolt's Chimney	L.G.Shadbolt, O.P.Shadbolt, A.C.MacLaren

Variation: K.Tarbuck, Collin June 3 1932

S	1907 May 25	4th/5th Gully to summit	T.Mears, J.Mackenzie
S	1907 Jun	Sligachan Gully & Parallel Chimneys Variation	A.P.Abraham, H.Harland

First descent 10 September 1911, A.C. MacLaren, L.S. Shadbolt

S	1907 Jun	Route II, Sgùrr a' Fionn Choire	A.P.Abraham, A.H.Binns, G.Bartrum, H.Harland
S	1907 Jun	Black Chimney	A.P.Abraham, H.Harland

Succumbed to extreme combined tactics and may not yet have received a free ascent.

S	1908 Aug 16	North Chimney, Bruach na Frithe	W.W.King, Dr. Inglis, Miss Inglis

'It was necessary to swing at the end of the rope from a dyke under the chockstones to the outside of the foremost chockstone.'

S	1909 Jun 19	Am Basteir Chimney	J.Martin, R.Mackenzie

Middle pitch; K.P. Scoones, 11 September 1910

S	1911 Aug 27	North Face, Am Basteir	K.P.Scoones, A.E.Scoones, J.Osborne Walker
S	1911 Sep 8	Left Gully	K.P.Scoones, H.Tomkinson, Miss D.S.Tomkinson
S	1907 Sep 8	MacLaren's Chimney	A.C. MacLaren, L.G. Shadbolt

Seems likely to have been climbed before by J.Mackenzie.

S	1911 Sep 9	Thomson and Jones Route	J.M.A.Thomson, H.O.Jones, B.C.Jones
S	1911 Sep 10	Sligachan Gully Buttress	J.M.A.Thomson, H.O.Jones, E.S.Reynolds, B.C.Jones

Archer Thomson wrote of the Cuillin '...their scale impressed us as magnificent, and their quality as excellent beyond previous experience in Britain.'

S	1913	Cooper's Gully	C.H.Cooper
S	1919	Fluting's Climb	Robertson Lamb, E.Roberts
S	1920 Jun 17	Knight's Peak, North Face	G.D.Abraham, H.Harland, G.Summers
S	1920 Aug 18	Lüscher's Route No. 2	Dr.E.Lüscher
S	1920 Aug 28	Lüscher's Route No. 1	Dr.E.Lüscher
S	1927 Jun 24	West Face Direct, Knight's Peak	F.W.Giveen, C.H.Cooper, D.R.Orr

Variation start: Red Slab Route, T.Low, G.Morfee, 27 July 1950

S	1934 Aug	Naismith's Route Direct	J.K.W. Dunn, J.G. Wilson
S	1944 Sep 10	Rudge and Wood's Route	W.L.Wood, E.C.W.Rudge
W	1947	Pinnacle Ridge	W.L. Wood and Party
S	1950 Jul 27	Red Slab Route	T.Low, G.Morfee
S	1960 Aug 18	King's Cave Wall/Outside Edge	C.J.S.Bonington, T.W.Patey
S	1960 Aug 18	West Wall Am Basteir	T.W.Patey, C.J.S.Bonington

These routes were done on the same day that the pair climbed Whispering Wall on Mhadaidh nearly 3hrs south along the Main Ridge.

W	1962 Dec 30	West Face, Knight's Peak	K.Bryan, N.Robb
S	1963 Jul 11	Thor	A.James, G.Reid

Technically a variation or, more likely, escape from Black Chimney

S	1963 Jul 12	Fria	A.James, G.Reid
W	1986 Feb 22	Lament	B.S.Findlay, G.Strange

Packed for a Traverse attempt the team lamented having no ice screws with which to tackle the

main ice-fall.

W	1986 Feb 28	North-West Face Route	P.Langhorne, Miss. J.Douglas
S	1989 Jul 12	Rainbow Warrior	S.Hill, T.Dickson
W	1993 Mar 31	Just a Boy's Game	C.Threlfall, P.McGuire
W	1994 Feb 22	Doctor's Chimney Right	C.Threlfall
S	1996 Sep	Hung, Drawn and Quartered	I.S.Dring, M.E.Moran

Probably the most impressive of all the chimneys in Skye.

W	1997 Feb 26	West Ridge of Knight's Peak	P.Franzen, M.E.Moran, S.Potter
W	1997 Feb 26	Flutings Climb	P.Franzen, M.E.Moran, S.Potter
S	1997 Jun 17	The Squeeze Box	M.E.Moran, A.Nisbet
W	1999 Mar 8	The Deadline	D.Ritchie, M.Shaw
W	1999 Mar 9	North Face, Am Basteir	D.Ritchie, M.Shaw
W	1999 Mar 13	Luscher's No.2	R.Bervie, M.E.Moran
W	1999 Dec 12	Am Basteir Chimney	N.Nelson, D.Ritchie
W	1999 Dec 15	Forked Chimney.	M.E.Moran (backroped)
W	2000 Feb 13	Deep Chimney	N.Marshall, D.Ritchie
W	2000 Feb 20	White Dreams	N.Marshall, D.Ritchie
W	2000 Feb 29	MacLaren's Chimney	C.Gardiner, N.Edwards, M.E.Moran
W	2000 Mar 4	Gingini Chiminee	M.Lates (unsec.)
W	2000 Apr 3	The Sickle	S.Broadbent, K.Wigmore
S	2000 Aug 3	Black Magic	G.Andrew, D.Morrison
W	2001 Jan 13	Luscher's No.1	J.Allott, M.Moran
W	2001 Dec 29	Doctor's Gully Left	D.Ritchie, N.McGougan
W	2002 Jan 1	North Chimney, Bruach na Frithe	D.Ritchie, N.McGougan
W	2002 Feb 24	Shadbolt's Chimney	D.Ritchie, M.Shaw
S	2002 Sep 15	Synchronicity	S.Kennedy, R.Hamilton
S	2002 Sept 22	Arbroath, Faded Message	D.Ritchie, N.McGougan
S	2002 Sept 22	Fairy Nuff, Adamant, Ladies Day	S.Kennedy, A.MacDonald
S	2002 Sep 29	Bedrock, Jacob's Ladder, Haribo,	
		High and Dry, Pink Umbrella	S.Broadbent, K.Wigmore, A.Baugh,
			G.Damerell
S	2003 April 18	Cuddy	S.Kennedy,R. Hamilton
S	2006	Captain Planet	E.Tressider, B.Fyffe

Direct Finish; Jun 2008 D.Macmanus, E.Tressider

W	2008 Jan 11	Hillary's Wake	M.Francis, R.Lawson
S	2008 Jul	No Regrets	M.Lates, M.Francis
S	2008	Wee Bitty Regret	M.Francis, M.Lates
S	2008 Jul	No Worries Mate	M.Lates, M.Francis, P.Cunningham
S	2008 Aug	Drag Queen	M.Lates, A.Lee-Browne
W	2008 Nov 25	Hung, Drawn and Quartered	N.Carter, M.E.Moran

'...the climbing was both brutal and spectacular, and undoubtedly rates as one of the most technical winter routes ever recorded in Scotland.'

S	2009 Sep 17	Big Worries Mate	M.Lates, R.Cutler
W	2010 Jan	Mike The Bhasteird	M.Francis, D.Williamson
W	2010 Dec 2	Shadbolt's Outer Variation	P.MacPherson, M.Moran, F.Blunt

Coire na Creiche

S	circa 1850s	Sgùrr Thuilm	Ordnance Survey party
S	1880 Apr	Bidein Druim nan Ràmh,	
		North Peak	W.W.Naismith
S	1883 Aug	Bidein Druim nan Ràmh,	
		Main Peak	L.Pilkington, H.Walker, E.Hulton
S	1887 Jul 1	Sgùrr a' Mhadaidh, all four tops	H.C.Hart, J.Mackenzie
S	1895 Sep 9	Waterpipe Gully	J.Kelsall, A.W.Hallitt

An exceptional event for the time by the two unknown Yorkshire climbers that resulted in one of the most amusing slanging matches recorded in mountaineering: 'As politely as possible (assuming the account to be serious) we desire to protest against the impression left by the description of the gully', wrote E.Gray and T.A.Falcon, to which Kellsall and Hallitt retorted; 'The politeness of the above is certainly beyond question, but the whole of it is a more striking tribute to the abilities of the writers as carpers and sneering sceptics, than as climbers'.

First Completely Direct Ascent by R.E.Thompson, A.T.Fraser, C.A.Wordsworth, C.J.Slade, G.R.Slade, 2 Jun 1899

S	1896 Sep 5	North-West Buttress	J.N.Collie, J.A.Parker, W.W.Naismith,
			E.B.Howell

S	1898 Aug 30	Foxes' Rake	H.Raeburn, A.Fraser, A.W.Russell
S	1907 Jun	The Spur and Summit Gullies	A.P.Abraham, G.Bartrum, A.H.Binns, H.Harland
S	1907 Jun	Slanting Gully	A.P.Abraham, G.Bartrum, A.H.Binns, H.Harland

Climbed Direct by J.M.A.Thomson, A.C.MacLaren, H.O.Jones, L.G.Shadbolt, 15 Sep 1911
A classic gully, far cleaner than most, with pitch after pitch of exacting climbing.

S	1909 (?)	Upper Rake	E.C.C.Baly
S	1911 Aug 10	Two Pitch Gully	N.C.Madan, H.E.L.Porter
S	1911 Sep 12	Archer Thomson's Route	J.M.A.Thomson, H.O.Jones, L.G.Shadbolt
S	1914 Jun 12	North Gully	H.Bishop, H.P.Cain, C.D.Yeomans
S	1918 Jul 28	Pye and Mallory's Route	D.R.Pye, G.H.L.Mallory, R.Mallory, L.G.Shadbolt
S	1937 Jul	South Gully	W.M.MacKenzie, A.M.MacAlpine, F.A.Oxley

Alternative to Pitch 9 on Right Wall by W.D.Brooker, C.M.Dixon, 4 Aug 1951

S	1939 Jun 4	Gauger's Gully	W.L.Wood, P.Greeman, W.H.Rae
S	1947 May 24	Waterpipe Corner	V.J.Wiggin, E.Wood-Johnson

With a total of 22 pitches this is a Scottish record. It was previously thought to be held by Clachaig Gully.

S	1949 Sep 20	Deep Gash Gully	H.G.Nicol, A.S.Parker

Had been attempted before by a number of quality climbers including Naismith (1898), Shadbolt and W.H.Murray. On the difficult second pitch Nichol described the climbing as '...exhausting, yet it required infinite delicacy and care.'

S	1950 Jul	Foxes' Folly	D.Leaver, A.Smee
S	1951 Aug 4	Fox Trap	C.M.Dixon, W.D.Brooker
S	1952 Jun 22	Shining Cleft	G.H.Francis, J.F.Adams, E.A.Wrangham

'They must have been in great form for it is truly a bold line. I consider it to be one of the finest of the early post-war routes in Skye. And to add to the prestige of that Cambridge first ascent, Wrangham's party did the ascent in hill-walking boots!' Malcolm Slesser, SMC Journal, 2006.

S	1952 Sep15	Central Gully	H.G.Nicol, I.H.Oliver, A.Grieve
S	1956 Aug 5	Dyke and Buttress Route	P.R.Stafford, A.C.Gilby
S	1958 May 30	Sanguinary Cracks	D.J.Temple, I.S.Clough
S	1958 Sep	Man Trap	N.Drasdo, C.M.Dixon
S	1960 Apr	Thunder Rib	R.Smith, G.Milnes
S	1960 Aug 18	Whispering Wall	T.W.Patey, C.J.S.Bonington
S	1963 Jul 28	Moon Raker	I.A.MacEacheran, I.Kennedy
S	1964 Aug 21-27	Goliath Buttress	J.Harwood, D.W.Robbins
S	1966 Aug 26	Clap Trap	D.Chapman, J.R. Sutcliffe
S	1967 May 14	Thor	C.Boulton, A.C.Cain
S	1968 May 25	Nero	T.Taylor, Miss E.Smith
S	1968 Jul 12	Vixen Groove	B.K.E.Edridge, D.C.Forrest
S	1969 Jun 24	Gargantua	J.Escott, G.Hardie
S	1972 Sep	Megaton	C.Boulton, P.Nunn, R.Toogood

Pitch 3 onwards by M.Boysen, P.Braithwaite, P.Nunn, Apr 1974

S	1972 Sep 18	Pig's Ear	B.Tibbett, B.Paterson
S	1974 May	Resolution	C.Rowland, S.Rowland
S	1974 Aug 28	Quark (1 pa)	C.Boulton, P.Nunn

FFA by T.Prentice, C.Fraser, Jun 1984

S	1976 May 27	Gauche	G.Evans, J.Harwood
S	1977 Sep 24	Gael Force	H.Henderson, R.G.Ross
W	1978 Feb 17	The Hose	I.Dalley, T.Anderson
W	1979	The Smear	J.Duff, D.Scott
W	1979	South Gully	A.C.Cain, G.Wallace
S	1980 Apr	Edgeway	C.Rowland, S.Rowland
S	1980 Apr	The Rent	C.Rowland, S.Rowland
S	1980 May	Revelation	B.Leadingham, M.Richardson, J.Smith
S	1980 May	Retribution	A.Livesey, P.Nunn, C.Rowland
S	1980 Jun 6	Nearer My God to Thee	J.R.MacKenzie, D.Butterfield
S	1980 Sep	Sinistra Crack	G.Reilly, A.Paul
S	1981	Waterpipe Slabs	C.Rowland, K.Hopper

The Basalt Staircase variation, 7 May 1982, B.Godkey

W	1983 Feb 20	North Gully	S.Kennedy, N.Morrison
W	1986 Feb 24	Waterpipe Gully	B.S.Findlay, G.Strange

Direct winter ascent by C.Downer, D.Scott, 28 Feb 1986

| W | 1986 Mar 1 | Icicle Factory | M.Fowler, T.Saunders |

An exceptional winter for Cuillin water-ice routes.

| S | 1990 Jul 14 | Hearthammer | G.Nicoll, K.Noble, A.Chamings |
| W | 1991 Feb 2 | Deep Gash Gully | M.Fowler, J.Lincoln |

'Scottish gully climbing at its incomparable best, a total adventure where we were forced to surpass ourselves in order to succeed.' Martin Moran describing what transpired to be the second winter ascent a week later.

W	1994 Mar 22	Stag Gully	C.Threlfall, J.Gregory, S.Hallay
W	1994 Dec 27	Stag Buttress	C.Threlfall, P.McGuire
W	1995 Jan 2	Central Buttress	C.Threlfall, B.Rogers

Right-Hand Groove by P.J.Biggar, B.G.Hard, 25 Feb 2001

W	1995 Mar 28	Stepped Buttress	C.Threlfall, P.McGuire
W	1998 Mar	Winter Gully	M.Lates, W.Dewar
W	1999 Dec 11	Whispering Wall	V.P.Ramsden, M.Fowler
W	2000 Mar 4	Cameron's Gully	I.D.Morrison, R.Simpson
W	2002 Jan 2	Gauger's Gully	D.Ritchie, N.McGougan
S	2004 May	What have I Becombe	D.Birkett, M.Edwards
W	2004 Dec	Slanting Gully (to Foxes Rake)	M.Lates, T.Hanly
W	2005 Dec	Thuilm Right	M.Lates, M.Francis
W	2006 Feb 18	Thuilm Left	M.Lates, B.Barnes
W	2006 Feb 19	Day Tripper	E.Brunskill, D.Morris
W	2006 Feb 23	West Buttress	R.McGuire, N.Urquhart
W	2006 Mar 21	Arrow Slot	N.Urquhart R.McGuire
W	2009 Feb 6	North West Chimney	D.Ritchie, N.McGougan
W	2010 Dec 12	Hosepipe Ban	M.Lates, M.Barratt

Coire a' Ghreadaidh

S	1871	Sgùrr a' Ghreadaidh	Foster Heddle
S	1877	Sgùrr nan Gobhar	Captain J.C.Macpherson (RE) of the OS
S	1887 Aug	Diagonal Gully	J.N.Collie, W.W.King
S	1898 Aug 20	North-West Ridge, (Sgùrr Eadar da Choire)	G.B.Gibbs, J.F.Dobson, W.W.King
S	1898 Aug 20	Chimney, West Summit Buttress (Ghreadaidh)	G.B.Gibbs, J.F.Dobson, W.W.King (in descent)
S	1908 Jun	Hidden Gully	F.Greig
S	1908 Sep 20	Branching Gully	W.Garden, J.R.Levack, W.A.Reid
S	1910 Sep 15	Eagle's Gully	E.W.Steeple, G.Barlow, H.E.Bowron, A.H.Doughty
S	1910 Sep 15	Vanishing Gully	E.W.Steeple, G.Barlow, H.E.Bowron, A.H.Doughty
S	1929 Jul	North-East Gully	P.M.Barclay, J.A.Ramsay
S	1936 Oct	North West Buttress Thormaid	Ascentionists not known
S	1947 Jul	Overhanging Gully	W.A.Greenwell, P.D.Roberts
S	1950 Aug 9	Goat's Gully	T.Shaw, C.M.Dixon
S	1952 Aug 15	Hidden Gully Buttress	J.Evans, T.Evans
S	1958 Jun 2	Aegis	H.MacInnes

MacInnes's friend Ian Clough made a second ascent a decade later, but the route has not been located since.

S	1965 Jun	Diamond Buttress	G.Martin, N.Smythe, D.Boston
S	1965 Jun 30	Hamish's Chimney	W.Poole, P.Gaff
S	1965 Jul 22	Ceo	J.Harwood, H.Small
S	1965 Jul 23	Gail	J.Harwood, H.Small
S	1965 Jul 23	Pincer	J.Harwood, H.Small
S	1965 Jul 24	Virgin Arete	J.Harwood, H.Small
W	1967 Dec 31	Diagonal Gully	W.Robertson, R.J.C.Robb
S	1968 Jun 16	Scimitar	J.Harwood, R.A.High
S	1970 Jul 10	Footrot	B.Taplin, D.Bain
S	1970 Jul 10	Verruca	B.Taplin, D.Bain

Direct Start by B.Taplin, M.Chalwin, 16 Jul 1970

| S | 1971 May 14 | Fosdyke | A.J.Gilbert, D.A.P.Steel |

Direct Finish by M.Lates, R.Lawson, 2005

W	1976 Jan 10	North-West Ridge	M.Don, R.J.C.Robb
S	1976 May 27	Trapist	G.Evans, J.Harwood
S	1976 May 27	Simplicity	G.Evans, J.Harwood
W	1978 Feb 17	North-East Gully	D.Rogerson, M.Eastwood
W	1986 Mar 2	White Wedding	T.Saunders, C.Watts, M.Fowler

Technically the FWA of Overhanging Gully

S	1992 Jun 20	Black Slab	J.R.MacKenzie, G.Cullen
S	1992 Jun 20	Soft Options	J.R.MacKenzie, G.Cullen
W	1993 Oct 14	North-North-West Spur	C.Threlfall, P.McGuire
W	1999 Dec 11	Hamish's Chimney	M.Lates, R.Lawson
S	2006 Jul	Baptist	I.McCabe, J.Shanks, J.Dyble
W	2004 Jan	Stag Do	S.Muir, R.Hewison
W	2009 Feb 8	Ice Trap	M.Lates, M.Francis

Coire na Banachdaich & Innaccessible Pinnacle

S	1873 Late Sum	Sgùrr na Banachdaich & Sgùrr Dearg	A.Nicolson, D.Macrae
S	1880 Aug 18	East Ridge, Inaccessible Pinnacle	C.Pilkington, L.Pilkington
S	1886 Aug 19	West Ridge, In Pinn	A.H.Stocker, A.G.Parker
S	1888?	North-West Corner, In Pinn	J.N.Collie, J.Mackenzie.

Direct start by H.Raeburn, J.Mackenzie, 6 Sep 1898

S	1890 Aug 22	Banachdich Gully	G.B.Gibbs and W.W.King. J.Mackenzie
S	1898 Aug 23	South Crack (top roped)	W.W.King

FFA by H.Harland, A.P.Abraham, A.H.Binns, late June 1906

S	1906	Window Buttress	J.N.Collie, J.Mackenzie
S	1906	North Wall of Banachdich Gully	J.N.Collie
S	1907	South Slabs	H.Harland, A.P.Abraham
S	1907 Jun	Deep-Cut Gully Buttress	A.G. Woodhead, H.E. Bowron, E.W. Steeple.
S	1909 Jul 31	Black Chimney	G.Barlow, H. B.Buckle, A.H.Doughty

Variation, Right Exit by H. & M.C. MacInnes, 1957 or 1958

S	1914 Jun 8	Bishop's Climb	H.Bishop, C.D.Yeomans
S	1921 June 28	Route I, Route II	A.S.Pigott, J.Wilding

Alf Pigott explains how he and John Wilding came to do both routes; having 'floated up the South Crack' and then 'washed down the short west side', they decided to investigate the steep southern face, which Pigott thought '...sufficiently broken to justify a start, so we put on our rubbers.'

S	1938 May 21	Evening Wall	Miss P.Campbell, A.J.Turner, A.B.Sutcliffe

Climbed but not named by Barlow pre-1923

S	1952 Aug 18	Burglar's Entrance	A.J.D.Wryder, J.E.Holliday
S	1953 Jun	Toolie Grooves	J.R.Marshall, C.L.Donaldson, G.Hood

Direct Finish by J. &. D.Preston, 23 Apr 2005

S	1957 Jul 19	Upper Window Buttress	A.D.Marsden, R.Redfern
S	1958 Jun 19	Melpomene	H.MacInnes, Miss C.Munday, Miss M.E.Elliot
S	1958 Jun 24	Aesculapius	H.MacInnes, J.A.Hartley, Miss M.C.Munday, Miss M.E.Elliot

The Hygeia Variations, Direct Start and Direct Finish by H.Insley, J.A.Hartley, 1958
FFA Direct Finish by C.Moody, W.Hood, 10 June 2006

S	1959 Jun 21	Valkyrie	W.S.Yeaman, W.Bonthrone
S	1962 Sep 11	Durham Slabs, Hadrian's Wall	K. Mosley, R. Wilson
S	1964 Aug 11	Varicose	J.Harwood
W	1968 Jan 2	Window Buttress	G.W.Wilkinson, R.Watters, G.Todd, S.Docherty
S	1970 Jul 23	Widow's Eye	R.O'Donovan, B.Marshall
W	1979 May 9	Banachdich Gully	R.Redwood, R.Manual
S	1980 May 18	Val	D.MacCallum, R.Milne
S	1980 Aug 23	Closer to the Edge	S. Scott, Miss S.Wheeler
W	1993 Dec 26	Goats Gully	C. Threfall, A. MacRuary
W	1994	Deep Cut Gully	D.Bisset, M.Francis, R.Macdonald
S	1999 Aug 8	The Naked Saltire	M.Lates, D.MacLachlan

Climbed the day after two young ladies stripped for a photo with only a saltire (and helmets!) to protect their modesty on top of the In Pinn.

S	2002 Aug 2	Grey Rib	C.Moody, C.Grindley
S	2005 Apr 23	Hippocratic Oath	J. & D.Preston
W	2006 Mar 15	Kibby's Route	T.Hanley, N.Urquhart
W	2007 Mar	Window Buttress	M.Airy, N.Kaczynski
W	2008 Dec 2	Playgrope	M.Francis, D.Bowdler
W	2010 Feb 18	The White Line	M.Lates, M.Nagle, C.Waddell

Coire Lagan
Upper Coire Lagan

S	1873 Late Sum	Sgùrr Alasdair	A.Nicolson, A.Macrae

'I had been told at Glen Breatal that another peak, a very beautiful one, had foiled the Ordnance men. This naturally stirred my desire to attempt it, which I did accompanied by a shepherd, Angus Macrae.'

S	1883 Autumn	South West Ridge, Sgùrr Alasdair	L.Pilkington, H.Walker, E.Hulton
S	1887 Jun 1	Sgùrr Theàrlaich	C.Pilkington, H.Walker
S	1887 Jun 2	Sgùrr MhicChoinnich	C.Pilkington, H.Walker, J.Heelis, J.Mackenzie
S	1887 Jul 4	Collie's Ledge	H.C.Hart, J.Mackenzie

See history section for an explanation of this intriguing misnomer.

S	1890 May 27	North Buttress, Sgumain	C.Pilkington, H.Woolley, C.Dent, G.Hastings
W	1892 Apr 14	An Stac Direct in descent	J.H.Gibson, J.H.Wicks, G.H.Morse, E.Carr
S	1892 Aug 8	Heathcote's Gully	J.N.Heathcote, Rev. G.Broke
S	1896 Jul 22	North-West Ramp	J. S & R.G.Napier and J.H.Bell
S	1896 Sep 3	Collie's Climb, Alasdair	J.N.Collie, E.B.Howell, W.W.Naismith
S	1898 Aug 8	King's Chimney	W.W.King, W.W.Naismith, W.Douglas

W.E.Corlett had made a remarkable descent by abseil 3 Aug 1889.

S	1907 Jun	Abraham's Climb	H.Harland, A.P.Abraham, A.H.Binns, G.L.Bartrum

Abrahams Direct (Stone Shoot Face) July 1937 W.M.MacKenzie, A.M.MacAlpine

S	1907Jun	West Buttress Route, Sgumain	A.G.Woodhead, H.E.Bowron, E.W.Steeple,R.Lamb and friend
S	1907 Oct	West Buttress Route, MhicChoinnich	G.D.&A.P.Abraham, H.Harland, A.W.Wakefield or S.W.Thomson

Variation Finish 2 Aug 1952 E. Byne, C. Ashborg, Miss W.E.Hill

S	1908 Jun	Ladies' Pinnacle, East Ridge	Mrs C.B.Phillip, Miss C.Prothero
S	1908 Aug 30	Gully B	H.B.Buckle, G.Barlow, A.H.Doughty
S	1908 Sep 1	Gullies C & D	H.B. Buckle, G. Barlow
S	1908 Sep/Oct	An Stac Chimney	F.Goggs, A.W.Russell
S	1909	Baly's Route	E.C.C.Baly
S	1912 Sep	East Corner	E.W.Steeple, G.Barlow
S	1913 Aug 1	Gully A	E.W.Steeple, G.Barlow, A.H.Doughty
S	1921 Jul	Final Tower Direct	E.W.Steeple, G.Barlow

Considered as harder than the Crack of Doom.

S	1924 Jul 22	West Trap Route	J.H.B.Bell, F.S.Smythe

Direct approach: 18 July 1946 A.Allsopp, R.G.Morsley

S	1925 Aug 4	Frankland's Gully	C.D.Frankland, Miss M.M.Barker, H.V.Hughes
S	1929 Early Sep	Mantelshelf Boulder	W.L.Coats

Not described in the text but one of the earliest of the Coire Lagan boulder problems.

S	1932 Jun 27	Wood-Johnson's Route	E.Wood-Johnson, C.J.A.Cooper, D.Lewers
S	1937 Aug 2	Barber's Route	B.K.Barber, M.Burton, G.Eisig, H.B.Law
S	1947 Aug 27	Lagan Route	D.Thomas, Mrs G.Goddard (Moffat)
S	1948 May 28	Jeffrey's Dyke	R.Jeffrey, Mrs Jeffrey, J.H.B.Bell, Mrs Bell, C.M.Allen
S	1949 Aug	Western Drainpipe	G.H.Francis, K.Norcross, A.R.Blair

Direct start T.W. Waghorn, P.G. White and C.J. Breeze August 1952

S	1950 Jul 15	Central Route	D.D.Stewart, D.N.Mill

S 1951 Jul 13 Sunset Slab J.D.Foster, J.L.Blake
Direct Exit: 31 May 1958, D.J. Temple, I.S. Clough. Yellow Groove Continuation: 30 June 1964, I.S. Clough, D.J.Temple, M.Battle, B.Fein. Yellow Walls Finish: 24 April 2005 J. & D. Preston.
S 1951 Jul 13 Superstition J.D.Foster, J.R.Stead, B.L.Blake
The Slant variation start: 1 Sep 1958, H.Greenbank, J.Wilkinson, D.Murray
Tam's Corner variation: 16 May 2005, S.Kennedy, T.Hamilton, R.Hamilton
S 1951 Sep 21 Direct Route, N.Buttress,
Sgùrr Sgumain D.D.Stewart, A.Colquhoun,
P.Vaughan
W 1952 Apr 2 Abraham's Route W.D.Brooker, C.M.Dixon, J.W.Morgan
Snake Variation:18 March 2006, M.Lates, D.Bowdler.
S 1952 Aug 25 Western Drainpipe Ridge P.G.White, T.W.Waghorn, C.J.Breeze
S 1955 Jul 29 Mistaken Crack G.S.Beattie, W.K.Davies, K.A.Sturrock
Variation to Third Pitch: Oedipus, 1958 H. MacInnes and party.
S 1956 Jun 9 Happy Returns A.M.Wood-Johnson, E.Wood-Johnson
S 1957 Styx H.MacInnes
New line on Third Pitch – Date and climbers unknown, may have been the following party. J.M. Mackenzie recorded the FFA in 1979 but the note 'Styx was Freed 1977' was added soon afterwards.
S 1957 Prometheus (3 pa) H.MacInnes, J.M.Alexander,
I.S.Clough
S 1957 Prokroustes (3 pa) H.MacInnes, I.S.Clough.
J.M.Alexander
Prokroustes was a robber who put travellers in his bed, stretching or lopping off their limbs so that they fitted it!
S 1958 May 29 Introduction I.S.Clough, D.J.Temple
S 1958 May 29 Theseus (3 pa) J.M.Alexander, T.R.Wilkinson
S 1958 Jun 9 Penitentiary Grooves H.MacInnes, I.S.Clough
FFA: 1971, D.Dinwoodie, B.Lawrie
S 1958 27 Jun Hemaphra and Ditus H.MacInnes, Miss M.C.Munday
S 1958 Priam H.MacInnes & party
S 1959 Apr 28 Willit J.McLean, I.S.Clough
S 1959 Apr 28 Lost Hope J.McLean, I.S.Clough
S 1959 Sep Sou'wester Cracks J.Wilkinson, G.J.Ritchie
S 1960 Aug 14 Lower Rib C.J.S.Bonington, T.W.Patey
S 1965 Aug Lethe W.Smith, J.McLean
S 1965 Aug 1 Laceration I.A.MacEacheran, J.Renny
S 1966 Jun 11 The Baron R.Ratcliffe, A.C.Willmott
S 1968 Jun 23 Purple Haze M.J.Guillard, J.R.Irvin
S 1968 Jun 24 Frostbite M.J.Guillard, J.R.Irvin
W 1970 Apr 11 Jeffrey's Dyke R.O'Donovan
W 1970 Apr 11 Gully A R.O.Donovan
S 1970 Jun 12 Reluctance A.Robertson, W.Tauber
S 1971 Jun 12 Grannie Clark's Wynd J.S.Shade, W.Tauber
W 1978 Feb The Twister C.Rowland, S.Rowland
W 1980 Feb 3 North-West Face C.Rowland, D.Jenkins
W 1981 Mar 1 Frankland's Gully P.Cairns, B.Ledingham, C.Rowland
W 1988 Apr 4 Early Bird M.Fowler, J.Lincoln
S 1988 May 3 The Klondyker A.Tibbs, D.Bearhop
S 1994 Jul 2 Raynaud's M.McLeod, C.Moody
S 1994 Aug 5 Vanishing Beads, Raven's Rib,
Mud Wrestler, Huffy Messiah,
Up the Down Stone Shoot,
Starless Bay, Flap Cracker C.Moody, A.Petrie
S 1996 Jul Blazing Saddles D.Hanna, S.Kennedy.
1997 Dec 31 In. Pinn. Fall M.Lates, D.Bowdler, M.Harmes,
A.Scott, K.Hughes
W 2001 Dec 31 B & C Gullies D.Ritchie, N.McGougan
W 2002 Feb 23 Gully D D.Ritchie, M.Shaw
S 2003 Apr 22 Hobo J.Lines
W 2004 Jan 2 BC Buttress D.Ritchie, M.Shaw
W 2004 Jan 29 CD Buttress D.Ritchie, M.Shaw
W 2005 Feb 13 Vent Du Nord D.Ritchie, D.McEachan
S 2006 May 8 Nuggets G. and K. Latter

S	2009 May 15	Curving Corner	I.Hey, M.Lates
S	2010 May 17	Sausage Sandwich	M.Lates, D.Windle, J.Windle
S	2010 May 17	Heinz Beans	M.Lates, D.Windle, J.Windle
W	2011 Mar 14	Gully E	M.Lates, M.Barratt

Sròn Na Cìche Coire Lagan Face

S	1904	The Finger	J.C.Thomson
S	1906	The Flake	J.N.Collie
S	1906 Jul	Collie's Route, Cioch(A' Chioch)	J.N.Collie, J.Mackenzie

Variation on Cioch Slab omitting the detour into Eastern Gully J.N.Collie, W.C.Slingsby, C.Phillip, G.Winthrop Young, J.Mackenzie, 1906.

Of outstanding historical significance. In 1899 Collie noticed a huge shadow on the face that he deduced could only be formed by the presence of some gigantic rocky tower. He was unable to return until July 1906. Mackenzie led to the top and named it A' Cioch. Collie was normally reserved and detested other people in the mountains but even he encouraged many friends to come and climb this unique obelisk.

S	1906 Aug 8	Cioch Gully & independent discovery of the Cioch	H.B.Buckle, G.Barlow

Recorded as climbed in winter, SMC. 1998; date and climbers unknown.

S	1906	Western Gully	J.N.Collie, J.Mackenzie

Initial direct pitches G. Barlow and friend (H.B. Buckle?), 1906

S	1907 Jun	Central Gully	A.G.Woodhead, E.W.Steeple, H.E.Bowron

East Wall and Central Gully Arete, July 30 1909, G.Barlow, H.B.Buckle, A.H.Doughty. Variation to 'unclimbable pitch' by right wall June 2 1935 M.B.Stewart, A.C.Borthwick, A.C.D.Small

S	1907	Amphitheatre Arete	J.N.Collie (J.Mackenzie?)

Amphitheatre Arete Variation, 5 September 1965, R.Turner, R.Howarth.

S	1907	Zigzag Route	J.N.Collie (J.Mackenzie?)
S	1907 Jun	Cioch Direct	H.Harland, A.P.Abraham

Variation to Cracks Pitch 25 June 1921, B.Martin, G.Wilson. Variation to Second Pitch, June 1933, Cambridge University M.C.

S	Same day	Cioch Nose	H.Harland, A.P.Abraham
S	1908 Aug	Little Gully	G.NBarlow
S	1908 Sep 3	West Central Gully and Arete	G.Barlow, H.B.Buckle
S	1909 Jun 20	Median	E.W.Steeple, H.E.Bowron

A daring frontal assault on the largest Cuillin rock face.

S	1911 Sep 13	Zigzag	L.G.Shadbolt, A.C.MacLaren, E.S.Reynolds
S	1911 Sep 13	Chimney and Crack	J.M.A.Thomson, H.O.Jones, B.C.Jones
S	1911 Sep 14	Archer Thomson's Route, Cioch Buttress	J.M.A.Thomson, H.O.Jones, L.G.Shadbolt, E.S.Reynolds, A.C.MacLaren, B.C.Jones

These three routes, along with several others throughout the Cuillin, were done by one of the strongest parties ever to climb in Skye.

S	1912 early Sep	Direct Route	E.W.Steeple, G.Barlow, A.H.Doughty
S	1912 early Sep	Chimney Route	E.W.Steeple, G.Barlow
S	1912 early Sep	Girdle Traverse of Sròn na Cìche	E.W.Steeple, G.Barlow

Variation: J.E.B.Wright, (W.Bruton?) June 1928.

The first of its kind on Skye, and no doubt inspired by similar lines on Lliwedd in North Wales.

S	1913 Sep	Eastern Gully, omitting the 2nd pitch	E.W.Steeple, G.Barlow

First complete ascent including the 2nd pitch J.Haggas, S.Thompson, 24 July 1938.

S	1914 Jun 15	Trap Face Route	J.B.Burrell, C.N.Cross

Variation: A.C.Cain, B.L.Dodson, P.Vaughan July 1950. Trap Face Route Direct (1976) is almost completely independent.

S	1915 Sept 14	Wallwork's Route	W.Wallwork, H.M.Kelly, J.Wilding

Variation from Second Ramp D. Thomas & Party, August 1969.

S	1918 Jul 31	Mallory's Slab and Groove	G.H.Mallory, D.R.Pye, L.G.Shadbolt

Variation to Second Pitch J.A.Ramsay?, 1932. Slab Corner Variation: I.Clough, G.Grandison, D.Pipes, 19 May 1958.

S	1918 Aug 6	Crack of Doom	D.R.Pye, L.G.Shadbolt

Direct Finish A.S.Pigott, J.Wilding, 27 June 1921. Direct Approach Miss B.Ritchie, C.D. Milner, 3 June 1936. Wall Variation to Crack Miss B. Ritchie, late June 1936.

H.B.Buckle, G.Barlow and A.H.Doughty had unsuccessfully attempted the route (which they named 'Hanging Gully') 5 May 1909.

| S | 1919 Late Aug | Cioch West | C.F.Holland, H.R.C.Carr, Miss D.E.Pilley |

Variation J.G.S.Smith 1951

| S | 1920/21/22 Aug | Parallel Cracks Route | E.W.Steeple, G.Barlow, A.H.Doughty |

Variations: M.J.Ball, C.G.W.Pilkington, W.O.M.Lutyens Sep1945; B.P.Williams, A.Maslin, 22 June 1953. Direct Start: J.Harwood, H.Small, D.J.Robbins July 1963.

S	1921 Jun 10	Slab Corner	A.Arthur, J.W.Arthur
S	1924 Jul 19	West Ridge of the Cioch	J.H.B.Bell, F.S.Smythe
S	1932 Jun 19	Cooper's Gangway	C.J.A.Cooper, E.Wood-Johnson, D.Lewers
S	1932 Jun 22	Central Slabs	E.Wood-Johnson, C.J.A.Cooper, D.Lewers

A fishing line was used to haul the rope rather than risk rope-drag!

| S | 1932 Jun | Engineers' Slant | D.L.Reid, E.H.Sale, J.D.Brown |

Cuillin exploration was no longer just for the privileged upper classes.

S	1932 Jul 22	Amphitheatre Wall	A.Horne, H.V.Hughes
S	1936 Aug 27	A.B.Route	A.Armitage, Miss H.Broadbent
S	1937 May 8	Coronation Route	S.Watson, G.C.Gray

This may be similar to, or even the same as 'Coronation', climbed by D.Stewart & party in 1953.

| S | 1937 Jul | Left Edge Route | W.MacKenzie, A.MacAlpine |
| S | 1944 | Arrow Route | I.Allan |

To disprove doubters Allan climbed the route again, scratching arrows with a scrap of rock as he ascended, hence the name. However, in 1928 the Lake District based guide J.E.B.Wright had already recorded; "The Cioch Slab, Central Face. Severe. An exhilarating climb in rubbers; and more so in boots." He climbed it twice: once solo and then, in boots, and trailed 200 feet (65m) of rope for a partner.

| S | 1946 Jul 19 | Diamond Slab | A.Allsopp, R.G.Morsley |

Direct Finish: J. Harwood, P. Thomas, 12 August 1964

S	1946 Jul 19	Apex Route	J.Wilkinson, D.W.Jackson, H.Ironfield
S	1946 Sep 21	Diamond Slab, West Route	A.Read, W.H.Turnbull
S	1947 May 17	Hangover Route	D.H.Haworth, G.J.Ritchie
S	1947 May 21	Crack of Double Doom	D.H.Haworth, I. Ap G.Hughes

Direct line above pitch 2: D.D. Stewart, D.N. Mill, I. Oliver September 1951.

S	1947 May 21	Doom Flake	D.H.Haworth, I. Ap G.Hughes
S	1947 Aug 21	East Wall Route	R.E.Davies, C.B.Machin
S	1949 Jun	Rib of Doom	C.M.G.Smith, A.Cleland
S	1949 Jun 9	Caravan Route	G.W.S.Pigott, J.A.Stewart, A.S.Pigott
S	1949 Jul 11	Integrity	D.H.Haworth, I. Ap G.Hughes

A magnificent classic breaking through overlaps and slabs above the Cioch.

Variation: P.Fletcher, B.Ripley, June 1962

	1951 Sep 21	Cioch Grooves	I.McNaught-Davis, G.H.Francis
S	1952 Jun 29	Petronella	G.H.Francis, E.A.Wrangham
S	1952 Sep 11	Boomerang	D.D.Stewart, D.N.Mill
S	1953 Jun 21	Magic Casement (aid)	M.M.Miller, G.H.Francis
S	1953 Jul	Jack-o' Diamonds	D.Leaver, C.E.N.Wilson
S	1953 Jul	Coronation	D.D.Stewart and party. (Possibly D.N.Mill and/or A.Colquhoun)

There is no indication the party were aware of Watson and Gray's 1937 'Coronation Route'

| S | 1954 May 21 | Slanting Crack (Cioch) | K.Deary. |
| S | 1956 Jul 16 | Bastinado (1 pa) | J.Cunningham, J.Allan, W.Smith |

The name is a punishment meted out by beating the soles of the feet with a stick!

FFA H.Hammill, A.Jones, 30 August 1975

Variation: D.Dinwoodie, C.MacLean, 25 July 1983

| S | 1956 Jul 16 | Trophy Crack | P.Walsh, H.MacKay |

The 'Trophy' was a piton marking the highest point previously reached by MacInnes. First free ascent of an E1 on this face.

| S | 1957 | Schadenfreude | R.D.Hinds, H.MacInnes, H.D.Parker, J.D.Small |
| S | 1957 | Prolepsis (aid) | H.MacInnes, T.Marsden, J.Haswell, R.E.Hinds |

Intricate aid route with sections possibly freed by Hang Free (1980).

S	1957 Aug 4	Kinloss Gully (3 pa)	I.S.Clough, R.Wilkinson
S	1957	Creag Dhu Grooves (aid)	H.MacInnes, I.S.Clough

An audacious route now climbed free at E3 5c. FFA G. Reagan, A (R.). McHardy, 1977

S	1957 Apr 1	Intermediate Traverse	A.D.Marsden, M.McNamara
S	1957 Jun 8	Strappado	H.MacInnes, A.D.Marsden, I.S.Clough

Strappado Direct (1980) is largely independent

S	1957 Jul	Central Route	D.Leaver, J.Gott

Direct Finish M.Lates, A.Pay, 11 May 2006

S	1958 May 29	Atropos (aid)	H.MacInnes, I.S.Clough

FFA (after rockfall) M.Fowler, P.Thomas, 1978

S	1958 May 30	Vulcan Wall (aid)	H.MacInnes, D.J.Temple, I.S.Clough

The route had been explored previously by John Temple, who then told MacInnes and Clough about it. When all three went off to make the ascent, Temple was astonished by the amount of aid the others used.

The Chambre Finish: G.Latter, D.Cuthbertson, 19 Jun 1980

S	1958 Jun 1	Depravity	H.MacInnes, I.S.Clough, D.Pipes
S	1958 Jun 4	Boreas Grooves	H.MacInnes, I.S.Clough, D.Pipes
S	1958	Ajax	H.MacInnes, A.N.Other
S	1958 Jul 27	Crembo Cracks (1 pa)	D.Gregory, R.Hutchison

Variations to several pitches, M.Priestman, A.Kassyk, 18 May 1980

S	1962 Aug 6	The Plunge (aid)	B.W.Robertson, E.Cairns
S	1963 Jul 15	Desire	J.R.Houston, W.Torrens
S	1964 Jun 20	Shangri-La	I.S.Clough, A.Nicholls
S	1964 Jun 27	Searcher	I.S.Clough, A.Nicholls
S	1965 Jul	Trojan Groove	I.Heys, K.Roberts.
S	1965 Jul	Spartan Groove	I.Heys, J.Firth

Direct Variation: P.Hunter, Miss S.Drummond, 8 Aug 1980

S	1965 Aug 9	The Snake	W.Sproul, J.Renny, J.Hall

Peg protection was commonplace and the route was considered as well protected. The opposite is now true with long run-outs between slung spikes.

S	1966 May 27/28	Pearly Gates	A.C.Willmott, R.Ratcliffe
S	1966 Jul 31	Grooves Eliminate (aid)	A.C.Willmott,F.Hart

FFA: The Nipple, Fowler and Thomas, 21 June 1977

W	1970 Feb 26	Little Gully	R.O'Donovan, M.Chalwin
S	1970 Jun 13	Fidelity	K.V.Crocket, D.M.Jenkins
S	1976 Sep 12	Trap Face Route Direct	J.Holmes, W.Trafford
S	1977 Jun 21	Dilemma	M.Fowler, P.Thomas
S	1978	FFA Overhanging Crack	M.Hamilton, G.Cohen

MacInnes & Clough are likely candidates to have first aided this stunning line but no record has been found which, equally, was not their style.

S	1978 Aug 25	Antonine Wall	A.Mitchell (unseconded)
S	1979 May	Enigma	M.Hamilton, D.Mullin
S	1979 May	Sternum	D.Gardner, G.Holden
S	1980 May 16	Strappado Direct	P.Hunter, C.Lees

Pitch 1: G.Szcua, C.Moody, 13 June 1988

S	1980 May 17	Hang Free	D.McCallum, R.Milne

Possible FFA Prolepsis (1957)

S	1980 May 17	Vanity	M.Priestman, A.Kassyk
S	1980 May 17	Krugerrand	P.Hunter, C.Lees

A busy day with 3 big routes on 3 separate parts of the face.

S	1980 May 18	Spock	P.Hunter, C.Lees
S	1980 Aug 9	Acapulco Wall	P.Hunter
S	1981 May 18	Ghost Riders	C.Dale, S.Cox
S	1982 Jun 12	Zephyr	D.Cuthbertson, D.McCallum

Only the second Cuillin E5

S	1982 Jun 19	Confession	D.Cuthbertson, G.Latter.
S	1982 Jun 19	Magic	D.Cuthbertson, G.Latter
S	1982 Jun 20	The Team Machine	D.Cuthbertson, G.Latter
S	1983 May 24	The Conjuror	R.Anderson, M.Hamilton
S	1983 Jul	Erotica	D.Dinwoodie, G.Livingston

Significantly the first 6b move in the Cuillin.

S	1985 Jun 2	Piety	N.Horn, C.Moody
S	1985 Jun	Stormy Petrel	S.Hill

S	1987 Jun 17	Prestidigitateur	R.Wightman, J.Topping
S	1988 Jun 13	Pocks	G.Szcua, C.Moody
	Pitch 2: C.Moody, N.Smith, 7 June 1992		
S	1989 Apr 21	The Highlander	G.Farquhar, G.Latter

The first E6 in the Cuillin takes a stunning line up the frontal arete of the Cioch.

W	1989 Apr 22	Amphitheatre Arete	M.MacLeod, B.Taylor

An interesting coincidence of a new winter route being climbed the day after the first Cuillin E6.

S	1989 May 20	Slanting Crack (Cioch Gully)	I.C.Halliday, W.A.Campbell
S	1990 Jul 22	Tennatte	G.Szuca
S	1990 Jul 22	Uhuru	T. Prentice, K.Howett
S	1990 Jul 23	Why	G.Szuca, A.Connolly
S	1990 Jul 24	Protect and Survive	G.Szuca
S	1990 Jul 25	Hindsight	G.Szuca, A.Connolly
S	1992 Jun	Banana	D.Griffiths, M.Roy
S	1992 Jun 16	Mistral Buttress	N.Horn, C.Moody
S	1994	The Joker	C.Moody

Probably climbed before.

S	1994 May 25	Slabby Wall Crack	D.Shepherd, J.Anderson
S	1994 Jul 31	Helen	S.Hill, C.Moody
S	2001	Clinging On	K.Howett, S.F.Muir
S	2002 Apr 6	Rat on a Stick	G.Ettle, L.Lyall
S	2002 Apr 6	C.D. Rom	G.Ettle, L.Lyall
S	2003 Jun	The Prize	B.Wear, J.Sutton

This is the ultimate power of the immortals in the film 'Highlander'.

S	2004 May	Venus Transit	J.Sutton, M.Meech
S	2004 Jun 8	The Gathering	D.Macleod

The Cioch again plays host to a leap in Cuillin standards bringing them back in line with the mainland once more.

S	2005 Jun 7	Box-King Route	I.King, B.Box
S	2005 Jun 25	Lowlander	C.Petigrew, T.Cooper
S	2008 May 12	Timerity	I.Taylor, T.Fryer
S	2009 Jul 16	Yanks	M.Lates, M.Clark

Coire a' Ghrunnda & Coire nan Laogh

S	1877	Sgùrr nan Eag	Captain J.C.Macpherson, OS Party
S	1889 Aug?	Thearlaich-Dubh Gap	J.N.Collie, W.W.King
S	1898 Aug 8	Thearlaich-Dubh Gap Gully	W.W.King, W.Douglas, W.W.Naismith
S	1898 Jul 4	Caisteal a' Garbh-choire	A.E.Robertson
W	1903 Apr 10	Thearlaich-Dubh Gap	H.Raeburn, W.N.Ling, C.W.Walker, H.Walker

'It was very cold here and the snow was being blown through the Gap, plastering the rocks and obscuring the holds. The climb was thoroughly interesting, and took the party just one hour.' Ling

S	1911 Jul	North Ridge, Caisteal a' Garbh-choire	W.W.Naismith, A.Arthur
S	1912 Aug	West, Central & East Gully (Coire nan Laogh)	S.W.Herford, J.Laycock

Unremarkable route, but a legacy to two of the finest rock climbers of the period. Herford's lead on Central Buttress on Scafell in 1914 was considered by far the most advanced rock climb in the world. Sadly, like many other talented climbers he was killed in the Great War (1916).

S	1912 Aug	West Gully (Alasdair)	E.W.Steeple, G.Barlow, A.H.Doughty
S	1919 Jul	Bower's Climb	G.S.Bower, J.Meldrum
S	1920/21/22	South Crag Gully, Green Recess Chimneys, Central Buttress, Trap Dyke Route, Far South Buttress, Central Route (Alasdair) Stack Buttress Direct & Red Wall Variant, North Crag Gully & Black Knight's Wall, Owl Buttress Left, Owl Chimney, Slab Buttress	E.W.Steeple, G.Barlow (last 2 routes with Doughty)

They camped at the crag each year and you get the impression of gents picking the fruits of a sun-soaked face on an annual basis.

S	1922	White Slab	E.W.Steeple, G.Barlow

Severe pitch below White Slab by E.A.M.Wedderburn, P.D.Baird, Jun 1933. Direct Finish by R.O'Donovan, M.Chalwin, 26 Jun 1970.
Steeple rated this classic, the final route they did, as the finest on the crag and incomparable at the grade

S	1932 Jun 25	Owl Buttress Right	D.Lewers, C.J.A.Cooper, E.Wood-Johnson
S	1947 May 23	Girdle Traverse of South Crag	V.J.Wiggin, E.Wood-Johnson
S	1948 May 14	Western Buttress	R.S.Dadson, B.Wilberforce Smith, H.Booth

The route had been climbed as high as the final pitch in 1938 and the record in the Glen Brittle House Log Book inspired the first ascent.

S	1950 Apr 14	White Slab Direct	G.H.Francis, J.M.Bowen

Oxford Variation by G.H.Francis, R.H.Hobhouse, P.F.Mitson, 28 Aug 1950. White Slab Variation by D.Leonard, N.Bowen, 8 Sep 1971

S	1950 Jul	Commando Crack	A.C.Cain, B.L.Dodson
S	1951 May 16	Quiver	J.Hammond, R.Morden

The first route on the buttress surprisingly ignored the corner of Grand Diedre opting instead for the steep wall and quivering legs.

S	1955 Jul 18	T-D Buttress, West Face	K.Bryan, R.Jamieson

Previously confused with Quiver.

S	1958 Jun 1	Grand Diedre & Direct Start	H.MacInnes, I.S.Clough, D.Pipes
S	1958 Jul 30	Lambda	R.C.Mason, T.Shallice
S	1958 Jul 30	Mu	R.C.Mason, T.Shallice
S	1963 Jul	Lumps	A. McKeith
S	1965 Jun	W.C. Route	I.S.Clough, Mrs N.Clough
S	1965 Jul 20	The Asp	J.McLean, W.Smith, W.Gordon
S	1965 Jul 20	Con's Cleft	J.McLean, W.Smith, W.Gordon

Two fine routes led by 'The New White Hope'. McLean bridged the gap between the old and new Creag Dhu members.

S	1968 May 20	Mega Route	J.R.Dempster, J.I.Wallace
S	1970 Aug 27	The Whet	M.G.Geddes, J.C.Higham, Miss A.C.Lamb
S	1976 Aug 5	Sundance	B.Dunn, A.Paul
S	1977 Aug 13	Oneshotbang	C.Higgins
S	1979 May 24	The Stag	S.C.Allen, P.Darbyshire
S	1980 May 4	Cuckoo Groove	R.Atkinson, D.Formstone
S	1980 Aug	Atlantis	K.Leinster, A. Paul
S	1984 May 28	Vagabond Crack	B.Molyneux, R.Reeve
S	1988 May 2	Gonzo Jamming	G.Jones, A.Waters
S	1988 May 2	Stormwatch	G.Jones, A.Waters
S	1992 May 17	Victoria Buttress	J.Tout, J.Andrew

Previously climbed in May 1991 by S.Kennedy and D.Ritchie but unnamed.

S	1992 May 17	Victoria Sponge	J.Tout, J.Andrew
S	1998 Jul	Rapid Progress	M.Lates, C.Scott
S	2002 Apr 6	A Walk On Part In The War	R.Durran, R.Pybus
W	2008 Jan 11	Grand Diedre	G.Briffet, P.Macpherson, M.Lates
W	2008 Mar 11	Eilidh's Ceilidh	P.Macpherson, M.Lates
S	2008 Jul 5	Crib Route, C.L. Route, Eilidh's on the Lash, Ruari's Rammy	M.Lates & P.Cunningham
S	2008 Sept 7	Owl Wall	M.Lates, J.Seal, J.Edwards
W	2009 Feb 4	West Gully	D.Ritchie & N.McGougan
S	2009 Jun 4	Eilidh's Ceilidh	M.Lates, A.Lee-Browne
W	2010 Jan 3	Green Recess Chimneys	N.Wilson, I.Stewart
S	2010 Sep 5	Swamp Fox	B.Hamilton, S.Kennedy
S	2010 Aug 15	Spear of Destiny	S.Kennedy, E.Rodger, B.Hamilton
S	2010 Aug 15	Domesday	E.Rodger, S.Kennedy, B.Hamilton
S	2011 Apr 22	Triple Whammy	S.Abbott, L.Taylor, N.Williams

Coir'-Uisg (Coruisk) Basin

S	1835 Sep 5	Bealach Mac an t-Soair, Druim nan Ràmh	C.Lesingham Smith, D.Macintyre
S	1859	Sgùrr na Stri	R.C.Weld

Weld spied the Inaccessible Pinnacle and wrote an article written in 1860 which summoned fellow

Alpine Club members to rid it of its inaccessibility. Had been climbed before.

S 1873 Sep 6   Sgùrr Dubh Mòr   A.Nicolson & friend
Followed by an epic night time descent down slabs and gullies to Coir'-Uisg.

S 1887 Jun 3   Sgùrr Dubh Beag   C.Pilkington, Horace Walker, J.Heelis, J.Mackenzie
The party had been drinking quite a lot of ale with painter Alfred Williams in his wooden cabin at Loch Scavaig, baulked at the stiff drop to the col, retreated to Scavaig and then made the long walk around the coast to Glen Brittle – presumably arriving sober?

S 1896 May 28   Dubh Ridge (bypassing the abseil) S. Williams, J. Mackenzie.
Completed direct by W.Douglas, J.Rennie, W.Lamont, 11 Jun 1896.

S 1896 Jun 2   North-East Ridge (Gars-Bheinn)   S.Williams, J.Mackenzie

S 1896 Sep 1   South-East Ridge
                 (Sgùrr a' Ghreadaidh)   J.N.Collie, E.B.Howell
Direct Route by W.A.Morrison, D.H.Menzies, early summer 1920
New Direct Line by W.Bruton, J.E.B.Wright, 10 Jun 1928.

S 1896 Sep 12   Sgùrr Coire an Lochain   J.N.Collie, E.B.Howell, W.W.Naismith, J.Mackenzie

S 1897 Aug 6   Brown's Climb   W.Brown, J.Rennie, W.Douglas, (H. Barrow?)

W 1903 Apr 11   Raeburn's Route
                 (Sgùrr Mhic Chòinnich)   H.Raeburn, W.N.Ling, C.W. & H.Walker

S 1910 Sep 14   Third-Fourth Gully   E.W. Steeple, G. Barlow, A.H. Doughty, H.E. Bowron.

S 1910 Sep 16   South-East Gully
                 (Sgùrr a' Mhadaidh)   E.W.Steeple, G.Barlow

S 1912 Aug 8   North-East Gully   C.O'Brien, E.L.Julian
By far the hardest route on Skye at the time, first repeated in 1951 and only at second attempt by a very good climber. 'We were forced to give up and retreated with a feeling of great respect for O'Brien & Julian, and a doubt about the Guide's classification.'

S 1912 Aug 11   O'Brien and Julian's Climb C.O'Brien, E.L.Julian
A very bold lead and remains the only route tackling this huge face head on.

S 1913   Eag Dubh Gully   E.W.Steeple, G.Barlow, A.H.Doughty
S 1913 Aug   Second-Third Gully   E.W.Steeple, G.Barlow, A.H.Doughty
S 1913 Aug   First-Second Gully   E.W.Steeple, G.Barlow
S 1913 Sep   North-East Ridge
                 (Sgùrr Thearlaich)   H.Raeburn and party
S 1913 Sep   Raeburn's Route
                 (Sgùrr Coire an Lochain) H.Raeburn, J.B.Meldrum & Wallwork brothers
Rum Doodle Variation by D.Yule, D.Hine, M.Anderson, 5 May 1984

W 1915 Apr   The Chasm   E.W.Steeple, G.Barlow
S 1919 Aug   The Chasm   E.W.Steeple, G.Barlow, A.H.Doughty
S 1920 Aug 14   Druim Pinnacle   Dr. Ery Lüscher
Approached by two abseils from Bidein.

S 1920 Aug   Terrace Gully   E.W.Steeple, G.Barlow, A.H.Doughty
S 1922 Aug   Terrace East Buttress   E.W.Steeple, G.Barlow
S 1924 Jul 28   Terrace West Buttress   E.W.Steeple, G.Barlow
S 1939 Jun   Slab Route   J.E.Byrom, P.Wigglesworth
S 1945 Jul 27   Bidein Direct from
                 Druim nan Ramh   G.H.Townend, R.L.Plackett, C.M.Plackett, G.C.Curtis
Variation by E.V.Reynolds, G.C.E.Wilson, H.W.Turnbull, Sep 1945

S 1949 Jun   Original Route, Coir'-uisg Buttress C.M.G.Smith, R.C.Putman
S 1949 Oct 23   Shelf Route   J.D.G.Davidson, F.R.Brooke
S 1950 Jul   Aladdin's Route   J.W.B.Barnes, H.Swift, D.Rich
S 1950 Jul 24   North-East Buttress   W.D.Brooker, C.M.Dixon
S 1950 Aug 1   Fluted Buttress   W.D.Brooker, C.M.Dixon
S 1950 Aug 7   Hourglass Crack   C.M.Dixon, T.Shaw
S 1951 Aug 8   Crack of Dawn   W.D.Brooker, C.M.Dixon
S 1951 Aug 12   Forgotten Groove   W.D.Brooker, C.M.Dixon
S 1953 Aug 13   Thunderbolt Shelf   T.W.Patey, W.D.Brooker
S 1953 Aug 15   South Twin, North Twin,
                 Midget Ridge, Clouded Buttress T.W.Patey, W.D.Brooker
S 1954 Jun 3   Black Cleft   C.M.Dixon, J.E.Monks

S	1954 Jun 4	Lost Arrow	C.M.Dixon, J.E.Monks
S	1954 Jun 4	The Bow	C.M.Dixon, J.E.Monks
S	1954 Jun 5	Pinnacle Face	R.Cra'ster, C.M.Dixon
S	1954 Jun 5	Gemini	C.M.Dixon, R. Cra'ster

Brooker and Dixon had made these prime cliffs of 'The Forgotten Corrie' virtually their own.

S	1957 Sep	Ladders	R.Smith
S	1957 Sep	Left Edge	R.Smith, H.Kindness

Quality and boldness as ever from Robin Smith on his first visit to Skye.

S	1958 Jun 25 & 27	St Andrew's Crack	L.J.Morris, M.J.Hill (3 pitches on 25th), W.Bonthrone (27th)
S	1958 Jun 27	Chemist's Constitutional	L.J. Morris, W. Bonthrone

A big new cliff is discovered in the Forgotten Corrie.

S	1958 Aug 22	Dawn Grooves	R.W.P.Barclay, W.D.Brooker
S	1959 Jun 19	Sue's Chimney	W.Bonthrone, Miss S.M.Bell, S.Yeaman
S	1960 May 21	Central Groove	D.J.Bennet, D.A Bennet, R.Cameron
S	1960 Jun	Coruisk Gully	S.Myles, F.Old, Q.Crichton
S	1960 Jul	Central Gully (Sgùrr Coire an Lochain)	J.G.Burns, D.N.Mill
S	1960 Aug 14	King Cobra	C.J.S.Bonington, T.W.Patey

King Cobra Direct by B.Davison, H.Day, 28 Jun 1992
Julian Lines describes a solo ascent in 'Skye is the Limit', SMC Journal 2004, which gives a good idea of the fear mere mortals will experience on a rope.

S	1961 May	Mayday	K.Bryan, M.Slesser
S	1962 Apr	Warsle	Mrs M.Wallace, M.Slesser
S	1962 May	Diagonal	K.Bryan, M.Slesser
S	1962 May 19	Coruisk Slabs	T.M.Lauren, J.Highet

Largely destroyed by a huge rockfall in the late 1990s.

S	1964 May	JMCS Buttress	B.Barclay, R.Chalmers

Variation by R.O'Donovan, A.McInnes, 23 May 1970

S	1965 May 30	Bee Cee Crack	B.Sproul, B.Cuthbert
S	1966 Jun 1	Rongwrong	R.A.Hobbs, P.L.Jackson
S	1966 Aug 25	Tenderfoot	D.Chapman, J.R.Sutcliffe
S	1966 Aug 25	Peridot	J.Harwood & R.A.High
S	1968 Jun 17	Magpie Cracks	J.Harwood & R.A.High
S	1968 Jun 19	Leviathan	J.Harwood, R.A.High
S	1968 Jul	Dwindle Wall	J.R.MacKenzie, R.Lambert
S	1968 Jul 17	The Happy Wanderer	J.R.MacKenzie, R.Lambert
S	1968 Jul 19	Skye Ride	R.Lambert, J.R.MacKenzie
S	1968 Jul 19	Phaeton	J.R.MacKenzie, R.Lambert
S	1969 Jun	Tinn Lamh Crack (1pa)	J.Barraclough, J.B.Cooper

FFA by J.Harwood, 1972
The Gaelic name refers to sore hands.

S	1969 Jun	Cocoa Cracks (aid)	J.Barraclough, J.B.Cooper
S	1971 Jun 3	Hanging Slab	J.A.Austin, D.G.Roberts

An intimidating line by the Yorkshire hardman.

S	1972 Jun 15	Micawber	S.J.E.Lyndsay, A.G.Skuce
S	1974 Jun 23	Mongoose	J.Lamb, P.Botterill

Direct Pitch (Mongoose Direct) by M.Fowler, P.Thomas, 20 Jun 1977

S	1975 May 29	Totie Lum, Stair Heid, Coruisk Corner	M.Easton, H.Henderson, G.Ross
S	1976 Aug 25	Thurman's Request & Duffy Variant	P.Moxon, J.Duffy
S	1977 Aug 12	Populace	N.Muir, A.Paul
S	1983 Jun 13	Paddy and Micks Route	Paddy Buckley, Mick Goad
S	1983 Jun 24	Lightfoot	M.Hamilton, R.Anderson, P.Whillance
S	1984 Apr 9	Lazy Layback	A.Shaw, J.Getley
S	1984 Aug 7	Widdle	S.Janik, J.Edie
S	1985	Rawhide	D.Bates, T.Walkington
S	1990 May 18-20	James' Crack, Assault Course Bimbo, Peterless Crack, Bryantless Crack, Witchless Corner	T.Walkington, A.Cunningham

S	1990 Jul 25-27	Sealsville, Nettie, Half Crack, Short Spur, Slabsville, No Pain Without Gain	G.Szuca, A.Connolly.

Mysterious selection of poorly recorded routes typical of Szuca. Disturbing the seal colony is also an issue in summer.

S	1994 May 24	Beached Whale	D.Shepherd, J.Andrew
W	1995 Mar 4	Exiguous Gully	M.Fowler, A.Cave
W	1996 Mar 16	O'Brien and Julian's Climb	B.Davison, A.Nisbet
S	1997 May 19	The Minke	G.Nicoll, M.Nicoll
S	1997 May 29	Outhaul	C.R.Ravey, J.S.Peden
S	1997 May 31	Reverse Thrust	R.Archbold, B.Findlay, G.Strange
S	1998 Jun	Lost Chord	J.Gillespie, A.Currie
S	1999 May 12	Half Century Crack	S.Brock, C.Heald
S	1999 Jul	Midge-a-mad-tosis	J.Buckley, N.Hunt, H.Richards, D.Bradburn
W	2002 Mar 1	Eag Dubh Gully	D.Ritchie, N.McGougan
S	2002 May	Coruisk Hut Crack	D.Smith
W	2004 Jan 17	Second-Third/First-Second Gully Combination	D.Ritchie, M.Shaw, N.McGougan
W	2005 Feb 12	Aladdin's Route	D.Ritchie, D.McEachan, N.McGougan
S	2007 May 2	Skye Wall	D.Birkett, A.Steele

A magnificent modern addition by one of the UK's top climbers.

S	2007 Jun 10	Swamp Donkey	R.McMurray, C.McGregor
S	2007 Jun 17	Paradise Found	P.Benson, G.Robertson
S	2007 Jun 18	Rainman	P.Benson, G.Robertson

A must-do route for aspiring mountain E5 climbers.

W	2008 Jan 12	Dawn Grooves	G.Robertson, M.Garthwaite
S	2008 May 3	Mrs Beaton, Firkin & Old Mortality	S.Johnson, G.Johnson
S	2008 May 24	The Yorkshireman's Debut	M.Barnard, M.Rycroft
S	2008 May 24	Rough Stuff	M.Barnard
W	2009 Feb 6	South-East Gully (Mhadaidh)	M.Fowler, M.Lates, D.Turnbull
W	2009 Mar	North-East Ridge (Thearlaich)	N.& L.Williams
W	2010 Mar 12	Springbank Gully	M.Lates, D.MacLachlan
S	2010 May 31	The Romp	M.Barnard, E.Boyd
S	2010 Jun	Coruisk Corner	D.Birkett, A.Mitchell
S	2010 Sep 25	Double Zero	S.Johnson, G.Johnson
S	2010 Sep 25	Fanny Cradock	M.Worsley, R.Duncan
S	2010 Sep 25	Ginger Nut	M.Worsley, R.Duncan
W	2010 Nov 30	Happy Go Lucky Route	F.Blunt, M.Lates
W	2010 Dec 2	Black Cleft	G.Robertson, G.Boswell
W	2011 Jan 10	Midget Ridge	D.Ritchie, N.McGougan

Blàbheinn & Clach Glas

S	1859 Summer	Blàbheinn	A.Swinburne, J.Nichol

Although traditionally listed this is only the first recorded ascent. Tourists had been guided up for many years before this.

S	1873 Sep 6	Great Gully and descent Willinks' Gully	G.H.Willink & brother
S	1887 May 29	Clach Glas	C.Pilkington, H.Walker, J.Heelis
S	1887 Jul 11	Clach Glas/Blàbheinn Traverse, South to North	W.P. & E.P.Marshall, J.Mackenzie

North to South by W.E.Corlett, E.R.Kidson, Jul/Aug 1890

S	1890 May 25	North Face Route	W.C.Slingsby, G.Hastings
S	1893 Jul 22	Half-Crown Pinnacle	W.W.Naismith, M.Mackenzie
S	1896 May 3	Arch Gully	G.D.Abraham, A.P.Abraham
S	1896 Sep 9	Naismith's Route	W.W. Naismith, J.A.Parker
S	1900 Jun	Sid's Rake, Clach Glas	S.Williams, D.Grant
S	1900 Jun	East Ridge, Blàbheinn	S.Williams, D.Grant

A winter description is first recorded in Simpson's SMC Climbers' Guide, 1969.

S	1905 Apr 22	Forked Pinnacle Ridge	W.I.Clark, T.E.Goodeve, H.Walker
S	1907 Jun	Consolation Gully	H.Harland, A.P.Abraham.

So-called because Harland and Abraham had failed to get up the still unclimbed Black Cleft.

S	1907 Aug 13	South-East Buttress	H.MacRobert, R.A.Brown,

S	1914 Jun	C-D Buttress	J.C.Thomson, J.R.Young
S	1914 Jun	South-East Route	J.C.Thomson, J.R.Young
S	1915 Jul 5	Central Buttress	W.N.Ling, E.Backhouse
S	1920 Jun	B Gully	G.D.Abraham, H.Harland, G.Summers
S	1923 Jun 8	North Face Direct	G.Sang, R.Burn
S	1927	Bealach Tower	R.Lamb & party
S	1958 Jun 12	Penelope	H.MacInnes
S	1961 Aug 24	Chock-a-Block Chimney	T.W.Patey, R.Harper
S	1967 Jun 17	Athain Slab Route, Athian Rib	H. Brown, W.W. Simpson, S.D. Menmuir
S	1967 Jul 21	The Horn	D.D.Stewart, D.J.Bennet

Direct pitches by I.S.Clough & party, 15 Sep 1968. FFA by P.Thomas, M.Fowler, 19 Jun 1977

S	1968 15 Jun	The Great Prow	T.W.Band, P.W.F.Gibbon, N.S.Ross, W.Tauber

This party from St Andrews University named the route 'The Splinter' beating the Clough and friends by two months. The Great Prow name was reported first though and has stuck ever since.
Twilight Slab Variation by A.J.Kennedy, G.Rooney, 6 Jun 1975
Splinter Finish by M.Lates, C.Moore, D.Moore 30 May 2010

S	1968 Sep	Left-Hand Buttress	A.Silvers, D.J.Walker
S	1968 Sep	Trundle Buttress	J.Greenwood, I.S.Clough
S	1968 Sep	Belinda, Birthday Groove, Canopy, Escalator Direct, The Hem, Judas, The Outsider, Scorpion, Sickle, Sidewinder, Virgo	I.S.Clough, J.Greenwood, A.Silvers, D.J.Waller

Sickle Variation Finish by S.Brown, G.Smith, 8 Sep 2005
The team were all friends through the Yorkshire cave rescue team and accumulated the biggest ever haul of new Cuillin routes (14) in a single period.

S	1968 Sep	Central Pillar	H.MacInnes, M.C.MacInnes
S	1968 Sep 16	Route One	H.MacInnes, M.C.MacInnes
S	1968 Sep 19	Clough's Cleft	H.MacInnes, M.C.MacInnes
S	1969	Hawse Pipe Chimney	H. MacInnes, M.C. MacInnes
S	1969	Access Gully	H.MacInnes, M.C.MacInnes
S	1969	Loss Leader	H.Macinnes, M.C.MacInnes
S	1969 May	Creep	I.S.Clough, H.MacInnes
S	1969 May	Bargain Offer	M.Boysen, D.Alcock
S	1969 May	Jib	M.Boysen, D.Alcock and I.Clough, H.MacInnes.

Climbed as two teams using different starts over the worrying crux band.

S	1969 Jun 16	South Buttress Gully	I.S.Clough, Mr & Mrs D.Adams
S	1972 Sep 2	Ecstasis	C.Boulton, P.Nunn, R.Toogood
S	1977 Jun 19	Stairway to Heaven	M.Fowler, P.Thomas

'It was a pity, we reflected, that the Skye cliffs are not worth a visit for those with hard rock-climbing in mind!'

S	1977 Aug	Gutter	I.Dalley, D.McCallum
S	1983 Aug 7	Eventide	M.McLeod, C.Moody
S	1987 Jul 19	Rosie's Stash	C.Moody
S	1989 May 18	Motown	S.Kennedy, M.MacCleod, A.Scrase
W	1991 Jan 12	B Gully	S.Kennedy, D.Ritchie
W	1994 Jan 3	Escape from Colditz	M.Lates, A.Fry, N.Bristow

Birthday Breakout: M. Lates, D.MacLachlan, March 8 2010

W	1994 Jan 8	The Crucifix	D.Litherland, M.E.Moran
W	1994 Jan 8	South-East Gully	D.Litherland, M.E.Moran
W	1994 mid-Jan	Sailaway	D.Bisset, M.Francis
S	1994 May	Mistaken Identity	R.McLaughlin, P.Stone
W	1995 Jan 26	The Big Ramp	M.E.Moran, J.Singh
W	1995 Mar 5	Serious Picnic	A.Cave, M.Fowler, C.Jones, D.Rcerz
W	1995 Mar 9	D Gully	D.Bunker, K.Law, M.E.Moran, A.Nolan
W	1995 Dec 23	Virgo	D.Ritchie, I.Stevenson
W	1996 Feb 14	Thrutcher's Groove	P.Bass, M.Lockley, M.Welch
W	1996 Mar 15	Birthday Groove	D.Ritchie, M.Shaw

W	1997 Jan 10	Teddy Bear's Gulch	M.E.Moran, M.Welch
S	1997 Jun 4	Finger in the Dyke	P.Thorburn, G.Farquhar, G.Latter
W	1998 Mar 8	Slighe à Bhodaich	D.Ritchie, N.Marshall
W	1998 Mar 10	Arch Gully	D.Ritchie, M.Shaw
W	1998 Dec 6	Penelope	D.Ritchie, M.Shaw
W	1999 Jan 16	The Cailliach	D.Ritchie, M.Shaw
W	1999 Dec 12	Chock-a-Block Chimney	M.Fowler, P.Ramsden
W	2000 Feb	North Face Route	A.Matthewson, L.Tidmarsh
W	2000 Mar 4	Clough's Cleft	F.MacCallum, M.Shaw, D.Ritchie
S	2000 Jul 1	The Whip	B.Bridgens, A.Hunt
S	2005 Jun 12	Where Eagles Dare	P.Mather, R.Mather
W	2007 Nov 23	MacLaren's Lament	M.Lates, M.Francis
S	2007 Jun 22	The Invisible Crack Adventure	M.Lates, M.Beeston
W	2009 Feb 2	North Face Direct	D.Ritchie M.Shaw
W	2009 Dec 22	Q Gully	M.Lates, M.Francis
W	2009 Dec 22	C Gully (descent)	M.Lates
W	2009 Dec 26	Ledge Route	D.Ritchie, M.Shaw
W	2010 Jan 10	The Great Prow	S.Richardson, I.Small
W	2010 Mar 8	South Buttress Gully	M.Lates, D.MacLachlan

Black Cuillin Outliers & Red Cuillin

S	1943 Jul 19	Odell's Route	N.E.Odell

Odell was more famous for his Everest exploits.

S	1953 Aug 22	Central Buttress	E.A.Wrangham

*Three new Very Difficult pitches were recorded right of Wrangham's route in 1968 by Gwen
Moffat & J & D Adams who opened up Glen Sligachan Buttress across the glen with Clough the
following season.*

S	1968 Jun 20	The Boojum	J.Harwood, R.A.High
S	1968 Jun 22	The Snark	J.Harwood, R.A.High
S	1976 Jun 1	Teflon	J.Harwood, G.Evans
S	1979 Apr 3	April Fools	P.Hunter, C.Lees
S	1980	Far East Buttress	A.C.Cain
S	1980	Cubs' Corner	A.C.Cain, B.Scout

Ginger Cain's partner was a boy scout working at the base in Kyle.

S	1980	Selig Gully	C.Rowland, K.Hopper
S	1980 May 3	Slow Riser	P.Hunter, C.Lees

Right-Hand Finish by J.Cooper & N.Smith, 9 Aug 1995

S	1981	Hand Jive	C.Rowland, P.Nunn
S	1981	Alpha Groove	C.Rowland, K.Hopper

Direct Finish by J.R.MacKenzie, G.Cullen, 1990

S	1981	Tapered Buttress	P.Nunn, A.Livesey

Alex is the brother of the better known climber, Pete Livesey.

S	1988	Skye Ride	J.R.MacKenzie, E.Jones
S	1988 Jun 1	Cunning Stunts	J.R.MacKenzie, E.Jones
S	1990	Cuckoo Waltz	G.Cullen, J.R.MacKenzie
S	1990	Streewise Dancer	J.R.MacKenzie, G.Cullen
S	1990 May 26	Rights of Passage	J.R.MacKenzie, G.Cullen
S	1990 May 27	Black Magic	J.R.MacKenzie, G.Cullen
S	1990 May 27	Flights of Fancy	M.Haltree, M.Frew, S.Price
W	1993	Selig Gully	R.MacDonald, S.Hill, D.Bisset, M.Francis
W	1994 Dec 7	Robbers' Fall	M.Lates
S	1995 Aug 7	Heart but no Sole	J.Cooper, N.Smith
S	1995 Aug 27	Zeke	N.Smith, J.Cooper
W	1998 Jan 4	Fiacaill Geal	M.Lates M.Francis
S	2006 Jul 2	The Yellow Jersey	R.Hamilton, S.Kennedy
W	2007 Feb 7	Wooly Gully	M.Lates, M.Beeston
W	2010 Jan 10	Creag Strollamus Burn	M.Lates

Ridge Traverses

S	1911 Jun 10	(Main) Cuillin Ridge	L.Shadbolt, A.MacLaren
S	1939 Jun 11	The Greater Traverse	I.C.Charleston, W.E.Forde
W	1965 Mar 1	(Main) Cuillin Ridge	D.Crabb, H.MacInnes, T.W.Patey, B.Robertson
W	1988 Apr 4	The Greater Traverse	J.G.McKeever, N.Robinson

SCOTTISH MOUNTAINEERING CLUB
SCOTTISH MOUNTAINEERING TRUST

Prices were correct at time of publication, but are subject to change

CLIMBERS' GUIDES

Arran, Arrochar and Southern Highlands	£15.00
Ben Nevis	£22.00
Glen Coe	£22.00
Highland Outcrops	£16.00
Lowland Outcrops	£22.00
North-East Outcrops	£22.00
Northern Highlands North	£22.00
Northern Highlands Central	£24.00
Northern Highlands South	£24.00
Scottish Rock Climbs	£24.00
Scottish Winter Climbs	£24.00
Scottish Sports Climbs	In preparation
Climbers' Guide carry pouch – from SMC website	£12.00

HILLWALKERS' GUIDES

The Munros	£23.00
The Corbetts & Other Scottish Hills	£23.00
The Cairngorms	£18.00
Central Highlands	£18.00
Islands of Scotland Including Skye	£20.00
North-West Highlands	£22.00
Southern Highlands	£17.00

SCRAMBLERS' GUIDES

Highland Scrambles North	£19.00
Skye Scrambles	£25.00

OTHER PUBLICATIONS

Ben Nevis – Britain's Highest Mountain	£27.50
The Cairngorms – 100 Years of Mountaineering	£27.50
A Chance in a Million? Avalanches in Scotland	£15.00
Hostile Habitats – Scotland's Mountain Environment	£17.00
Scottish Hill Names	£16.00
Munro's Tables	£16.00
The Munroist's Companion	£16.00

Visit our website for more details and to purchase on line:
www.smc.org.uk

Distributed by:
Cordee Ltd, 11 Jacknell Road,
Dodwells Bridge Industrial Estate, Hinkley LE1 7HD
(t) 01455 611185 (e) sales@cordee.co.uk
www.cordee.co.uk